B

Elem
Rudiments

2nd Edition

# of Music

Answer Book

edited by

Kathleen Wood

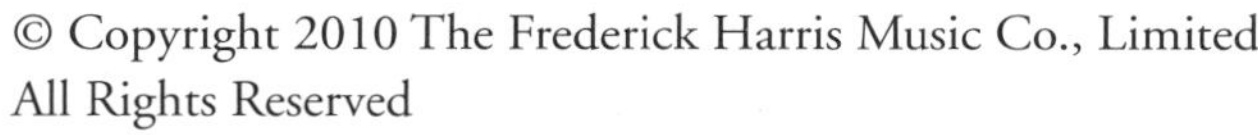

19 18 17 16 5 6 7 8 9 10

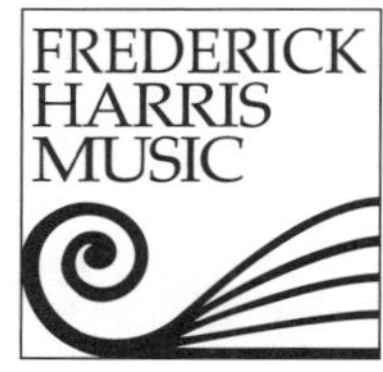

CHAPTER 1

NOTATION

B I A EXERCISES (p. 7)

1. Write the following notes in the treble clef.

a) F on a line	f) F in a space
b) A in a space	g) B on a line
c) G on a line	h) D in a space
d) C in a space	i) G in a space
e) E on a line	j) middle C

a) b) c) d) e) f) g) h) i) j)

2. Write the following notes in the bass clef.

a) B in a space	f) D on a line
b) F on a line	g) G in a space
c) middle C	h) F in a space
d) A on a line	i) G on a line
e) E in a space	j) C in a space

a) b) c) d) e) f) g) h) i) j)

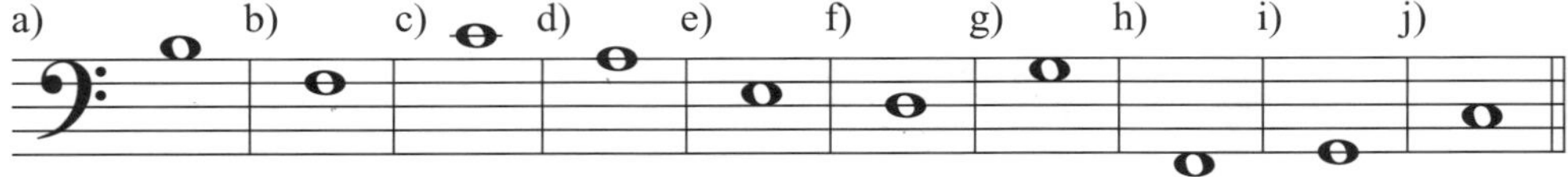

3. Name each of the following notes.

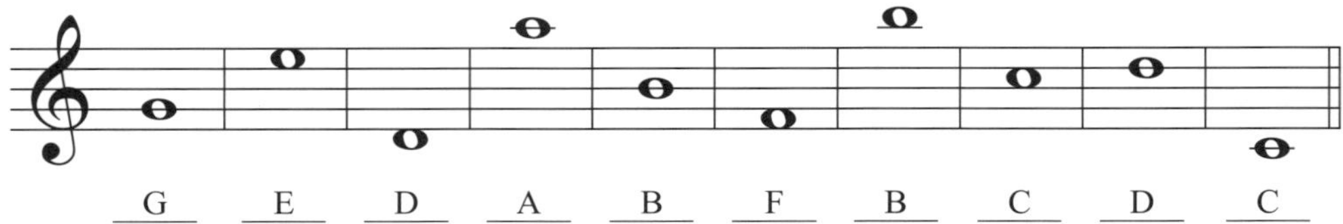

4. Name each of the following notes.

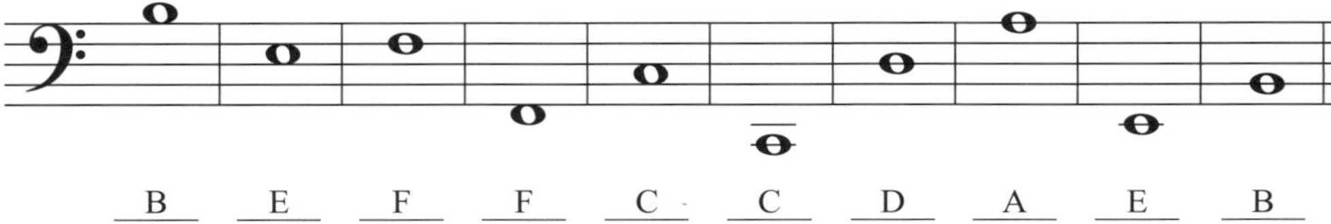

5. Name each of the following notes.

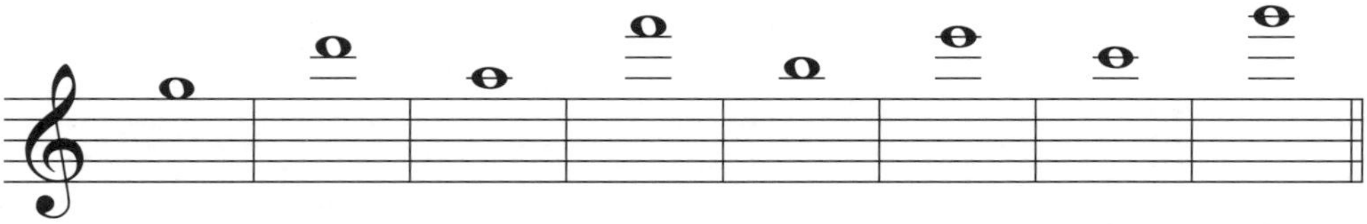

G D A F B E C G

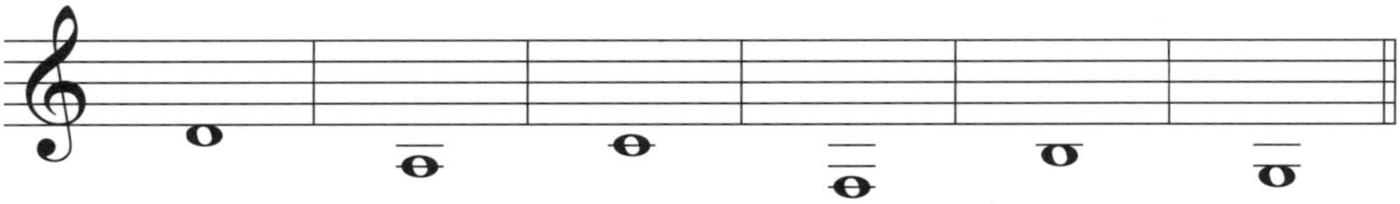

D A C F B G

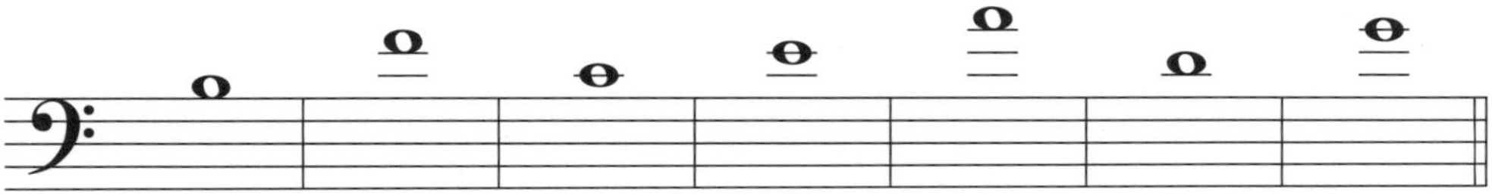

B F C E A D G

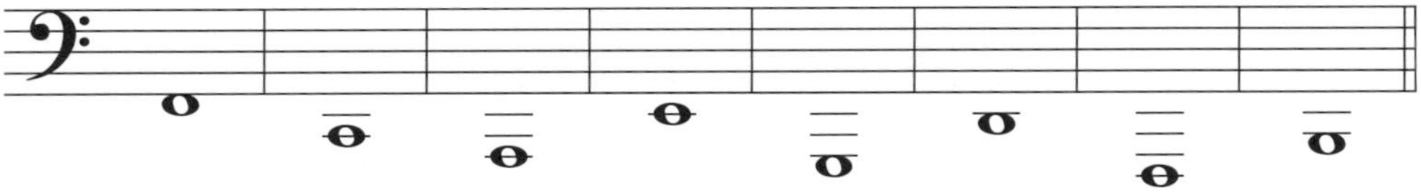

F C A E G D F B

6. Name each of the following notes.

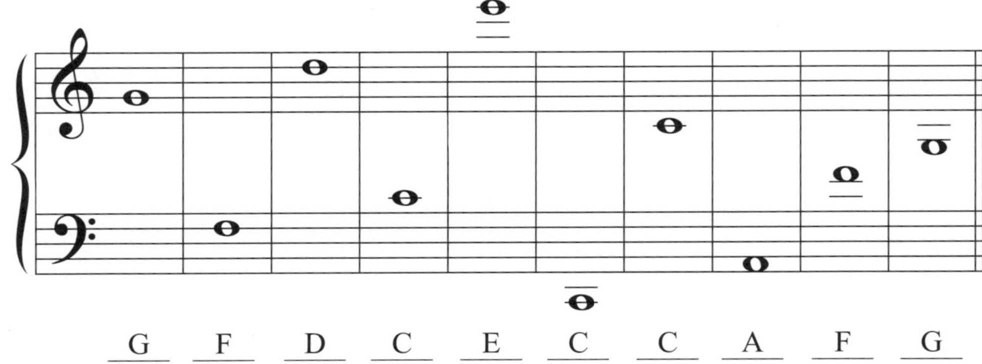

G F D C E C C A F G

A MORE EXERCISES (p. 9)

1. Name each of the following notes.

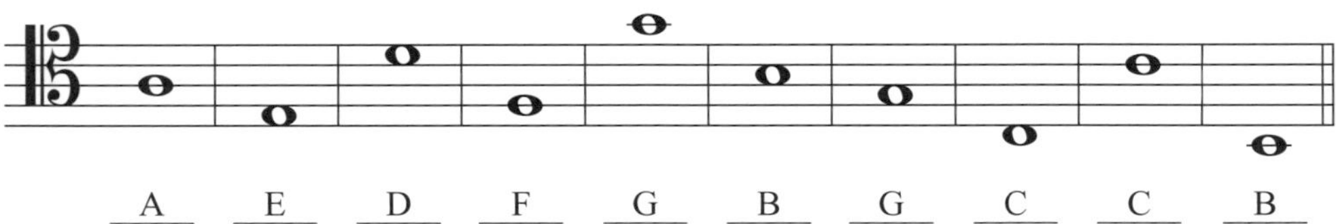

2. Name each of the following notes.

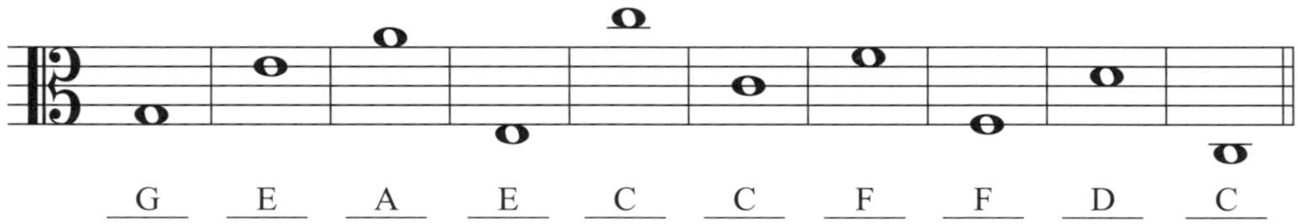

3. Write the following notes in the alto clef.

a) A on a line	f) B in a space
b) G on a line	g) A in a space
c) D in a space	h) middle C
d) F on a line	i) G in a space
e) E in a space	j) E on a line

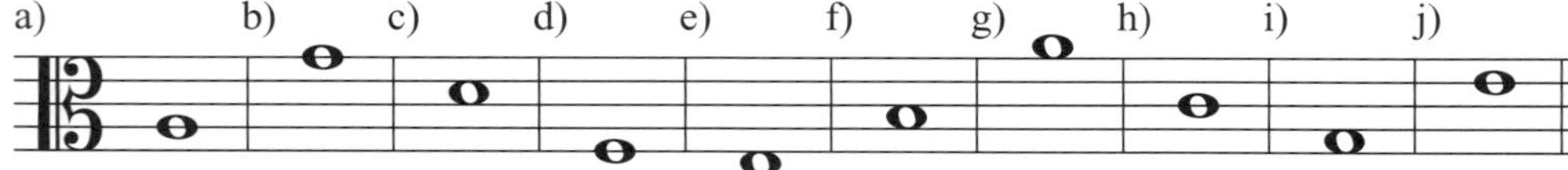

4. Write the following notes in the tenor clef.

a) D on a line	f) F on a line
b) G in a space	g) middle C
c) A on a line	h) F in a space
d) E in a space	i) B in a space
e) D in a space	j) E on a line

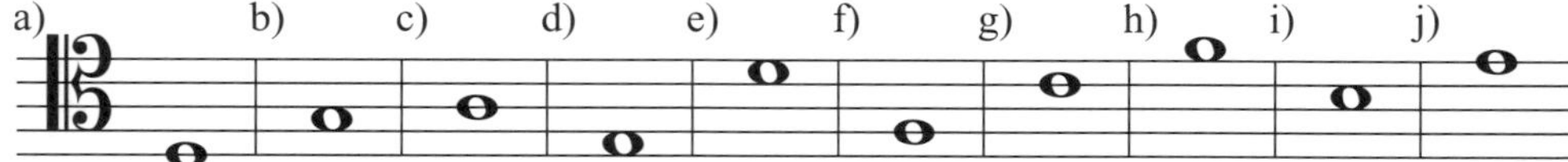

B I A EXERCISES (p. 12)

1. Write *one* note that is equal to the value of each of the following.

a) 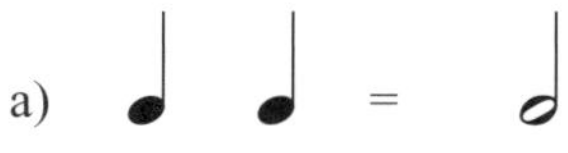

d) 

b) =

e) =

c) =

f) =

2. Write *one* rest that is equal to the value of each of the following.

a) =

f) =

b) =

g) =

c) =

h) =

d) =

i) =

e) =

j) =

3. Write *three* notes that are equal to the value of each of the following.

a) 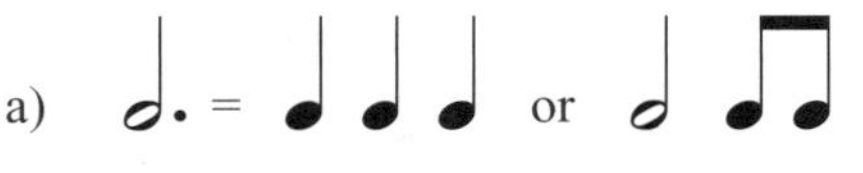

c) 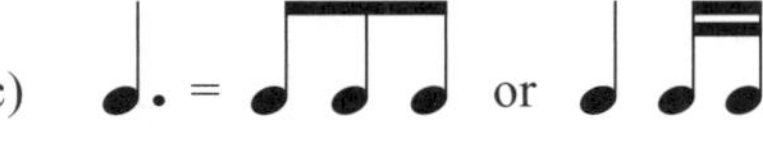

b) 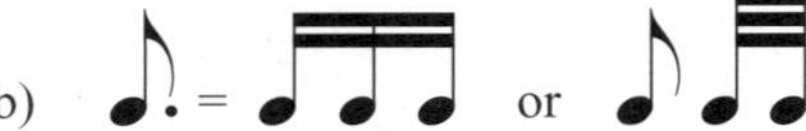

d) 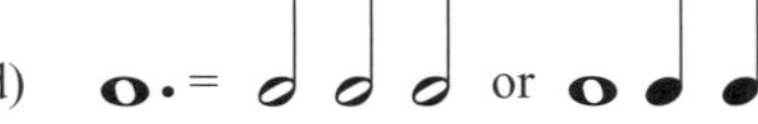

4. Write *two* rests that are equal to the value of each of the following.

a) =

c) =

b) =

d) =

5. Complete the following statements.

a) 2 quarter notes	=	4	eighth notes
b) 1 half note	=	2	quarter notes
c) 3 eighth notes	=	6	sixteenth notes
d) 1 quarter note	=	4	sixteenth notes
e) 2 eighth notes	=	1	quarter note
f) 4 sixteenth notes	=	2	eighth notes
g) 2 half notes	=	1	whole note
h) 1 whole note	=	8	eighth notes
i) 4 thirty-second notes	=	2	sixteenth notes
j) 2 sixteenth notes	=	1	eighth note
k) 1 dotted quarter note	=	3	eighth notes
l) 3 half notes	=	1½	whole notes
m) 4 half notes	=	1	breve note
n) 6 sixteenth notes	=	12	thirty-second notes
o) 1 dotted half note	=	3	quarter notes

6. Write a single note (or dotted note) that is equal to the value of each of the following.

a) 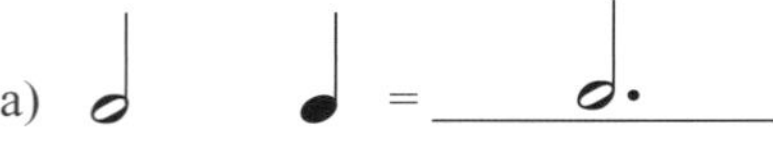

b)

c) 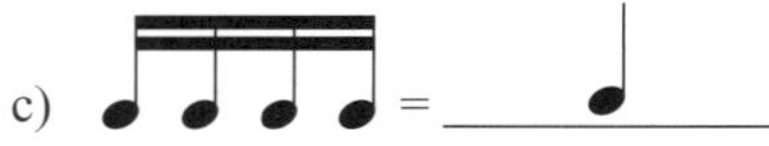

d) 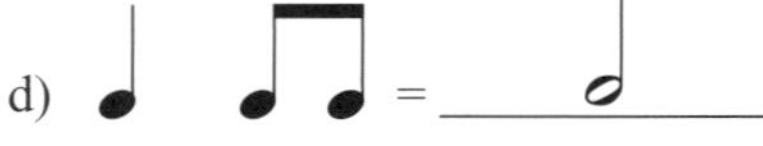

e)

f)

g) 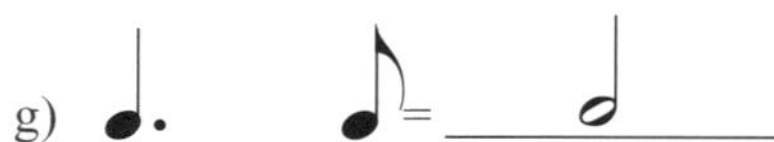

h) 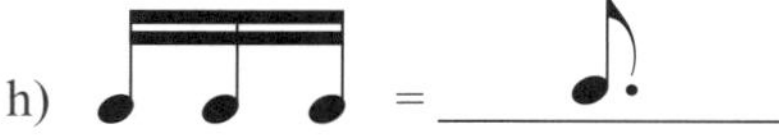

i)

j)

7. Write a single rest (or dotted rest) that is equal to the value of each of the following.

a)
b)
c)
d)
e)
f)
g)
h)

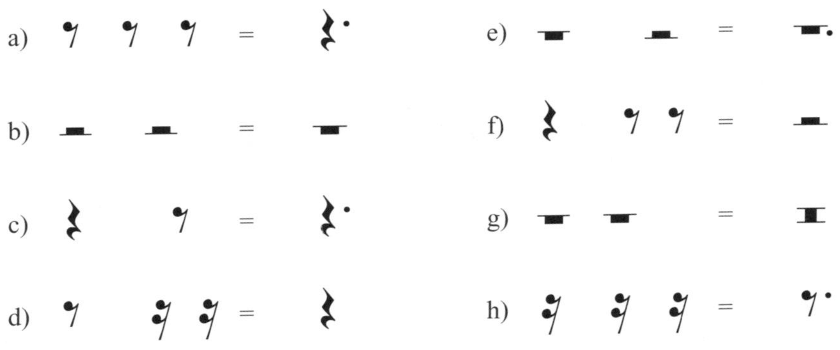

8. Write a single note (or dotted note) that is equal to the value of each of the following.

a)
b)
c)
d)
e)
f)

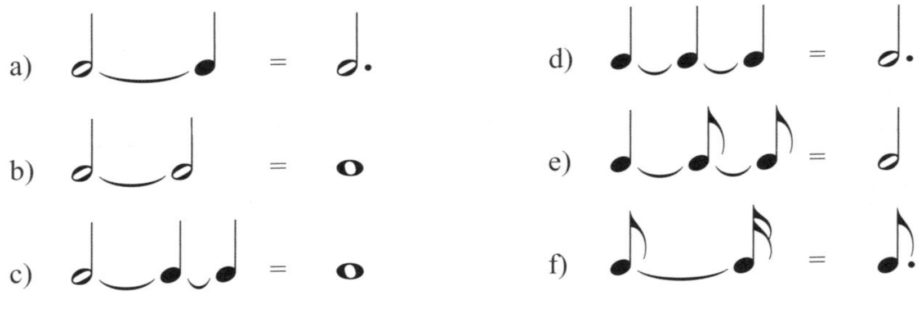

I A MORE EXERCISES (p. 15)

1. Write *three* notes that are equal to the value of each of the following.

a)
b)
c)
d)

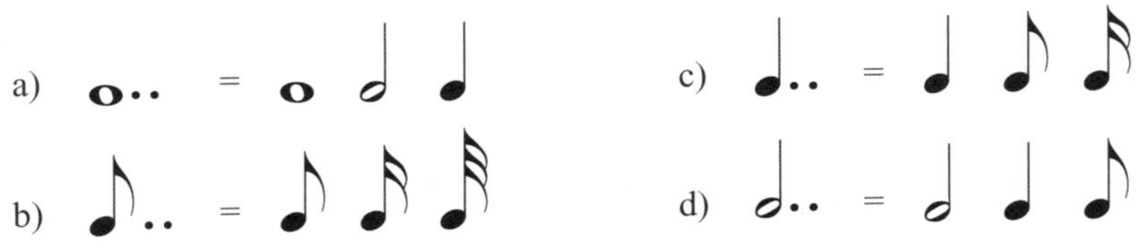

2. Write a single double-dotted rest that is equal to the value of each of the following.

a)
b)
c)
d)

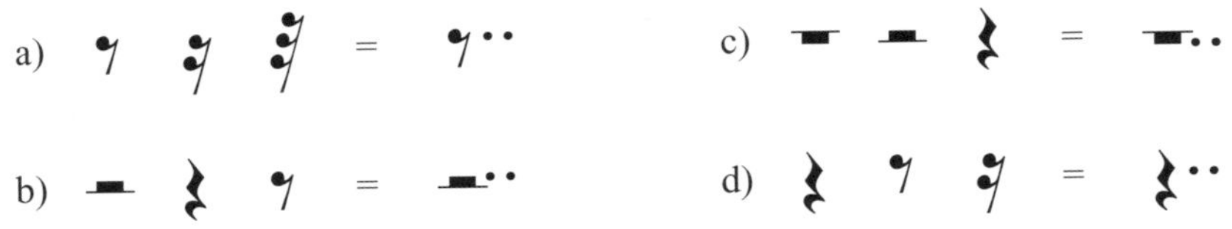

B I A EXERCISES (p. 17)

1. State whether each of the following is a diatonic semitone, a chromatic semitone, or a whole tone.

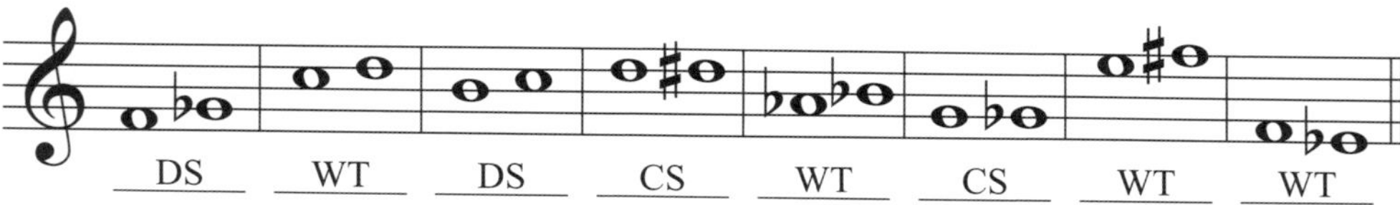

2. Write a chromatic semitone above each of the following notes.

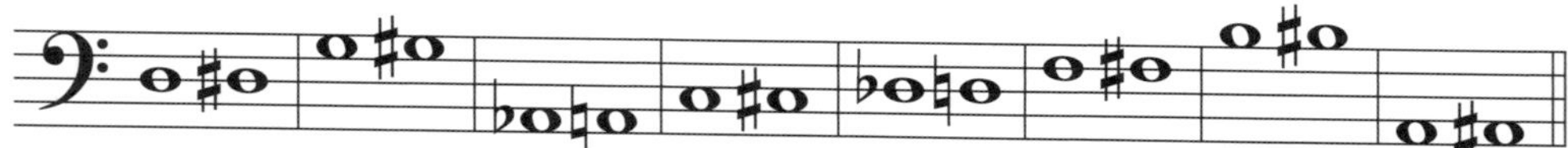

3. Write a diatonic semitone above each of the following notes.

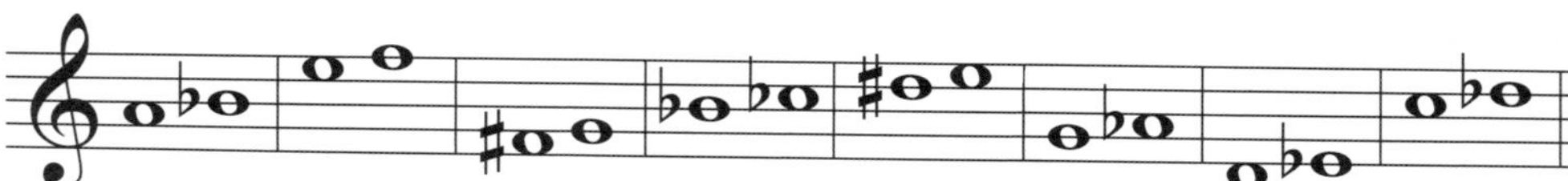

4. Write a chromatic semitone below each of the following notes.

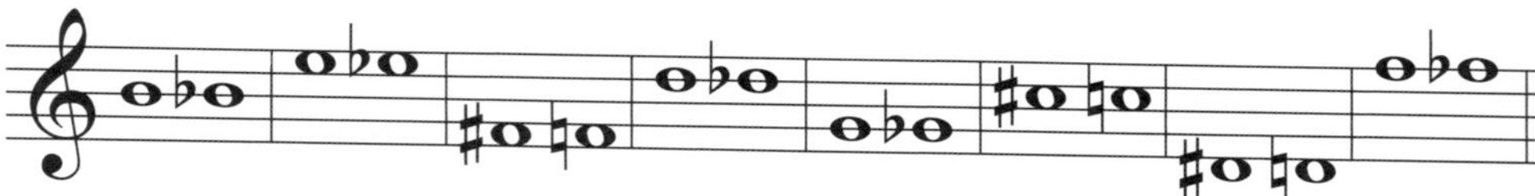

5. Write a diatonic semitone below each of the following notes.

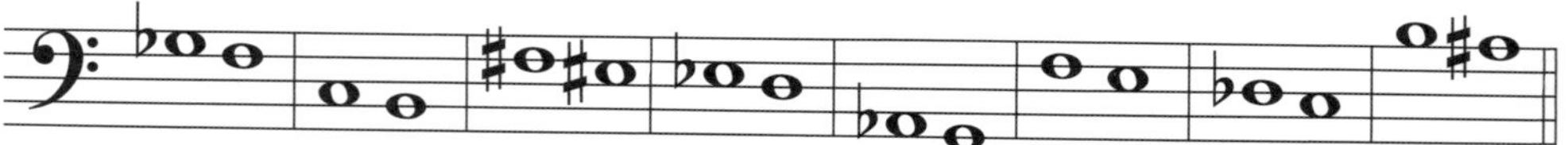

6. Name all the whole tones found between pairs of white keys on the piano.

C–D, D–E, F–G, G–A, A–B

7. Name all the whole tones found between pairs of black keys on the piano.

C♯–D♯, F♯–G♯, G♯–A♯ or D♭–E♭, G♭–A♭, A♭–B♭

8. Write a whole tone above each of the following notes.

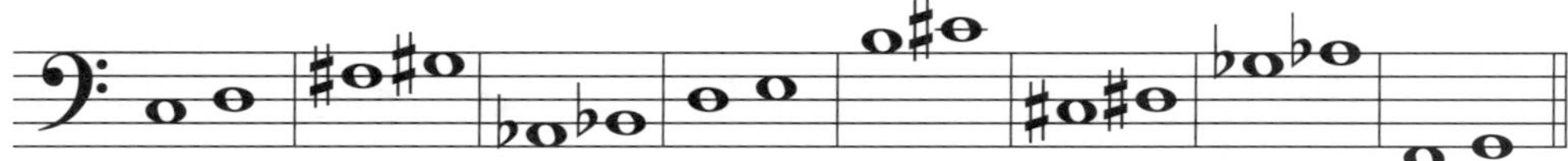

9. Write a whole tone below each of the following notes.

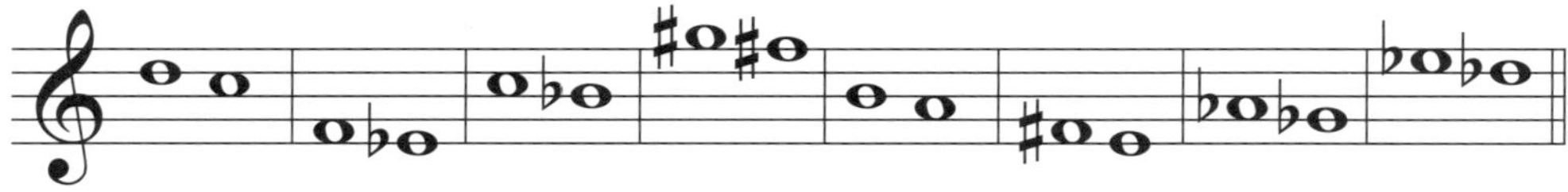

10. For each of the following notes, write a note that is enharmonically equivalent.

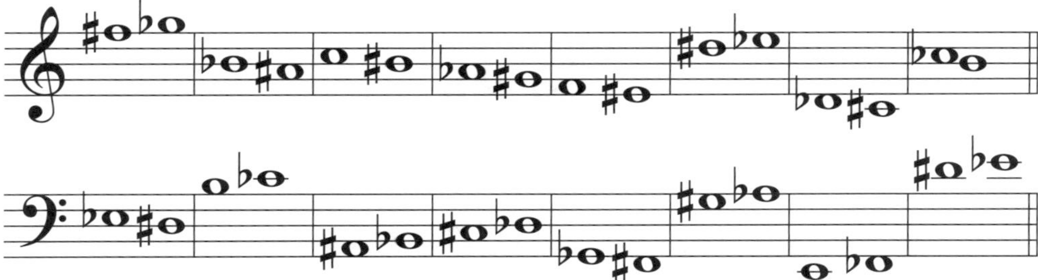

I A MORE EXERCISES (p. 19)

1. Complete the following statements.

a) To raise a ♮ one semitone, you use a ____♯____.

b) To lower a ♯ one semitone, you use a ____♮____.

c) To lower a ♮ two semitones, you use a ____𝄫____.

d) To raise a ♭ one semitone, you use a ____♮____.

e) To lower a ♮ one semitone, you use a ____♭____.

f) To raise a ♭ two semitones, you use a ____♯ or ♮♯____.

g) To raise a ♯ one semitone, you use a ____𝄪____.

h) To lower a ♯ two semitones, you use a ____♭ or ♮♭____.

i) To lower a ♭ one semitone, you use a ____𝄫____.

j) To raise a ♮ two semitones, you use a ____𝄪____.

c) E major in quarter notes

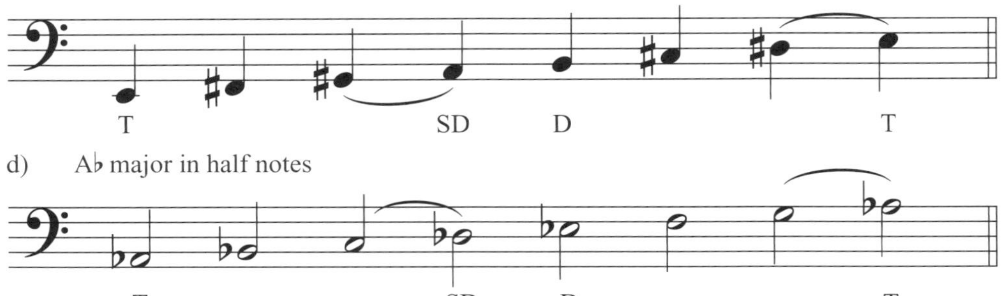

3. Write the following scales in the treble clef, ascending and descending, using the correct key signature for each. Mark each semitone with a slur, and label the tonic, subdominant, and dominant notes.

a) E major in whole notes

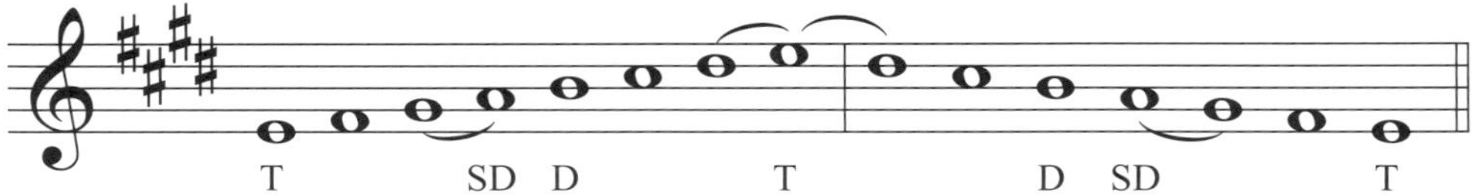

b) A♭ major in dotted half notes

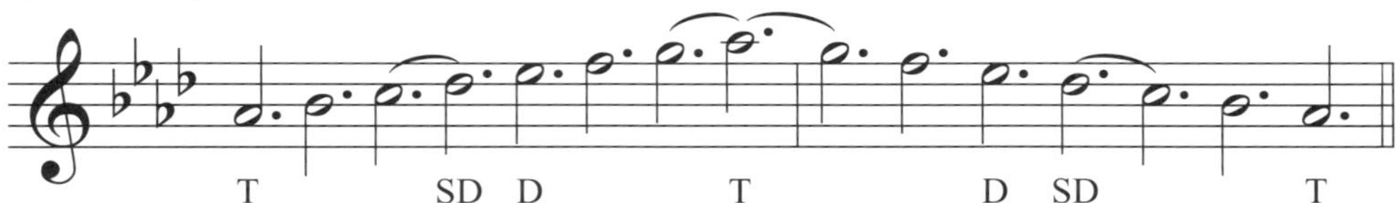

c) C major in half notes

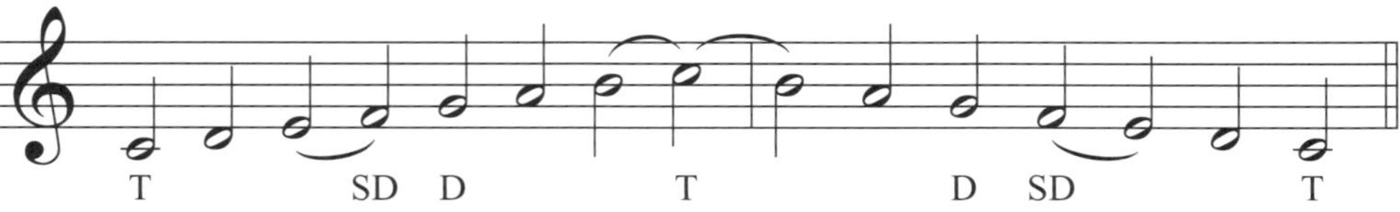

d) B♭ major in pairs of eighth notes

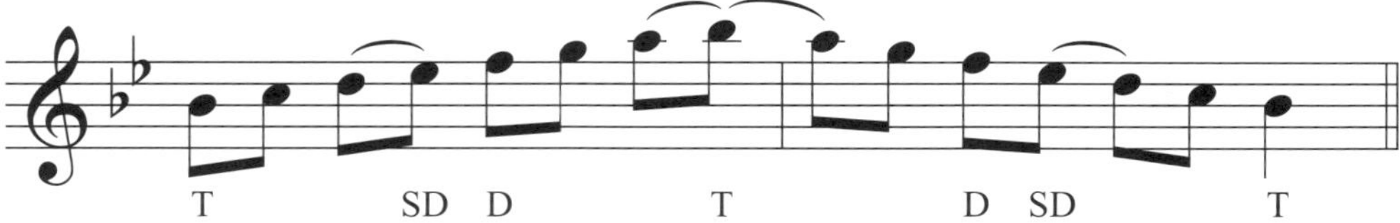

e) D major in quarter notes

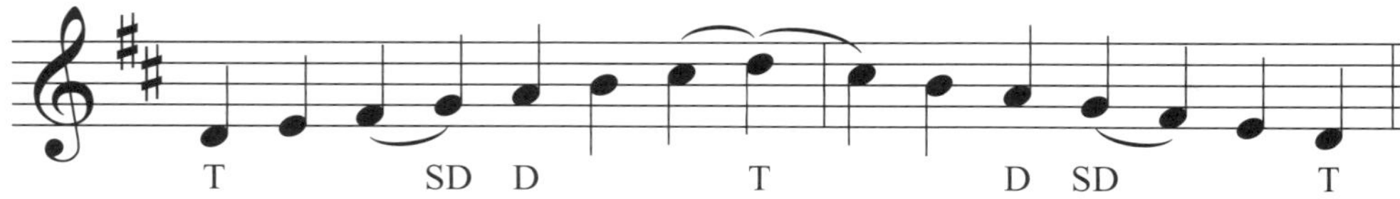

4. Write the following scales in the bass clef, ascending and descending, using the correct key signature for each. Mark each semitone with a slur, and label the tonic, subdominant, and dominant notes.

a) E♭ major in half notes

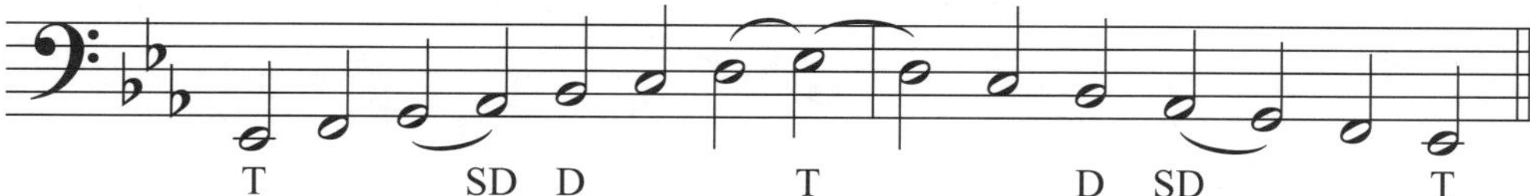

b) G major in pairs of eighth notes

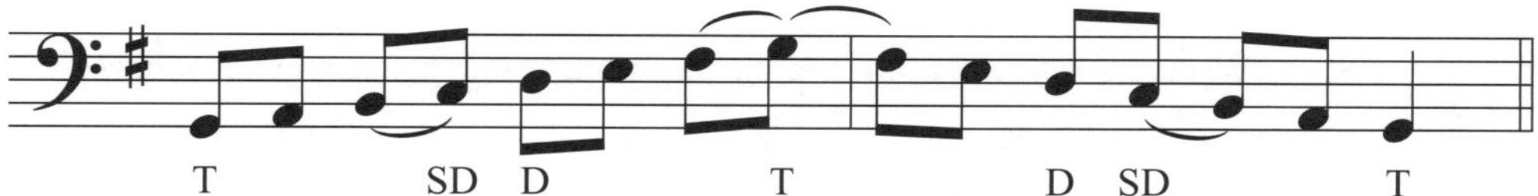

c) F major in dotted quarter notes

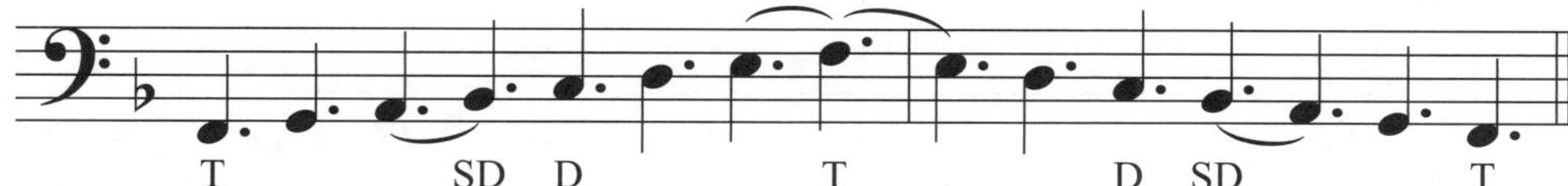

d) A major in whole notes

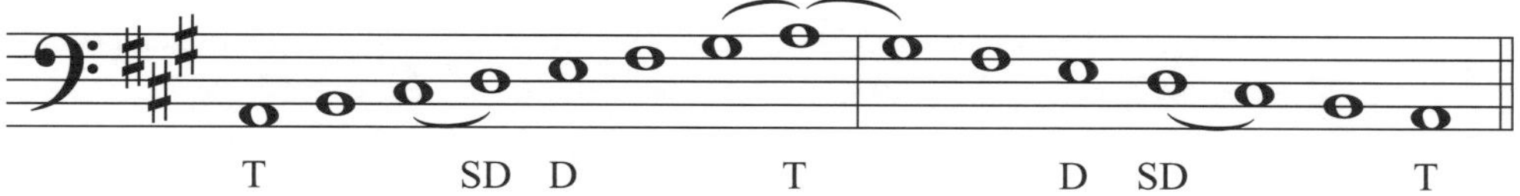

5. Write the following key signatures in the treble clef.

a) A♭ major
b) E major
c) B♭ major
d) D major

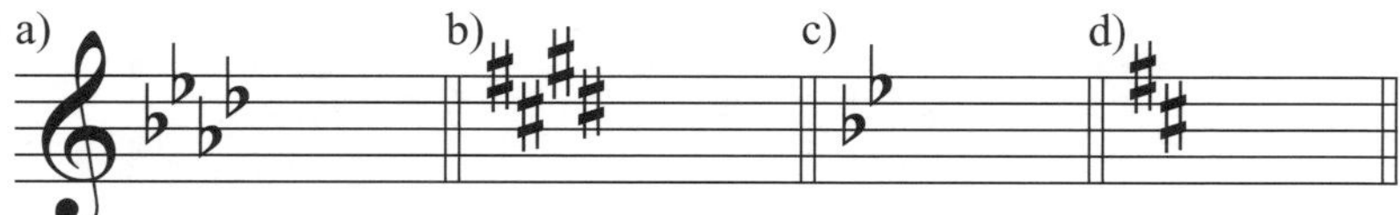

6. Write the following key signatures in the bass clef.

a) F major
b) A major
c) E♭ major
d) G major

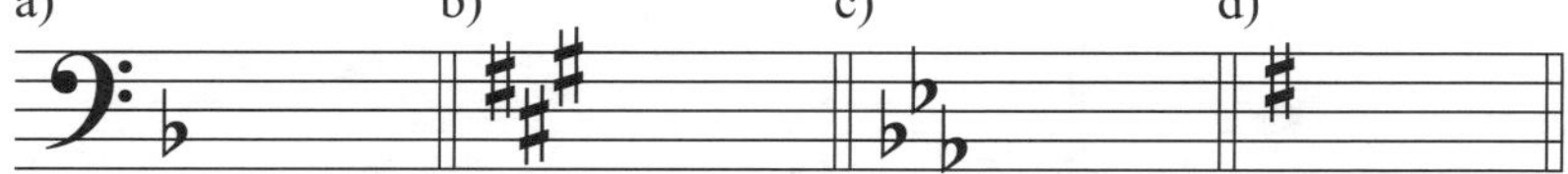

7. Write the following notes in the treble clef, using the correct key signature for each.

a) the tonic of F major
b) the tonic of E♭ major
c) the dominant of D major
d) the subdominant of B♭ major
e) the dominant of A major
f) the dominant of G major
g) the tonic of A♭ major
h) the subdominant of E major

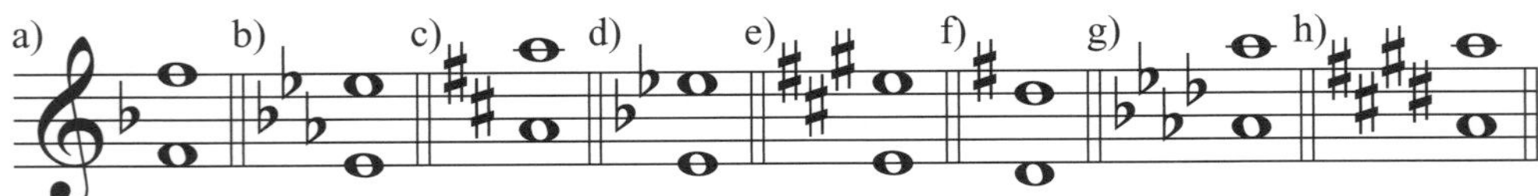

8. Write the following notes in the bass clef, using the correct key signature for each.

a) the tonic of E major
b) the dominant of B♭ major
c) the subdominant of F major
d) the subdominant of D major
e) the dominant of A♭ major
f) the tonic of C major
g) the subdominant of G major
h) the dominant of E♭ major

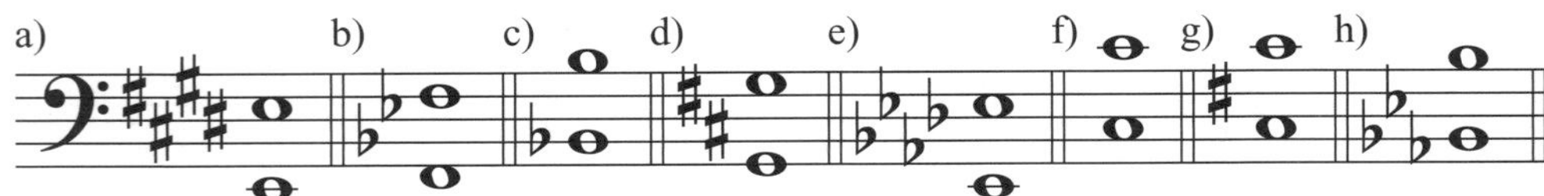

9. Write the following notes in the treble clef, using accidentals instead of a key signature.

a) the tonic of G major
b) the subdominant of F major
c) the dominant of D major
d) the dominant of B♭ major
e) the subdominant of C major
f) the tonic of B♭ major
g) the dominant of E major
h) the subdominant of E♭ major

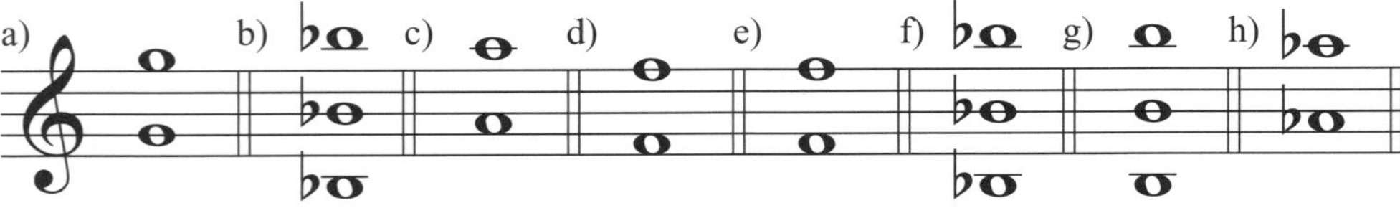

10. Write the following notes in the bass clef, using accidentals instead of a key signature.

a) the tonic of A major
b) the dominant of C major
c) the dominant of E♭ major
d) the subdominant of G major
e) the subdominant of B♭ major
f) the dominant of F major
g) the subdominant of A major
h) the tonic of D major

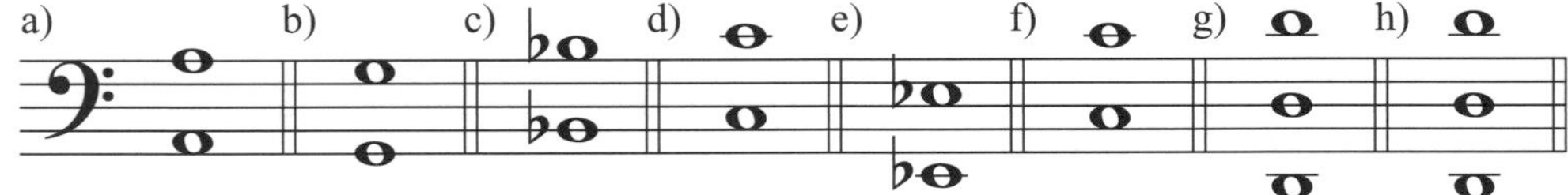

11. Fill in the blanks to complete the following sentences.

a) The key signature of D major is 2 sharps F♯, C♯.

b) The tonic of E♭ major is E♭.

c) The key signature of A♭ major is 4 flats B♭, E♭, A♭, D♭.

d) The major key that has three sharps is A major.

e) [treble clef, one sharp] is the key signature of G major.

f) The major key that has two flats is B♭ major.

g) The order of the first four sharps is F♯, C♯, G♯, D♯.

h) Semitones occur between 3rd and 4th, and 7th and 8th in every major scale.

i) The dominant of C major is G.

j) The names of the flats in E♭ major are B♭, E♭, A♭.

k) The key signature of E major is 4 sharps F♯, C♯, G♯, D♯.

l) D is the subdominant of A major.

m) The major key that has four flats is A♭ major.

n) The fifth note of any scale is called the dominant.

o) F is the dominant of B♭ major.

p) [bass clef, one flat] is the key signature of F major.

q) The order of tones and semitones in every major scale is T, T, ST, T, T, T, ST.

r) E♭ is the subdominant of B♭ major.

s) The key that has no sharps or flats is C major.

t) A scale can be divided into two tetrachords.

Opt.

I A MORE EXERCISES (p. 28)

1. Write the following notes in the treble clef, using the correct key signature for each.

a) the mediant of B major
b) the dominant of F♯ major
c) the tonic of G♭ major
d) the submediant of D major
e) the supertonic of A major
f) the leading note of E♭ major
g) the subdominant of C♯ major
h) the dominant of A♭ major
i) the supertonic of B♭ major
j) the leading note of E major

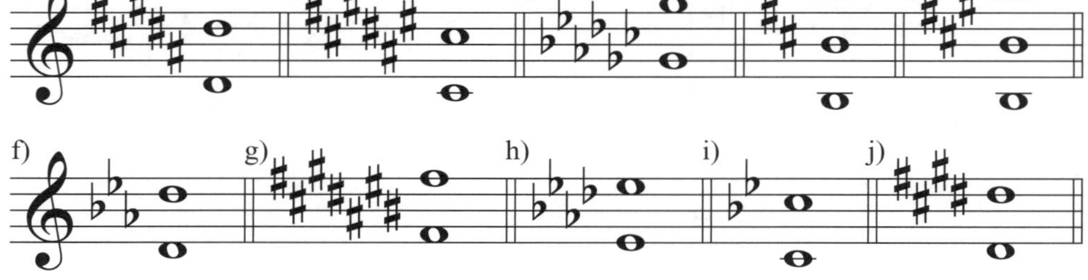

2. Write the following notes in the bass clef, using the correct key signature for each.

a) the tonic of D♭ major
b) the submediant of F major
c) the supertonic of C major
d) the dominant of E♭ major
e) the leading note of G major
f) the mediant of F♯ major
g) the subdominant of A major
h) the submediant of A♭ major
i) the mediant of B♭ major
j) the tonic of B major

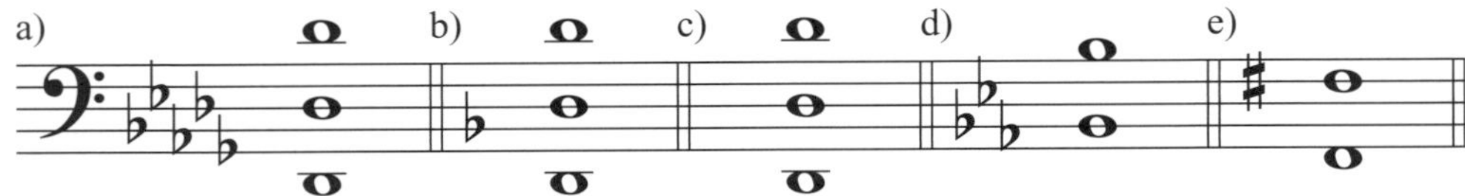

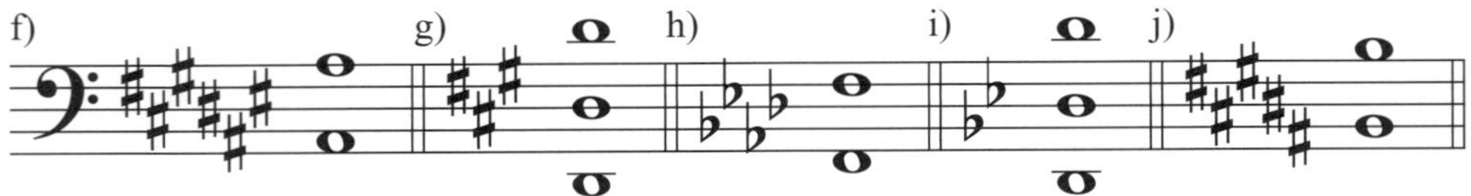

3. Write the following notes in the treble clef, using accidentals instead of a key signature.

a) the subdominant of C major
b) the tonic of E♭ major
c) the dominant of D major
d) the mediant of A major
e) the submediant of G major
f) the dominant of B major
g) the supertonic of A♭ major
h) the leading note of C♯ major

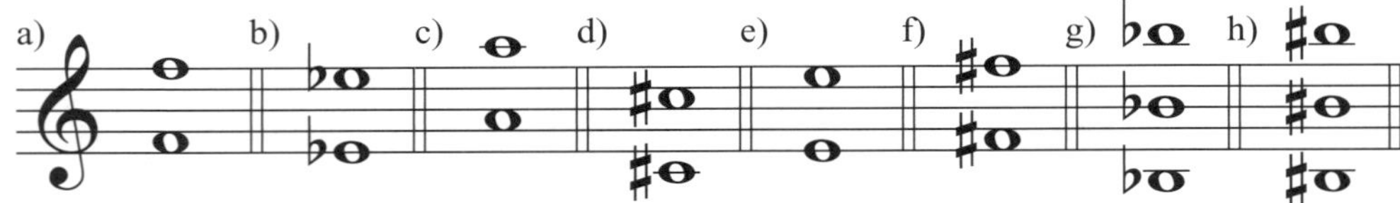

4. Write the following notes in the bass clef, using accidentals instead of a key signature.

a) the leading note of A major
b) the supertonic of G♭ major
c) the dominant of E major
d) the submediant of B♭ major
e) the mediant of C♯ major
f) the leading note of B major
g) the supertonic of D major
h) the subdominant of G major

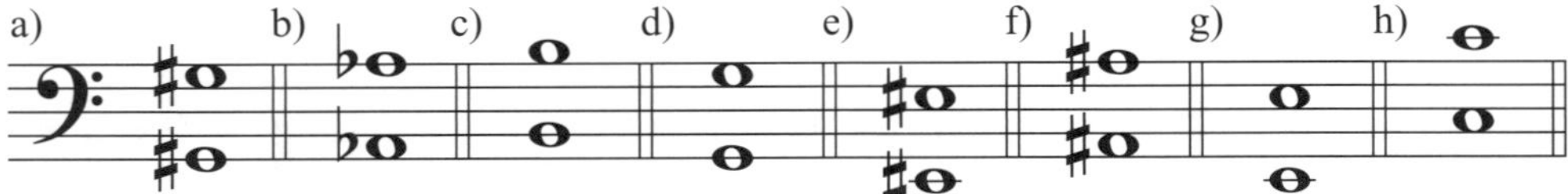

5. List the order of the sharps as they appear in a key signature.

F♯ C♯ G♯ D♯ A♯ E♯ B♯

6. List the order of the flats as they appear in a key signature.

B♭ E♭ A♭ D♭ G♭ C♭ F♭

7. For each of the following, name the major key and the technical degree name of the given note.

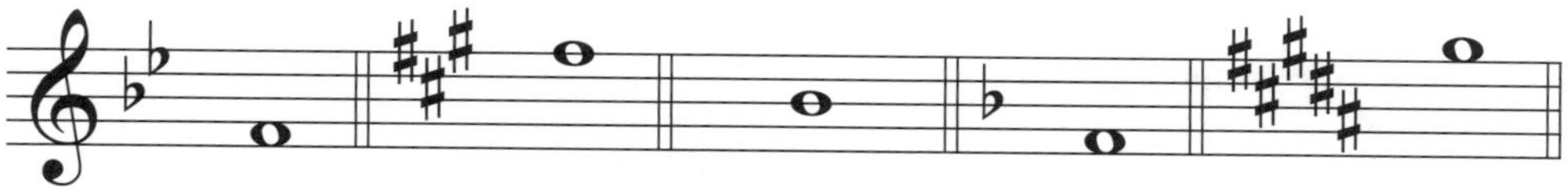

key:	B♭	A	C	F	B
degree:	dominant	submediant	leading note	tonic	submediant

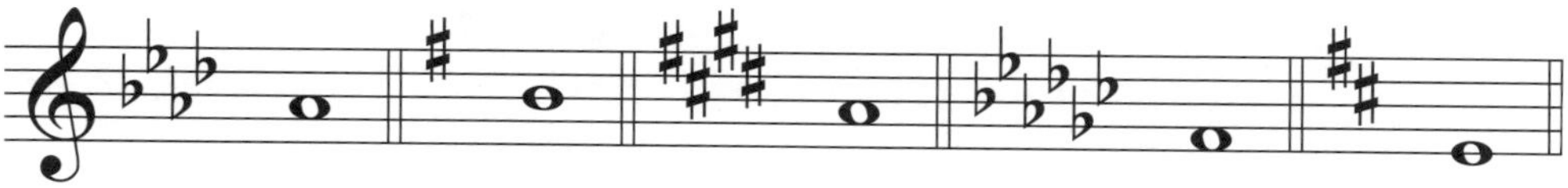

key:	A♭	G	E	G♭	D
degree:	tonic	mediant	subdominant	leading note	supertonic

8. For each of the following, name the major key and the technical degree name of the given note.

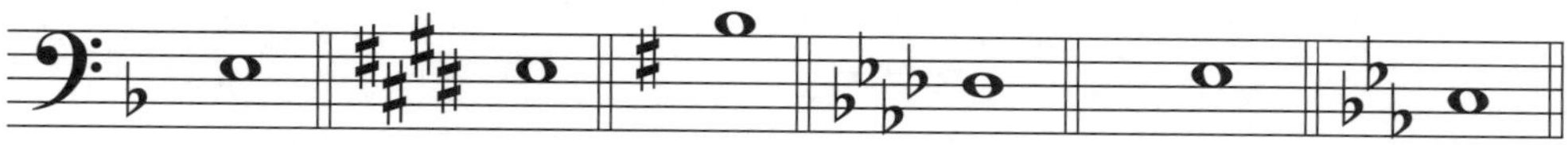

key:	F	E	G	A♭	C	E♭
degree:	leading note	tonic	mediant	subdominant	mediant	submediant

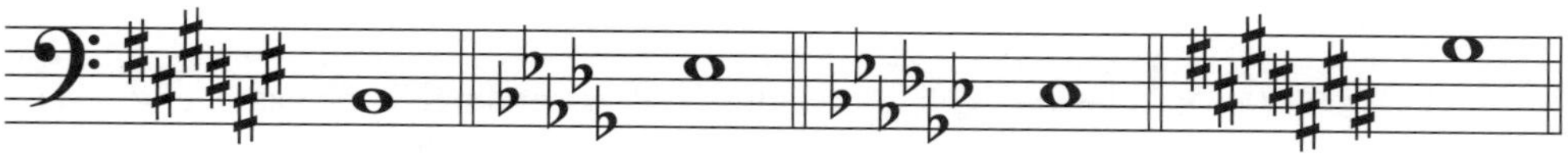

key:	F♯	D♭	G♭	C♯
degree:	subdominant	supertonic	subdominant	dominant

9. Write the following scales, ascending and descending, in the treble clef. Use accidentals instead of a key signature, and mark the semitones with slurs.

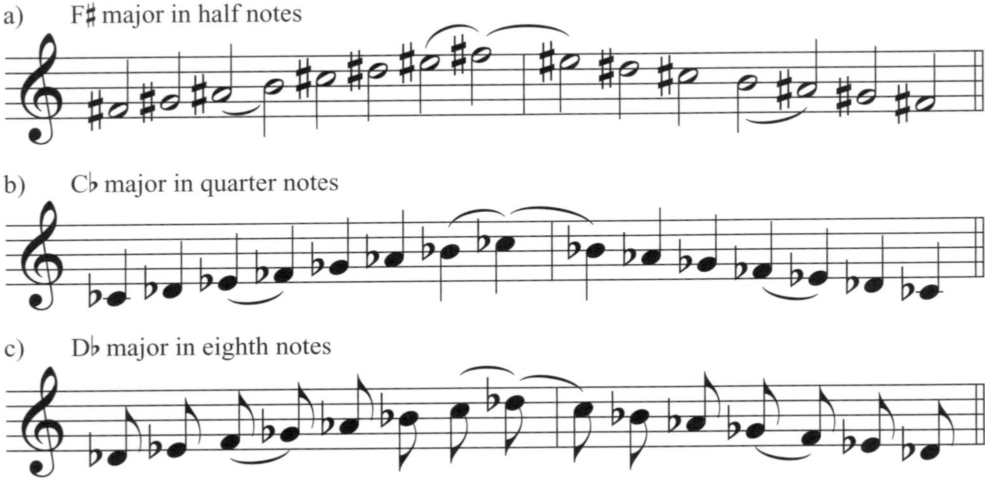

10. Write the following scales, ascending and descending, in the treble clef. Use the correct key signature for each, and mark the semitones with slurs.

a) C♯ major in sixteenth notes

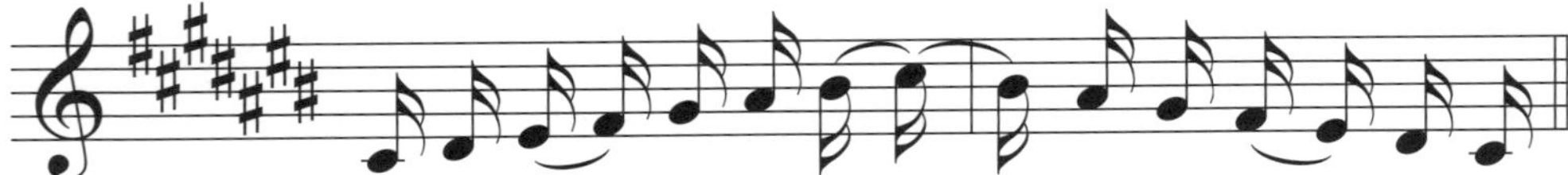

b) B major in half notes

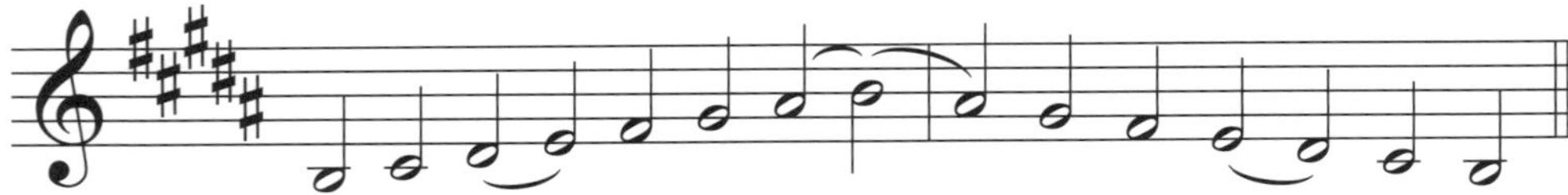

c) G♭ major in whole notes

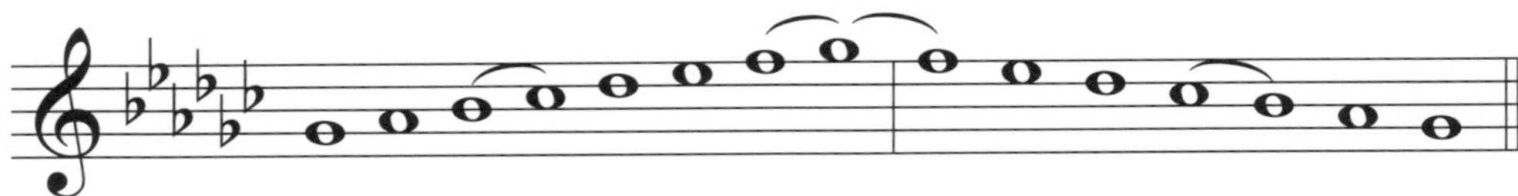

11. Write the following scales, ascending and descending, in the bass clef. Use accidentals instead of a key signature, and mark the semitones with slurs.

a) B major in quarter notes

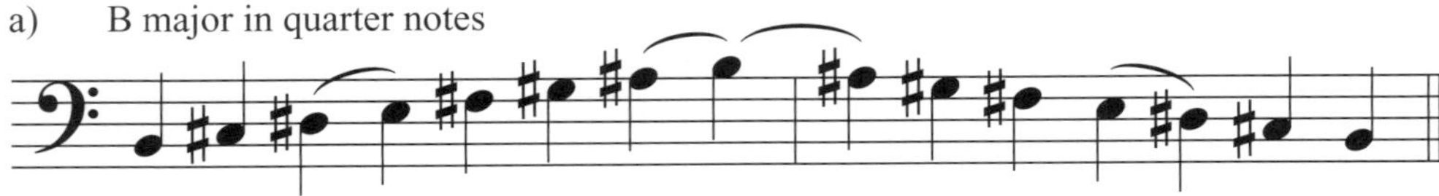

b) C♯ major in eighth notes

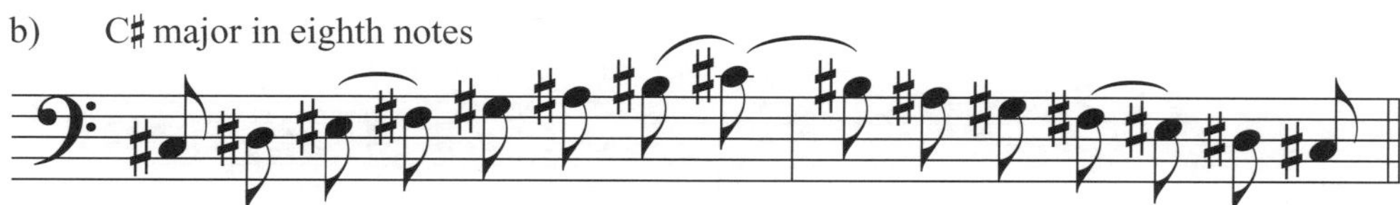

c) G♭ major in dotted half notes

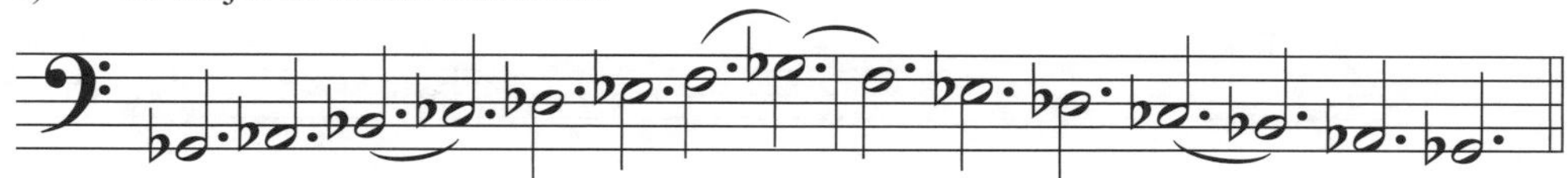

12. Write the following scales, ascending and descending, in the bass clef. Use the correct key signature for each, and mark the semitones with slurs.

a) F♯ major in dotted quarter notes

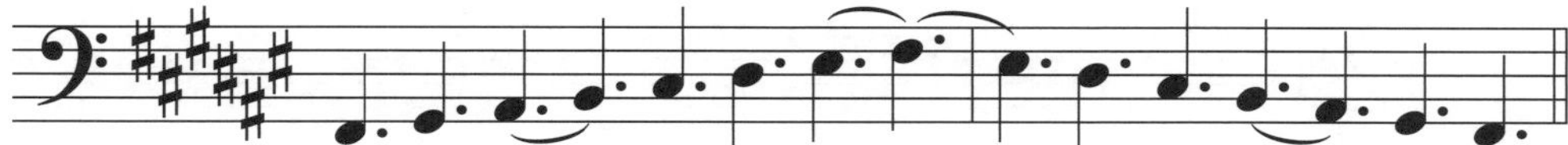

b) D♭ major in whole notes

c) C♭ major in sixteenth notes

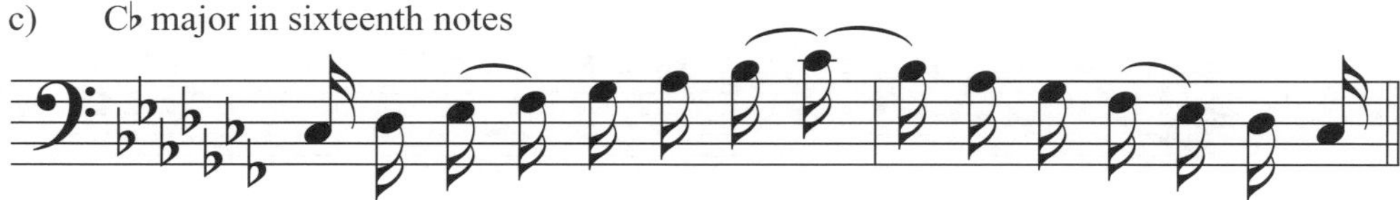

13. Write the following scales in the treble clef, ascending only. Use the correct key signature for each. Use whole notes.

a) the major scale whose key signature is five flats
b) the major scale whose dominant is G♯
c) the major scale whose leading note is A♯
d) the major scale whose key signature is six flats
e) the major scale whose supertonic is G♯
f) the major scale whose mediant is E♭
g) the major scale whose subdominant is F♯
h) the major scale whose submediant is G♯
i) the major scale whose leading note is F
j) the major scale whose mediant is G

a) b)

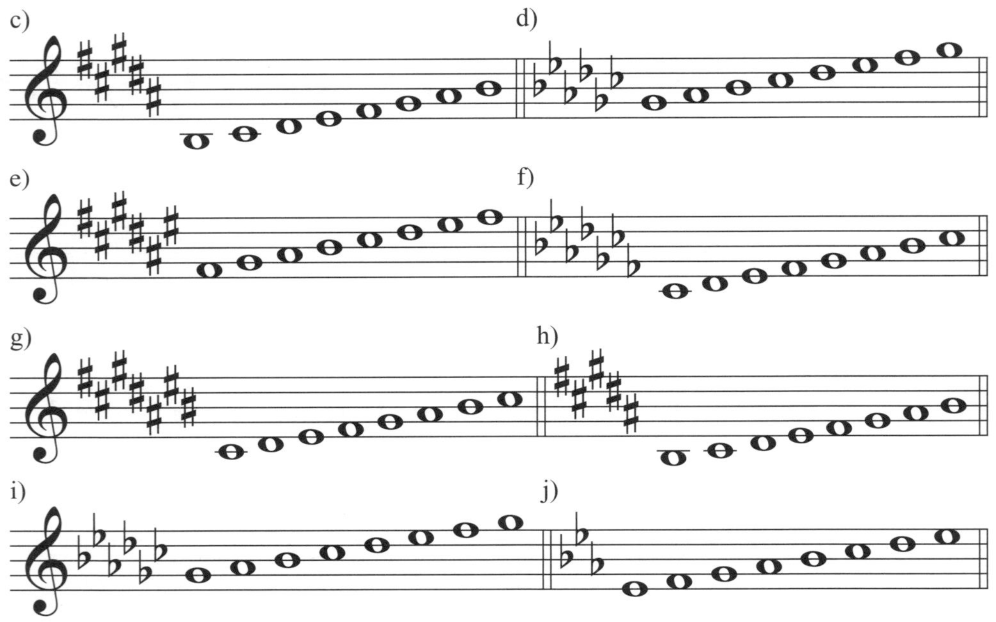

A STILL MORE EXERCISES (p. 32)

1. Write the following scales in the alto clef, ascending and descending. Use the correct key signature for each, and mark the semitones with slurs. Use whole notes.

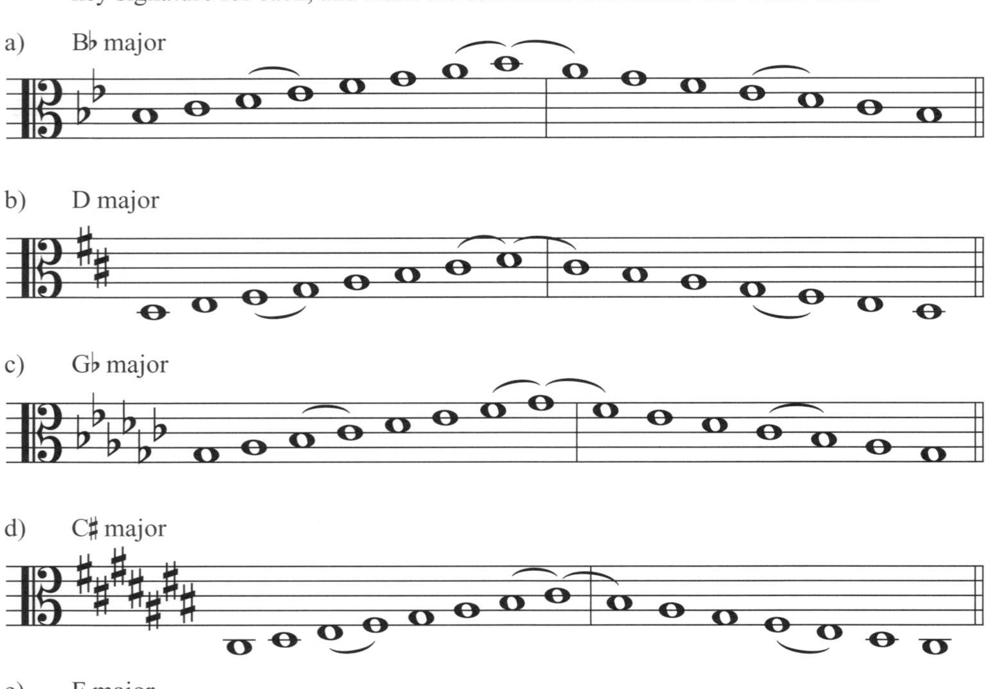

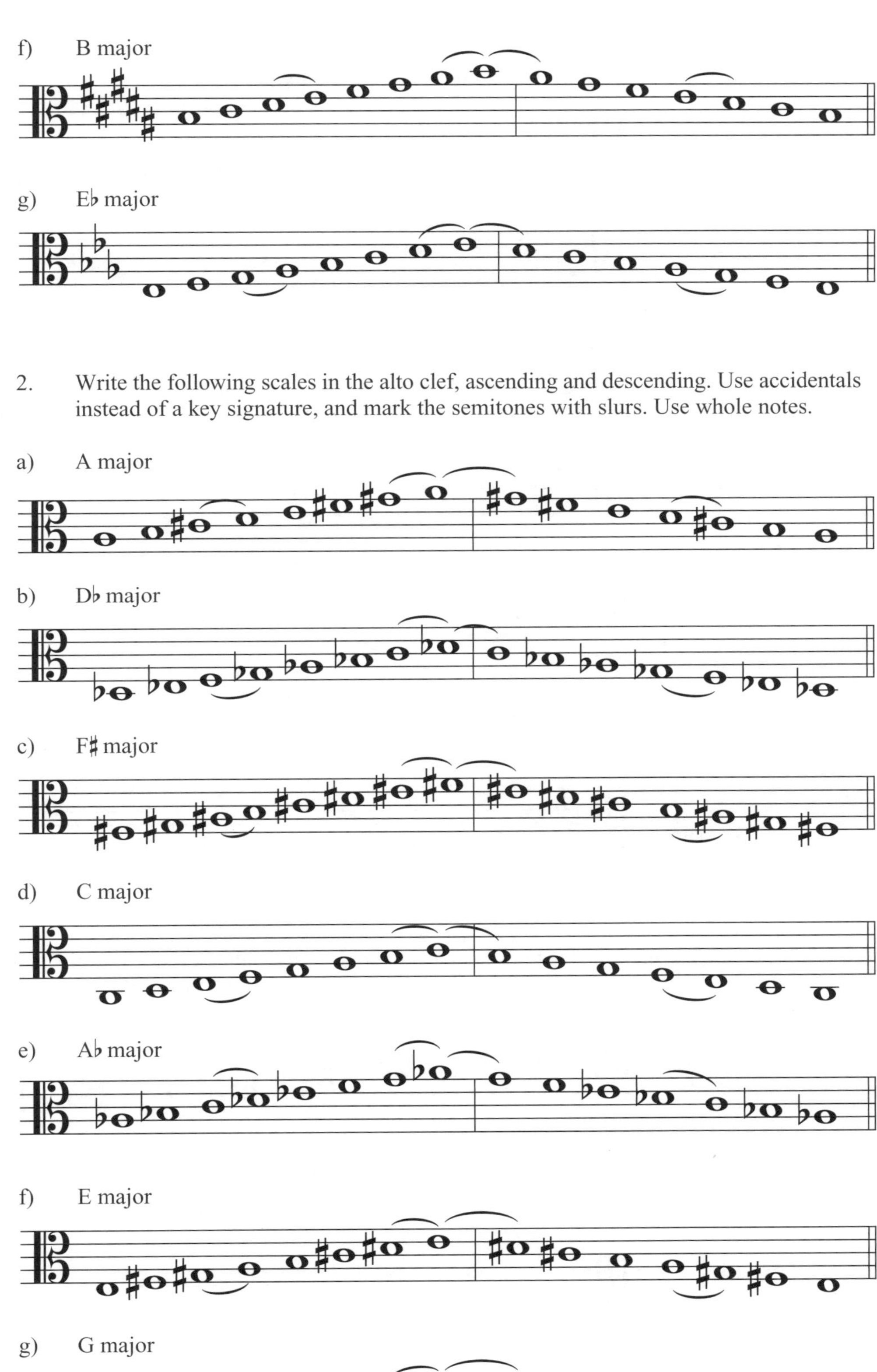

2. Write the following scales in the alto clef, ascending and descending. Use accidentals instead of a key signature, and mark the semitones with slurs. Use whole notes.

3. Write the following scales in the tenor clef, descending only. Use the correct key signature for each, and mark the semitones with slurs. Use whole notes.

a) C major

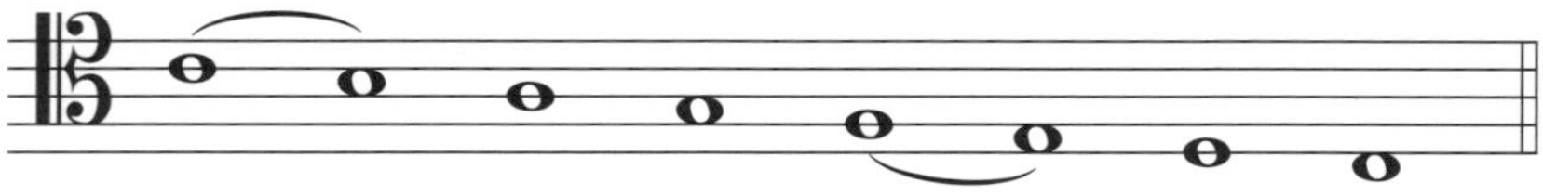

b) E major

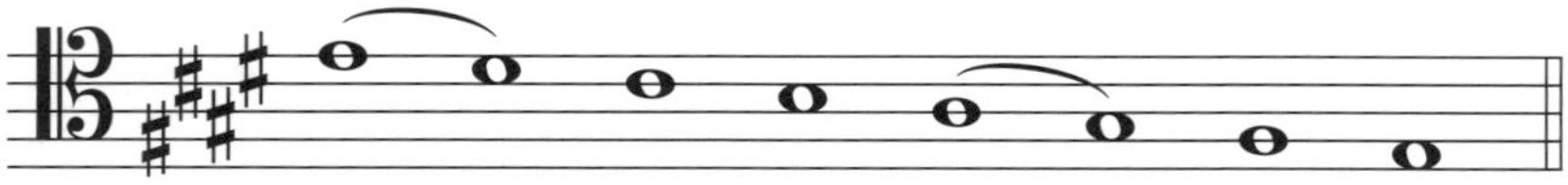

c) G major

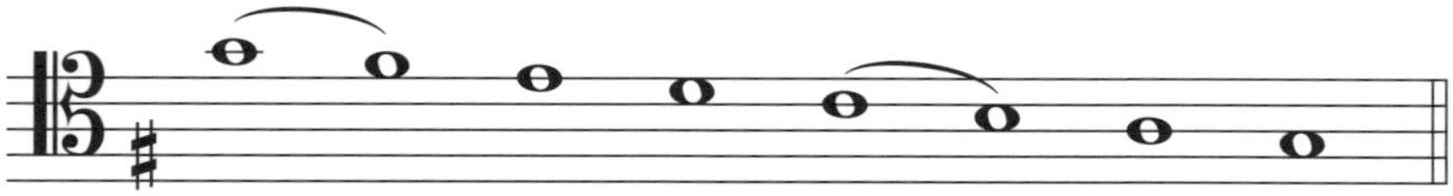

d) A major

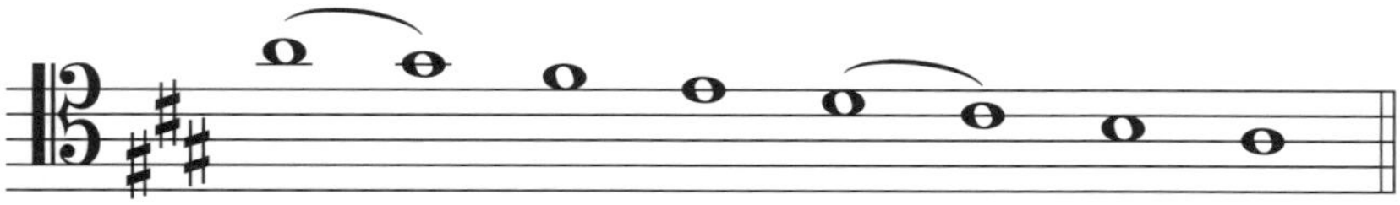

e) D♭ major

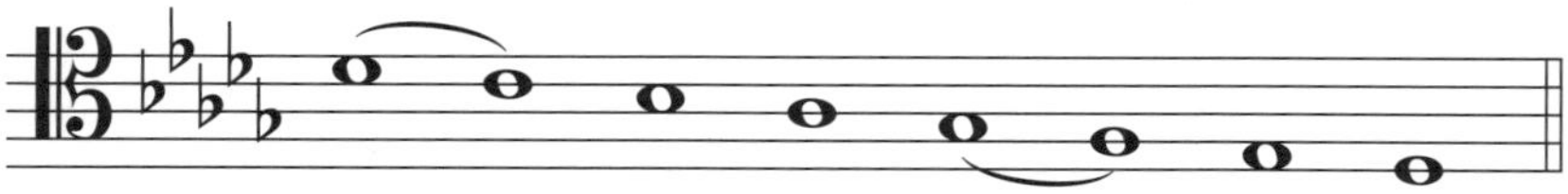

f) F♯ major

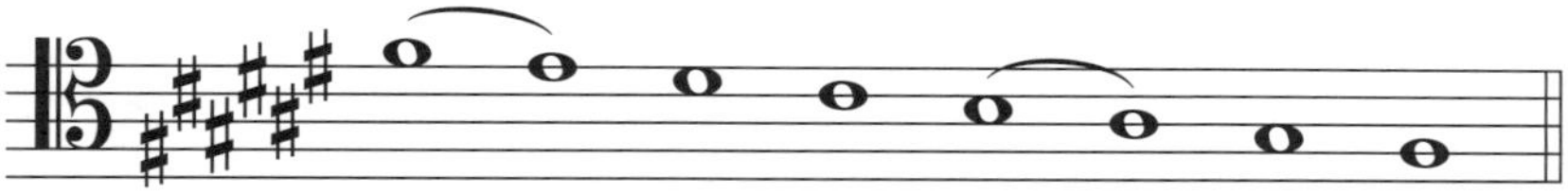

g) A♭ major

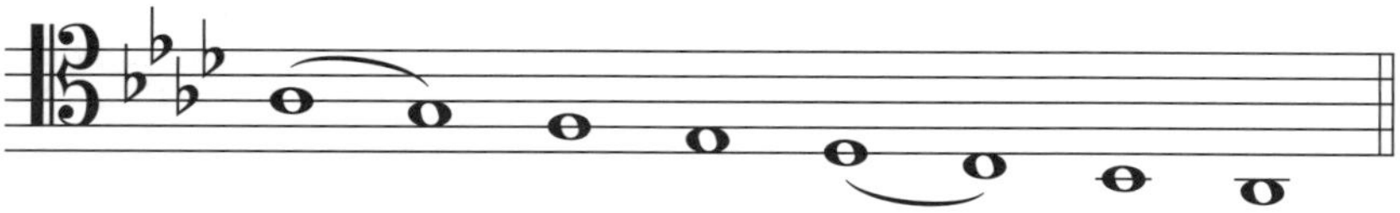

4. Write the following scales in the tenor clef, descending only. Use accidentals instead of a key signature, and mark the semitones with slurs. Use whole notes.

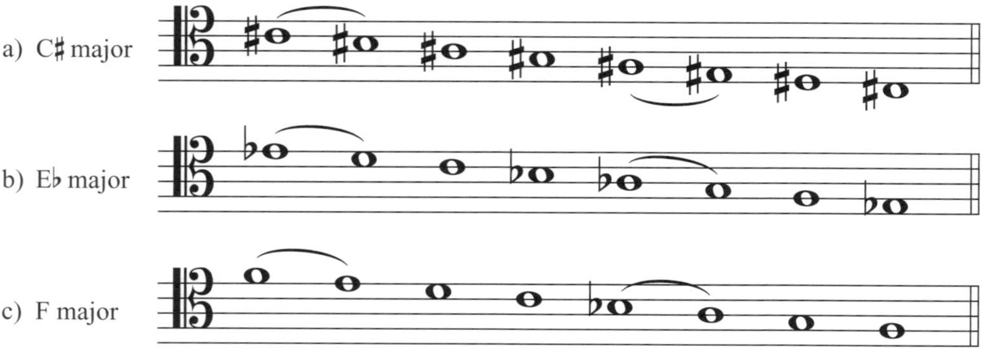

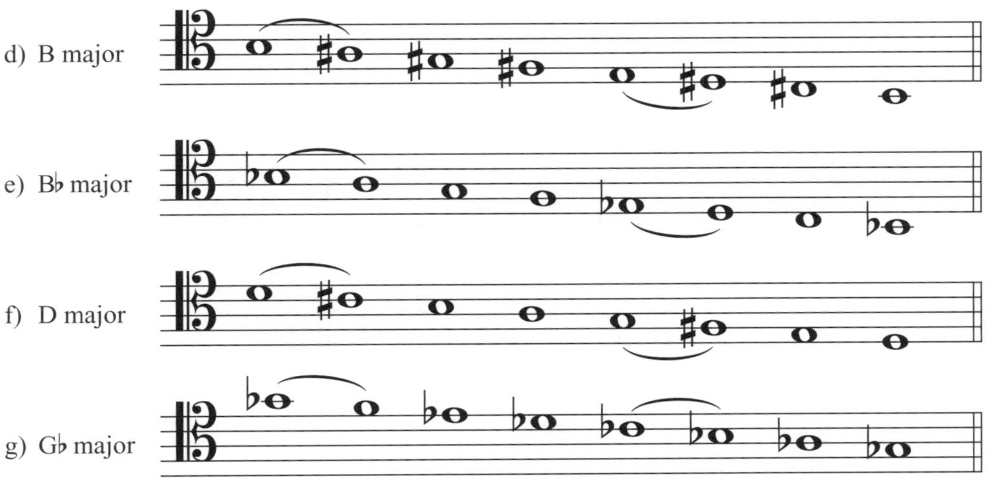

5. Write the following scales in the bass clef, ascending and descending. Use the correct key signature, and mark the semitones with slurs. Use whole notes.

a) B♭ major, from dominant to dominant

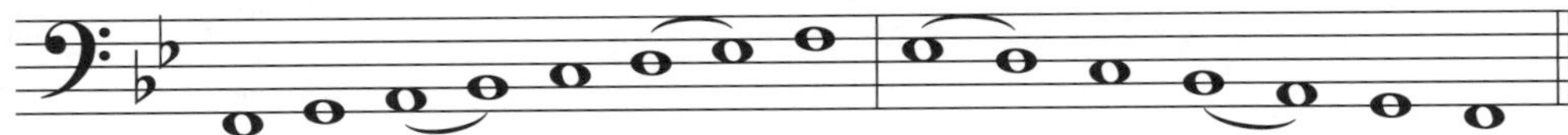

b) E major, from supertonic to supertonic

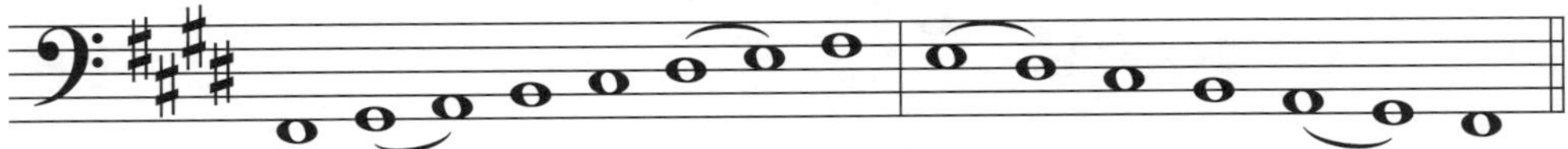

c) D♭ major, from subdominant to subdominant

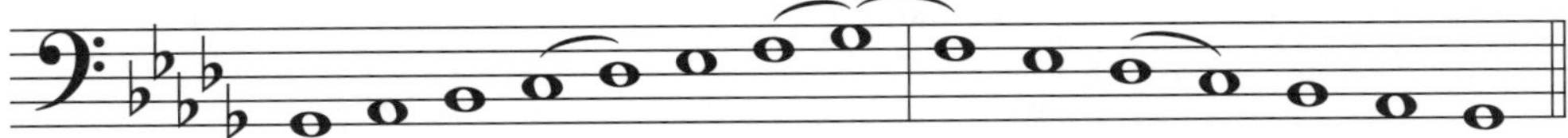

d) G major, from submediant to submediant

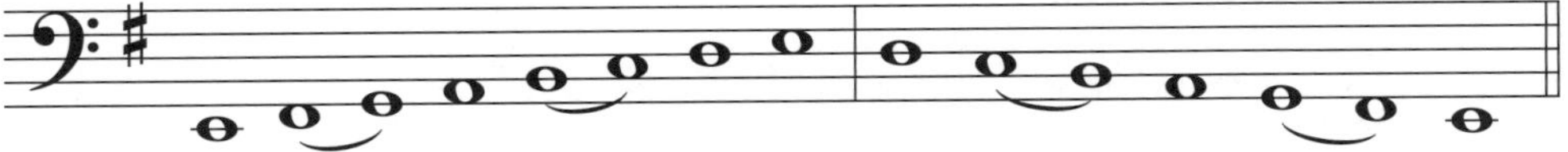

e) C♯ major, from tonic to tonic

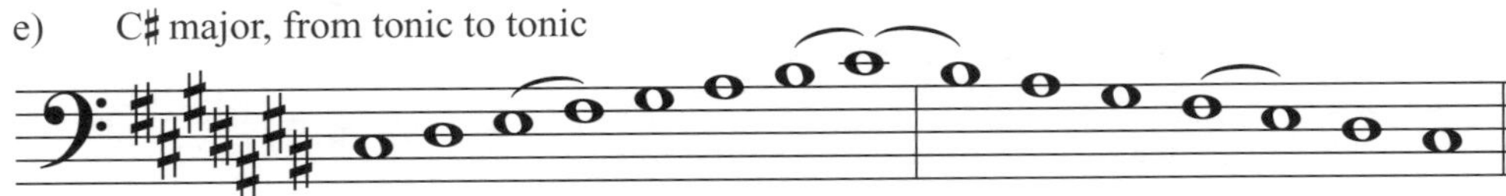

6. Write the following scales in the treble clef, ascending and descending. Use accidentals instead of a key signature, and mark the semitones with slurs. Use whole notes.

a) A major, from mediant to mediant

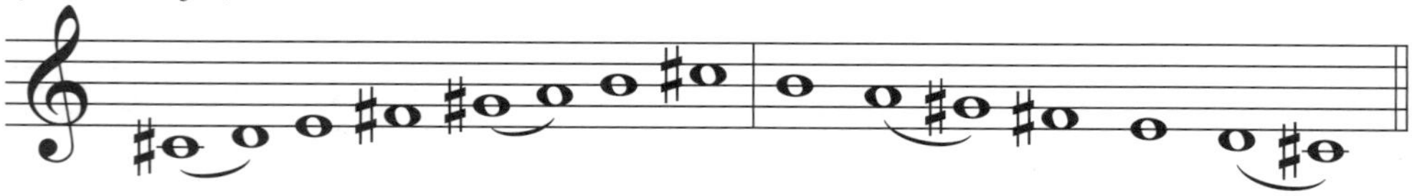

b) F♯ major, from tonic to tonic

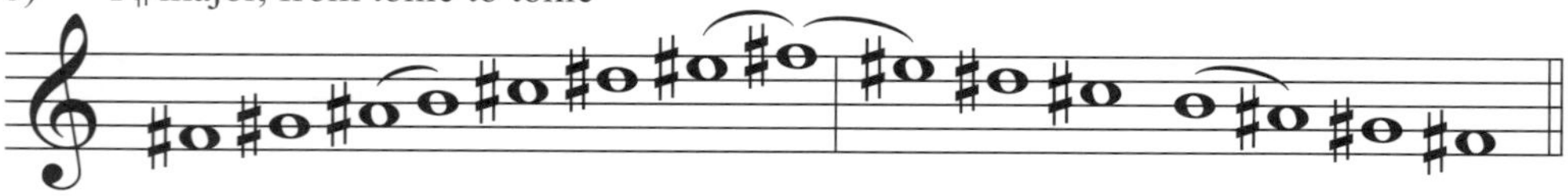

c) E♭ major, from dominant to dominant

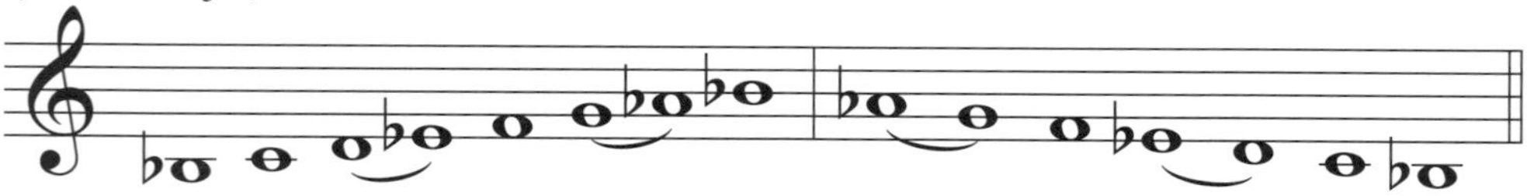

d) D major, from leading note to leading note

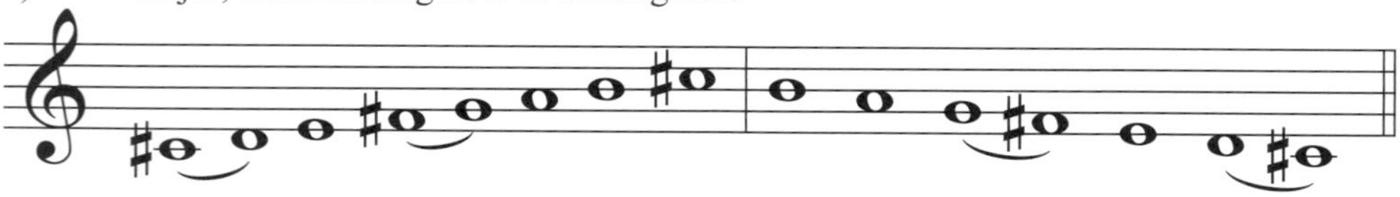

e) B major, from supertonic to supertonic

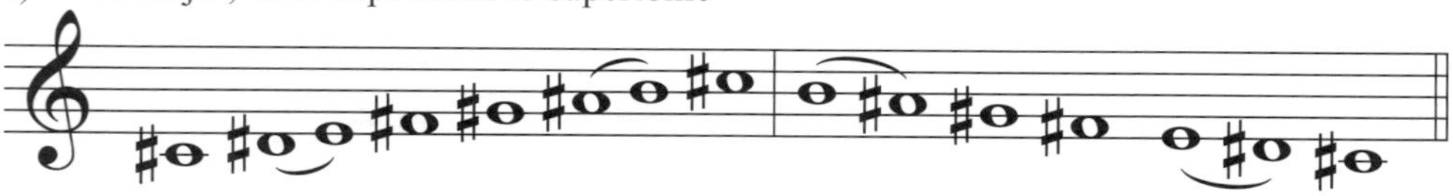

7. Write the following scales in the alto clef, ascending and descending. Use the correct key signature, and mark the semitones with slurs. Use whole notes.

a) A♭ major, from dominant to dominant

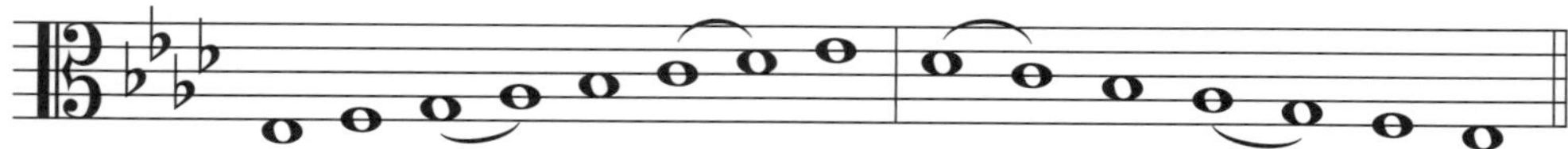

b) F♯ major, from leading note to leading note

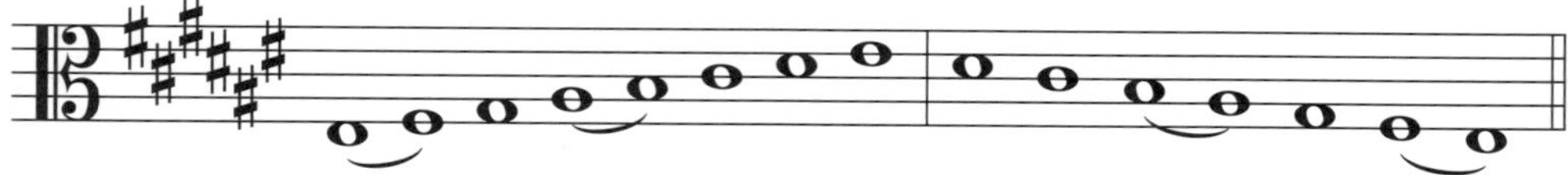

c) G♭ major, from supertonic to supertonic

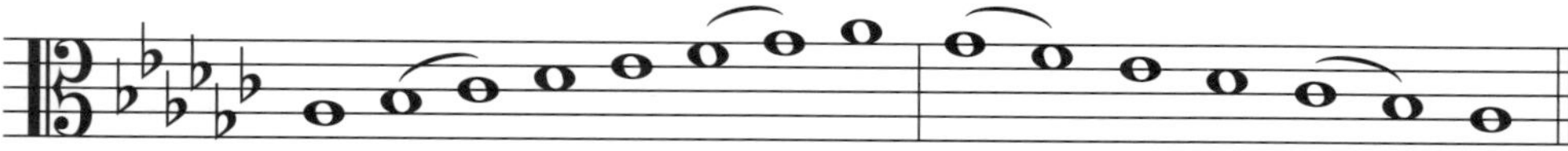

d) B major, from subdominant to subdominant

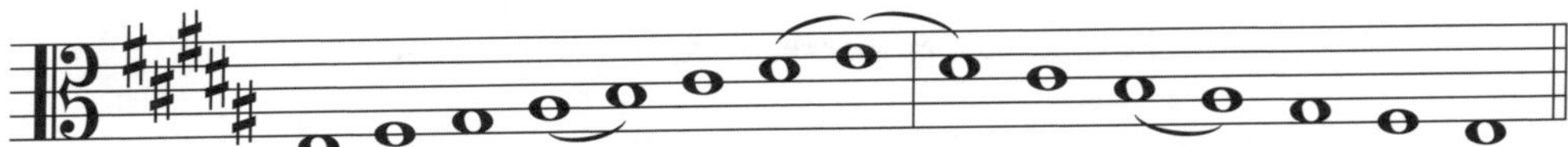

e) A major, from submediant to submediant

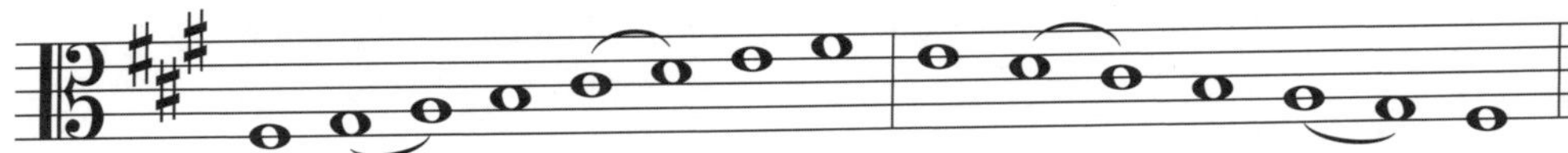

8. Write the following scales in the tenor clef, ascending and descending. Use accidentals instead of a key signature, and mark the semitones with slurs. Use whole notes.

a) D♭ major, from tonic to tonic

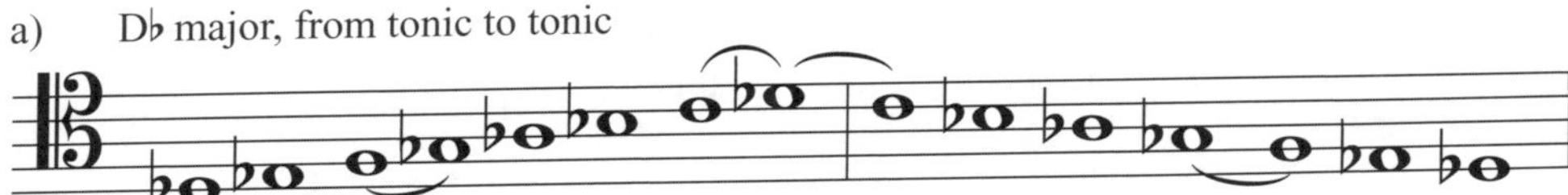

b) E major, from submediant to submediant

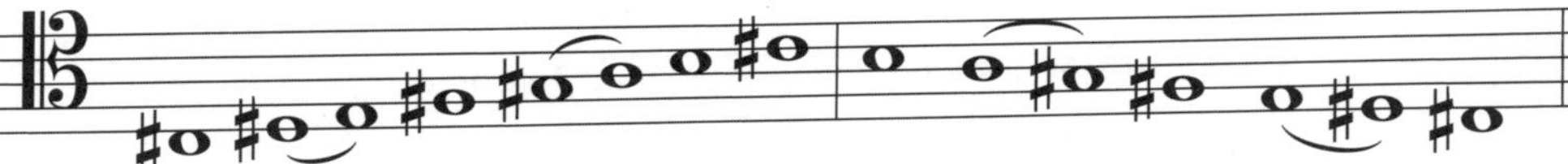

c) F major, from mediant to mediant

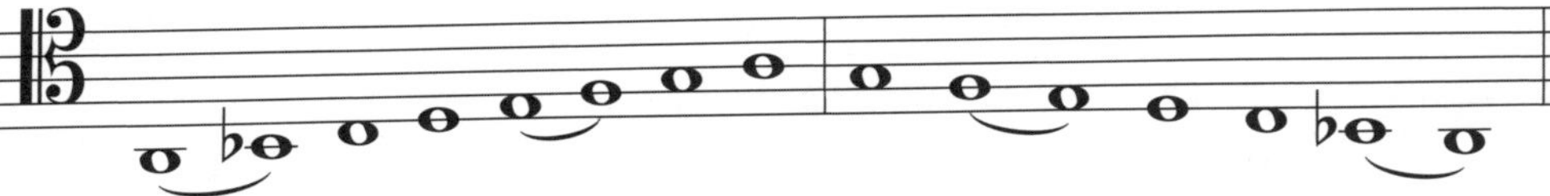

d) C♯ major, from supertonic to supertonic

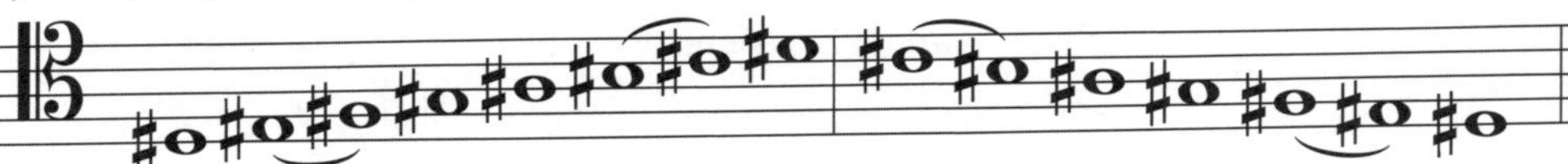

e) B♭ major, from leading note to leading note

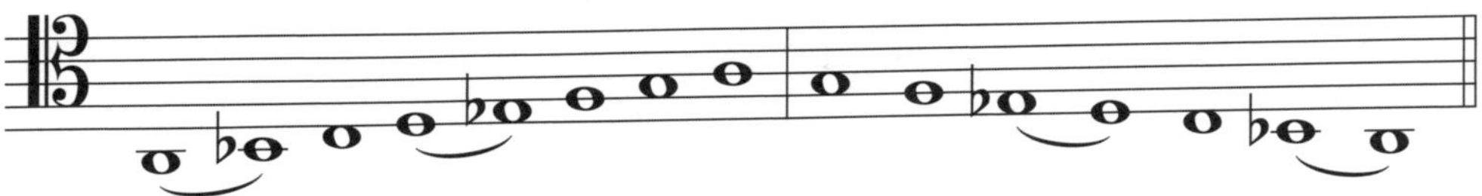

B I A EXERCISES (p. 45)

1. Name the relative major of the following minor keys.

a) C♯ minor E major
b) A minor C major
c) F minor A♭ major
d) B minor D major
e) G minor B♭ major
f) E minor G major

2. Name the relative minor of the following major keys.

a) A major F♯ minor
b) E♭ major C minor
c) F major D minor
d) E major C♯ minor
e) G major E minor
f) B♭ major G minor

3. Fill in the blanks to complete the following sentences.

a) The minor key whose key signature is one sharp is E minor.
b) The key signature of B minor is 2 sharps F♯, C♯.
c) The key signature of A major is 3 sharps F♯, C♯, G♯.
d) The major key whose key signature is four flats is A♭ major.
e) The subdominant of D minor is G.
f) The minor key whose key signature is three sharps is F♯ minor.
g) The key signature of E♭ major is 3 flats B♭, E♭, A♭.
h) The dominant of F♯ minor is C♯.
i) The major key whose key signature is two flats is B♭ major.
j) The key signature of F minor is 4 flats B♭, E♭, A♭, D♭.
k) The minor key whose key signature is two flats is G minor.
l) The major key whose key signature is one sharp is G major.
m) The key signature of C♯ minor is 4 sharps F♯, C♯, G♯, D♯.
n) The dominant of B minor is F♯.
o) The key signature of F major is 1 flat B♭.
p) The key signature of D minor is 1 flat B♭.
q) The major key whose key signature is four sharps is E major.
r) The minor key whose key signature is three flats is C minor.
s) The key signature of D major is 2 sharps F♯, C♯.
t) The subdominant of C♯ minor is F♯.

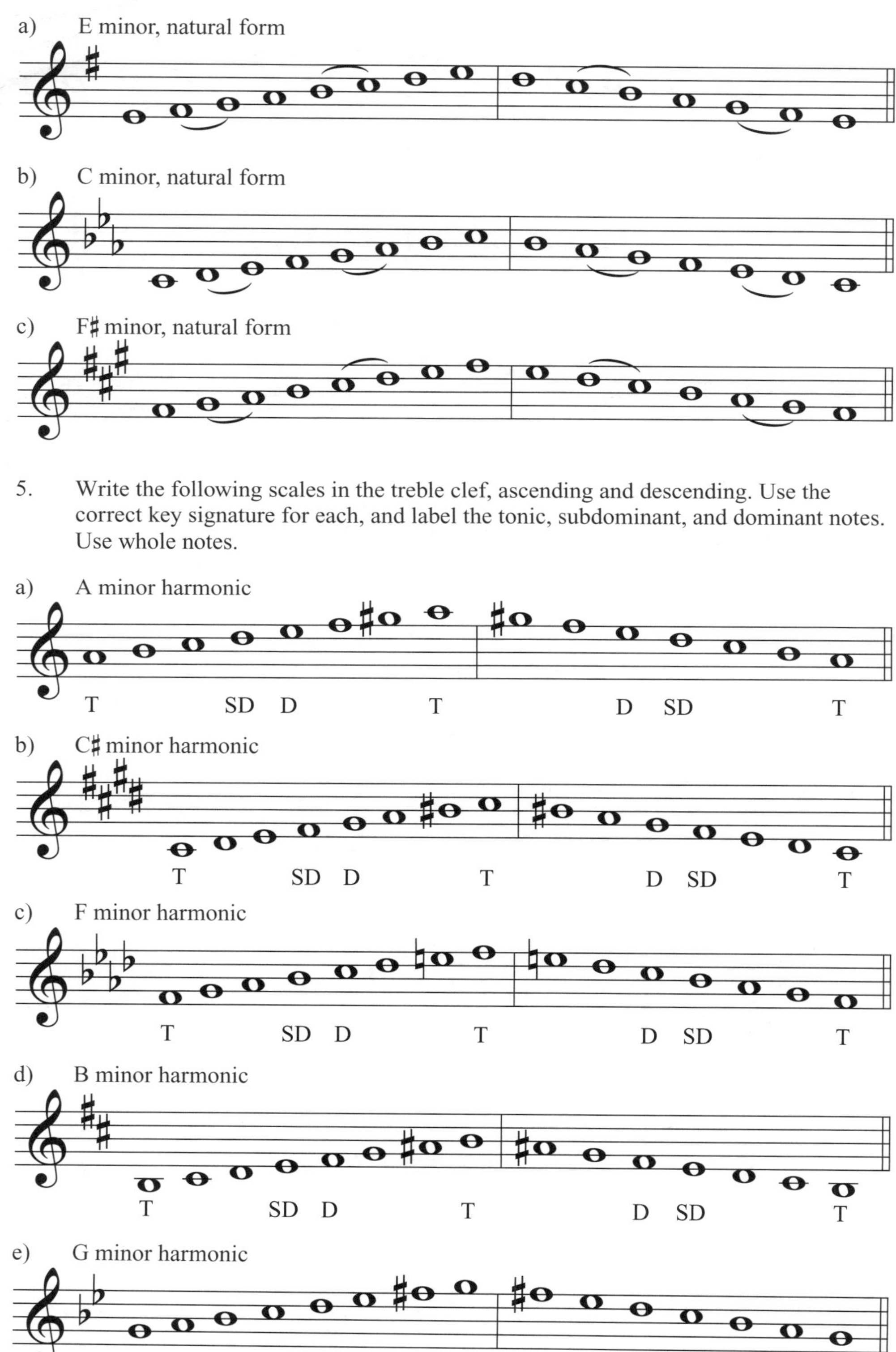
4. Write the following scales in the treble clef, ascending and descending. Use the correct key signature for each, and mark the semitones with slurs. Use whole notes.
a) E minor, natural form
b) C minor, natural form
c) F♯ minor, natural form
5. Write the following scales in the treble clef, ascending and descending. Use the correct key signature for each, and label the tonic, subdominant, and dominant notes. Use whole notes.
a) A minor harmonic
T SD D T D SD T
b) C♯ minor harmonic
T SD D T D SD T
c) F minor harmonic
T SD D T D SD T
d) B minor harmonic
T SD D T D SD T
e) G minor harmonic
T SD D T D SD T

6. Write the following scales in the bass clef, ascending and descending. Use accidentals instead of a key signature. Use whole notes.

a) D minor melodic

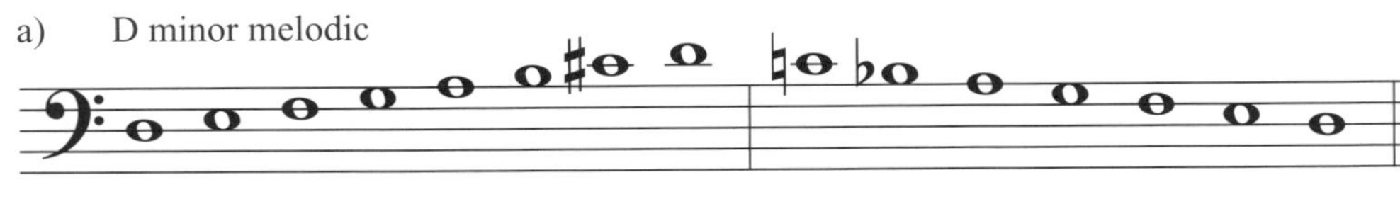

b) E minor melodic

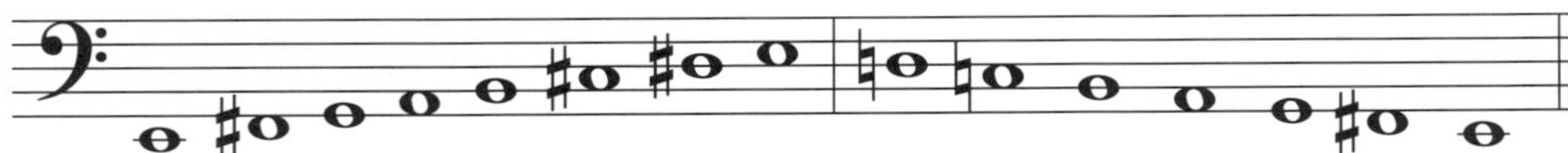

c) C minor melodic

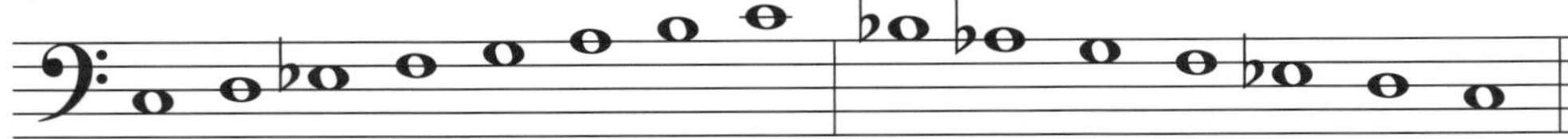

d) F♯ minor melodic

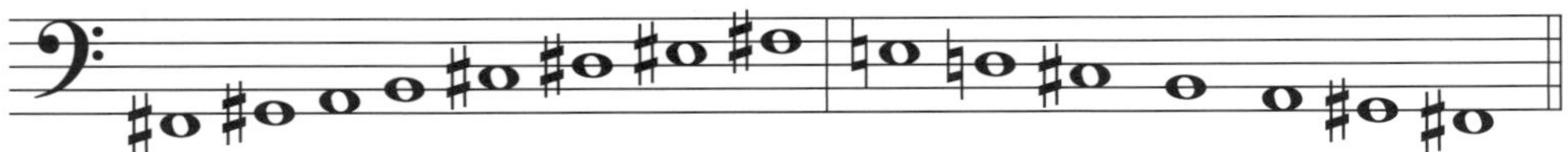

7. Write the following scales in the treble clef, ascending and descending. Use accidentals instead of a key signature, and label the tonic, subdominant, and dominant notes. Use whole notes.

a) D minor, natural form

b) B minor, natural form

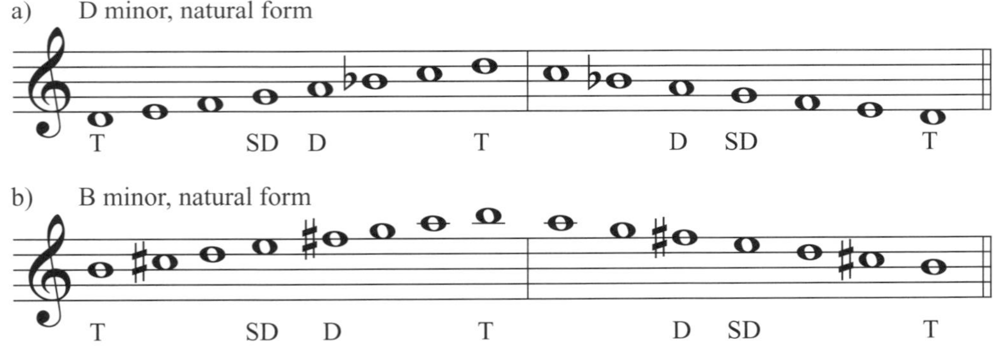

c) F minor, natural form

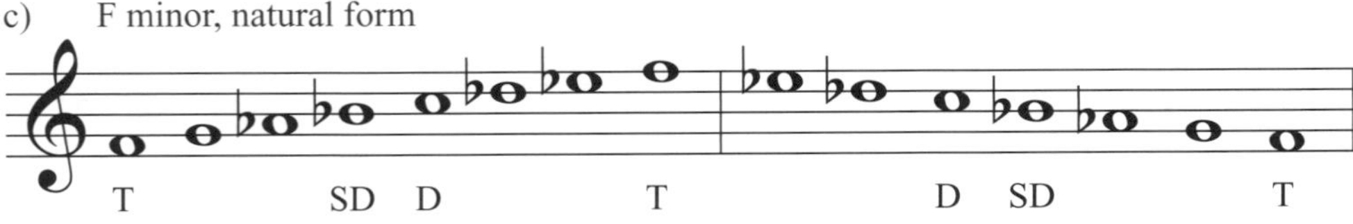

8. Write the following scales in the bass clef, ascending and descending. Use the correct key signature and label the tonic, subdominant, and dominant notes. Use whole notes.

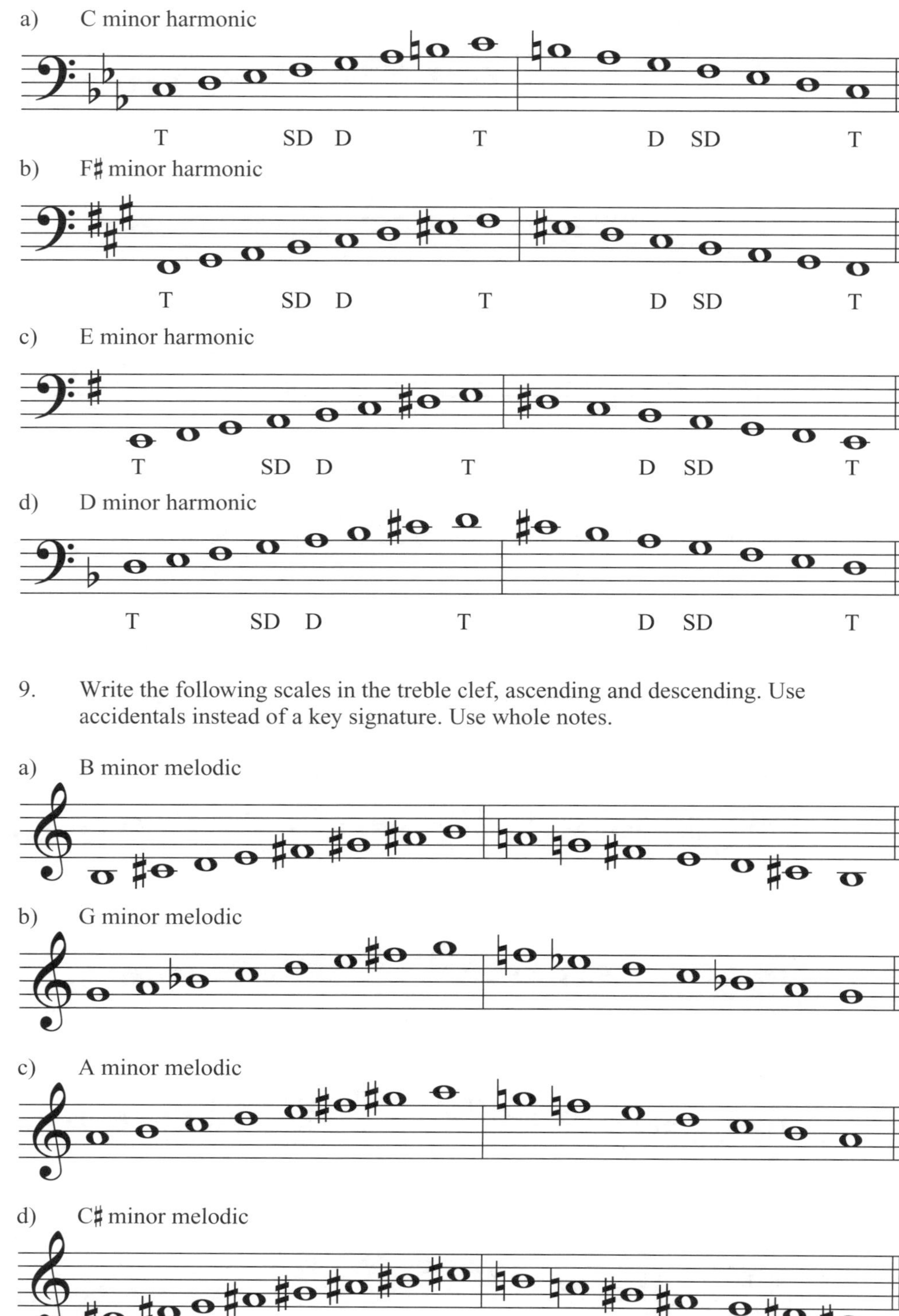

10. Write the following scales in the bass clef, ascending and descending. Use the correct key signature for each, and mark the semitones with slurs. Use whole notes.

a) G minor, natural form

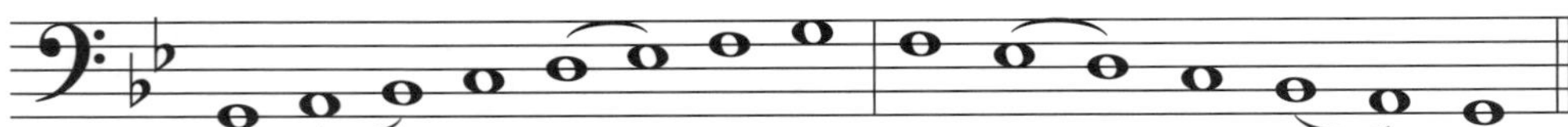

b) A minor, natural form

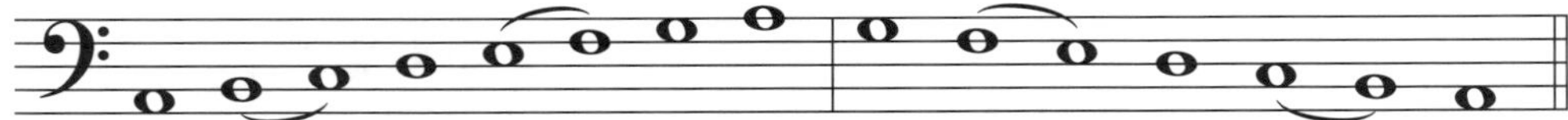

c) C♯ minor, natural form

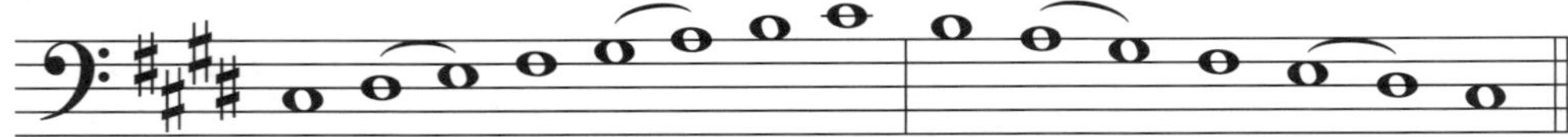

d) F minor, natural form

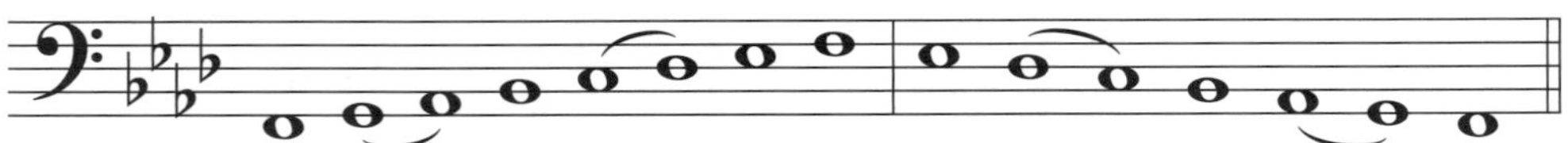

11. Write the following scales in the treble clef, ascending and descending. Use accidentals instead of a key signature, and mark the semitones with slurs. Use whole notes.

a) E minor harmonic

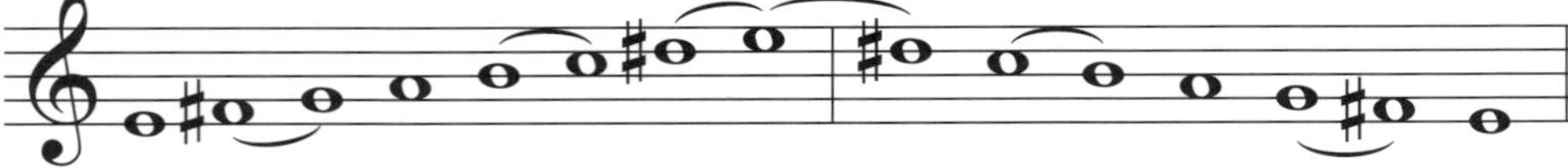

b) D minor harmonic

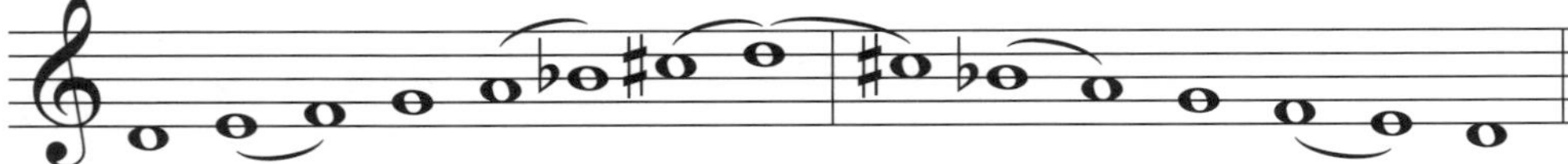

c) F♯ minor harmonic

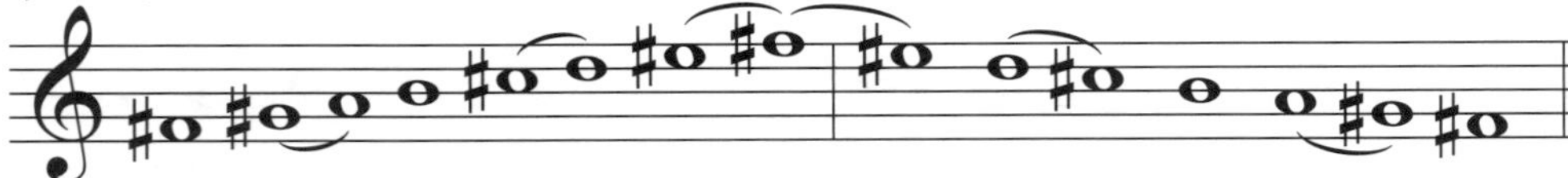

d) C minor harmonic

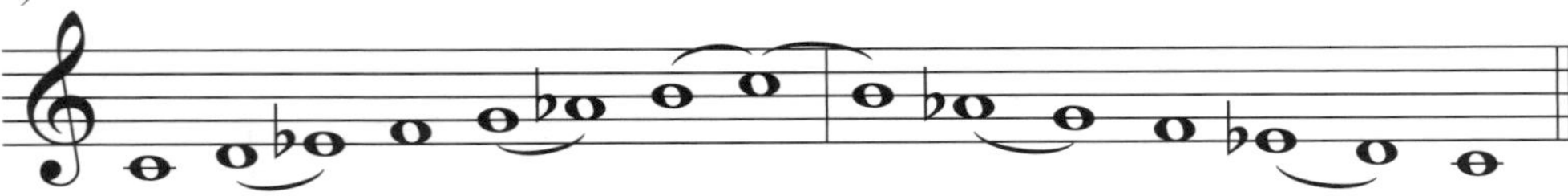

12. Write the following scales in the bass clef, ascending and descending. Use the correct key signature for each, and mark the semitones with slurs. Use whole notes.

a) B minor melodic

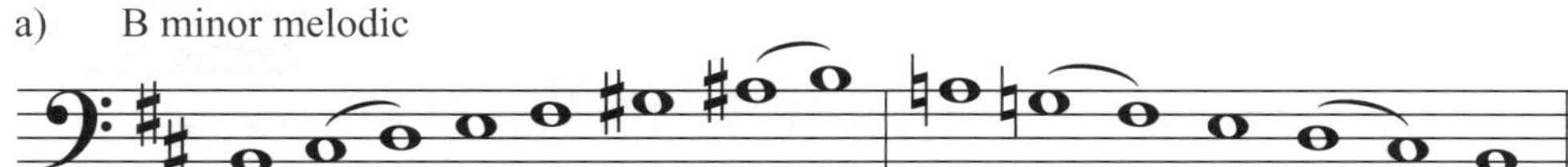

b) F minor melodic

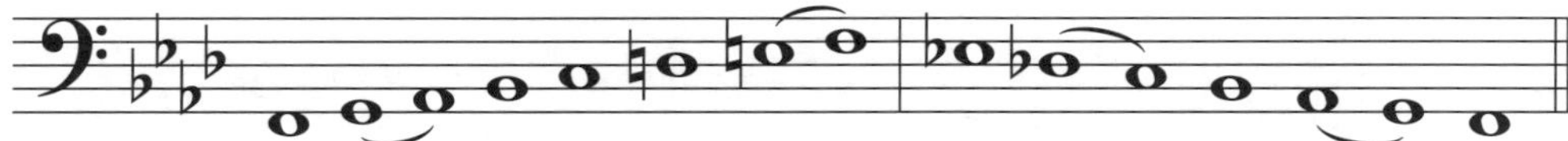

c) C♯ minor melodic

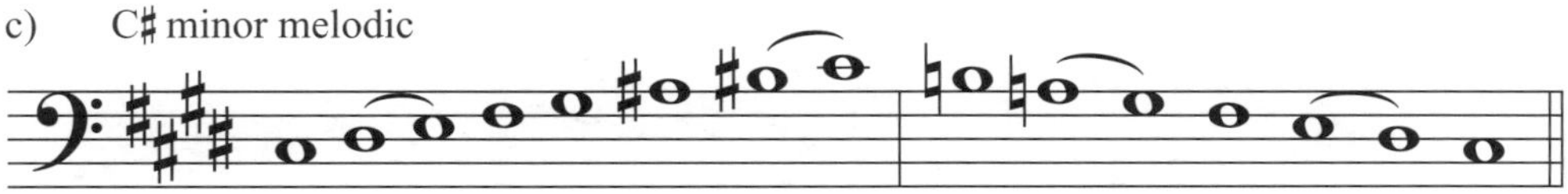

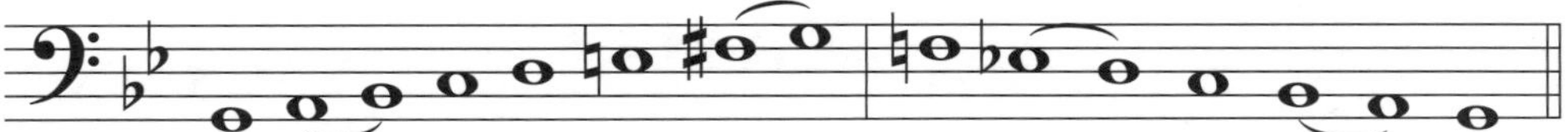

d) G minor melodic

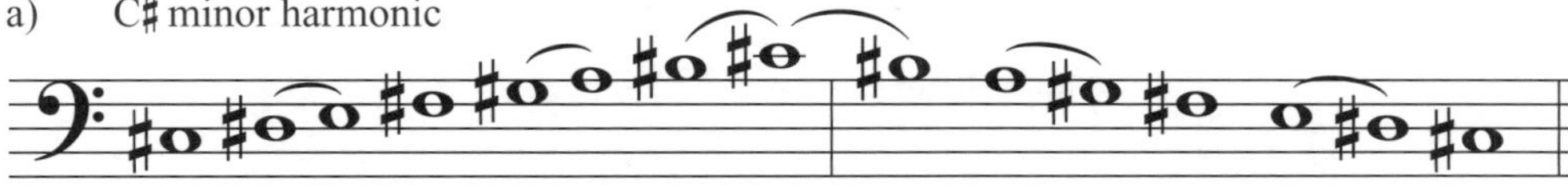

13. Write the following scales in the bass clef, ascending and descending. Use accidentals instead of a key signature, and mark the semitones with slurs. Use whole notes.

a) C♯ minor harmonic

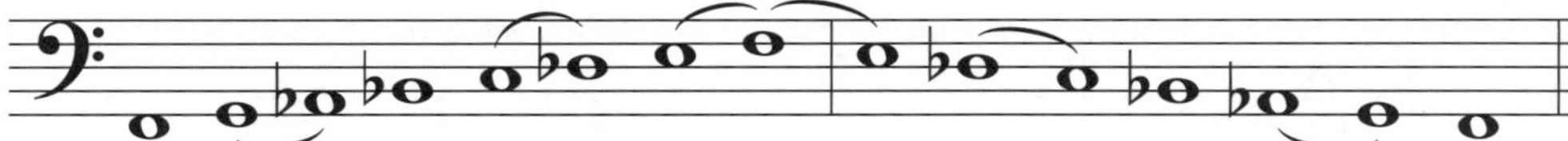

b) F minor harmonic

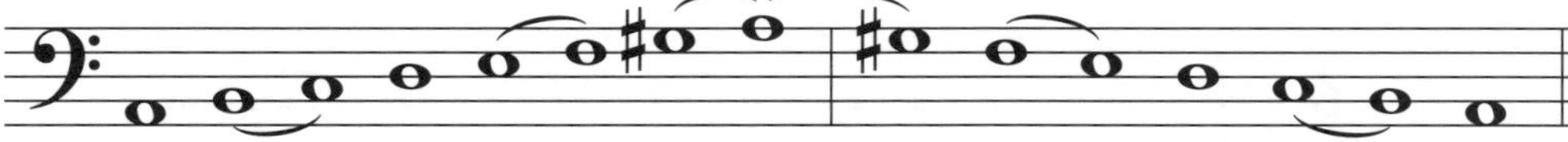

c) A minor harmonic

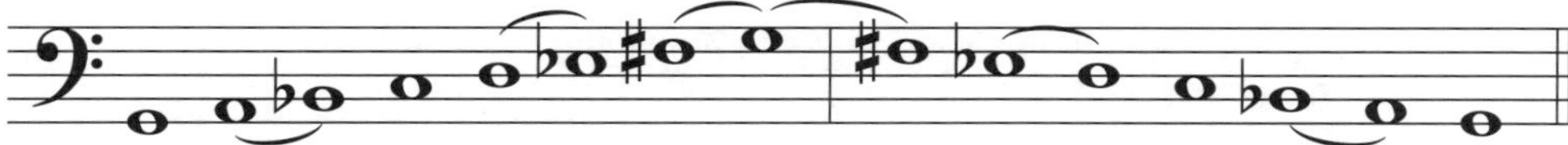

d) G minor harmonic

14. Write the following scales in the treble clef, ascending and descending. Use the correct key signature for each, and mark the semitones with slurs. Use whole notes.

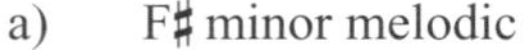

a) F♯ minor melodic

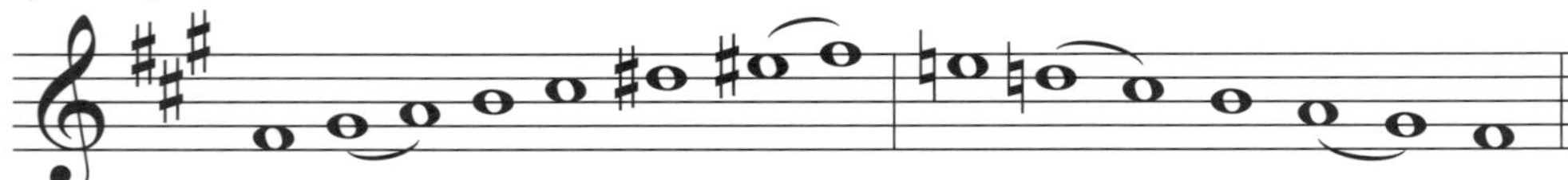

b) C minor melodic

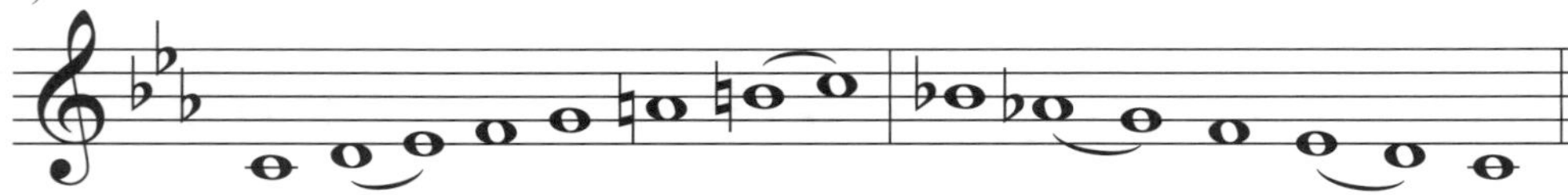

c) D minor melodic

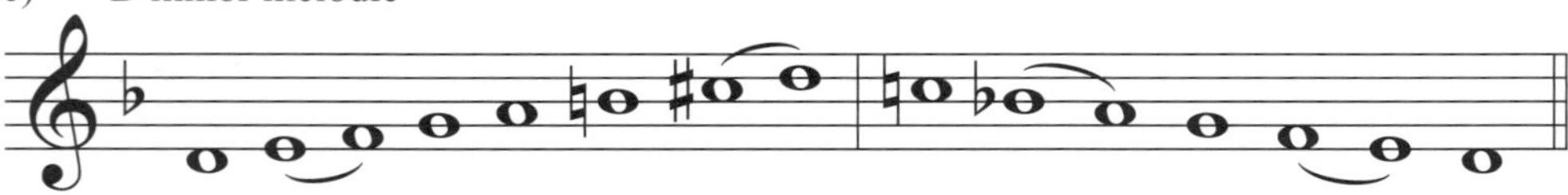

d) E minor melodic

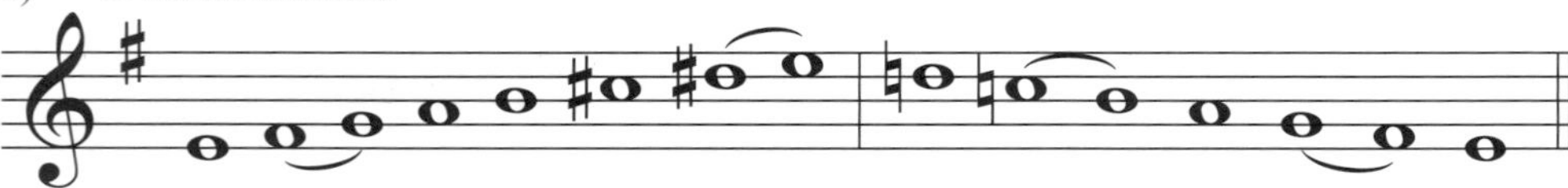

I A **MORE EXERCISES** (p. 52)

1. Write the following scales in the treble clef, ascending and descending. Use the correct key signature for each, and mark the semitones with slurs. Use whole notes.

a) G♯ minor, natural form

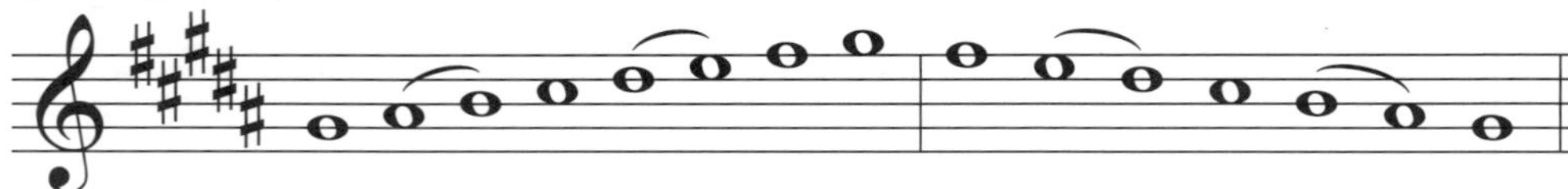

b) the natural minor scale whose key signature is six flats

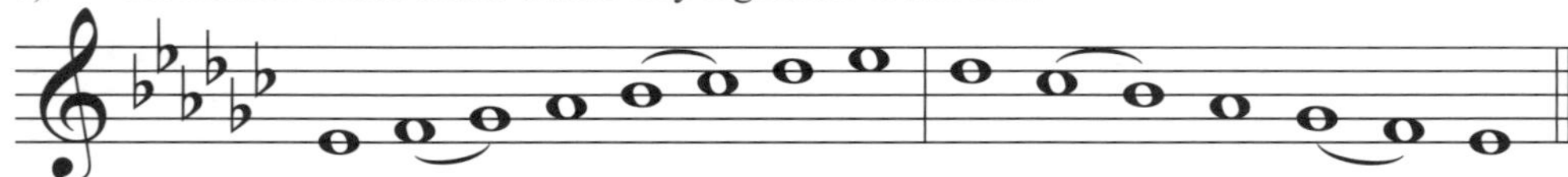

c) A♭ minor, natural form

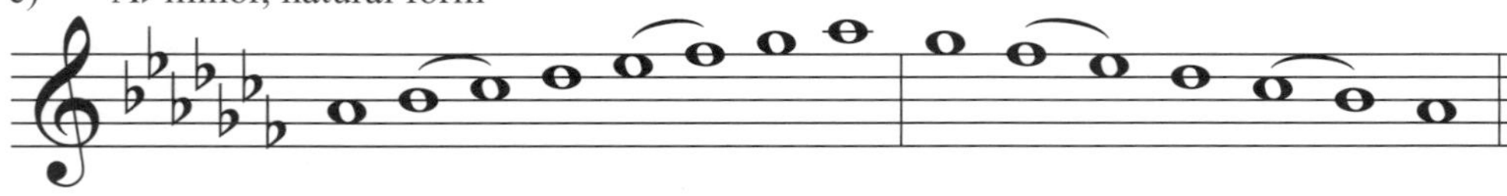

d) the natural minor scale whose key signature is six sharps

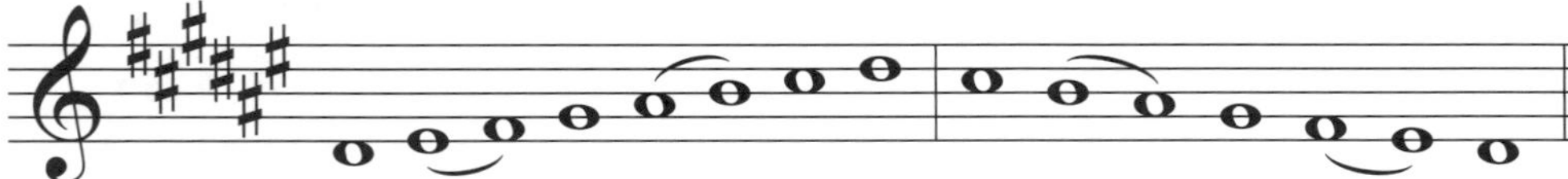

2. Write the following scales in the bass clef, ascending and descending. Use accidentals instead of key signatures, and mark the semitones with slurs. Use whole notes.

a) B♭ minor, natural form

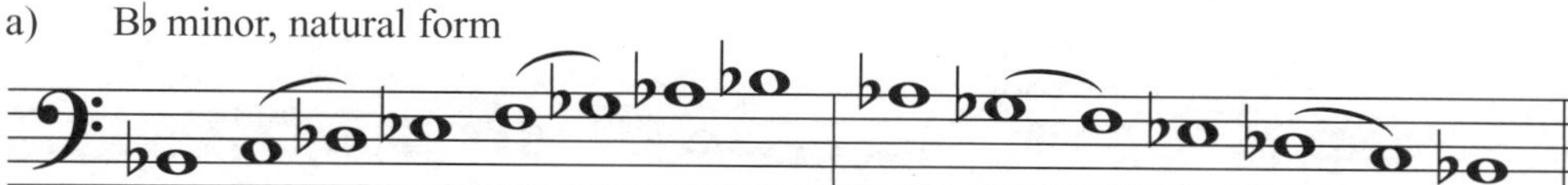

b) the natural minor scale whose relative major is E

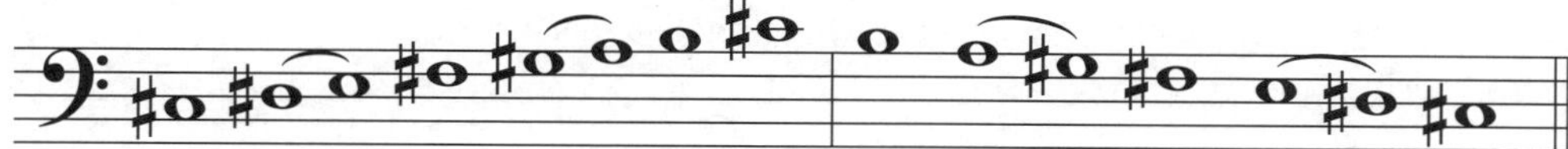

c) A♯ minor, natural form

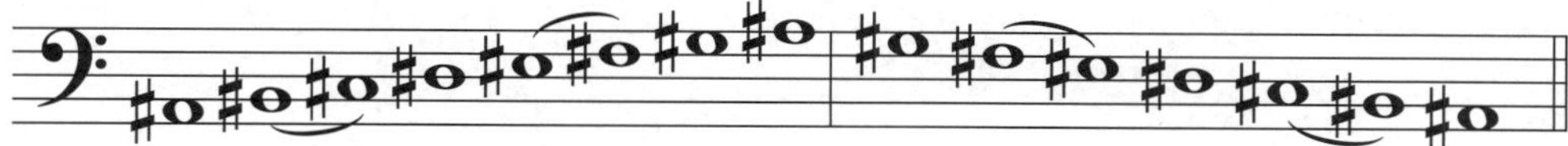

d) the natural minor scale whose relative major is A♭

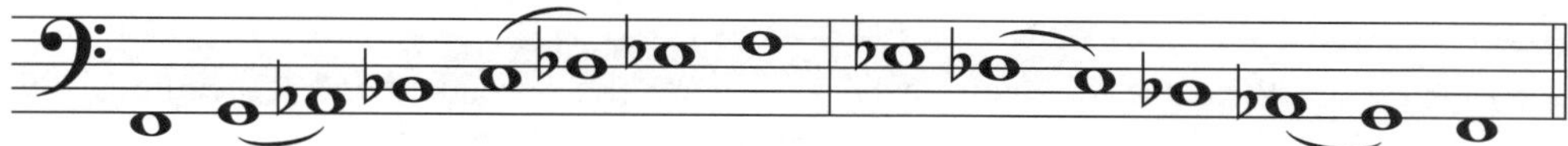

3. Write the following scales in the treble clef, ascending and descending. Use the correct key signature for each, and mark the semitones with slurs. Use whole notes.

a) D♯ minor melodic

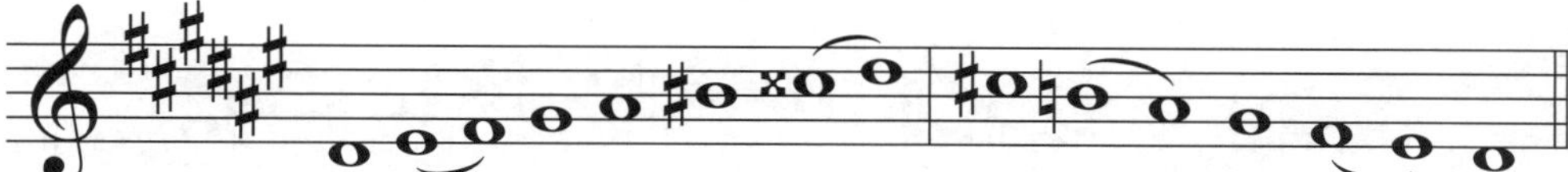

b) the melodic minor scale whose relative major is D♭

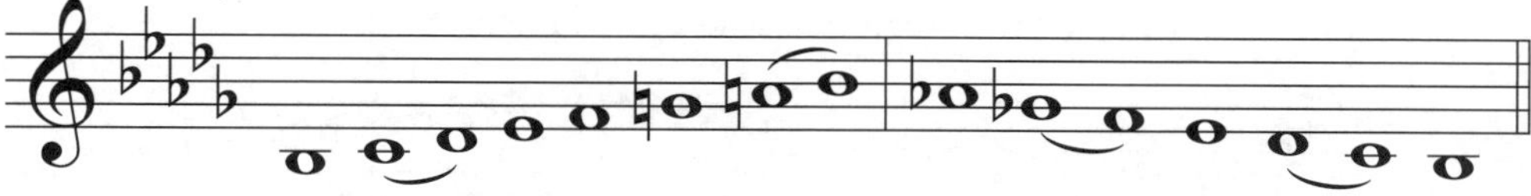

c) the melodic minor scale whose key signature is seven flats

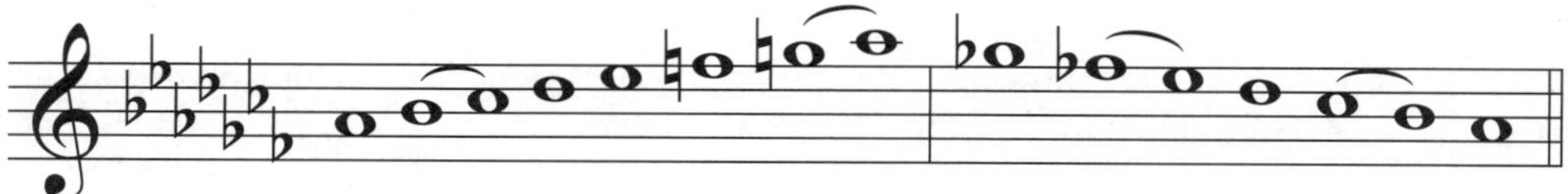

4. Write the following scales in the treble clef, ascending and descending. Use accidentals instead of a key signature, and mark the semitones with slurs. Use whole notes.

a) A♯ minor melodic

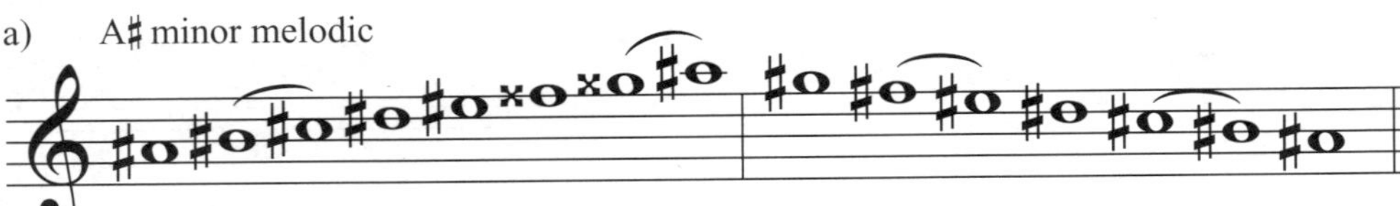

b) the melodic minor scale whose relative major is G♭

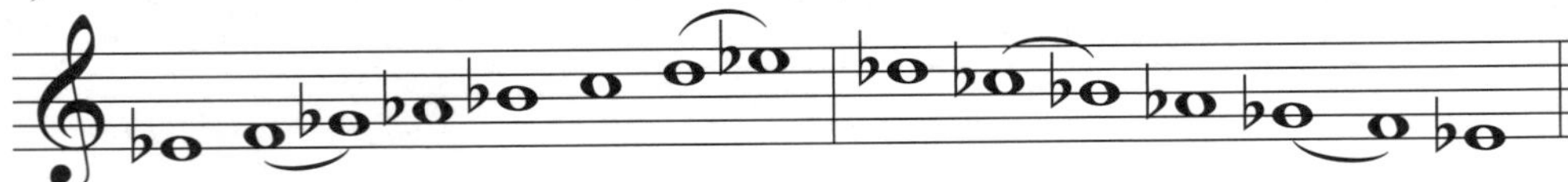

c) the melodic minor scale whose key signature is five sharps

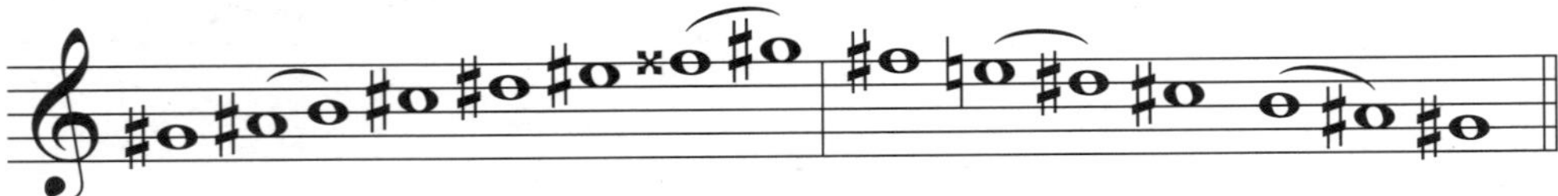

5. Write the following scales in the bass clef, ascending and descending, using accidentals instead of a key signature. Use whole notes.

a) B♭ minor melodic

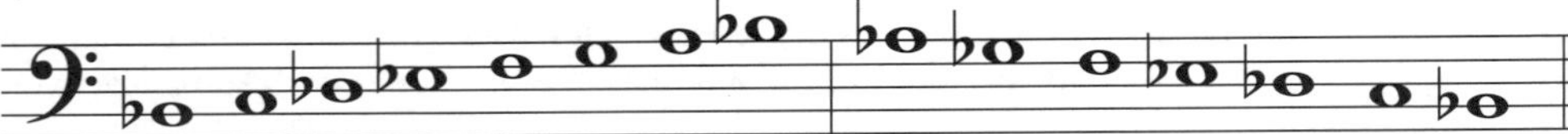

b) the melodic minor scale whose relative major is F♯

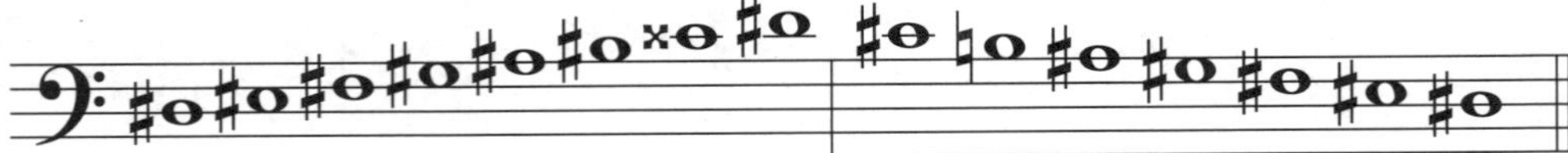

c) the melodic minor scale whose key signature is seven flats

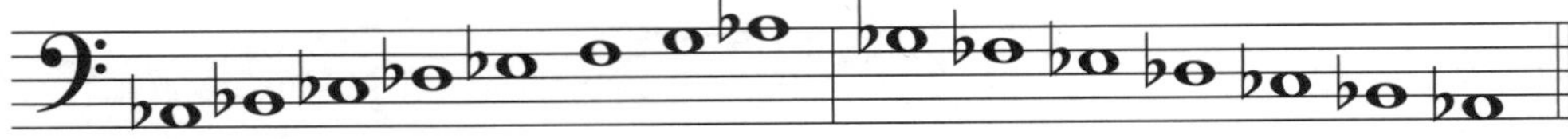

6. Write the following scales in the bass clef, ascending and descending, using the correct key signature for each. Use whole notes.

a) E♭ minor harmonic

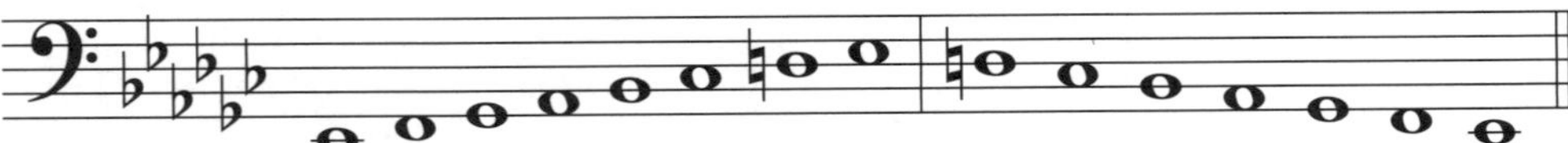

b) the harmonic minor scale whose relative major is B

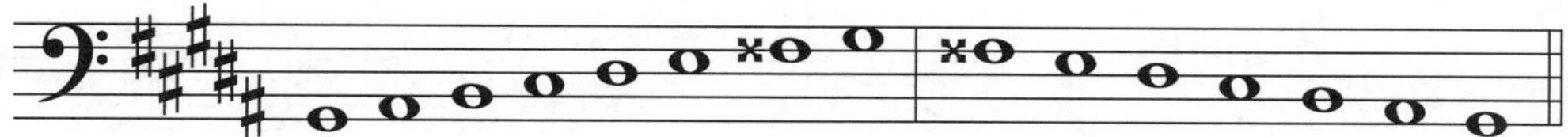

c) the harmonic minor scale whose key signature is seven sharps

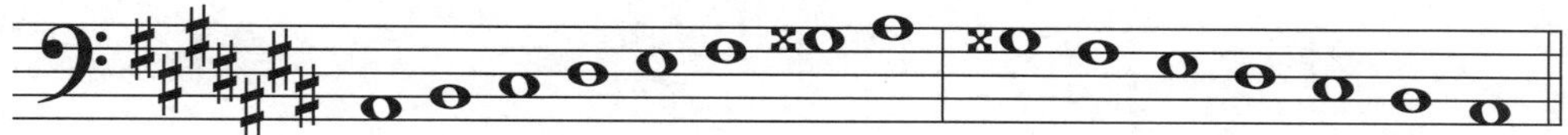

7. Write the following scales ascending and descending, in the bass clef, using the correct key signature for each. Use whole notes.

a) the melodic minor scale whose supertonic is D

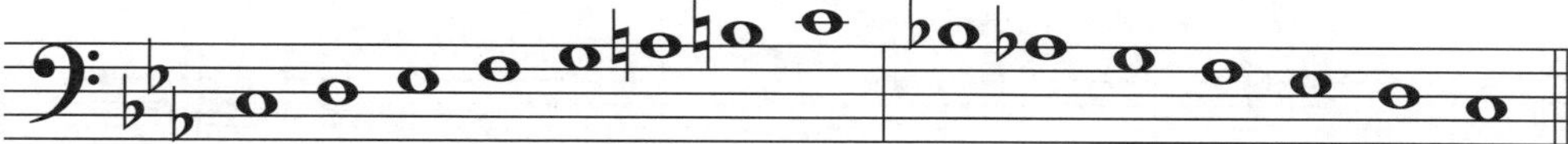

b) the harmonic minor scale whose dominant is B♭

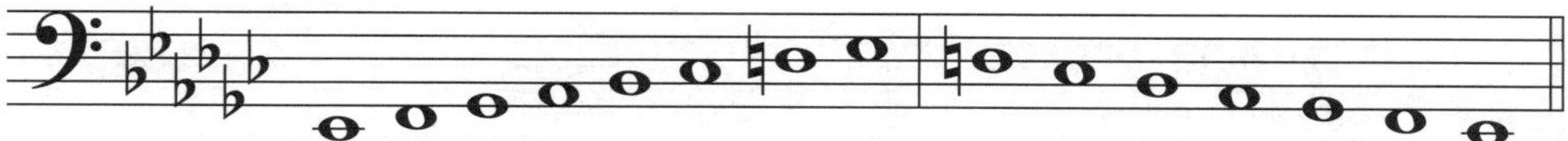

c) the melodic minor scale whose leading note is G♯

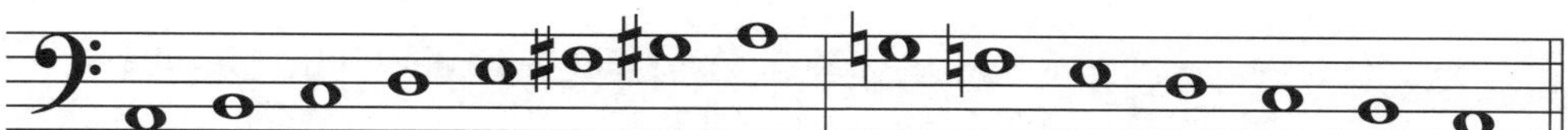

d) the harmonic minor scale whose subdominant is E♭

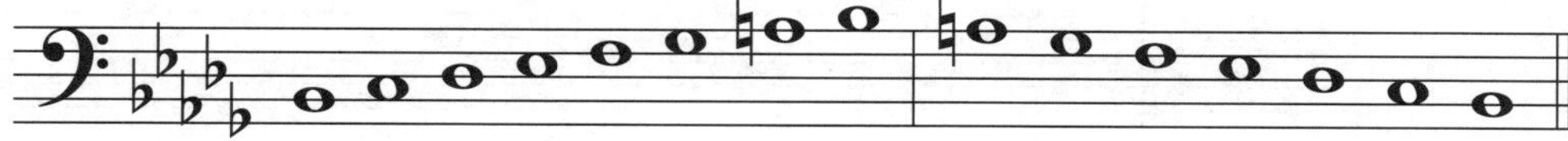

e) the harmonic minor scale whose mediant is A

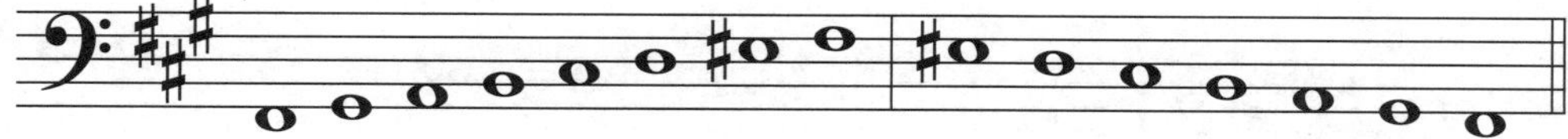

8. Add the proper clef, key signature, and accidentals where necessary, to complete the following scales.

a) G♭ major

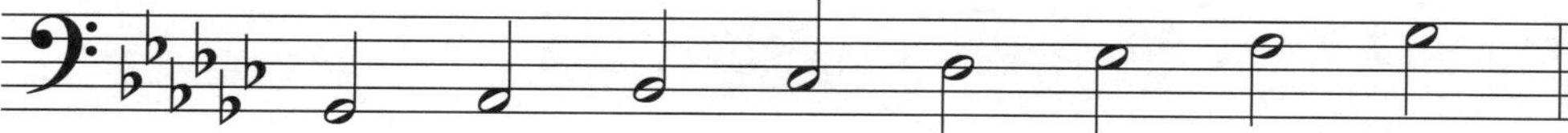

b) E major

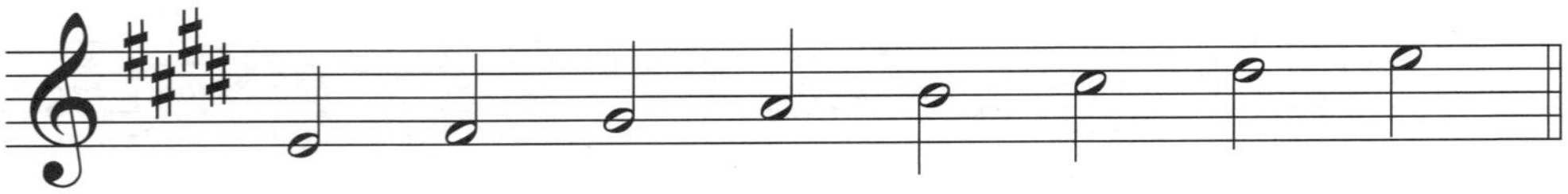

c) G minor melodic

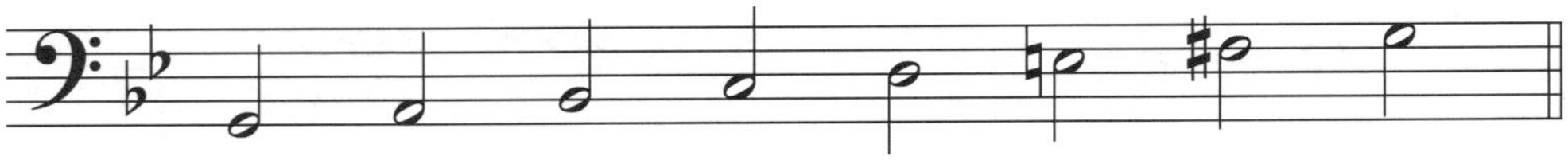

d) E♭ major

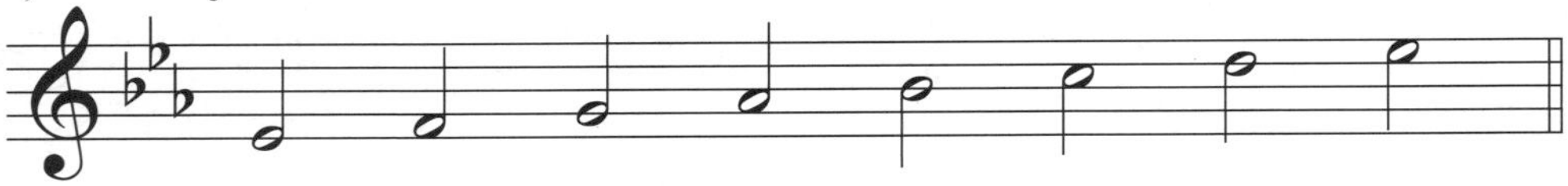

e) E minor harmonic

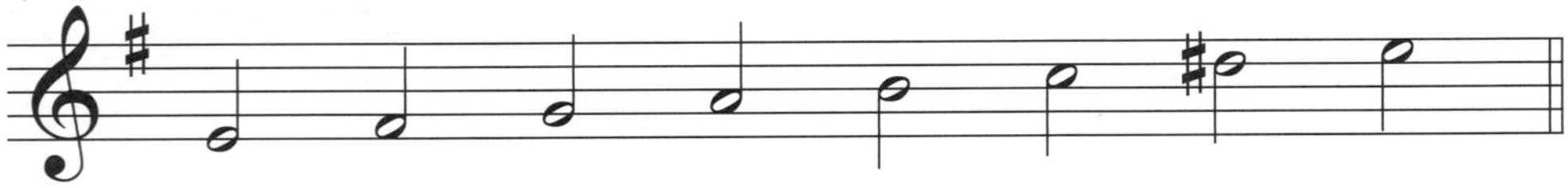

f) G♯ minor harmonic

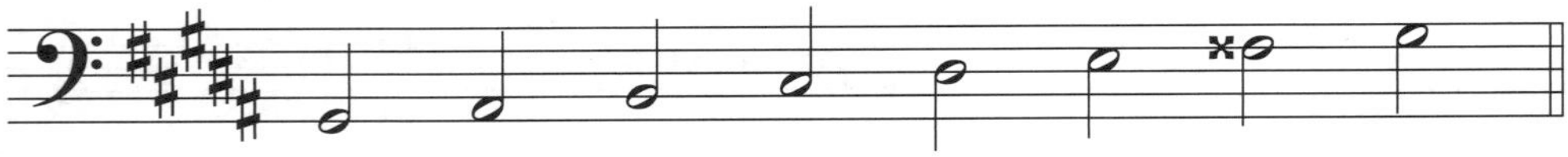

9. Write the following scales in the bass clef, ascending only, using the correct key signature for each. Use whole notes.

a) B major

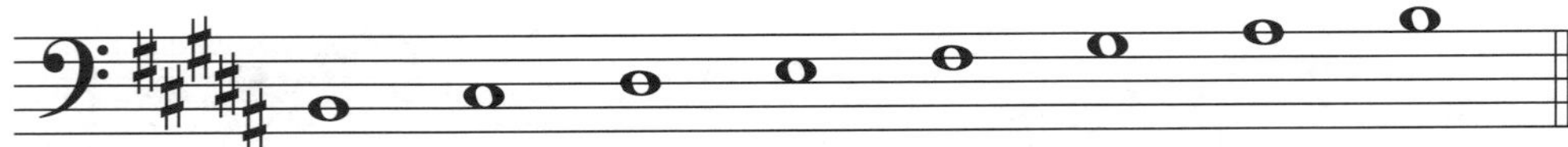

b) the major scale that is enharmonically equivalent to B major

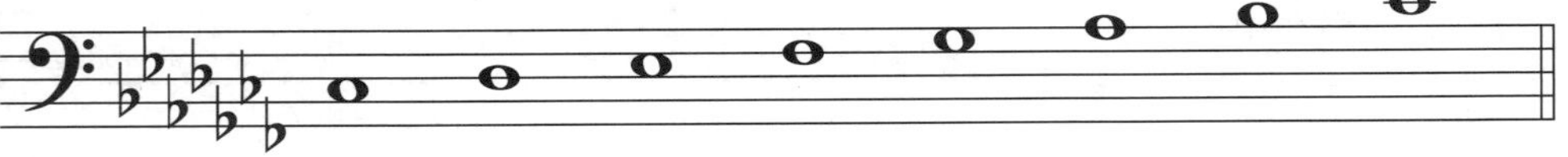

c) D♭ major

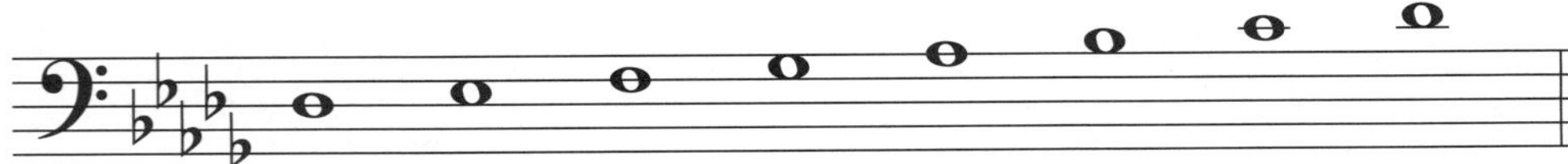

d) the major scale that is enharmonically equivalent to D♭ major

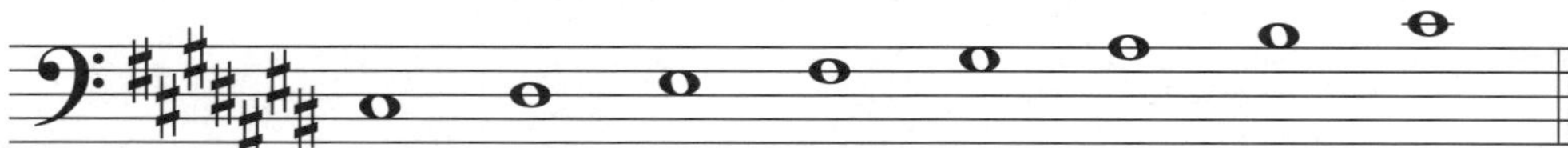

e) F♯ major

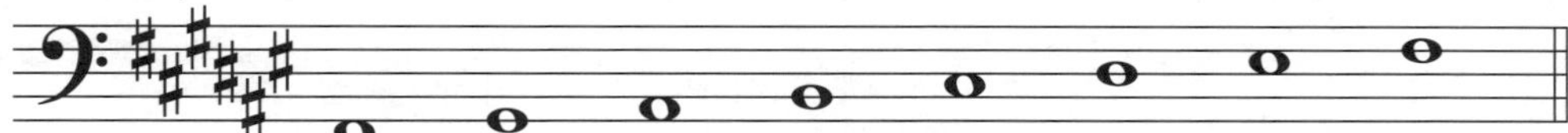

f) the major scale that is enharmonically equivalent to F♯ major

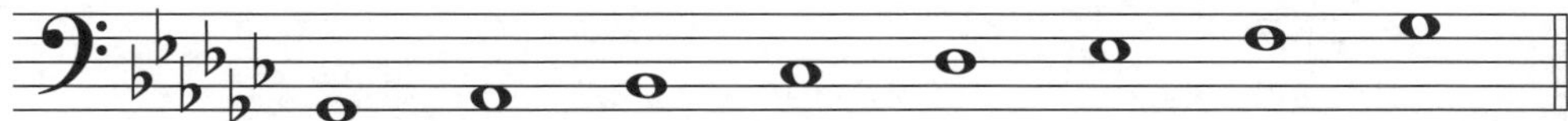

10. Write the following scales in the treble clef, ascending and descending, using the correct key signature for each. Use whole notes.

a) A♭ minor, natural form

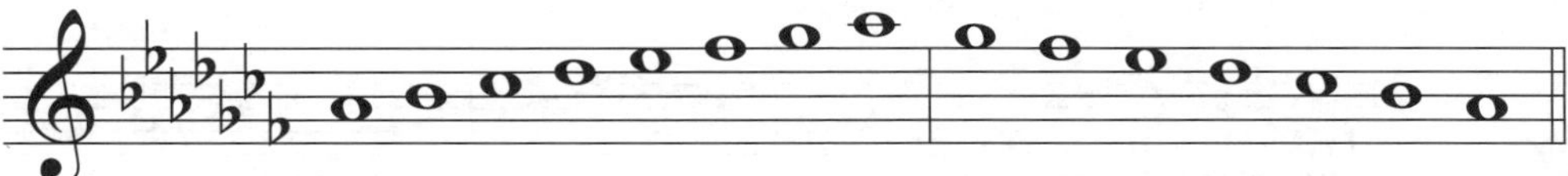

b) the minor scale that is enharmonically equivalent to A♭ minor, natural form

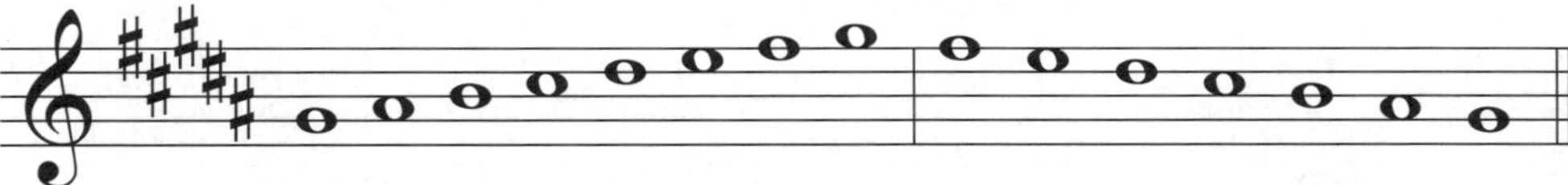

c) D♯ minor harmonic

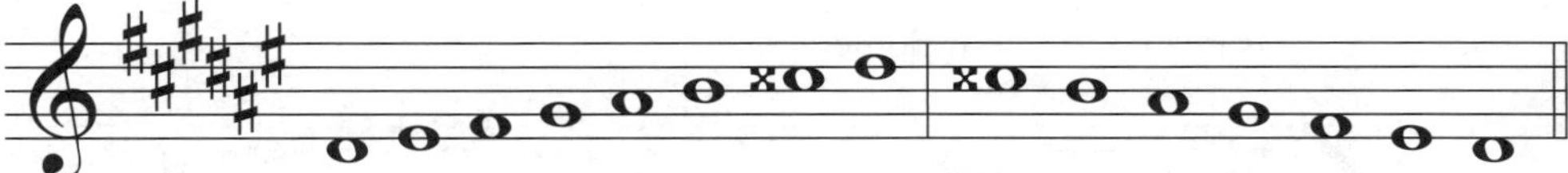

d) the minor scale that is enharmonically equivalent to D♯ minor harmonic

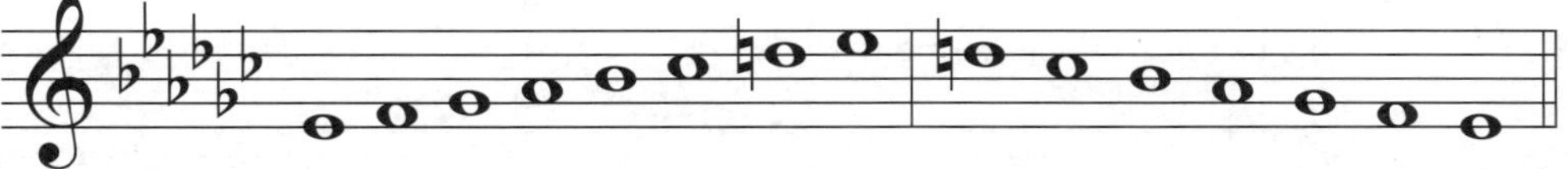

e) A♯ minor melodic

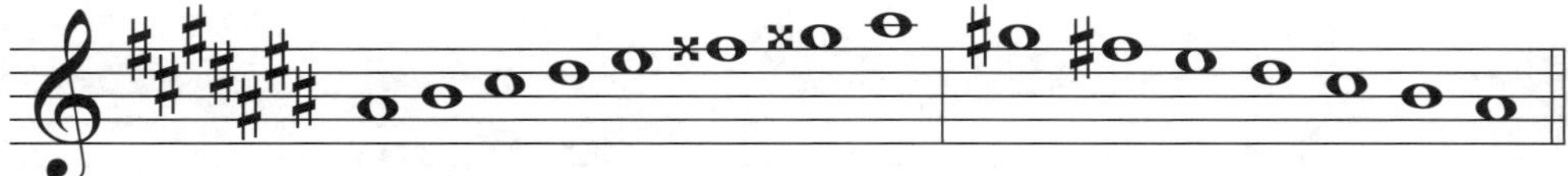

f) the minor scale that is enharmonically equivalent to A♯ minor melodic

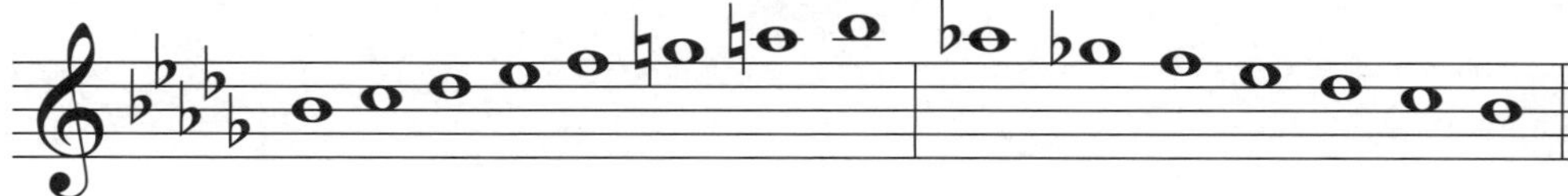

11. Write the following scales in the treble clef, ascending and descending, using the correct key signature for each. Use whole notes.

a) A♭ major

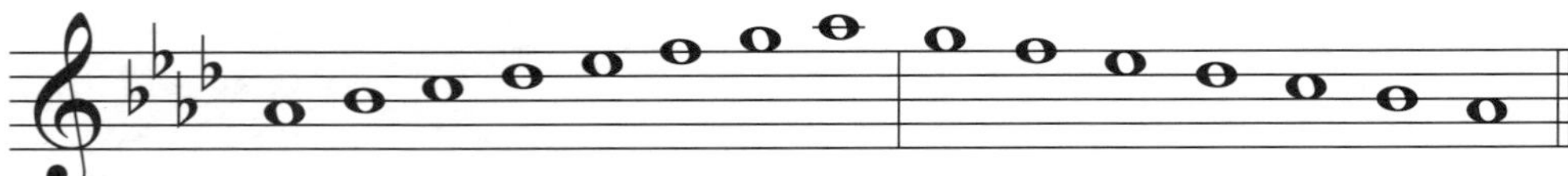

its relative minor, harmonic

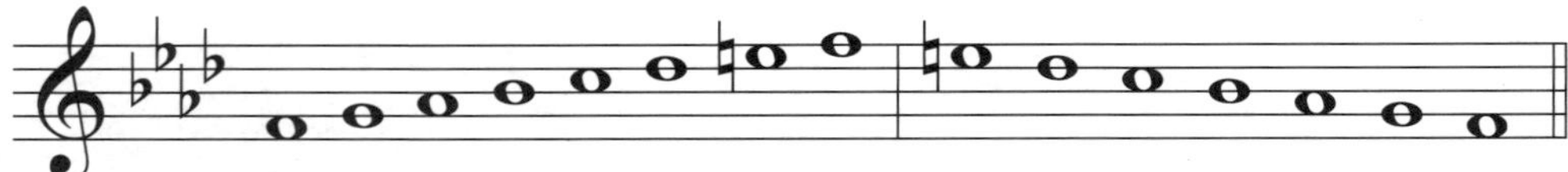

its tonic minor, melodic

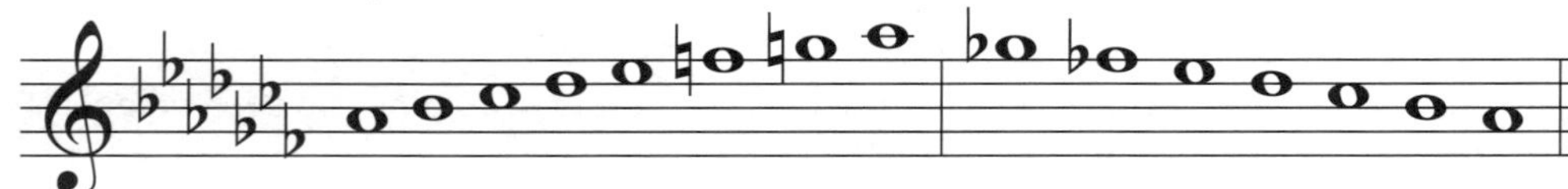

its enharmonic minor, melodic

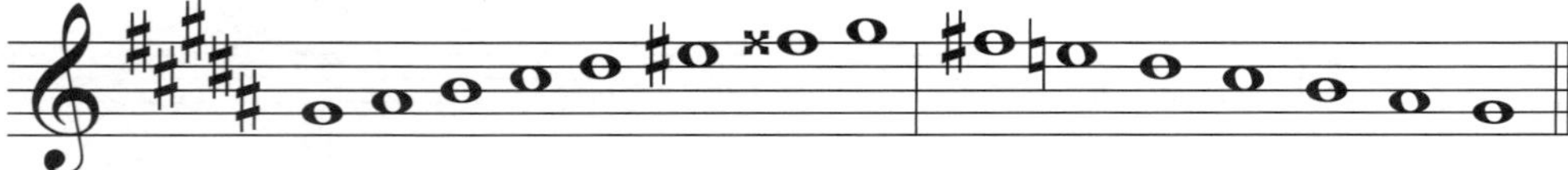

b) B♭ major

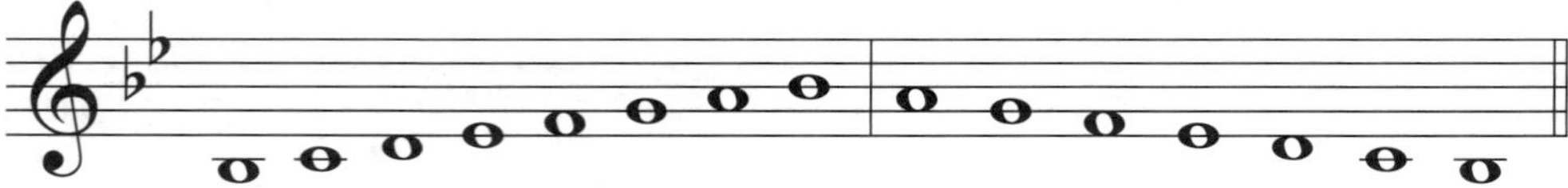

its relative minor, melodic

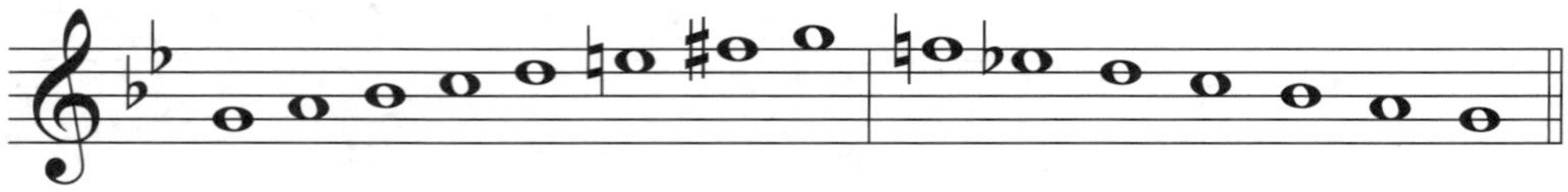

its tonic minor, harmonic

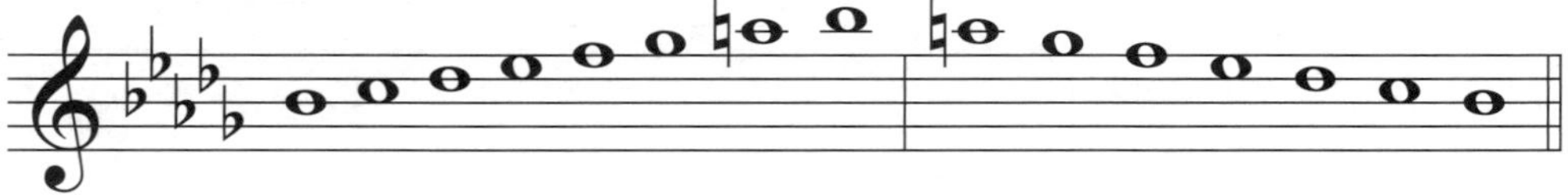

its enharmonic minor, harmonic

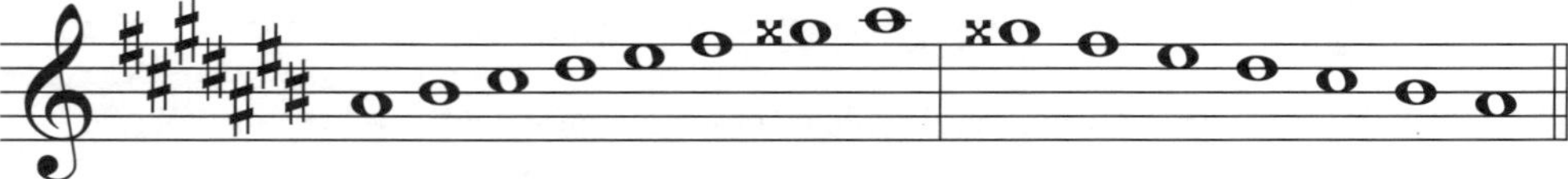

c) C♯ minor, natural form

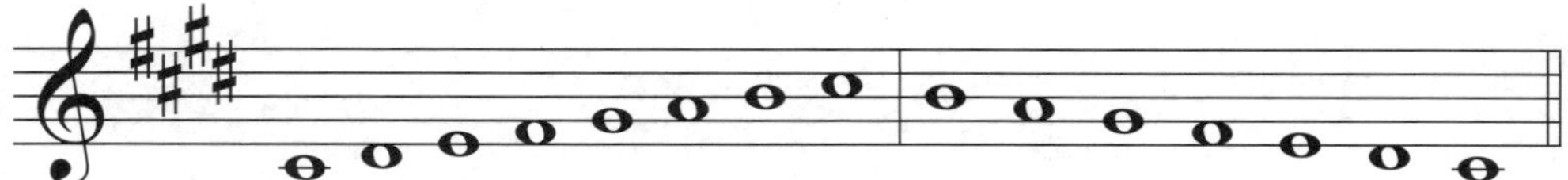

its relative major

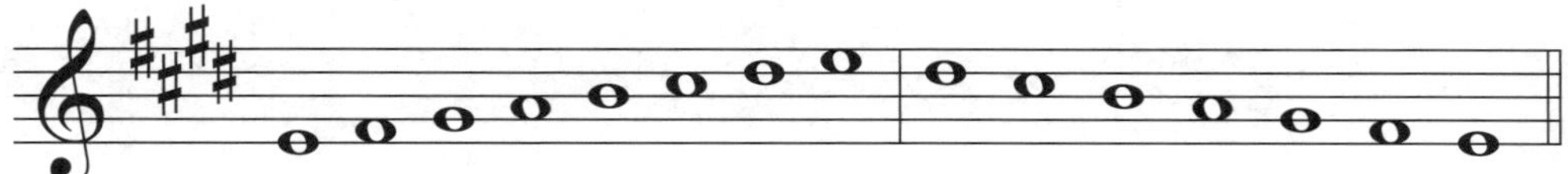

its tonic major

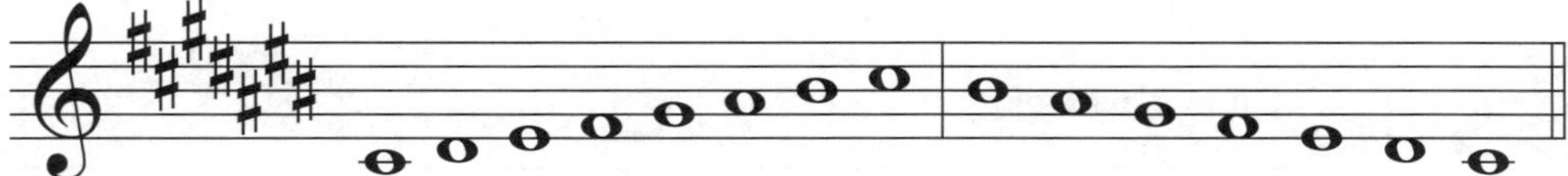

its enharmonic major

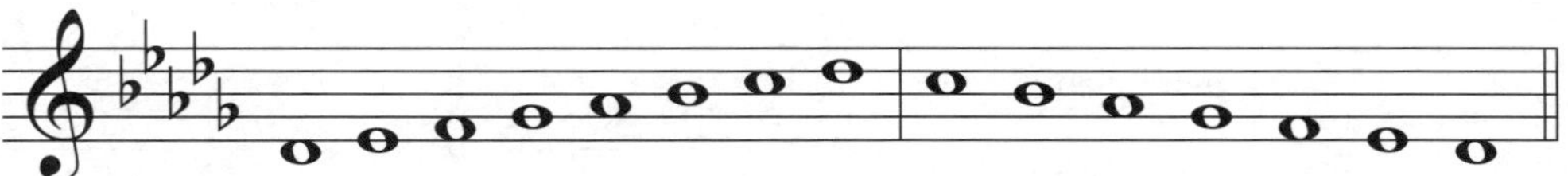

State the relationship between the third and fourth scales in each section of question 11. The scales are enharmonically equivalent.

12. Fill in the blanks to complete the following sentences.

a) Name the minor scale whose key signature has six sharps. D♯ minor

b) Name the minor scale that is the enharmonic equivalent of a). E♭ minor

c) Name the relative major scale of a). F♯ major

d) Name the major scale that is the enharmonic equivalent of c). G♭ major

e) Name the enharmonic minor scale of d). F♯ minor

f) State the relationship of d) to b). G♭ major is the relative major of E♭ minor

g) State the relationship of e) to c). F♯ minor is the tonic minor (or parallel minor) of F♯ major

A STILL MORE EXERCISES (p. 59)

1. Write the following scales in the given clefs, ascending and descending. Use the correct key signature for each. Use whole notes.

a) E♭ minor, natural form

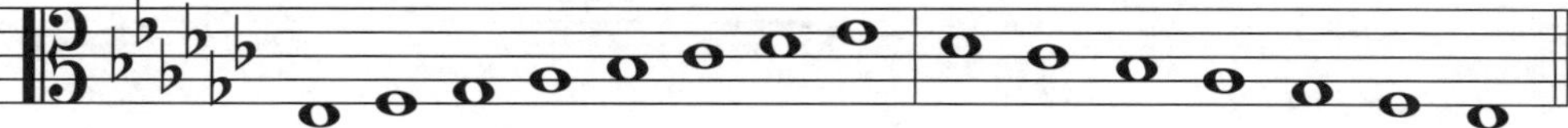

b) C minor, natural form

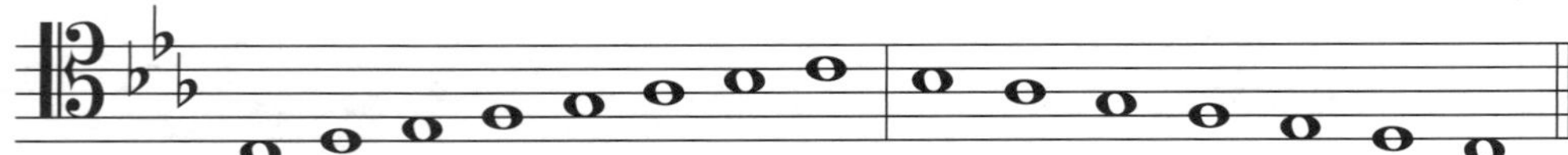

c) A♯ minor, natural form

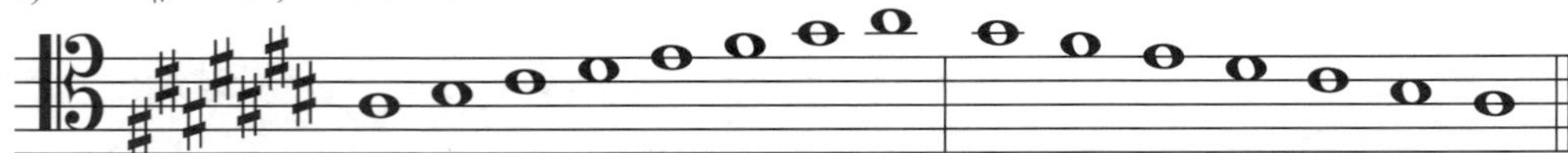

2. Write the following scales in the given clefs, ascending and descending. Use accidentals instead of a key signature. Use whole notes.

a) F minor, natural form

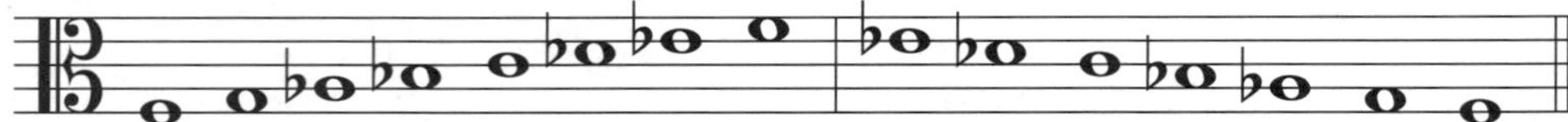

b) G minor, natural form

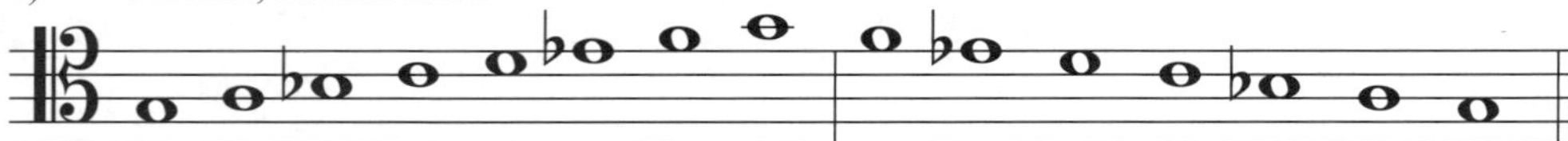

c) C♯ minor, natural form

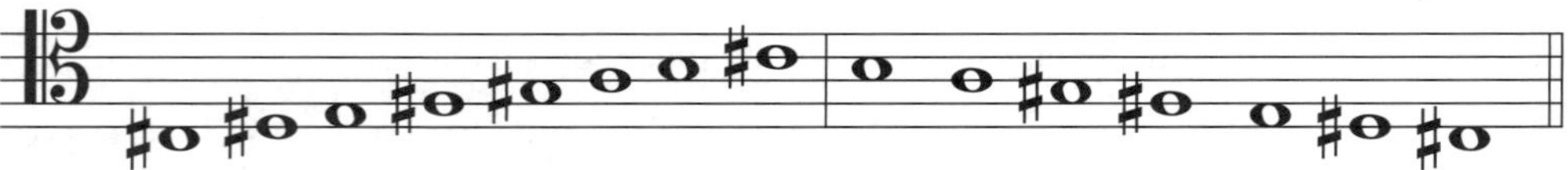

3. Write the following scales in the alto clef, ascending and descending, using the correct key signature for each. Use whole notes.

a) A♭ minor harmonic

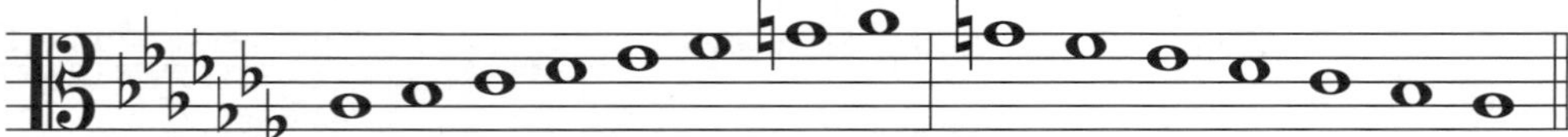

b) B minor melodic

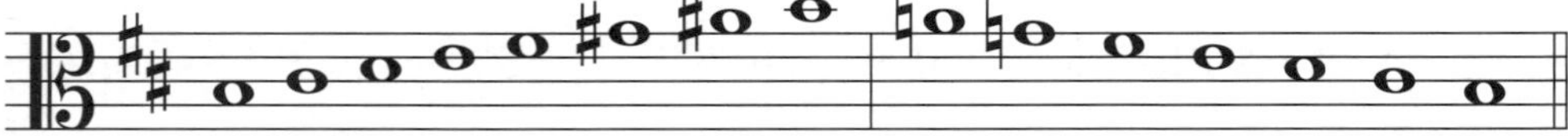

c) D♯ minor harmonic

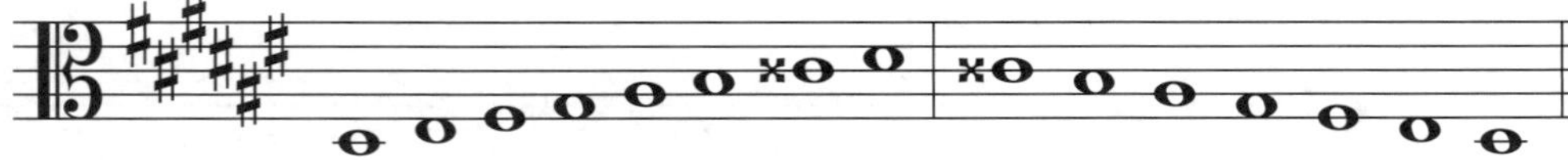

d) G minor harmonic

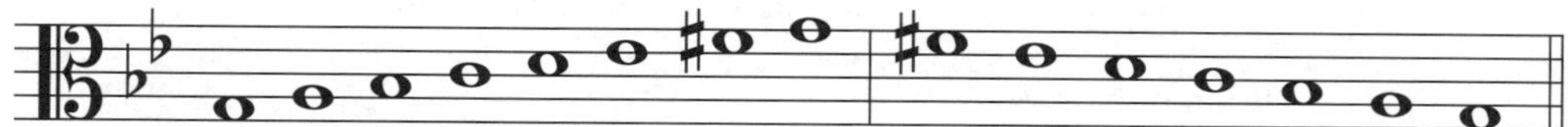

4. Write the following scales in the tenor clef, ascending and descending, using the correct key signature for each. Use whole notes.

a) C minor melodic

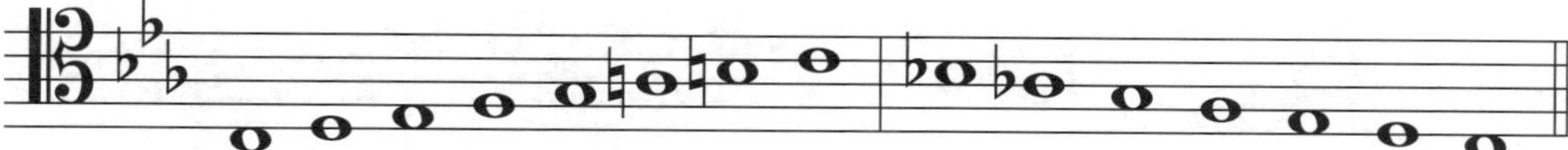

b) G♯ minor harmonic

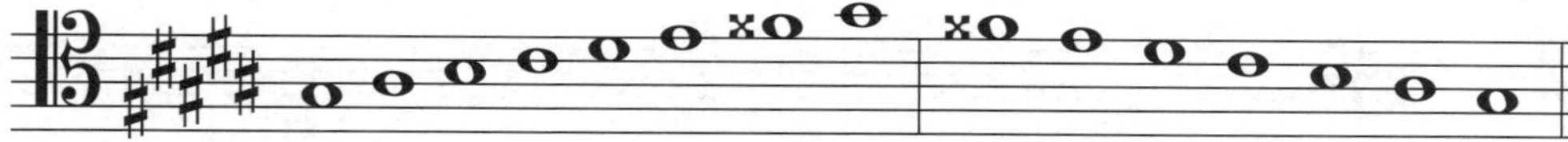

c) E minor melodic

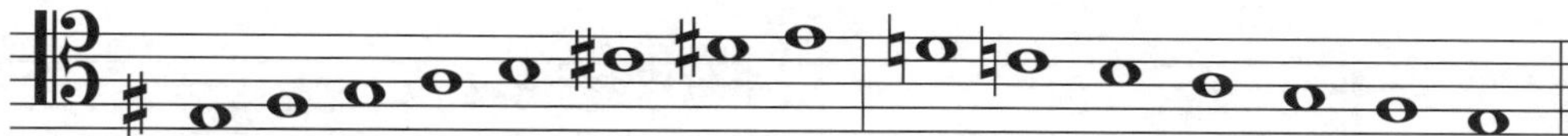

d) F♯ minor melodic

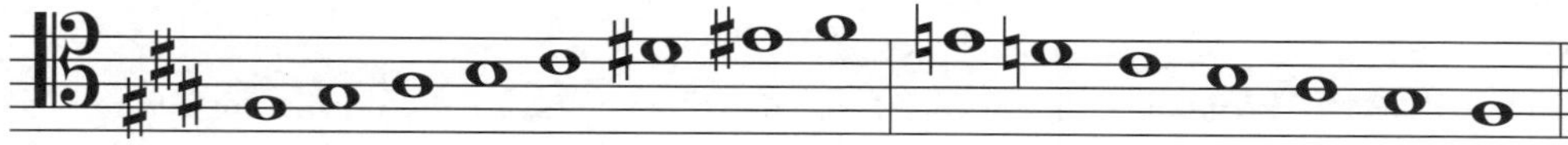

5. Write the following scales in the alto clef, ascending and descending, using accidentals instead of a key signature. Use whole notes.

a) C minor harmonic

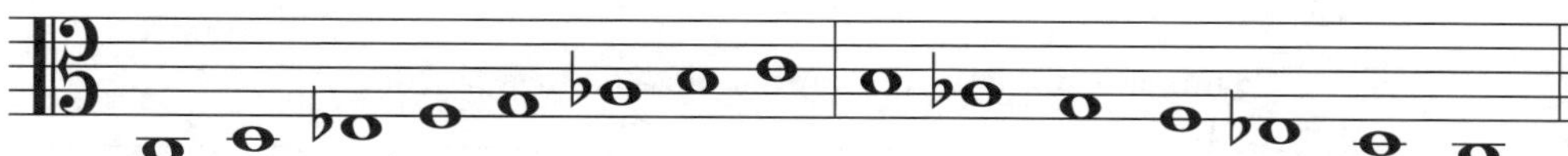

b) E minor harmonic

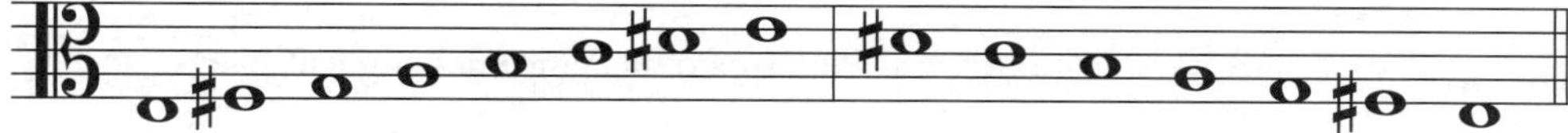

c) D minor melodic

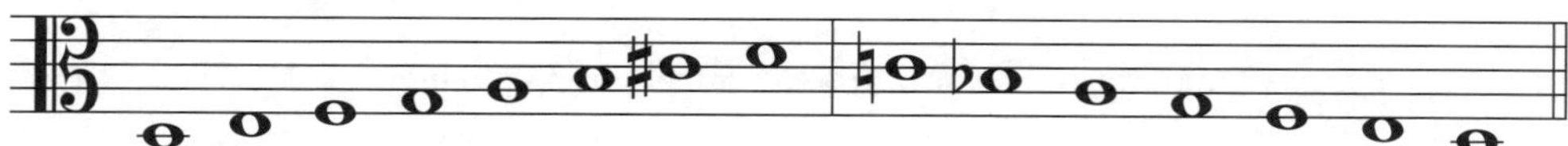

d) F♯ minor harmonic

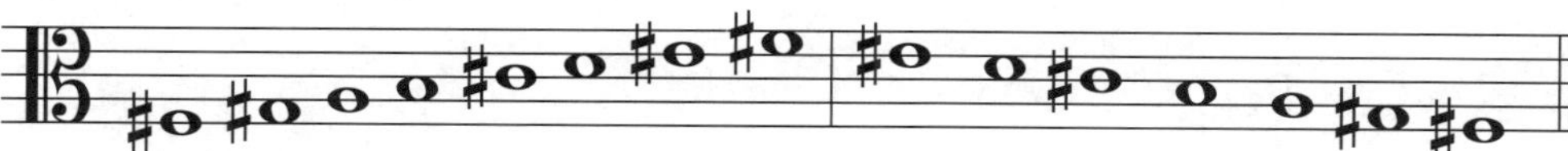

6. Write the following scales in the tenor clef, ascending and descending, using accidentals instead of a key signature. Use whole notes.

a) B minor harmonic

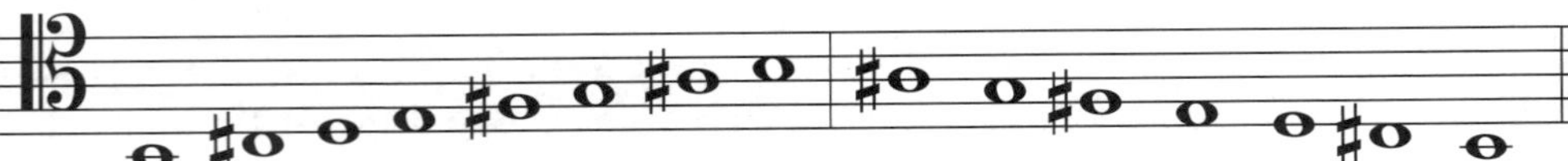

b) E♭ minor harmonic

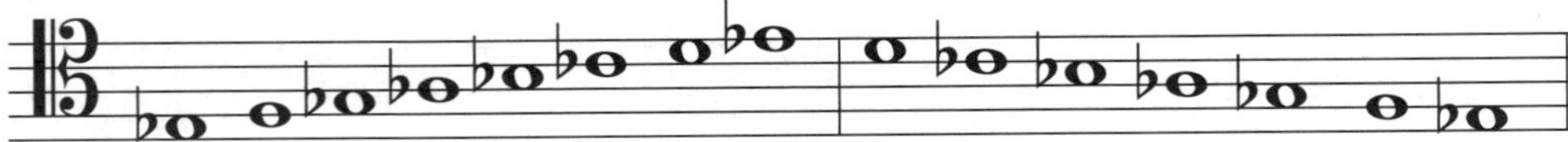

c) A♭ minor melodic

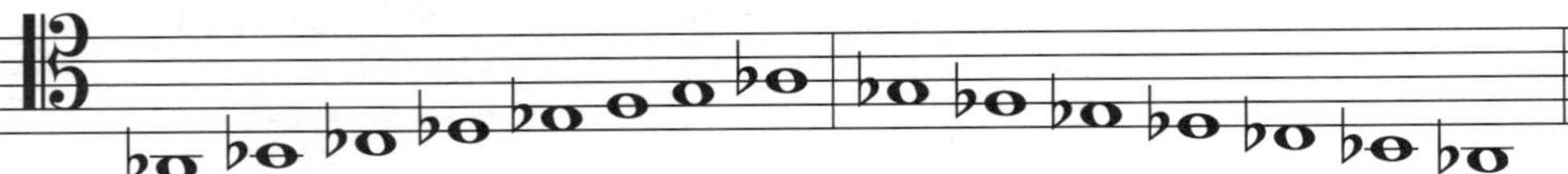

d) C♯ minor harmonic

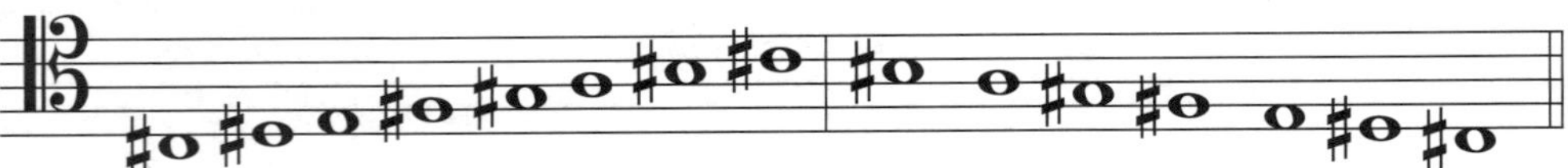

7. Write the following scales in the given clefs, ascending and descending. Use the correct key signature for each. Use whole notes.

a) D♯ minor, natural form, from supertonic to supertonic

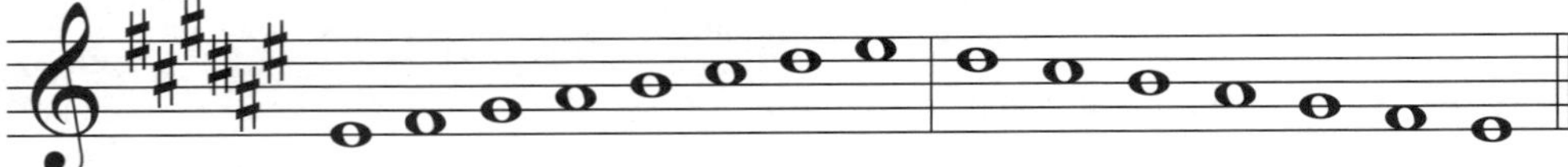

b) G♯ minor, natural form, from submediant to submediant

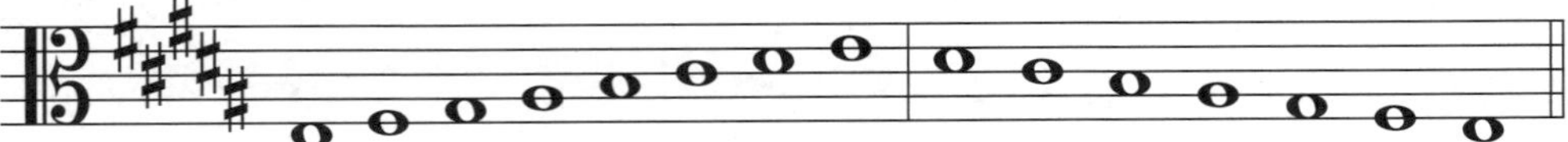

c) A♭ minor, natural form, from subdominant to subdominant

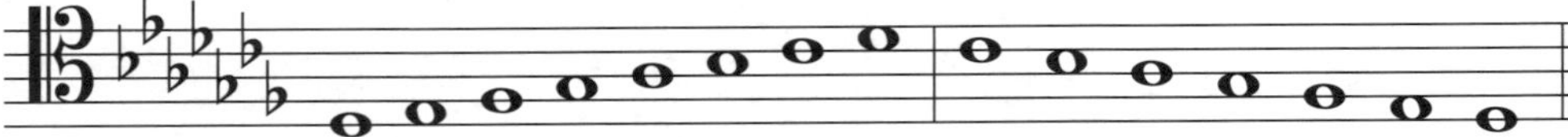

d) F♯ minor, natural form, from dominant to dominant

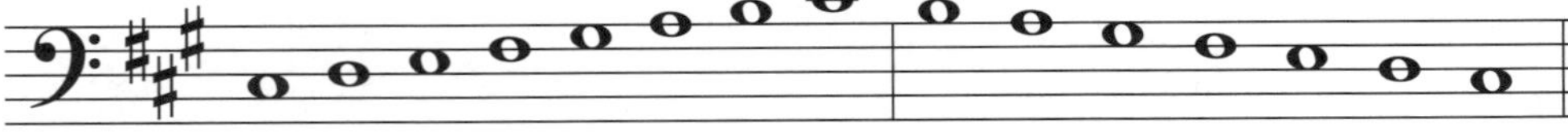

e) B♭ minor, natural form, from mediant to mediant

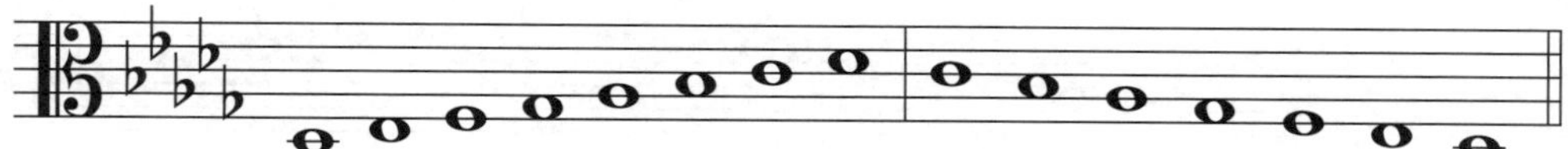

8. Write the following scales, ascending and descending, in the bass clef. Use the correct key signature for each, and mark the semitones with slurs. Use whole notes.

a) G♯ minor melodic, from dominant to dominant

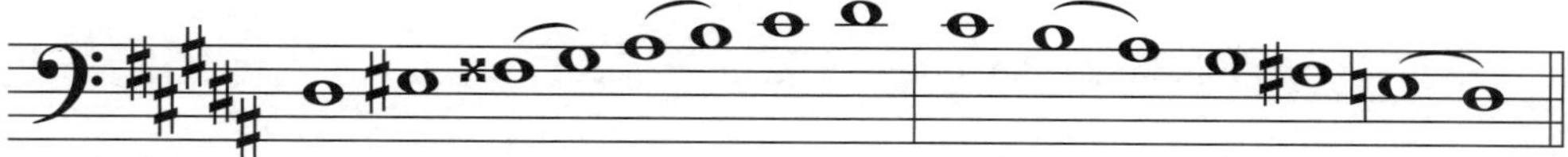

b) C♯ minor harmonic, from subdominant to subdominant

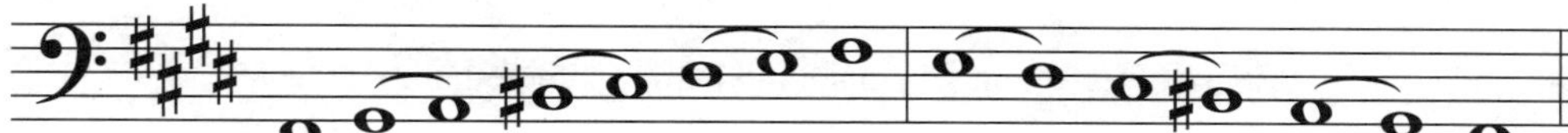

c) E minor harmonic, from dominant to dominant

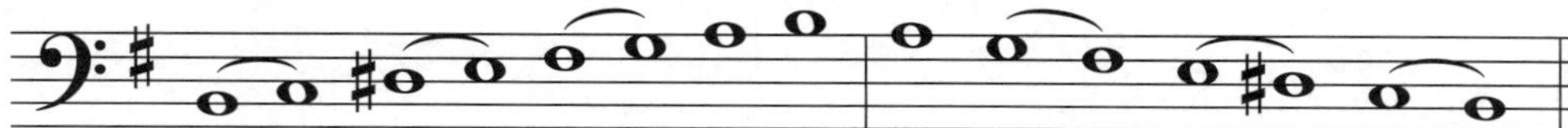

d) B♭ minor melodic, from tonic to tonic

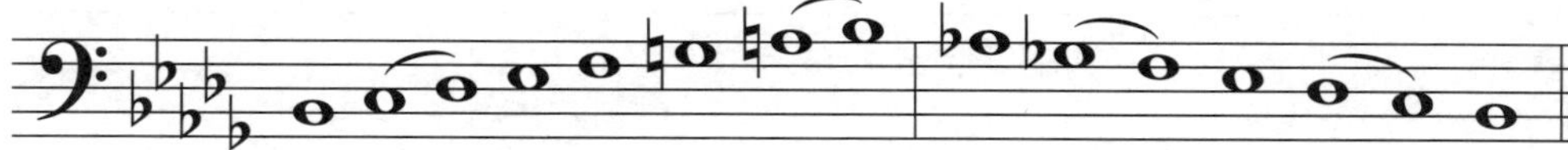

e) F♯ minor harmonic, from subdominant to subdominant

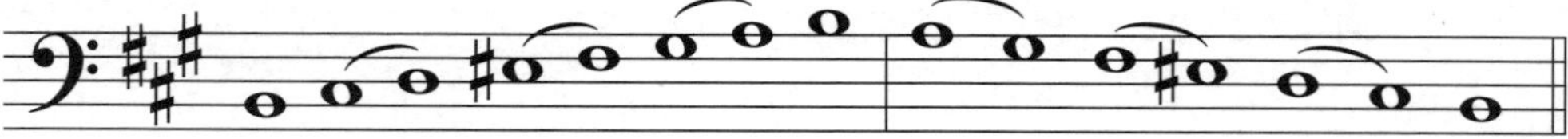

9. Write the following scales in the alto clef, ascending and descending, using the correct key signature for each. Use whole notes.

a) A minor melodic, from subdominant to subdominant

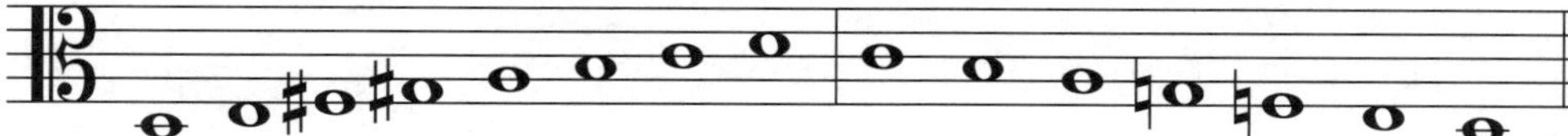

b) F minor harmonic, from leading note to leading note

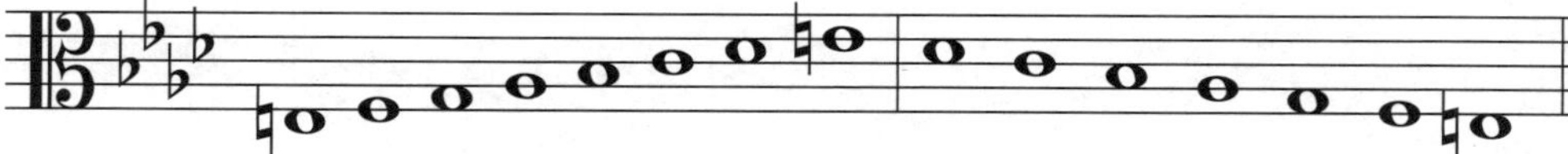

c) G♯ minor harmonic, from mediant to mediant

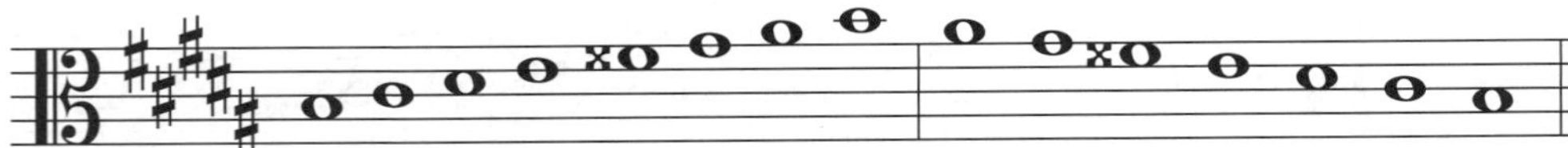

d) B minor harmonic, from leading note to leading note

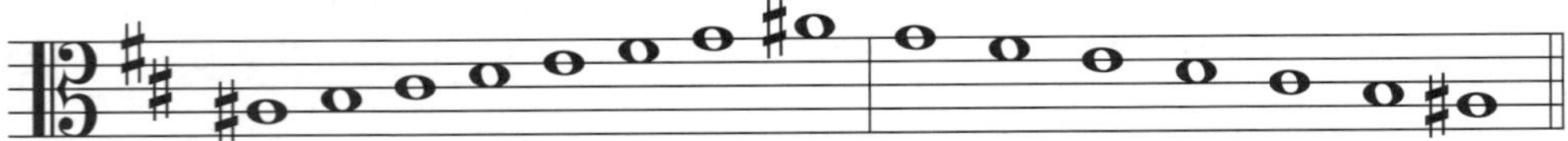

e) C minor melodic, from supertonic to supertonic

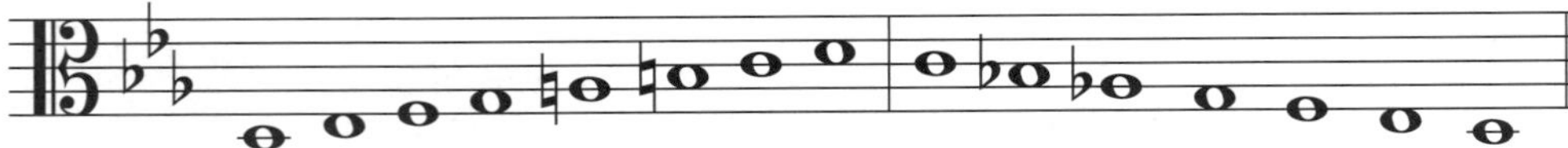

f) E♭ minor harmonic, from submediant to submediant

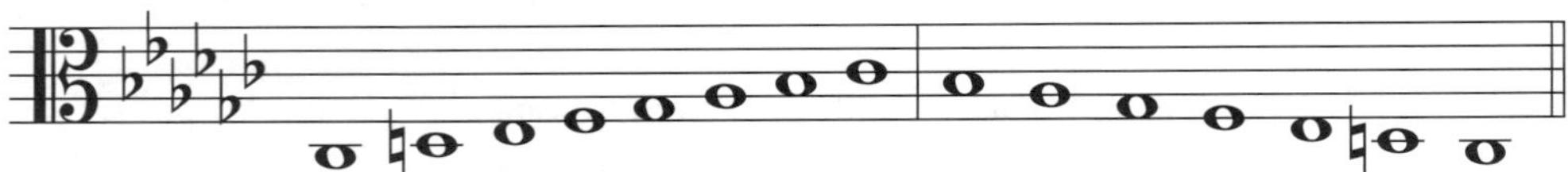

g) D minor harmonic, from dominant to dominant

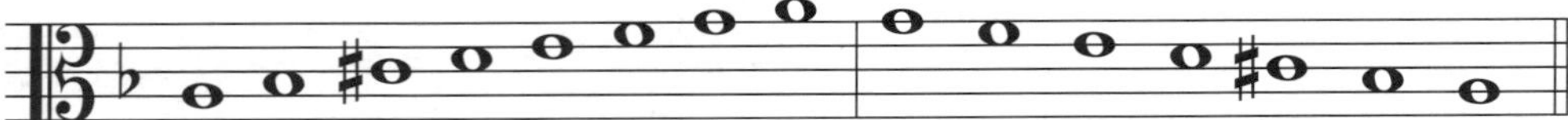

h) F♯ minor melodic, from supertonic to supertonic

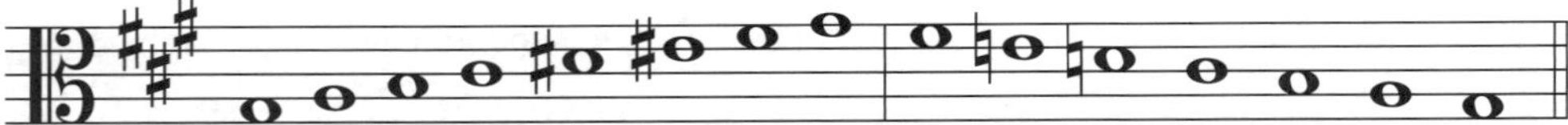

i) B♭ minor harmonic, from subdominant to subdominant

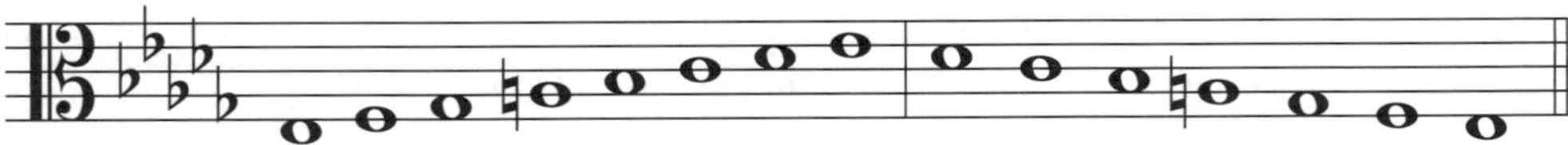

10. Add the proper clef, key signature, and accidentals where necessary to complete the following scales.

a) D major, from mediant to mediant

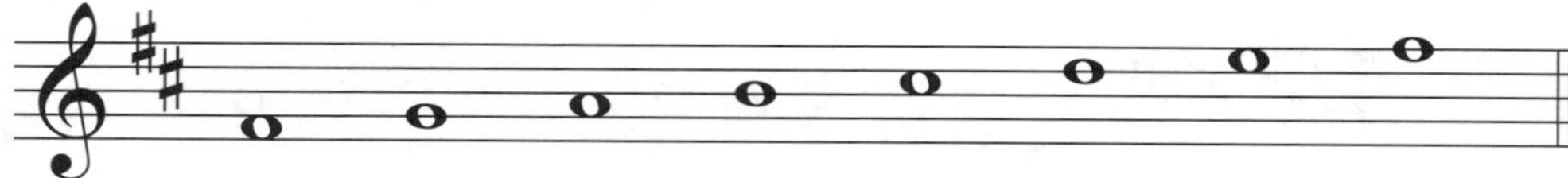

b) G minor melodic, from submediant to submediant

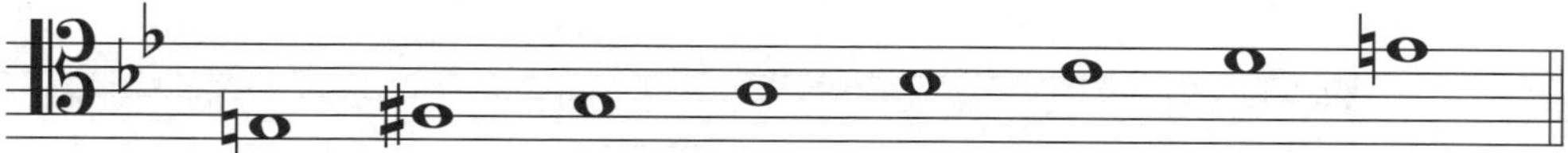

c) C♯ major, from submediant to submediant

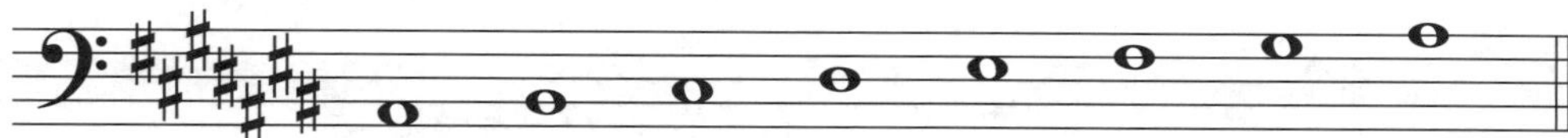

d) F♯ minor harmonic, from tonic to tonic

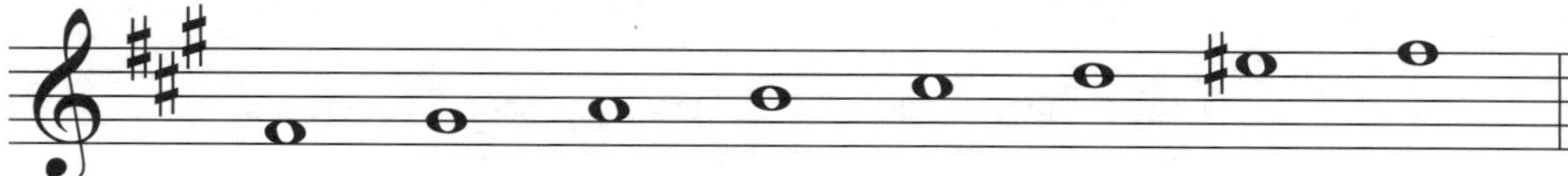

e) A minor melodic, from tonic to tonic

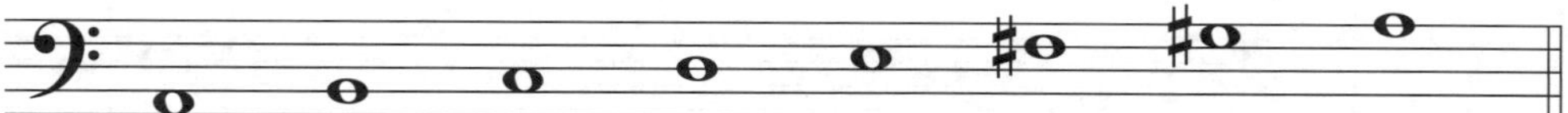

f) E minor melodic, from mediant to mediant

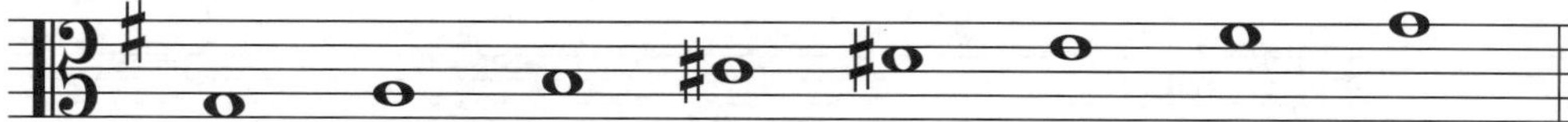

g) B♭ major, from dominant to dominant

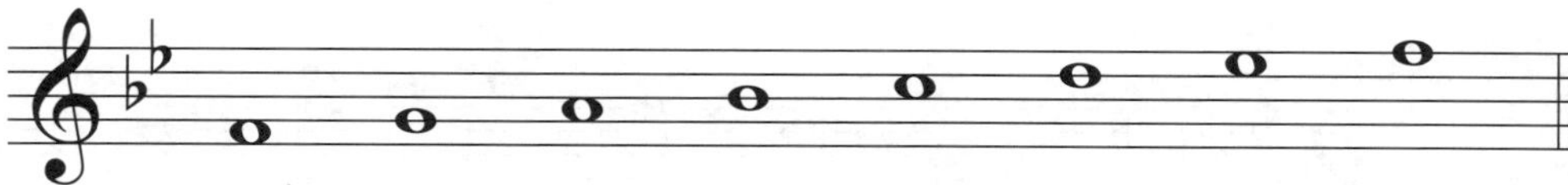

h) C minor harmonic, from mediant to mediant

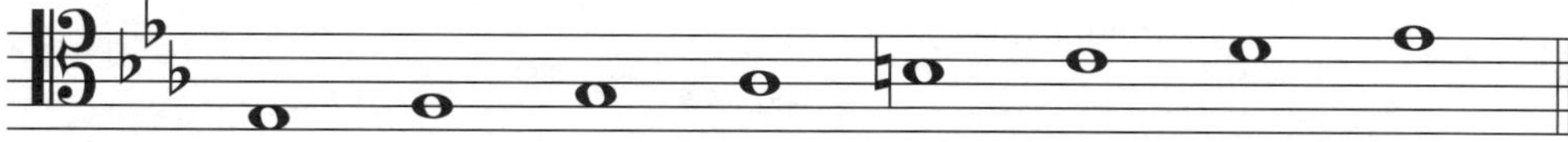

i) F minor harmonic, from supertonic to supertonic

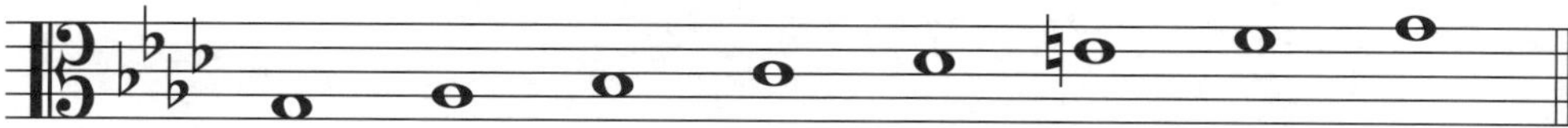

11. Write the following scales in the tenor clef, ascending and descending, using the correct key signature for each. Use whole notes.

a) the major scale whose key signature is seven flats

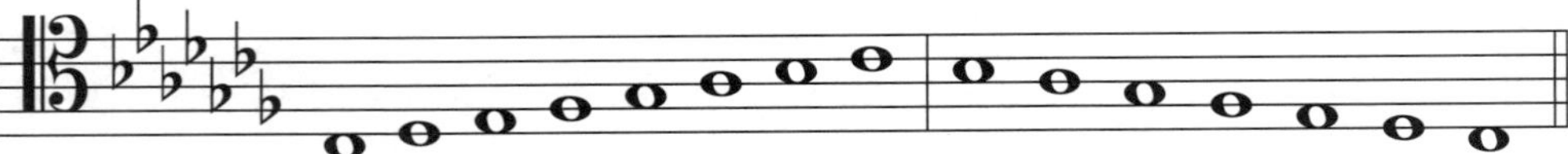

b) its relative minor, harmonic

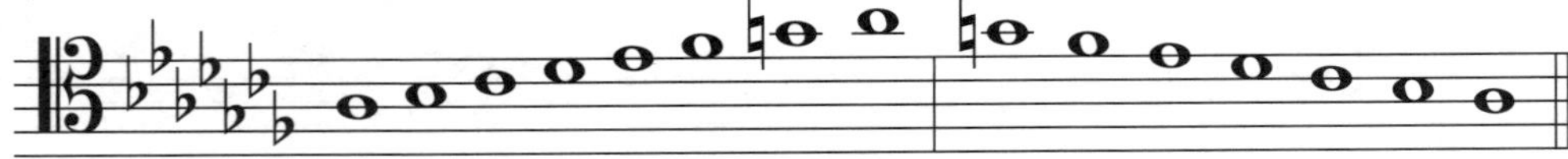

c) its enharmonic minor, melodic

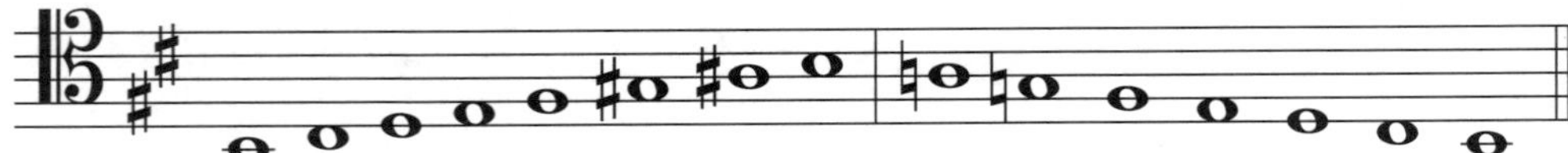

12. Write the following scales in the bass clef, ascending and descending, using the correct key signature for each. Use whole notes.

a) the harmonic minor scale whose key signature is four sharps

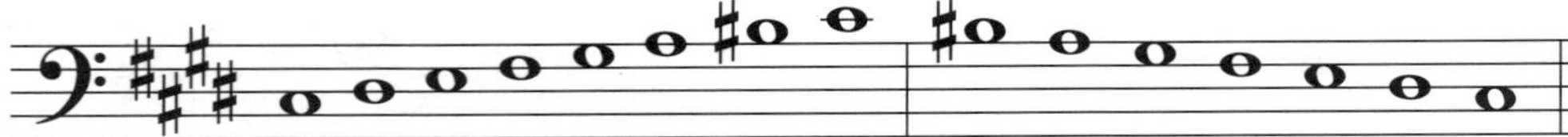

b) its relative major

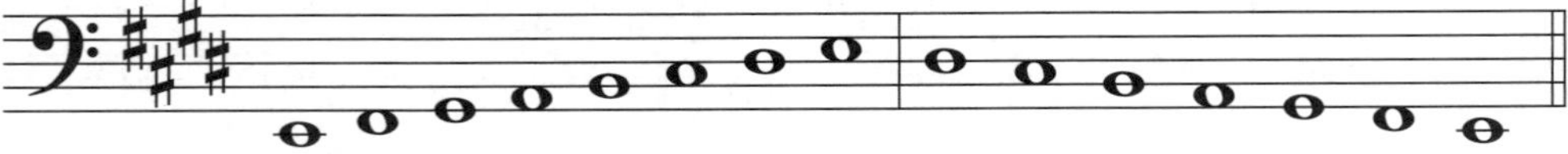

c) its tonic major

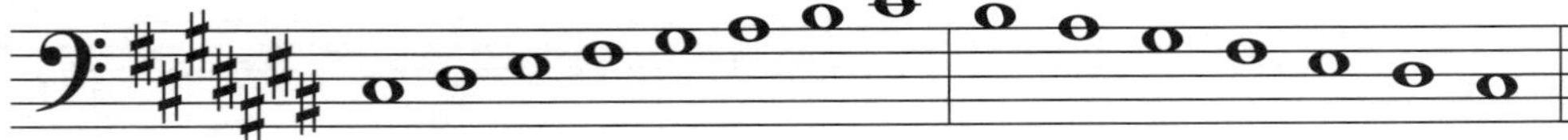

d) its enharmonic major

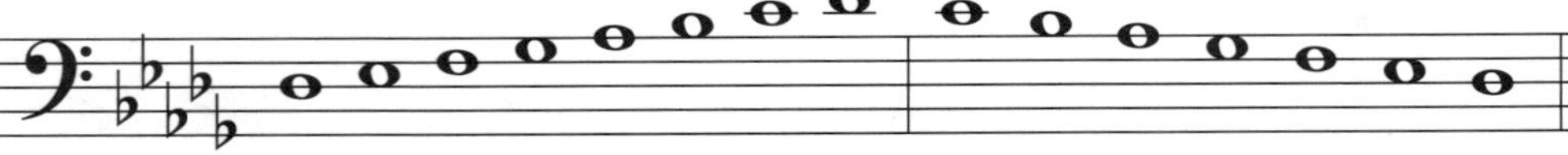

13. Write the following scales in the treble clef, ascending and descending, using the correct key signature for each. Use whole notes.

a) E♭ major

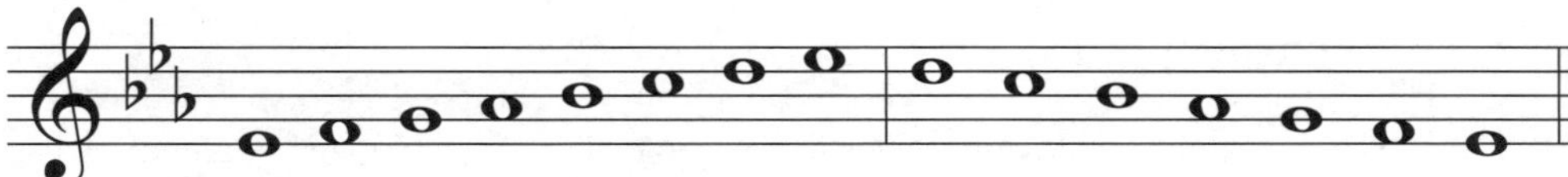

b) C minor, harmonic

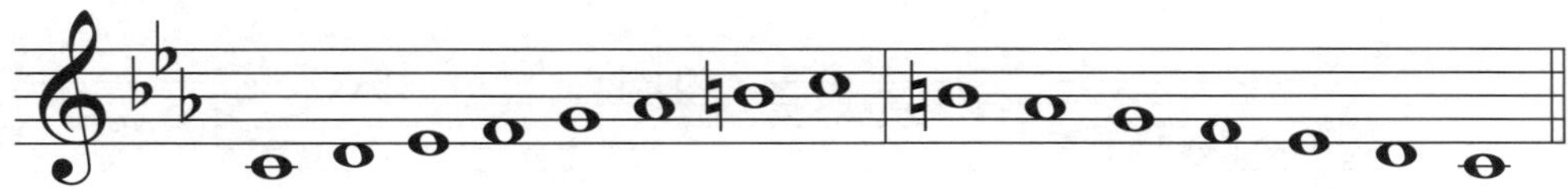

c) E♭ minor, melodic

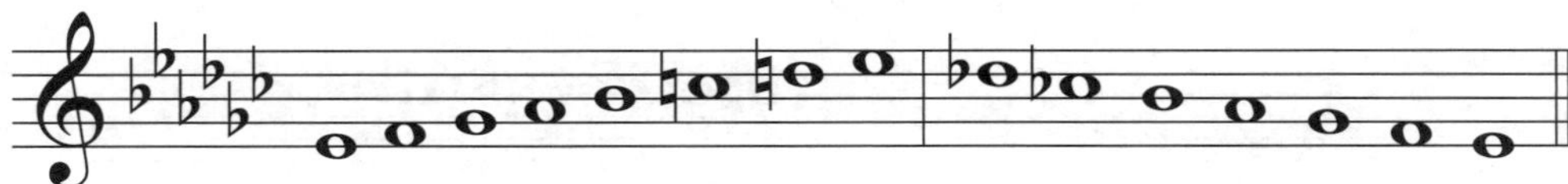

d) D♯ minor, harmonic

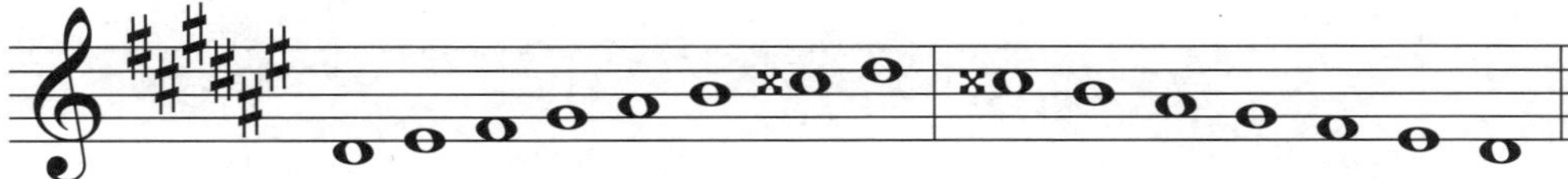

State the relationship of the first scale in question 13 to each of the others.

relationship of a) to b) a) is relative major of b)

relationship of a) to c) a) is tonic major of c)

relationship of a) to d) a) is enharmonic tonic major of d)

CHAPTER 3

OTHER SCALES AND MODES

I A EXERCISES (p. 69)

1. Write the following scales in the treble clef, ascending and descending, using accidentals. Use whole notes.

a) chromatic scale starting on G

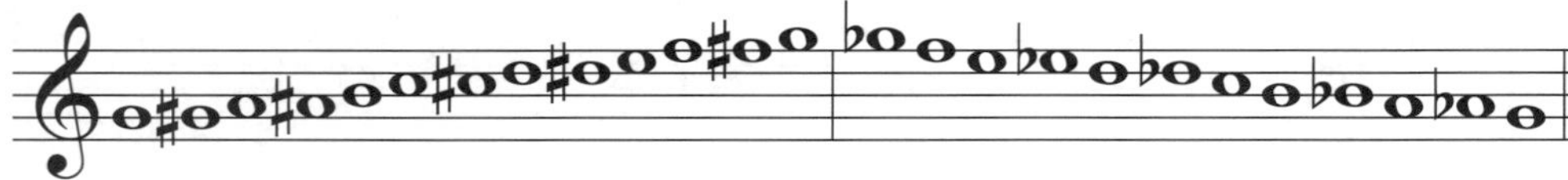

b) chromatic scale starting on F

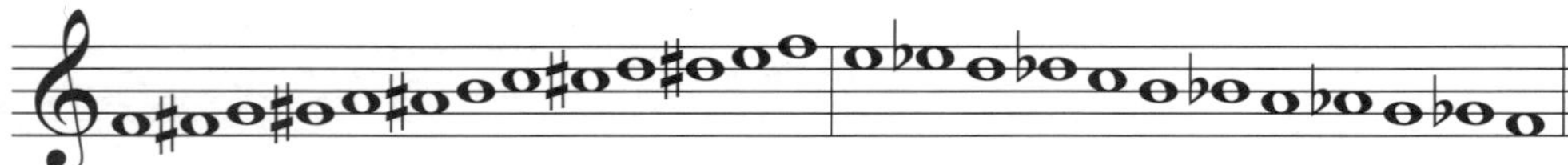

c) chromatic scale starting on F♯

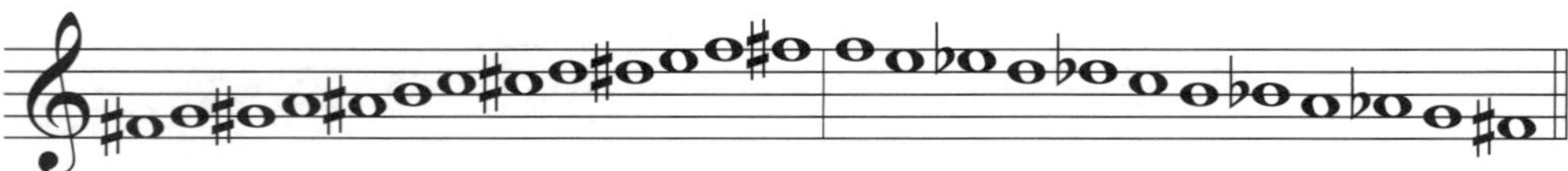

2. Write the following scales in the bass clef, ascending and descending, using accidentals. Use whole notes.

a) chromatic scale starting on A

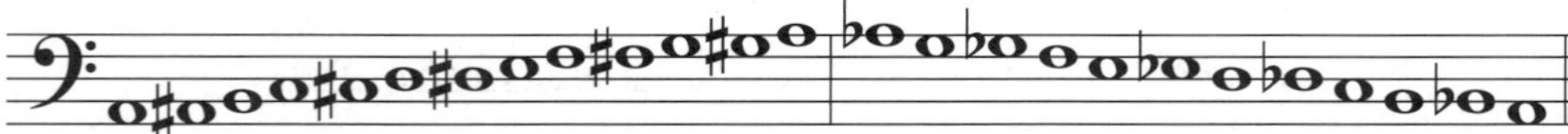

b) chromatic scale starting on B

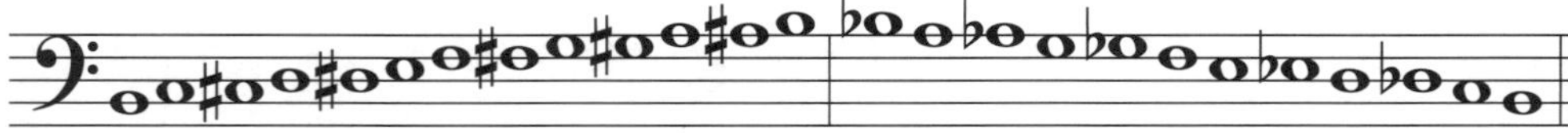

c) chromatic scale starting on E♭

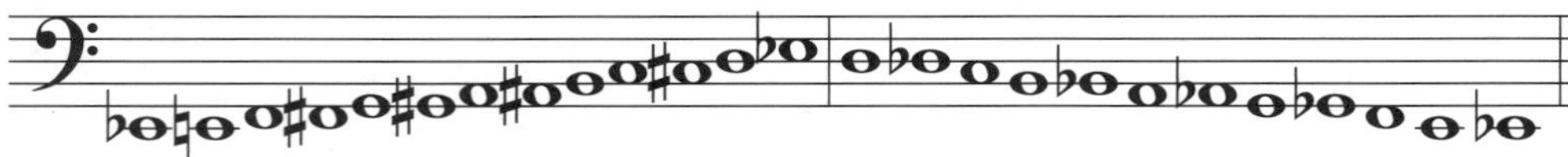

3. Add accidentals to each of the following to create chromatic scales.

a)

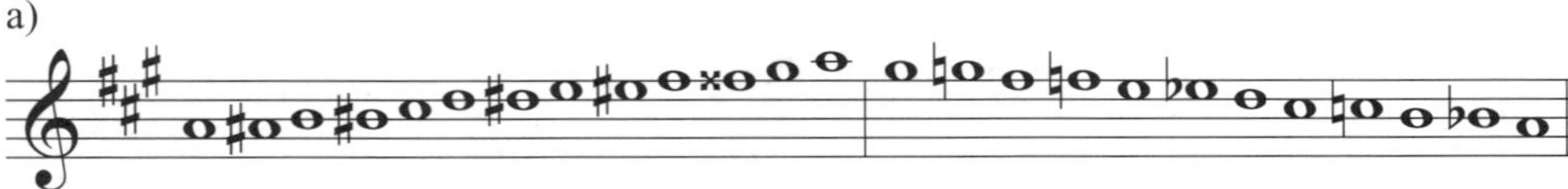

b)

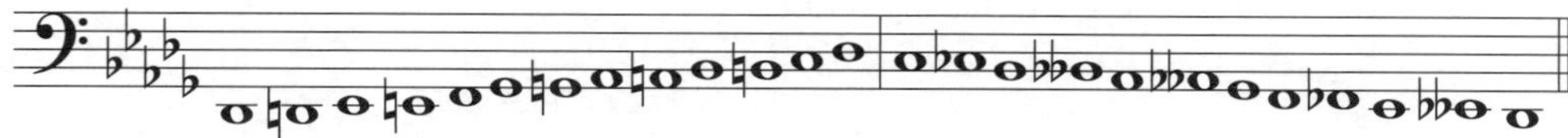

c)

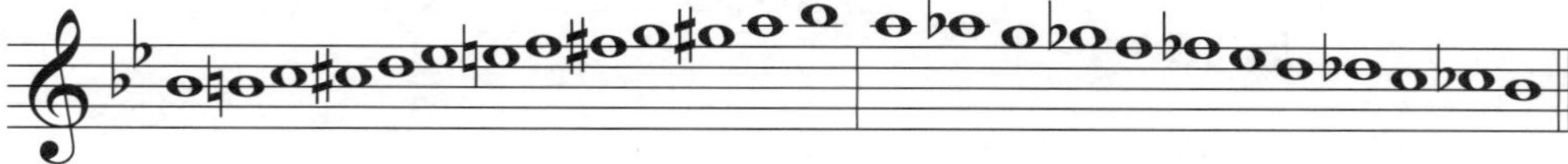

d)

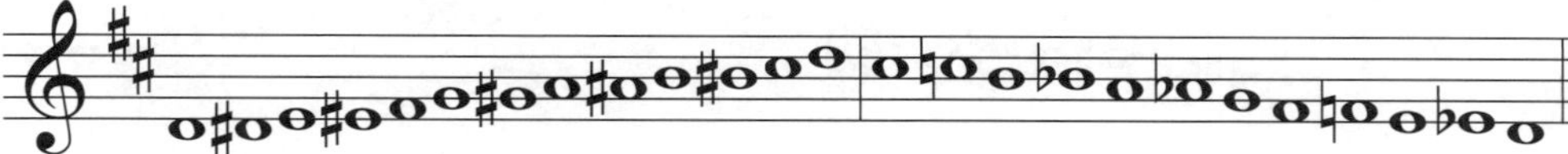

4. Write the following scales in the treble clef, ascending and descending, using key signatures. Use whole notes.

a) chromatic scale starting on B♭

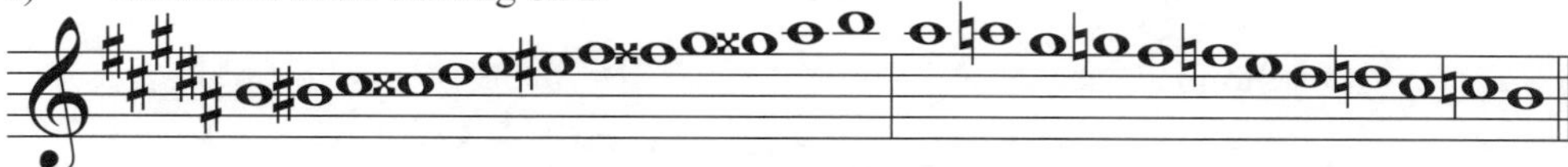

b) chromatic scale starting on D

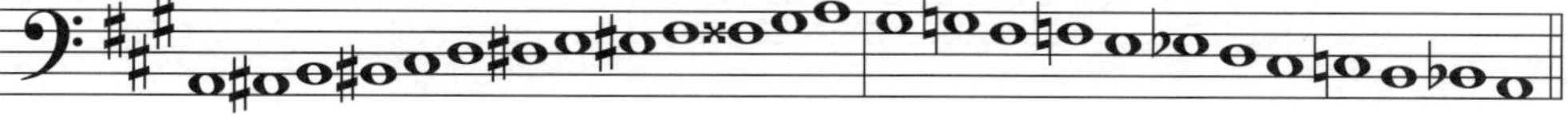

c) chromatic scale starting on B

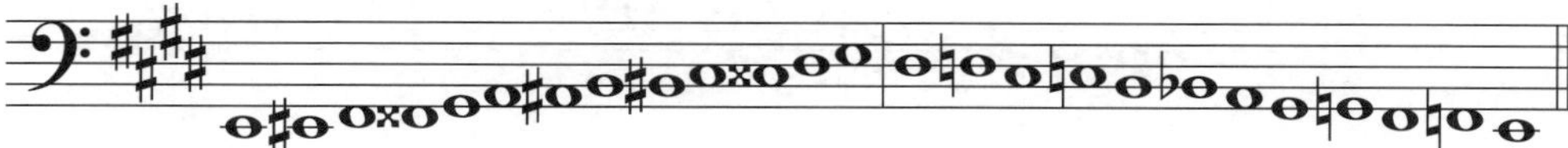

5. Write the following scales in the bass clef, ascending and descending, using key signatures. Use whole notes.

a) chromatic scale starting on A

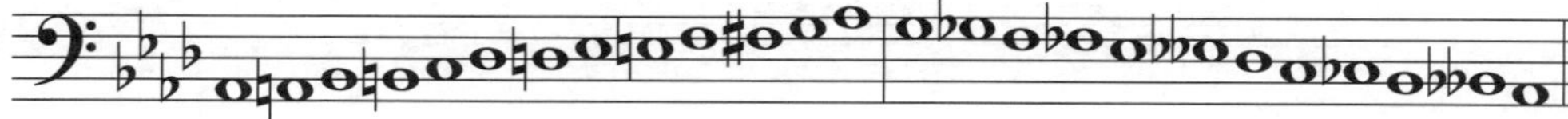

b) chromatic scale starting on E

c) chromatic scale starting on A♭

A MORE EXERCISES (p. 71)

1. Write the following scales in the given clefs, ascending and descending, using accidentals. Use whole notes.

a) chromatic scale starting on F♯

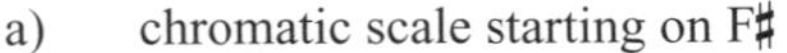

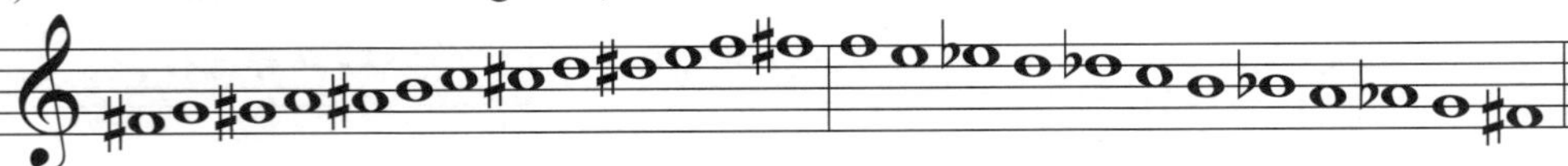

b) chromatic scale starting on D

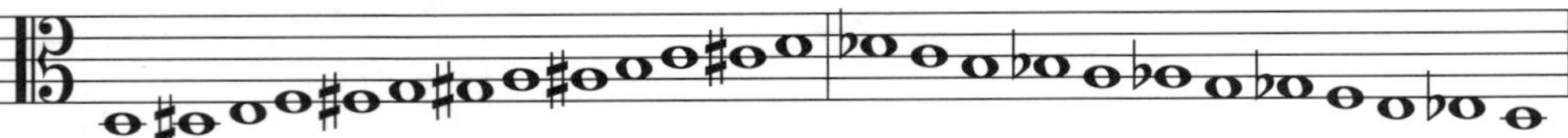

c) chromatic scale starting on B♭

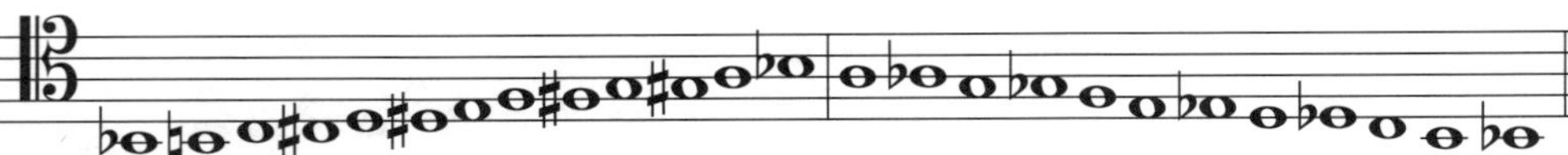

d) chromatic scale starting on D♭

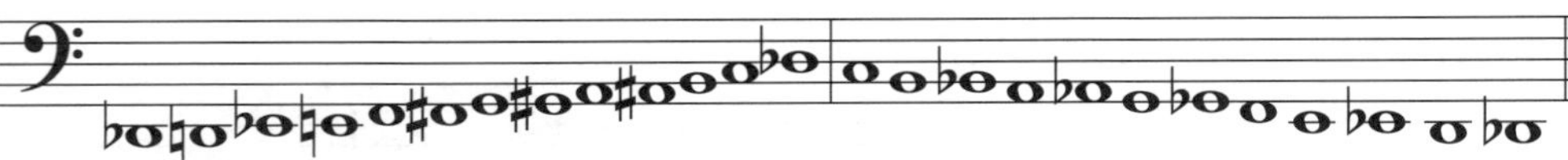

2. Write the following scales in the given clefs, ascending and descending, using key signatures. Use whole notes.

a) chromatic scale starting on C♯

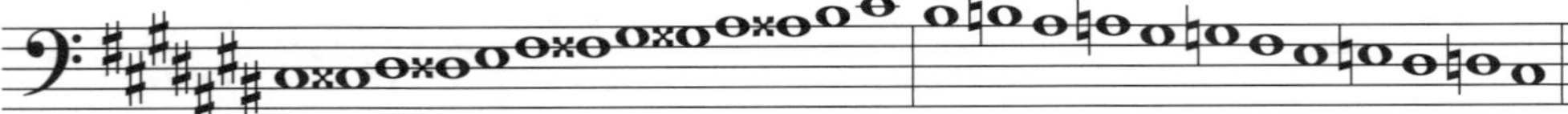

b) chromatic scale starting on A♭

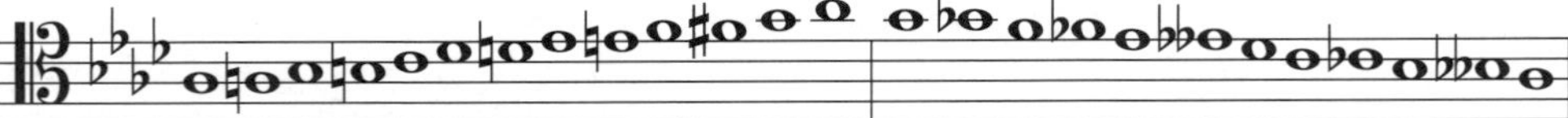

c) chromatic scale starting on E

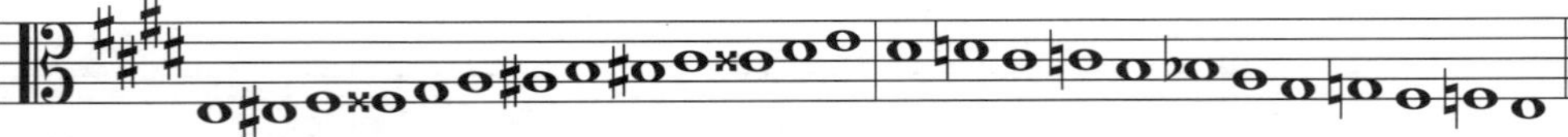

d) chromatic scale starting on G♭

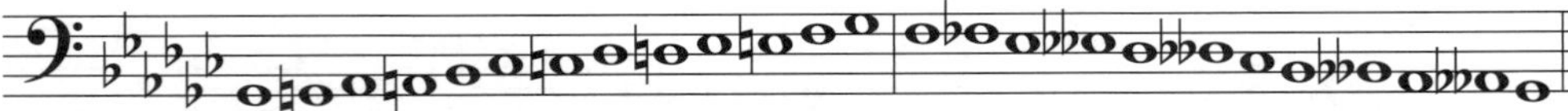

I A EXERCISES (p. 73)

1. Change each of the following major 2nds into a diminished 3rd by respelling one of its notes enharmonically.

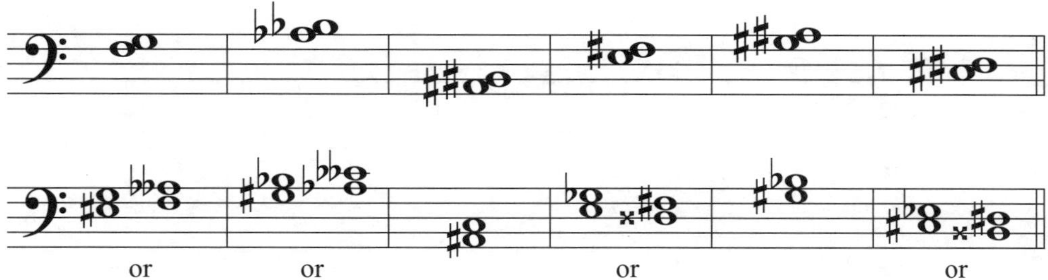

2. Change each of the following diminished 3rds into a major 2nd by respelling one of its notes enharmonically.

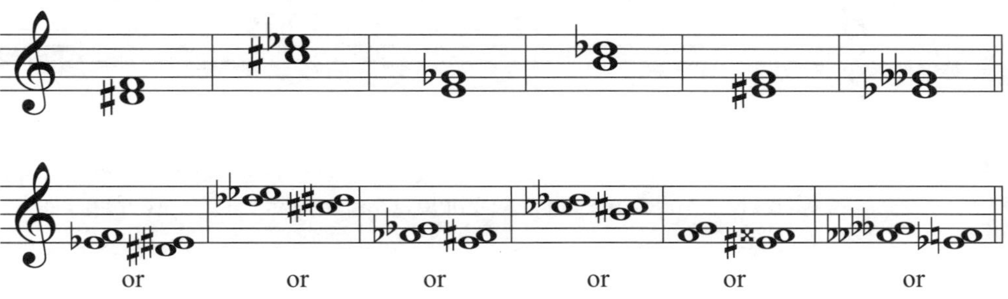

3. Add accidentals to each of the following to create whole-tone scales. Do not alter the first note of each scale.

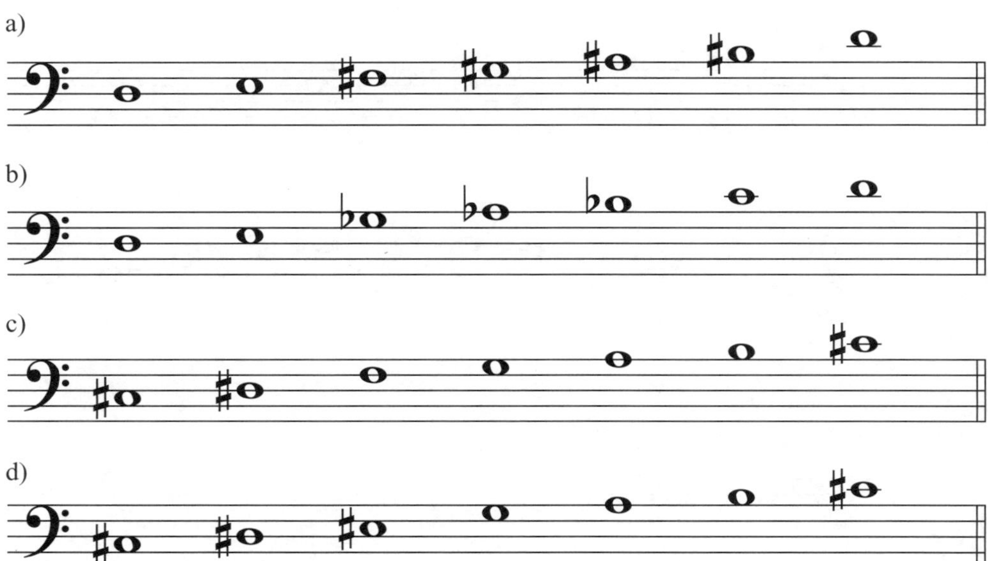

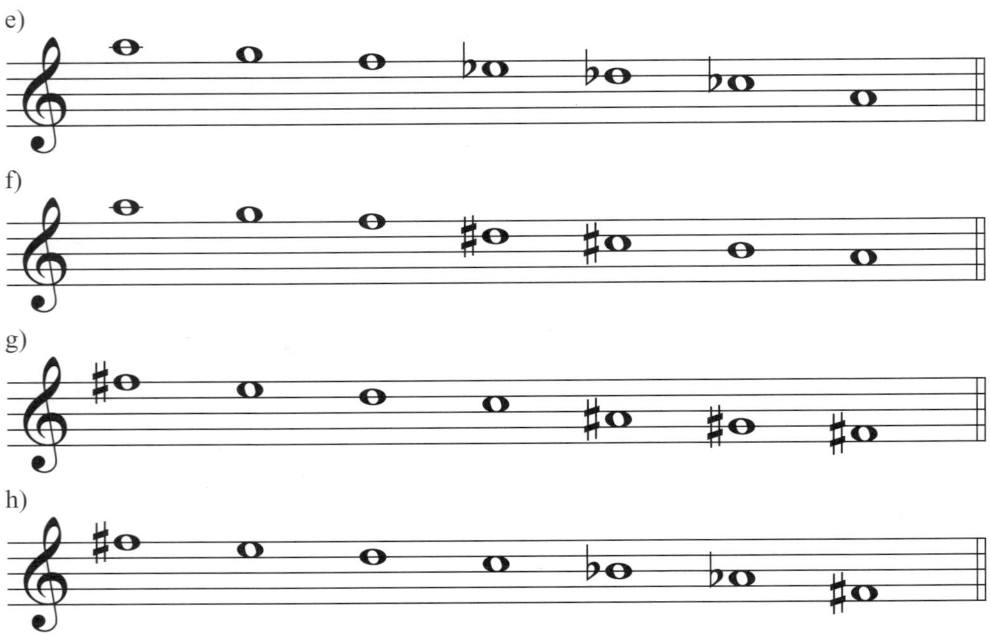

4. Write a whole-tone scale in the treble clef, ascending and descending, beginning on each of the following notes. (Sample answers. Other spellings are possible.)

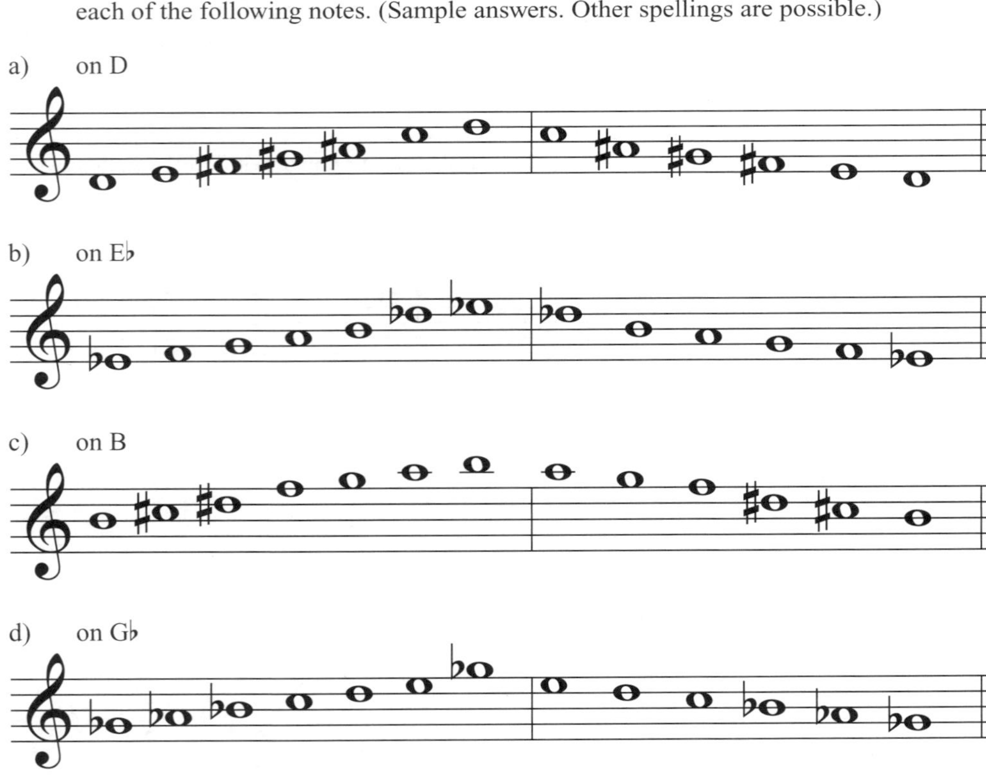

5. Write a whole-tone scale in the bass clef, ascending and descending, beginning on each of the following notes. (Sample answers. Other spellings are possible.)

a) on A

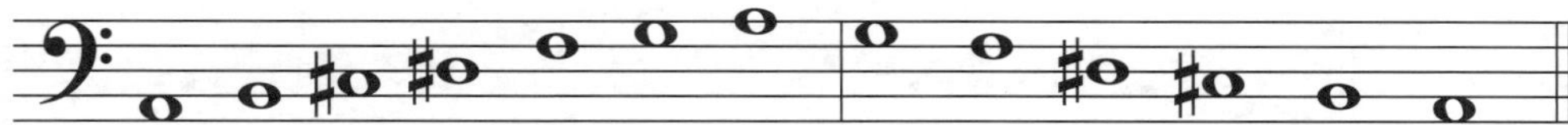

b) on E

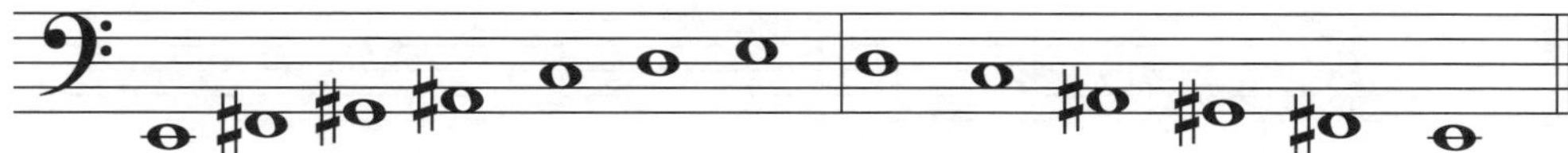

c) on F♯

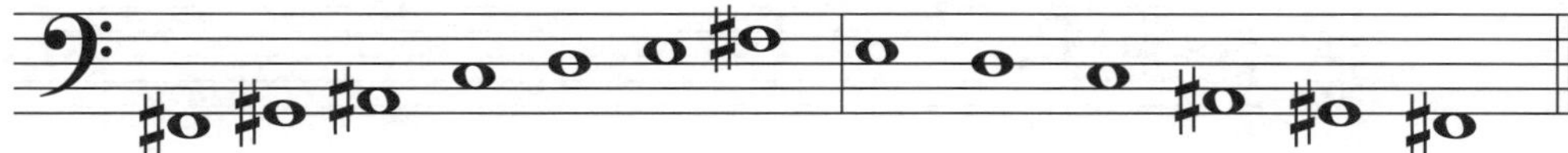

d) on C♯

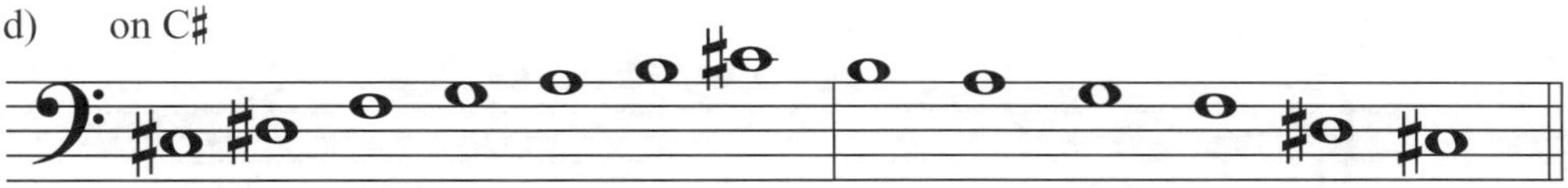

A MORE EXERCISES (p. 76)

1. Write a whole-tone scale in the tenor clef, ascending and descending, beginning on each of the following notes. (Sample answers. Other spellings are possible.)

a) on D♭

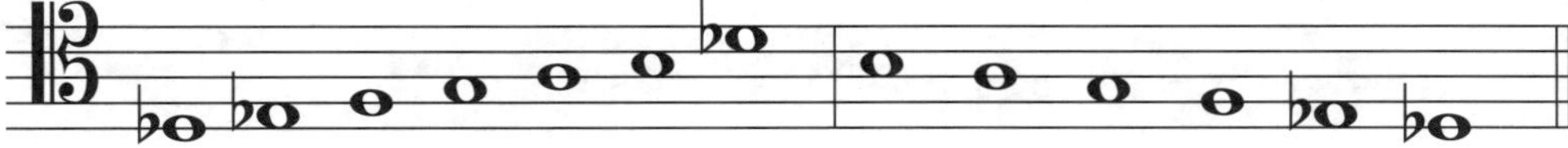

b) on F♯

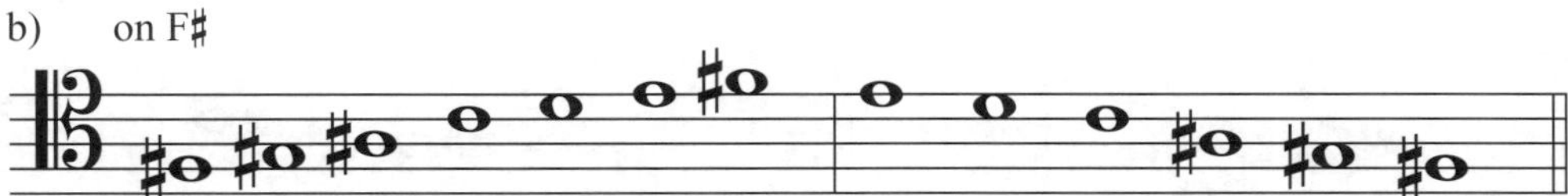

c) on A

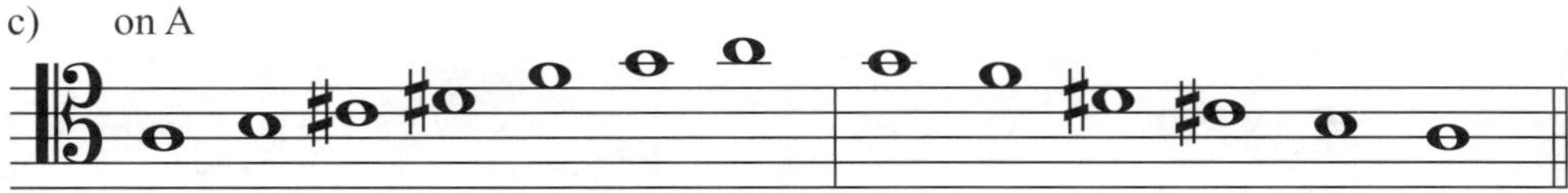

d) on B♭

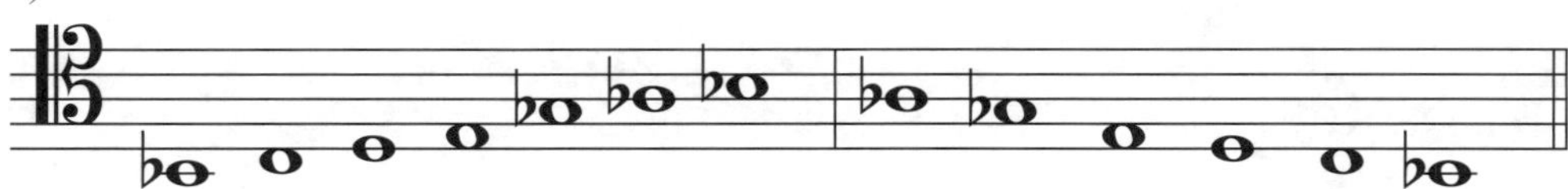

2. Write a whole-tone scale in the alto clef, ascending and descending, beginning on each of the following notes. (Sample answers. Other spellings are possible.)

a) on G

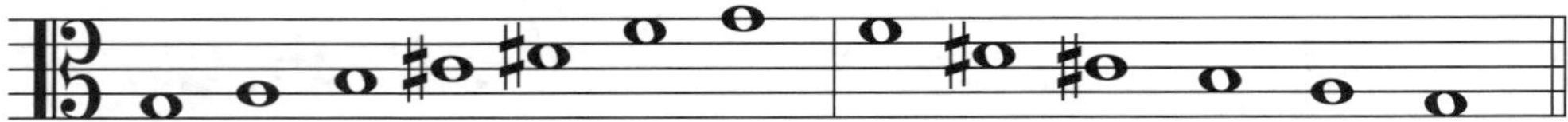

b) on A♭

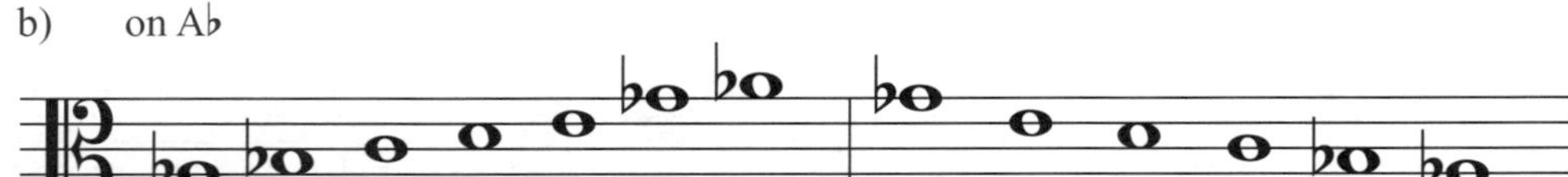

c) on C♯

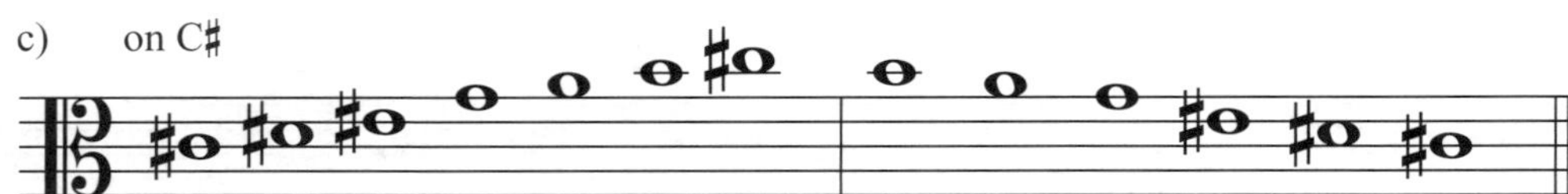

d) on B

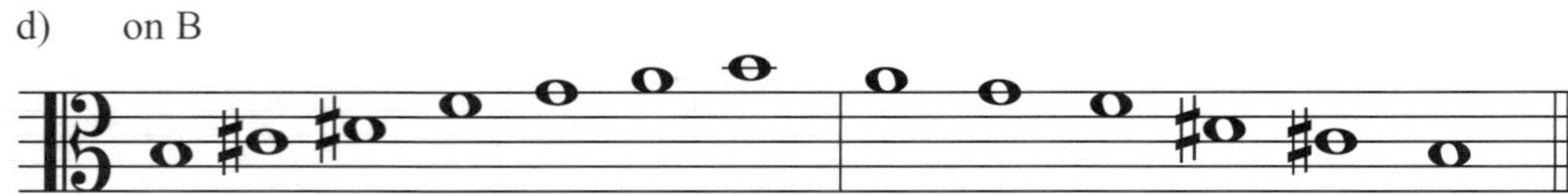

I A EXERCISES (p. 77)

1. Add accidentals to each of the following to create blues scales. Do not alter the first note of each scale.

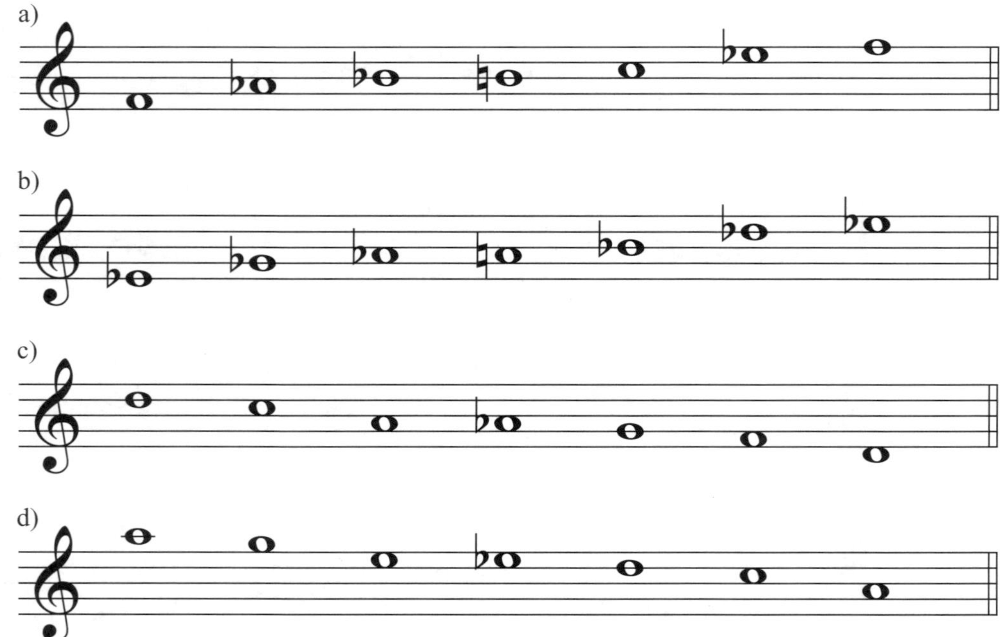

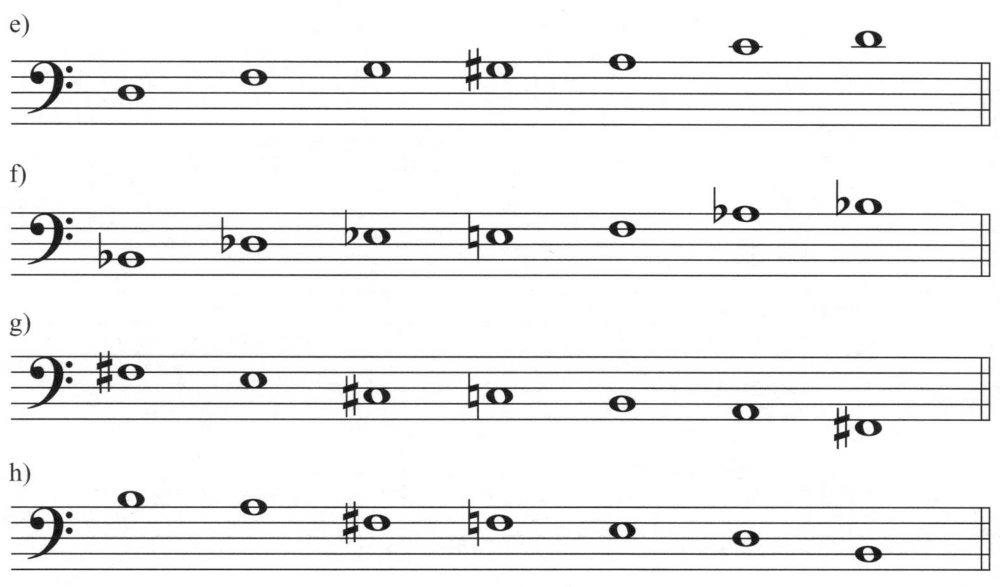

2. Write the following blues scales in the treble clef, ascending only.

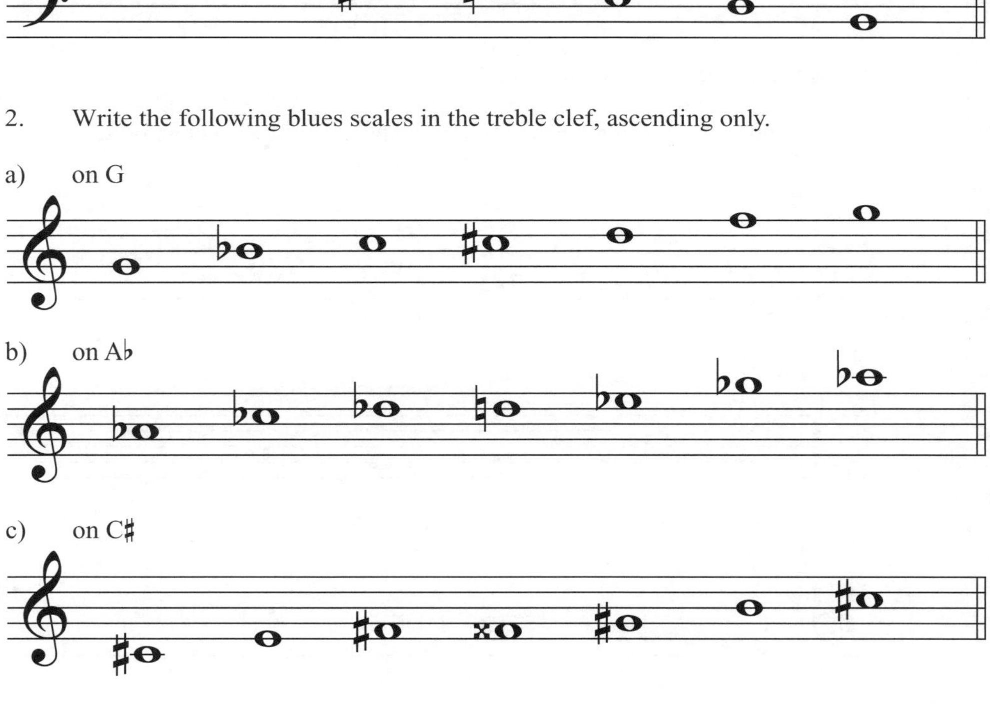

3. Write the following blues scales in the bass clef, descending only.

a) on E

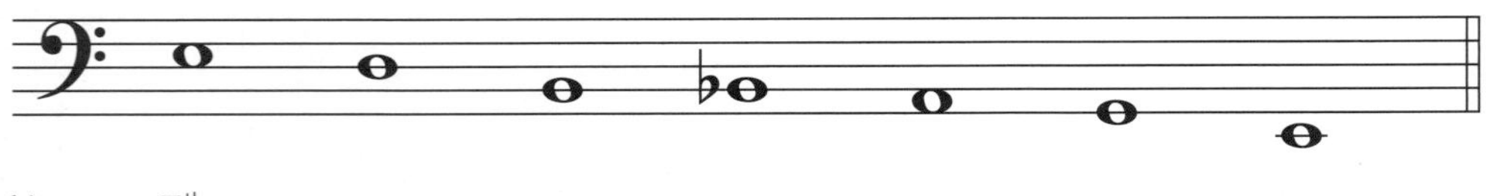

b) on F♯

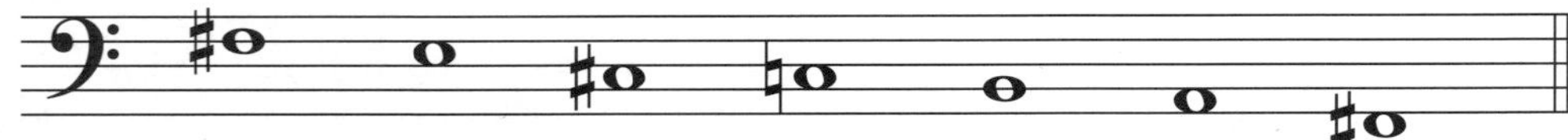

c) on B♭

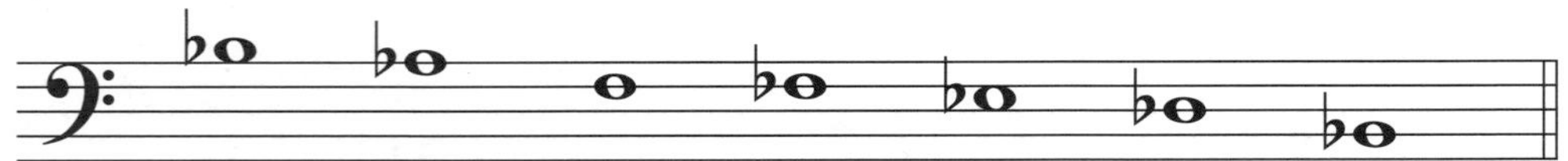

A MORE EXERCISES (p. 79)

1. Write the following blues scales in the given clefs, ascending only.

a) on D♭

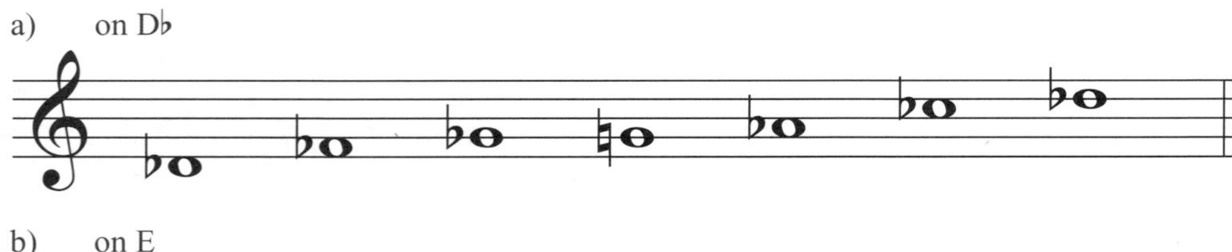

b) on E

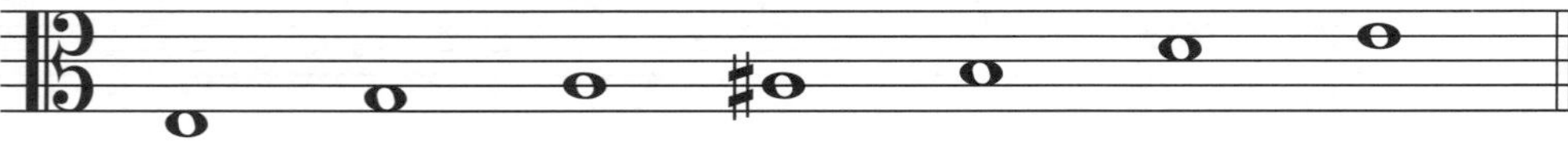

c) on E♭

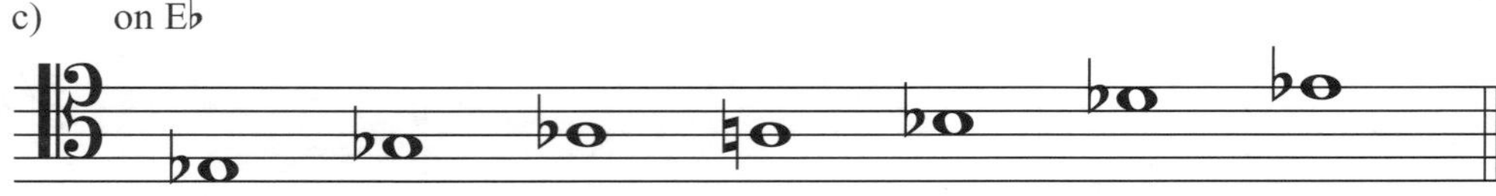

d) on F♯

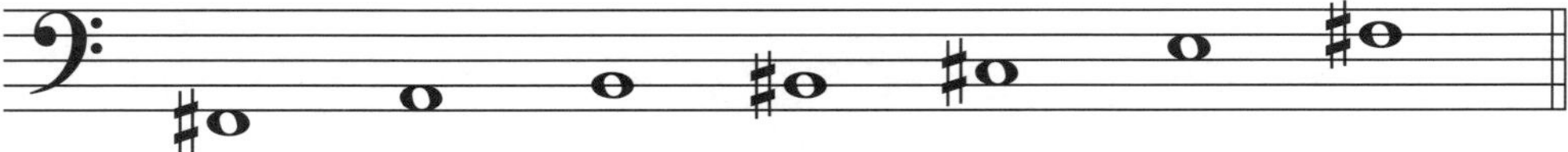

2. Write the following blues scales in the given clefs, descending only.

a) on A♭

b) on B♭

c) on C♯

d) on B

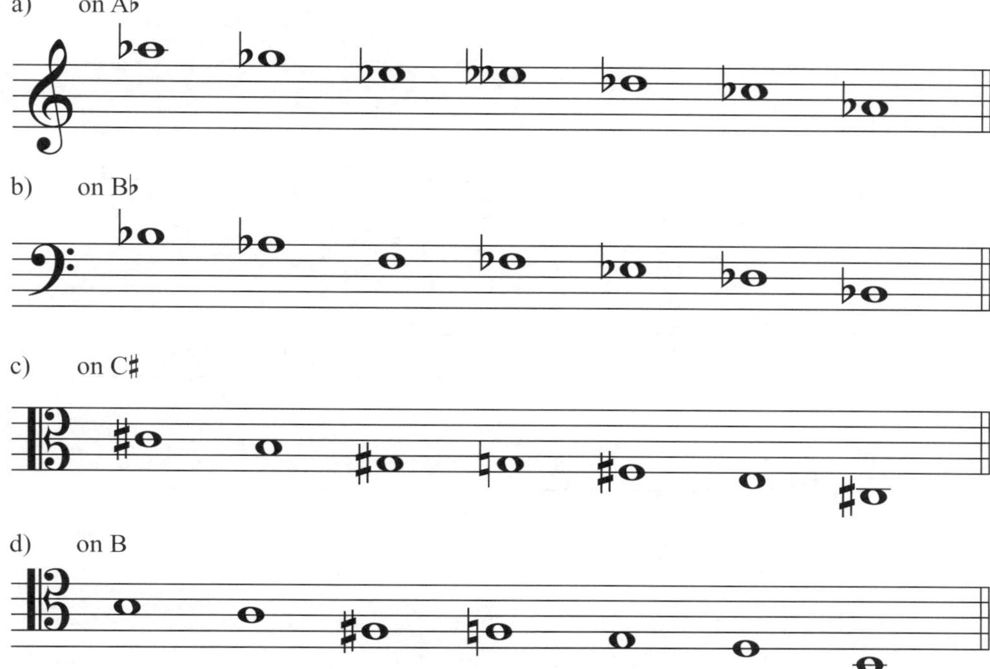

I A EXERCISES (p. 81)

1. Add accidentals to each of the following to create octatonic scales. Do not alter the first *two* notes of each scale.

a)

b)

c)

d)

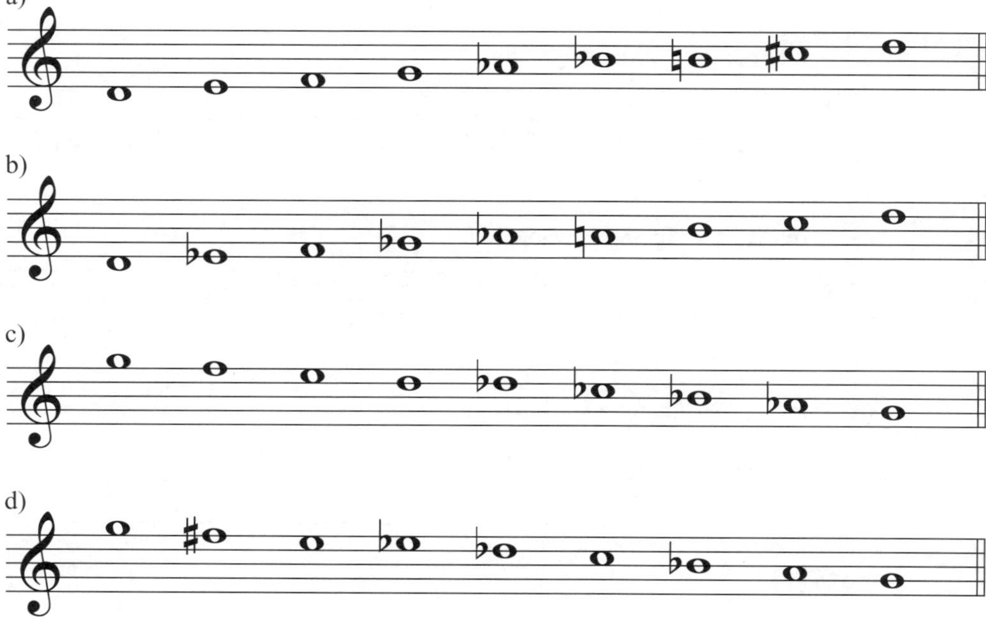

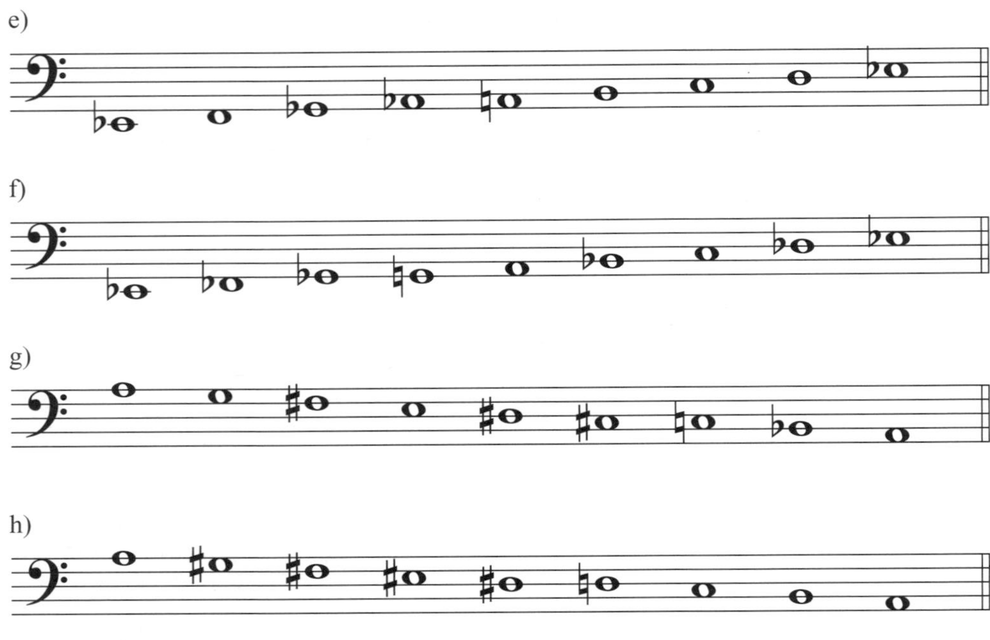

2. Write each of the following octatonic scales in the bass clef, ascending and descending. (Sample answers. Other spellings are possible.)

a) on E, starting with a semitone

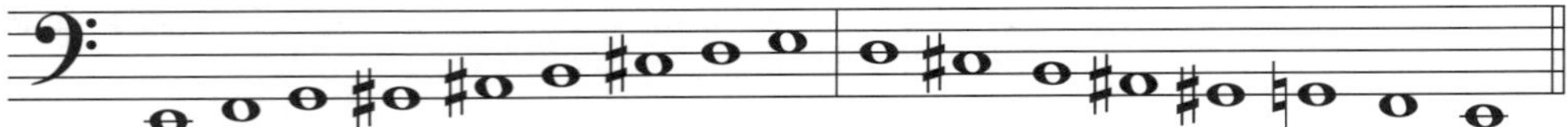

b) on F, starting with a whole tone

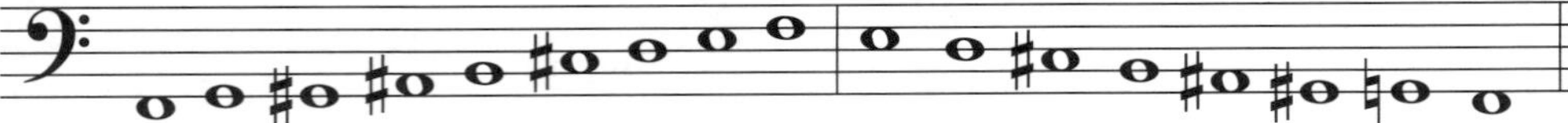

c) on A♭, starting with a whole tone

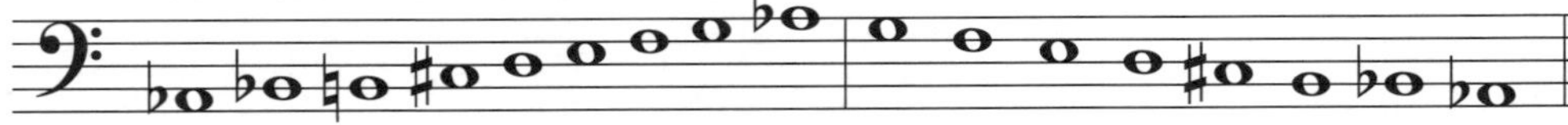

d) on C♯, starting with a semitone

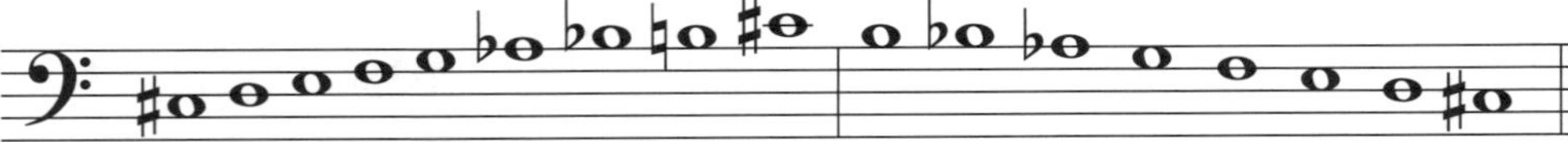

3. Write each of the following octatonic scales in the treble clef, ascending and descending. (Sample answers. Other spellings are possible.)

a) on B, starting with a whole tone

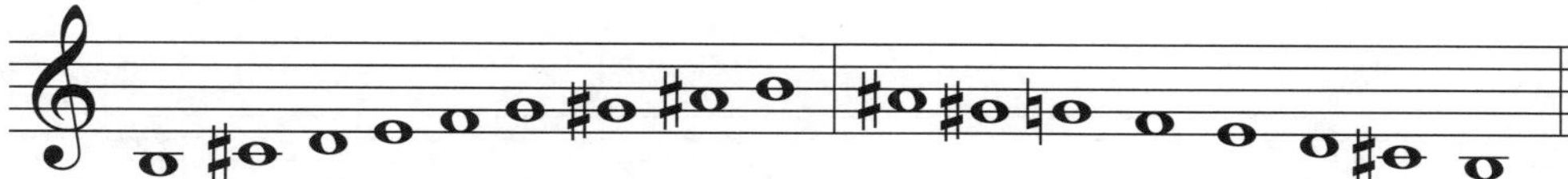

b) on C, starting with a semitone

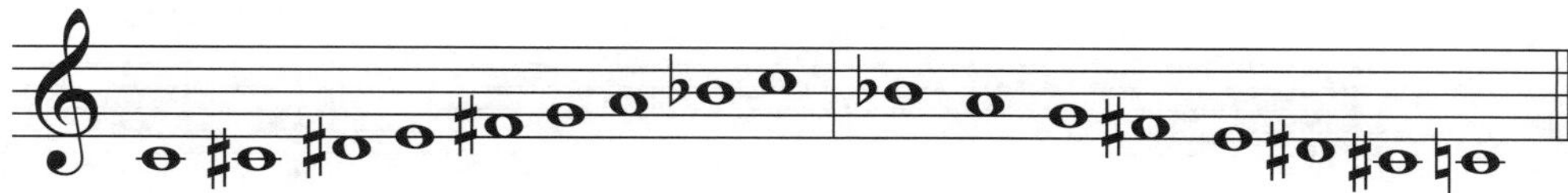

c) on F♯, starting with a whole tone

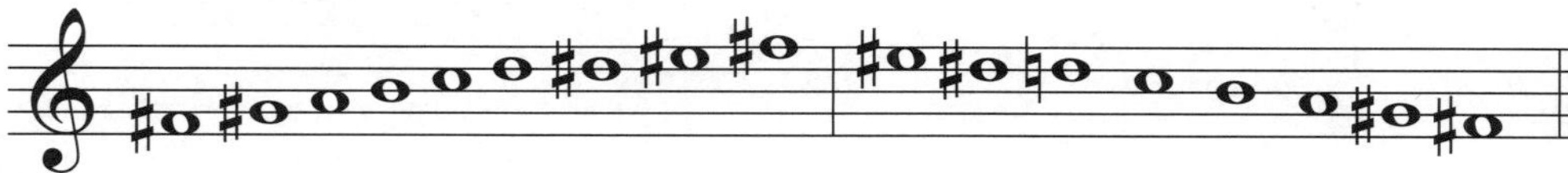

d) on B♭, starting with a semitone

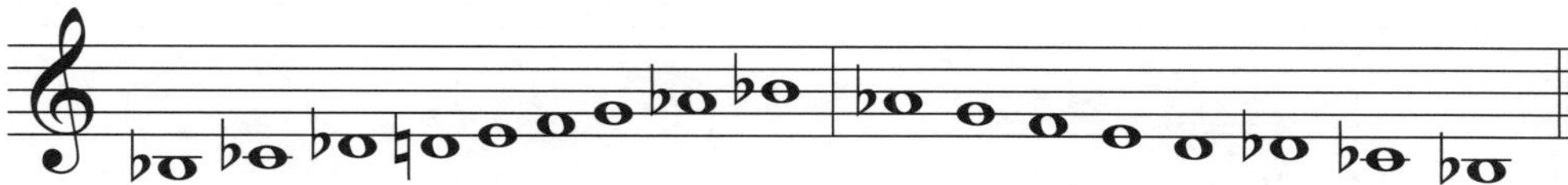

A MORE EXERCISES (p. 83)

1. Complete each of the following octatonic scales. (Sample answers. Other spellings are possible.)

a)

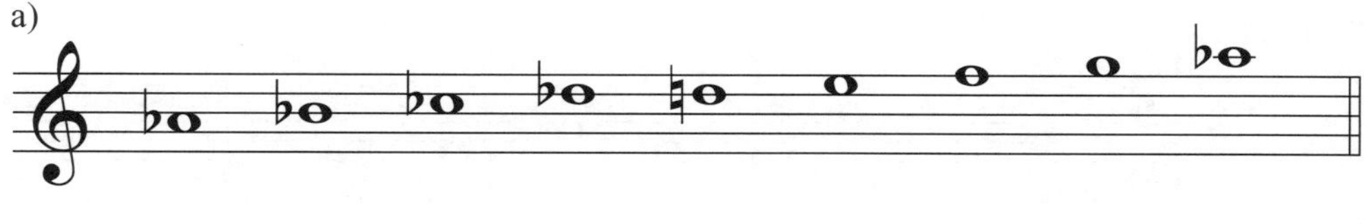

b)

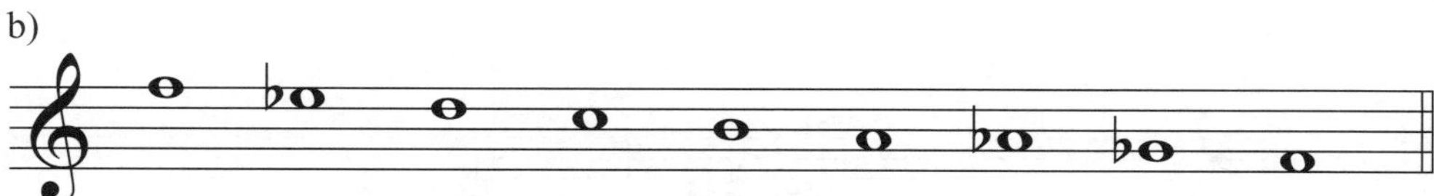

c)

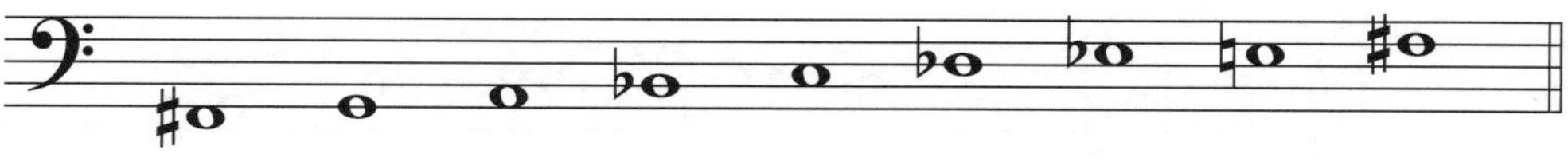

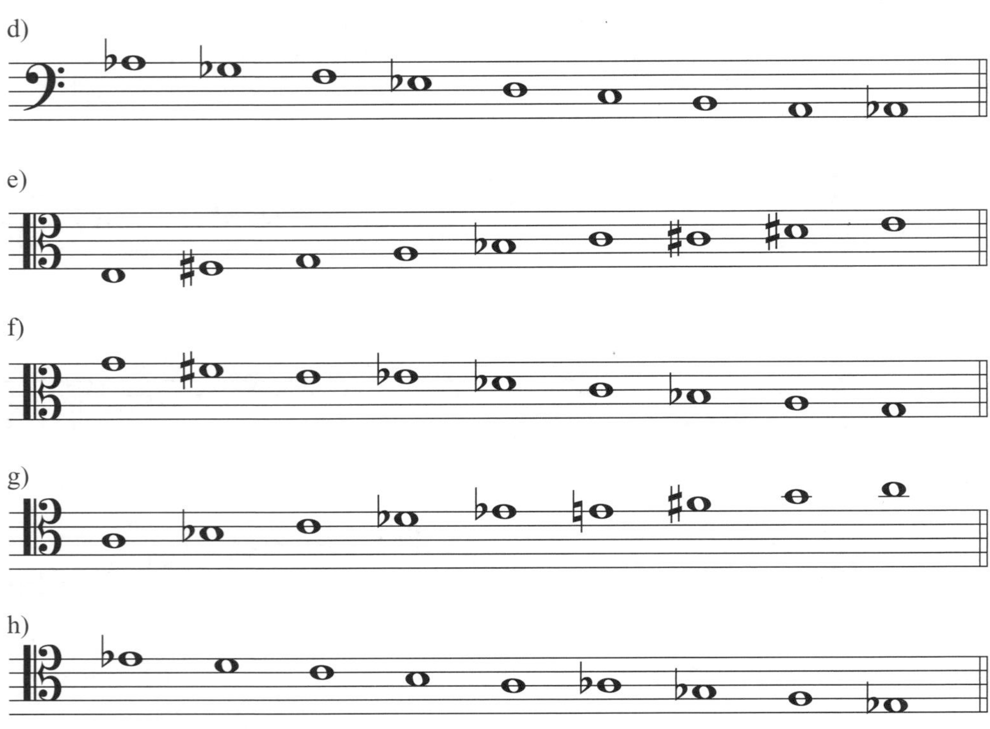

I A EXERCISES (p. 87)

1. Write the following major pentatonic scales in the treble clef, ascending and descending, using accidentals.

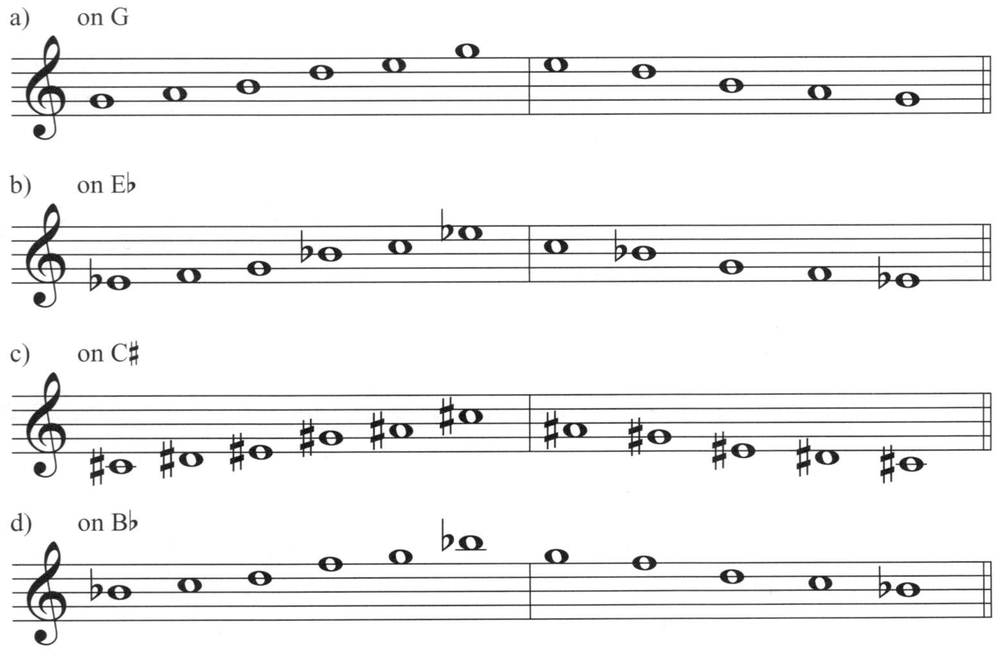

2. Write the following minor pentatonic scales in the bass clef, ascending and descending, using accidentals.

a) on F

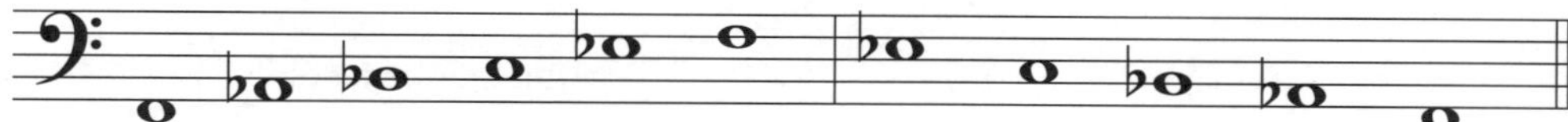

b) on A♭

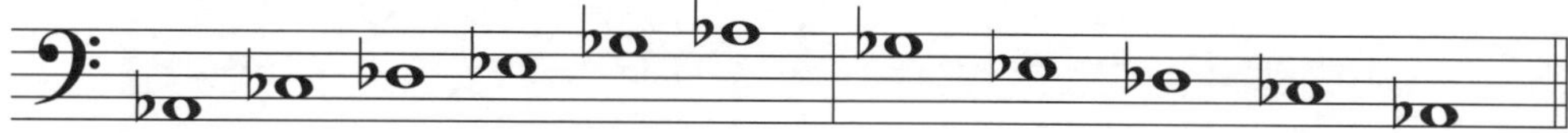

c) on D♯

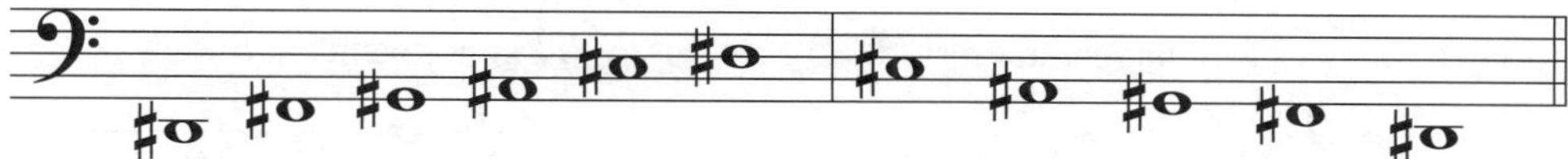

d) on E

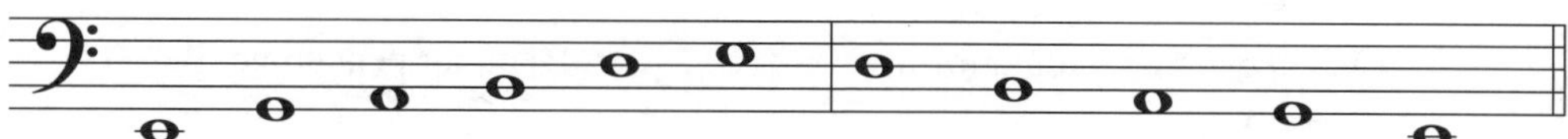

3. Write the following major scales in the bass clef, ascending only, using the correct key signature for each. Then write major pentatonic scales starting on the same notes and using the same key signatures.

Example: G major G major pentatonic

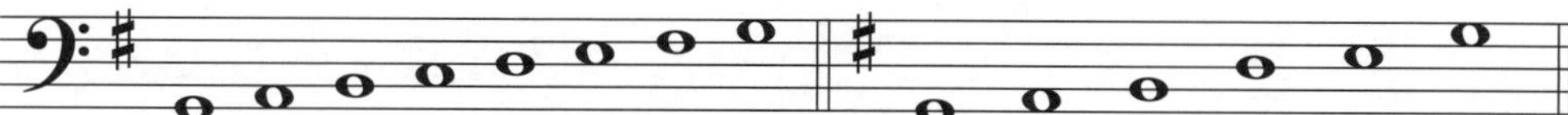

a) A major A major pentatonic

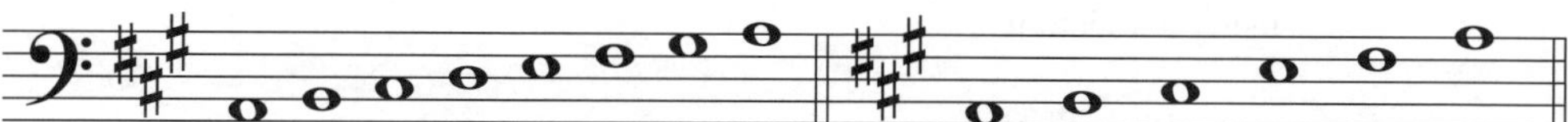

b) D♭ major D♭ major pentatonic

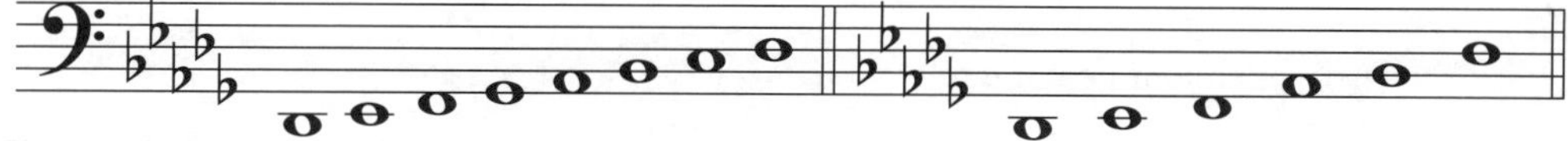

c) B major — B major pentatonic

d) E major — E major pentatonic

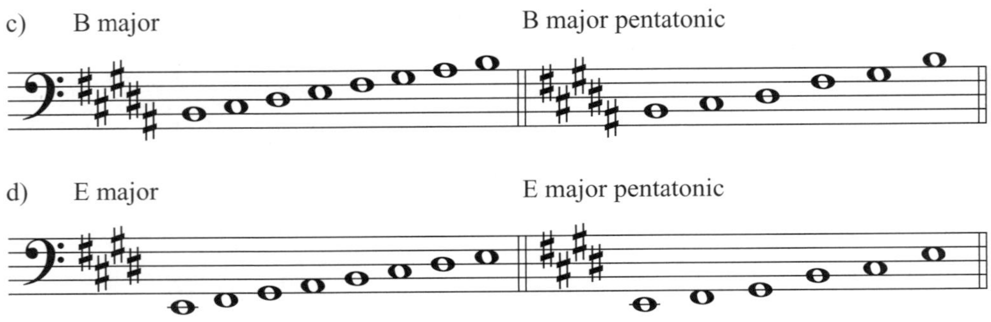

4. Write the following minor scales in the treble clef, descending only, using the correct key signature for each. Then write minor pentatonic scales starting on the same notes and using the same key signatures.

a) F♯ minor, natural form — F♯ minor pentatonic

b) B♭ minor, natural form — B♭ minor pentatonic

c) E♭ minor, natural form — E♭ minor pentatonic

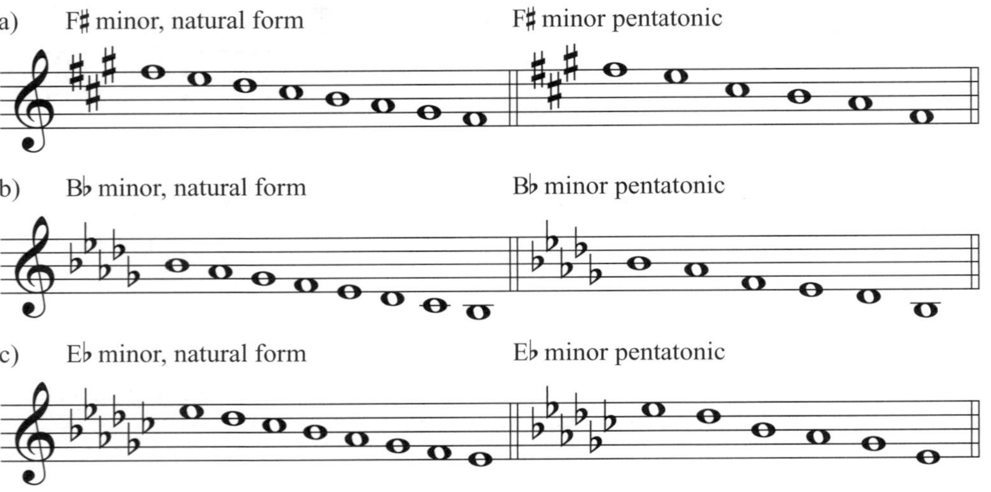

A MORE EXERCISES (p. 89)

1. Write the following pentatonic scales in the given clefs, ascending and descending, using accidentals.

a) B minor pentatonic

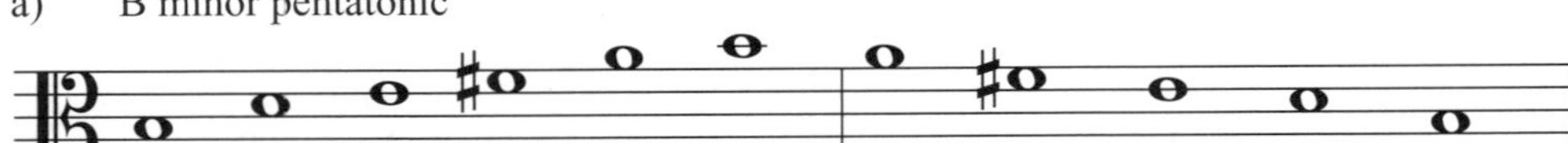

b) A♭ major pentatonic

c) E minor pentatonic

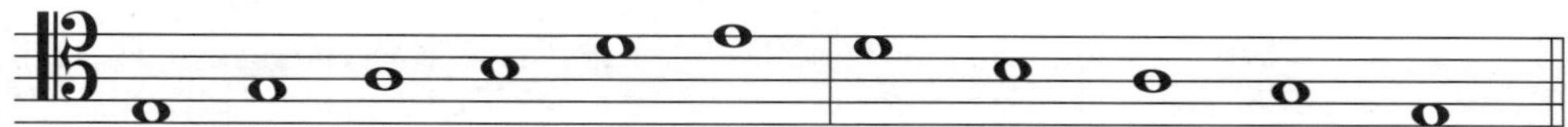

d) D♭ major pentatonic

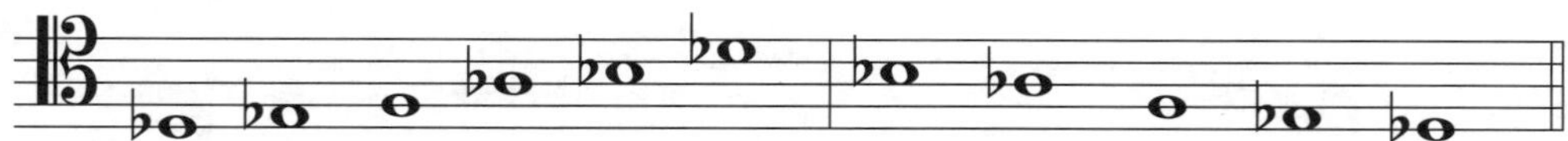

2. Write the following pentatonic scales in the given clefs, ascending and descending, using a key signature for each.

a) G♭ major pentatonic

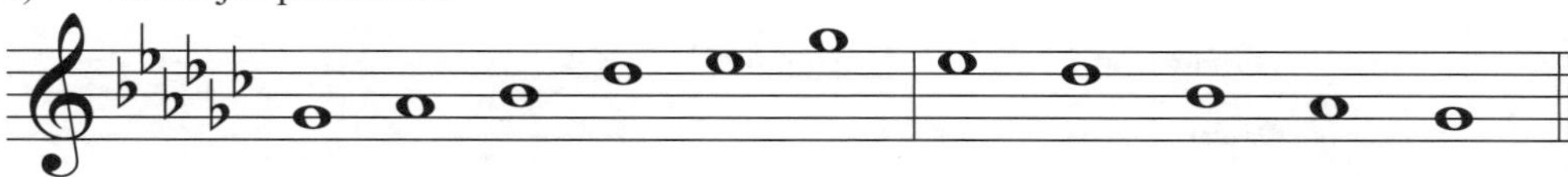

b) E♭ major pentatonic

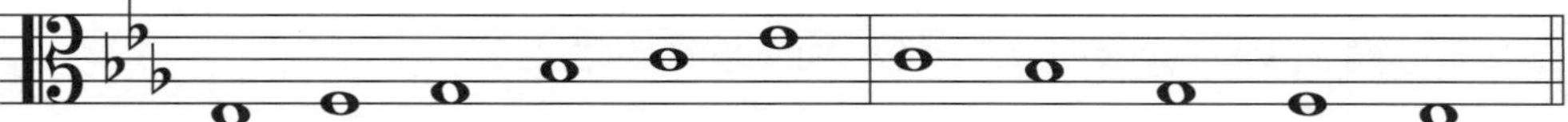

c) F♯ minor pentatonic

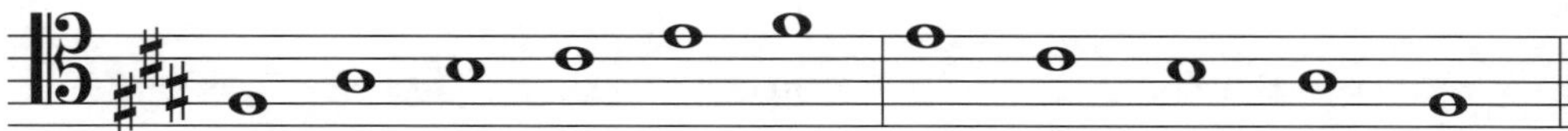

d) G minor pentatonic

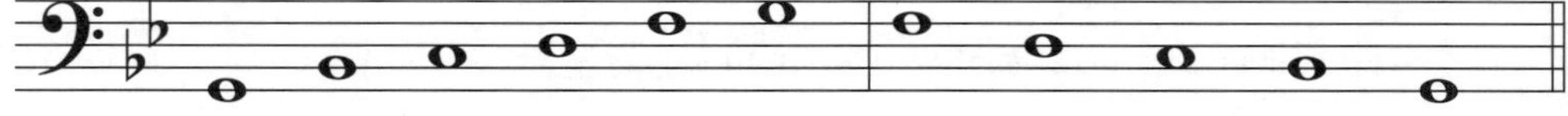

A EXERCISES (p. 96)

1. Write the following major scales in the given clefs, ascending and descending. Use the correct key signature and start on the specified degree for each scale. Identify the equivalent mode in each case.

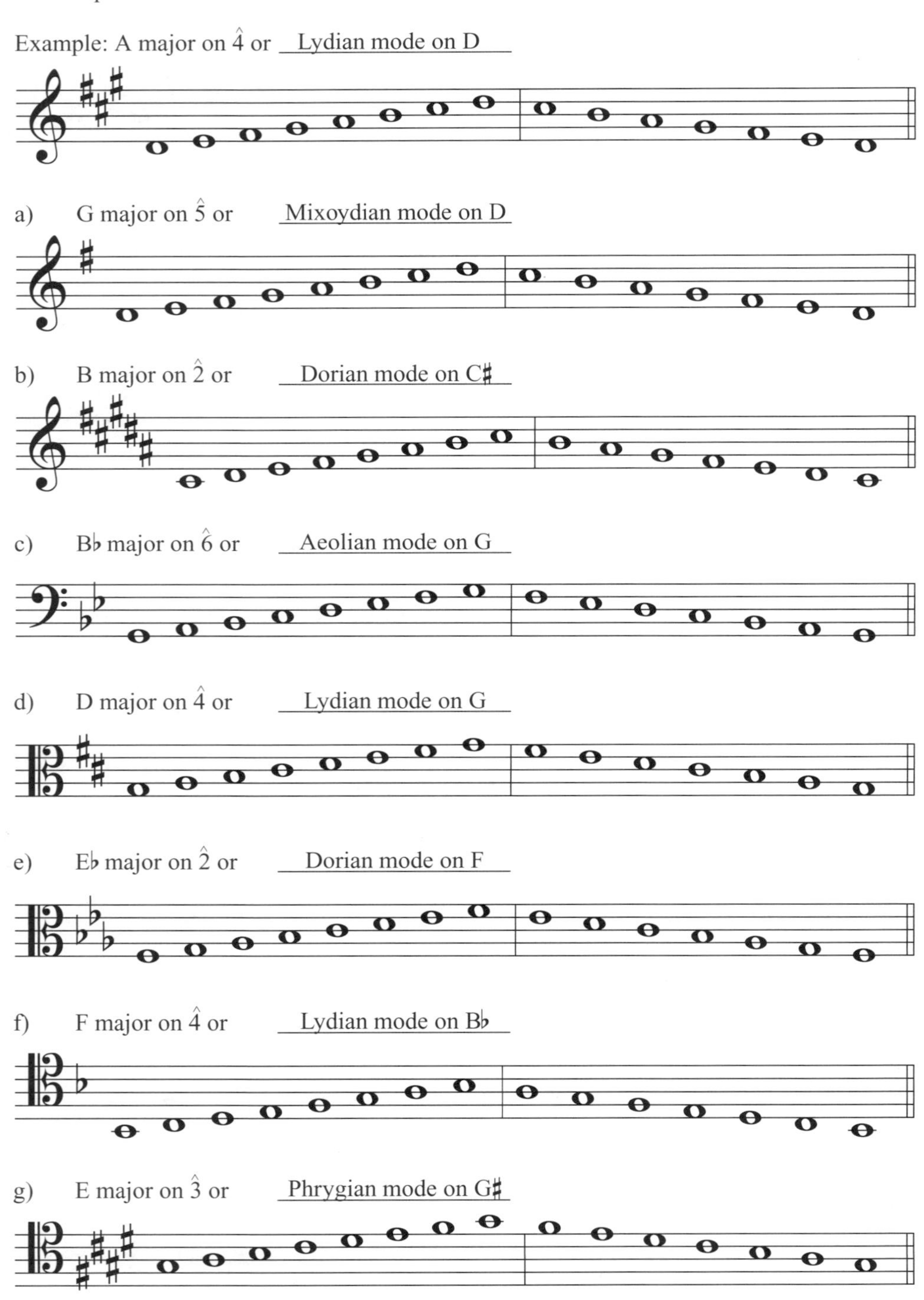

2. Write the following modes in the given clefs, ascending and descending. Use accidentals instead of key signatures. Identify the equivalent major scale and its starting degree in each case.

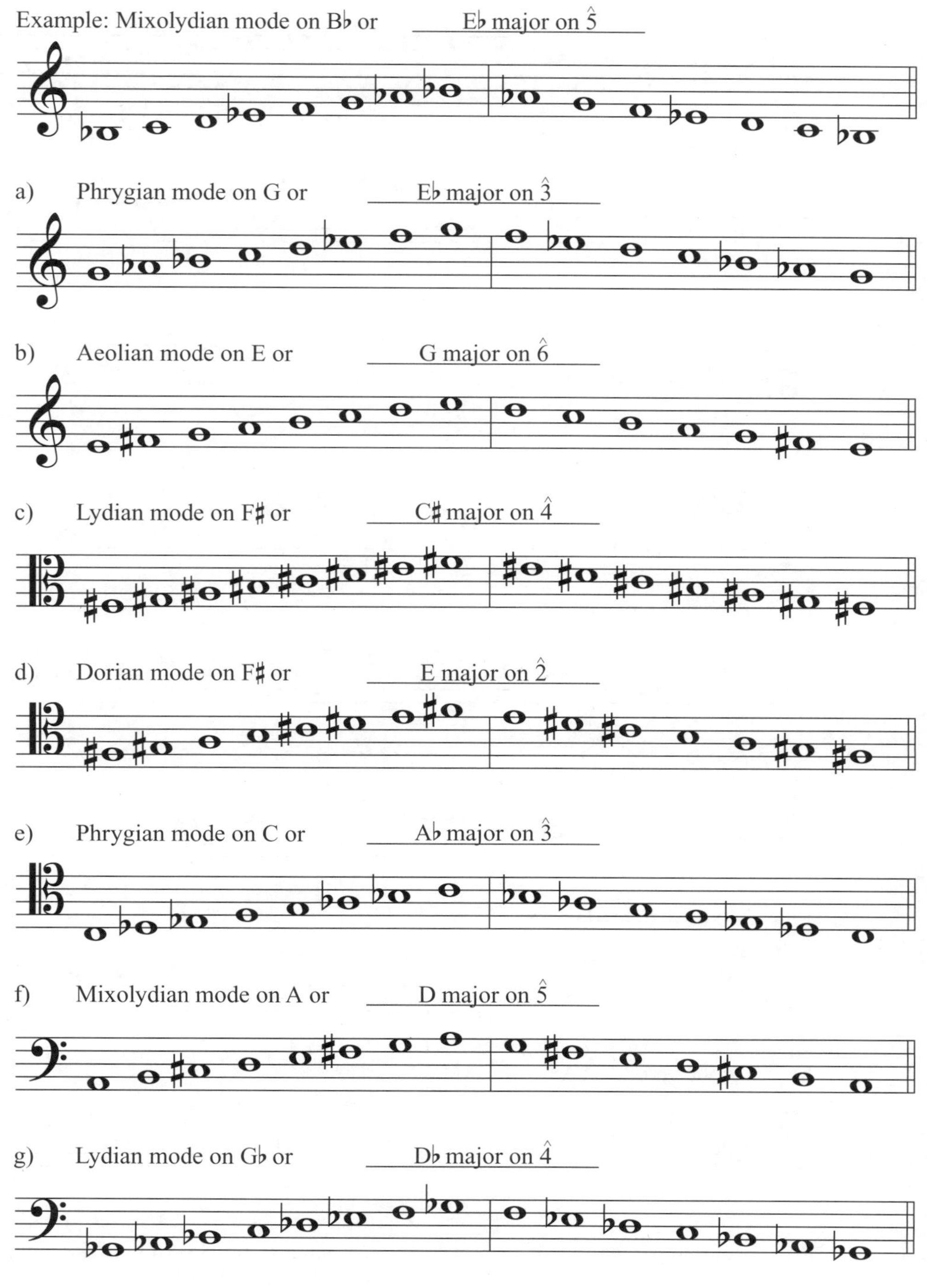

3. Write the following modes in the given clefs, ascending and descending. Use key signatures and add any necessary accidentals.*

a) Lydian mode on B♭

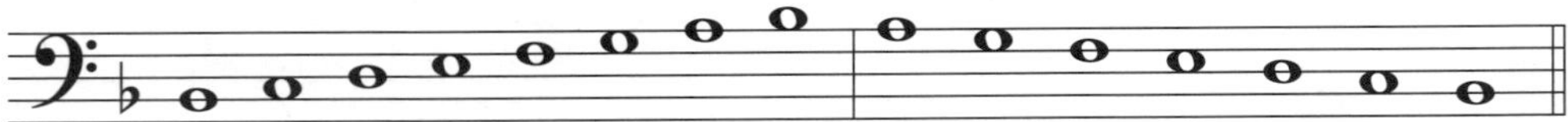

b) Dorian mode on C

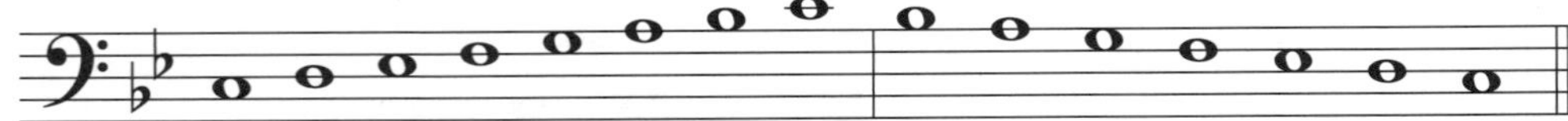

c) Phrygian mode on F♯

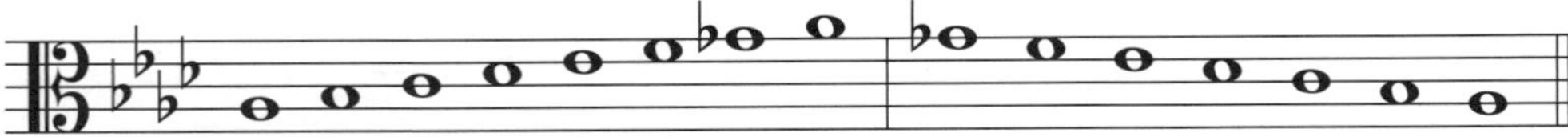

d) Lydian mode on E

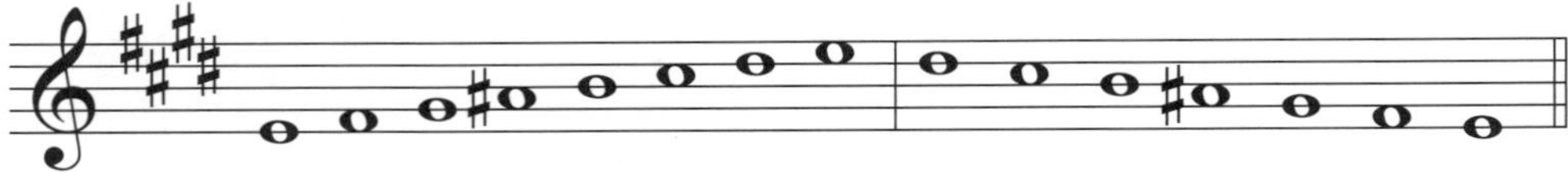

e) Phrygian mode on B♭

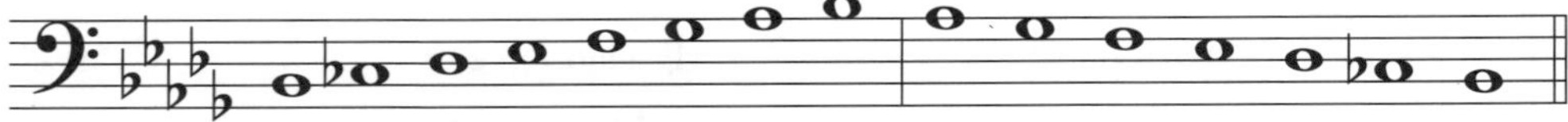

f) Dorian mode on E

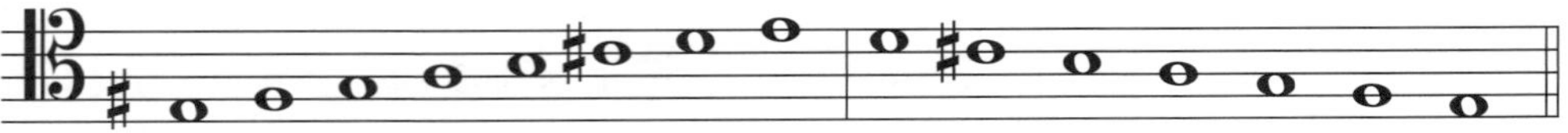

g) Mixolydian mode on A

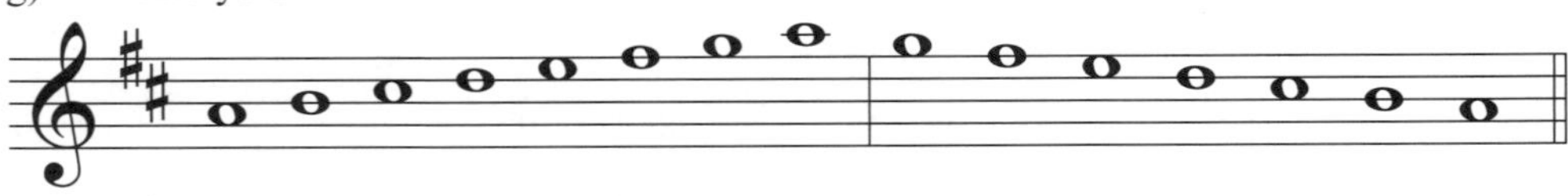

h) Aeolian mode on A♯

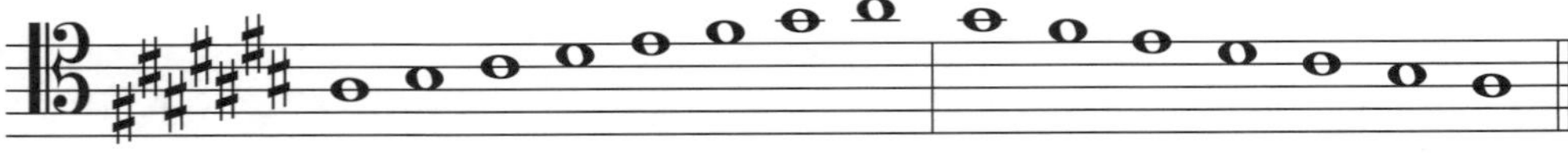

* Refer to paragraph 14, "Major and Minor Modes," pp. 94–96 in *Elementary Rudiments of Music,* which explains alternate ways of writing these modes.

I A REVIEW: IDENTIFYING SCALE TYPES

EXERCISES (p. 99)

1. Name each of the following scales as major, natural minor, harmonic minor, melodic minor, whole-tone, chromatic, blues, octatonic, major pentatonic, or minor pentatonic.

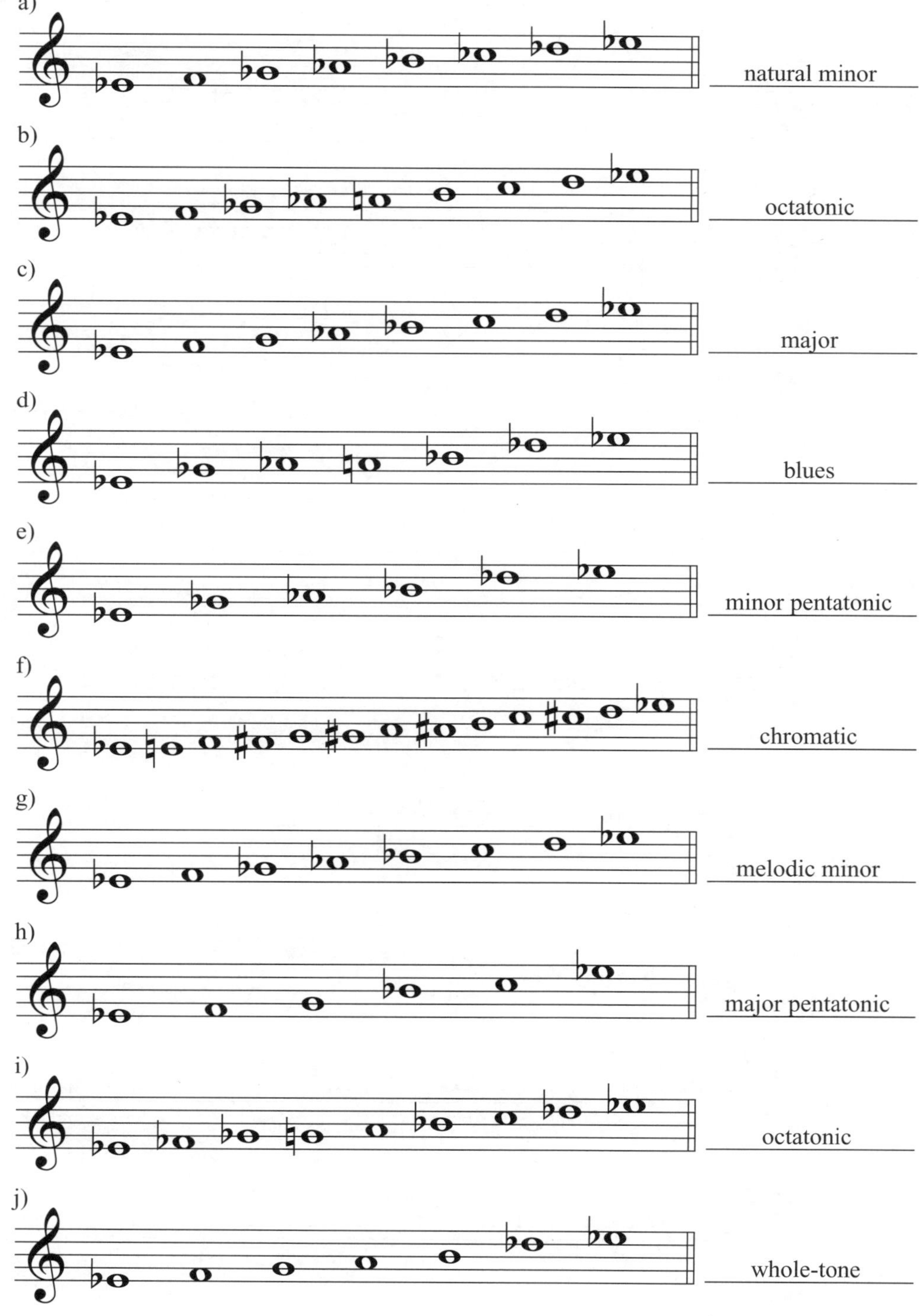

2. Name each of the following scales as major, natural minor, harmonic minor, melodic minor, whole-tone, chromatic, blues, octatonic, major pentatonic, or minor pentatonic.

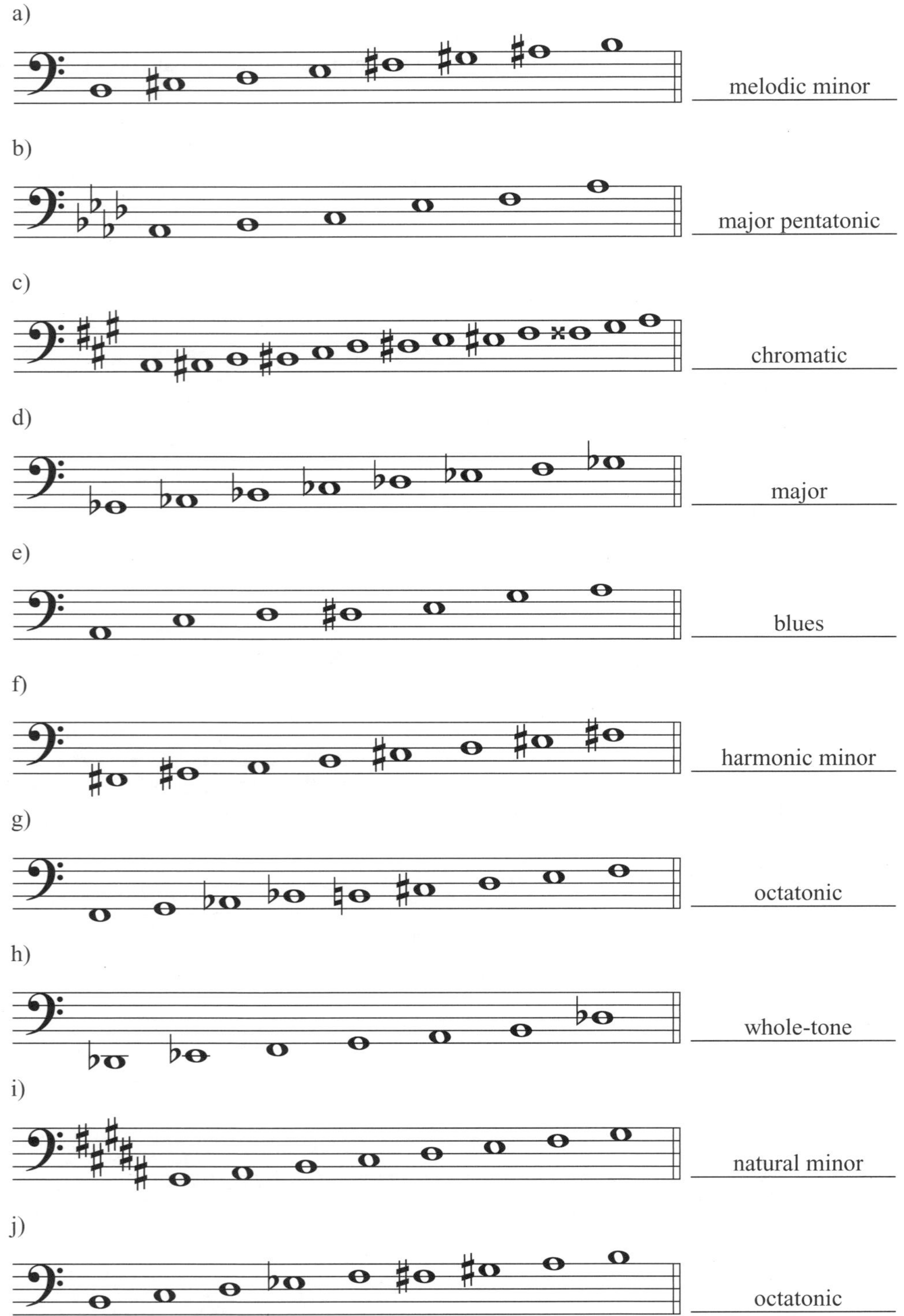

3. Name each of the following scales as major, natural minor, harmonic minor, melodic minor, whole-tone, chromatic, blues, octatonic, major pentatonic, or minor pentatonic.

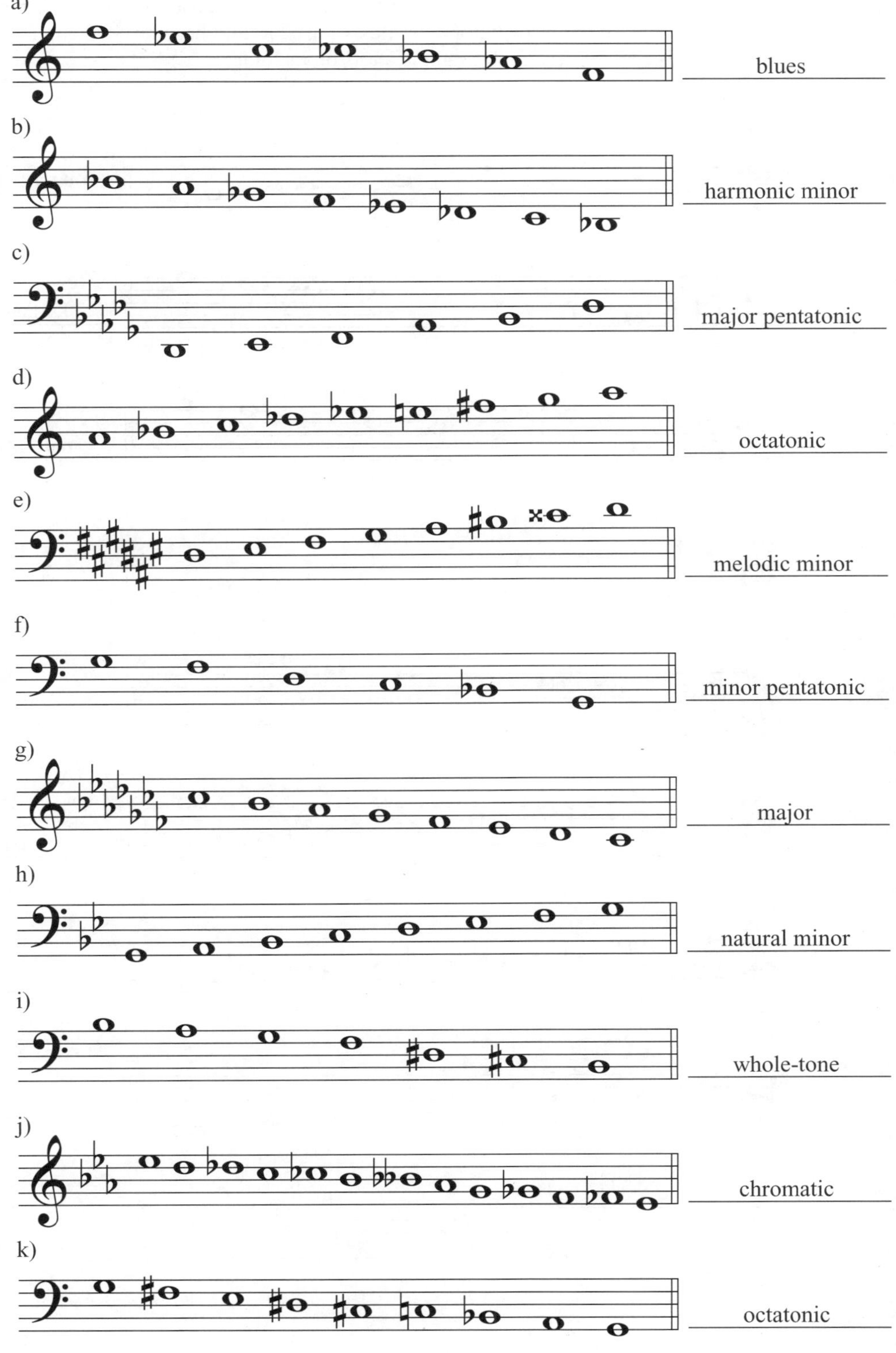

A MORE EXERCISES (p. 102)

1. Identify each of the following as major, minor (specify natural, harmonic, or melodic), whole-tone, chromatic, blues, octatonic, or pentatonic (specify major pentatonic or minor pentatonic) scales, or as Dorian, Phrygian, Lydian, or Mixolydian modes. Each example starts on its tonic.

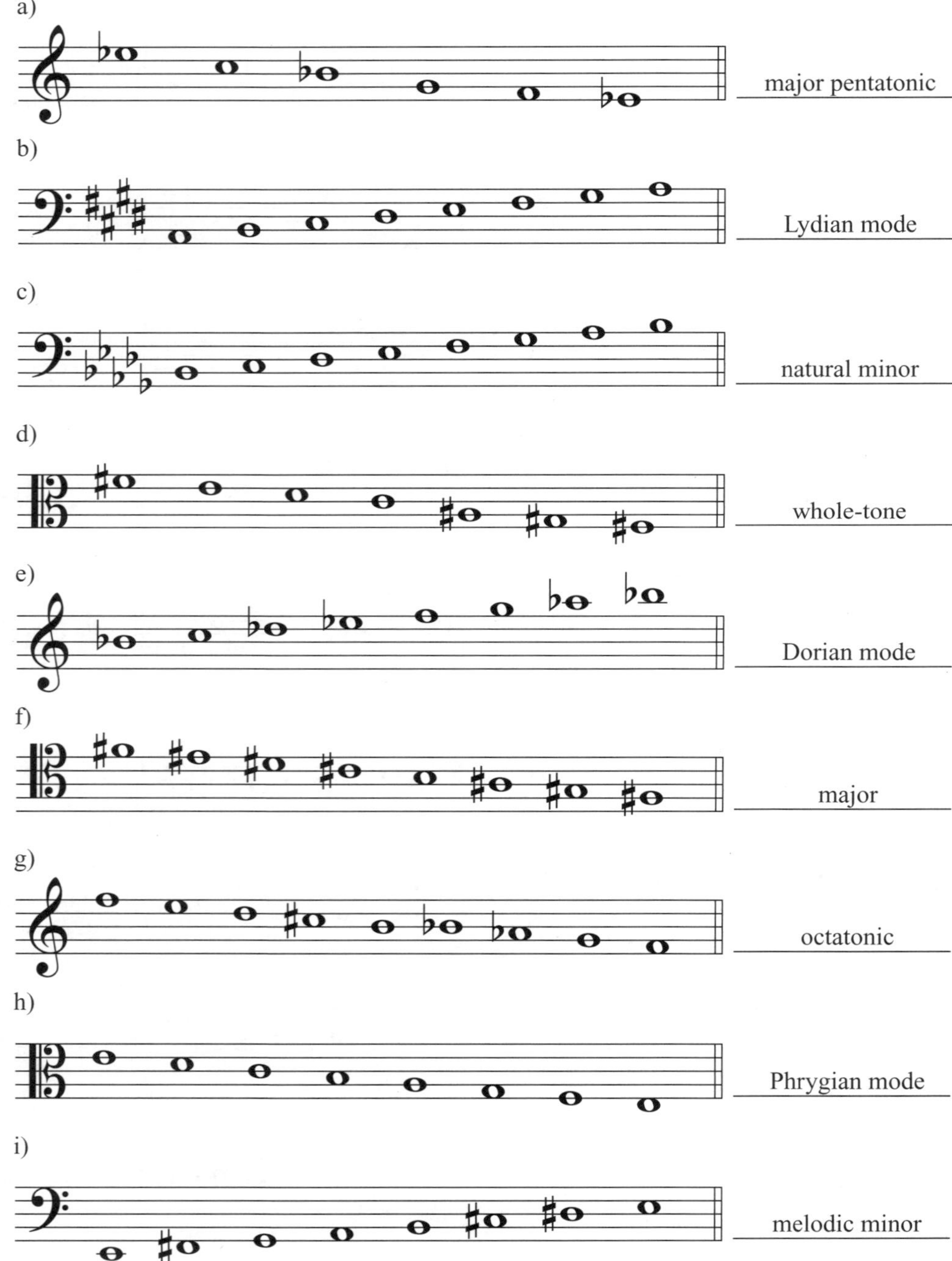

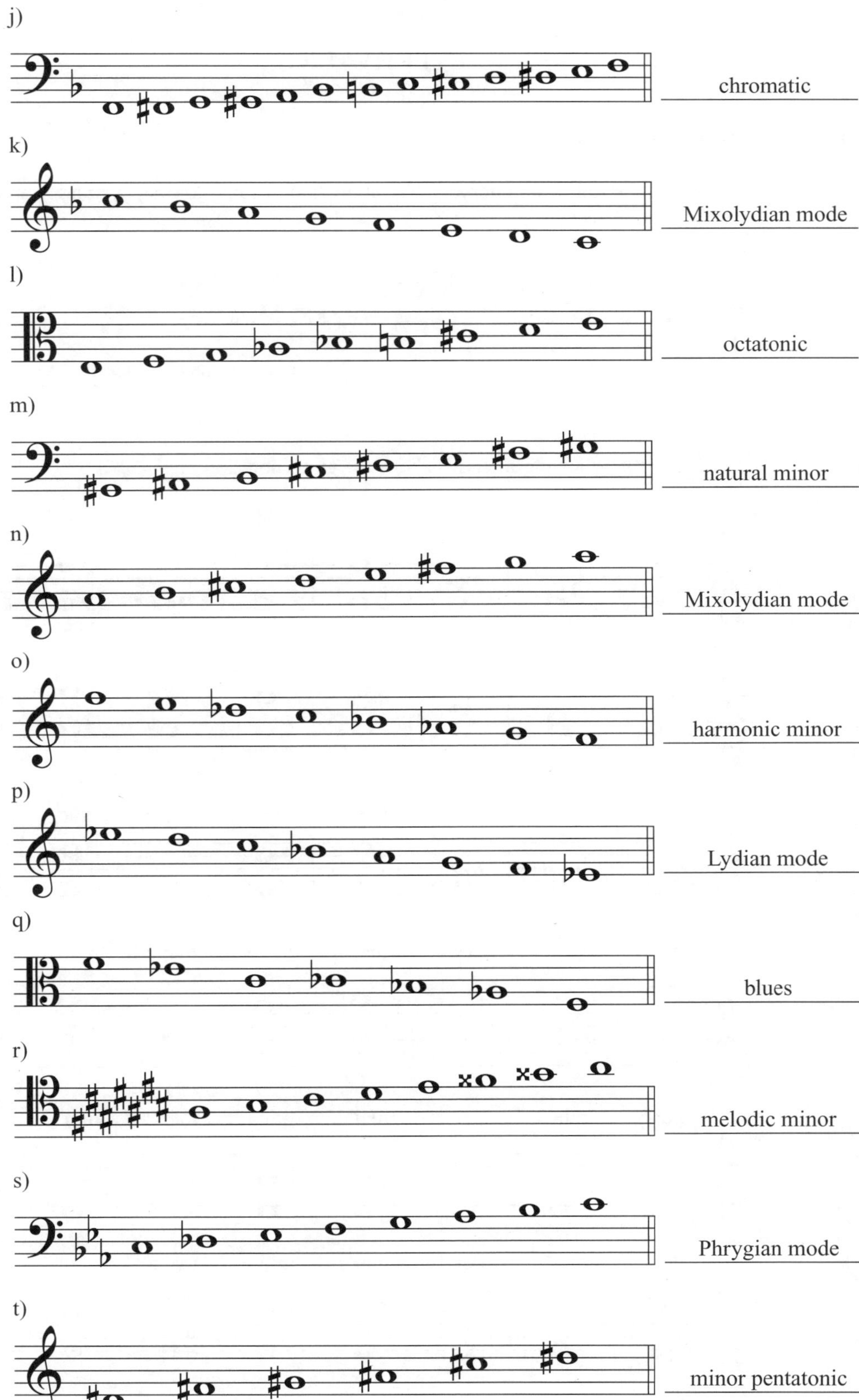
j)
chromatic
k)
Mixolydian mode
l)
octatonic
m)
natural minor
n)
Mixolydian mode
o)
harmonic minor
p)
Lydian mode
q)
blues
r)
melodic minor
s)
Phrygian mode
t)
minor pentatonic

CHAPTER 4

INTERVALS

B I A EXERCISES (p. 107)

1. Name the following intervals. Use abbreviations: maj for major, min for minor, and per for perfect.

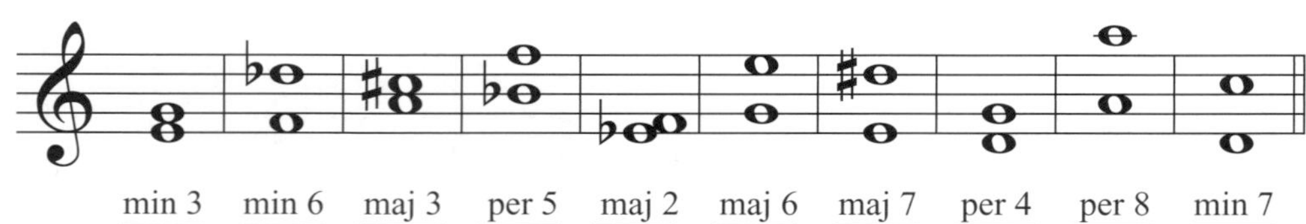

2. Write the following intervals above the given notes.

a) per 8 min 3 per 4 maj 7 min 6 maj 2 min 7 min 2

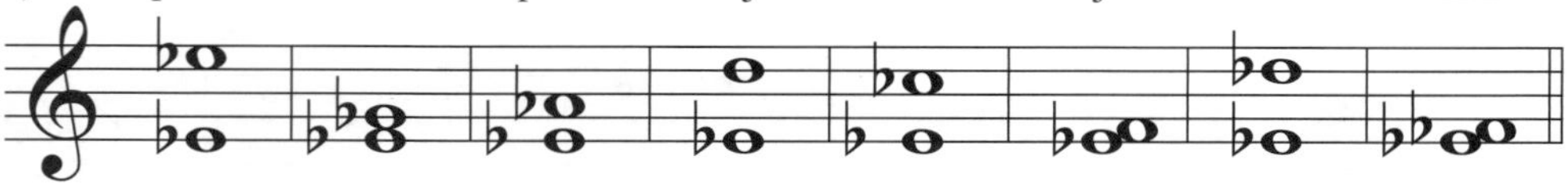

b) per 8 min 3 per 4 maj 7 min 6 maj 2 min 7 min 2

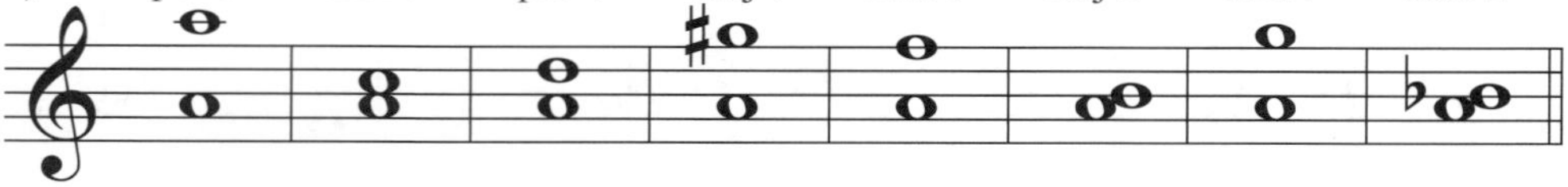

c) per 8 min 3 per 4 maj 7 min 6 maj 2 min 7 min 2

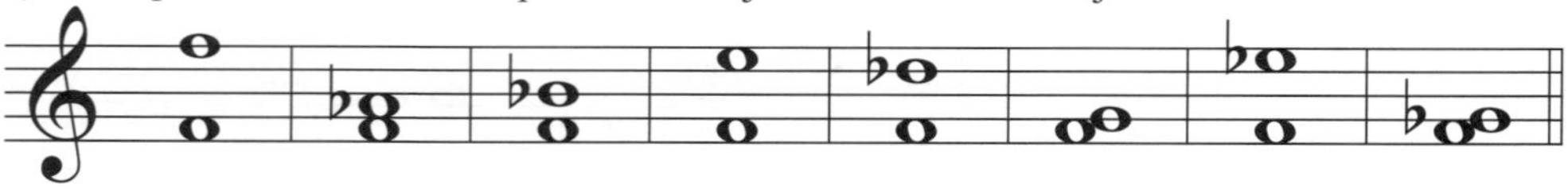

d) per 8 min 3 per 4 maj 7 min 6 maj 2 min 7 min 2

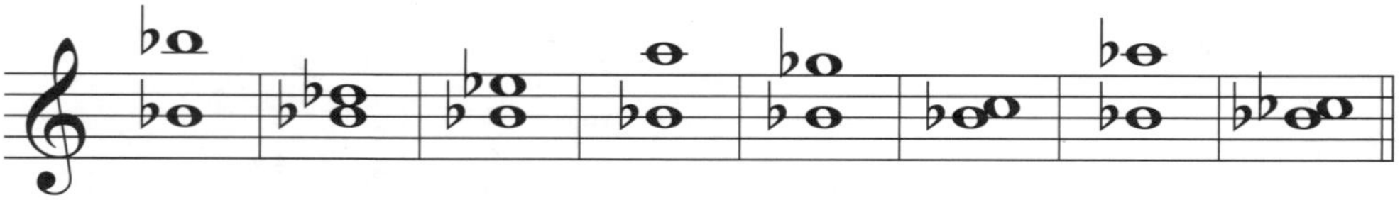

e) per 8 min 3 per 4 maj 7 min 6 maj 2 min 7 min 2

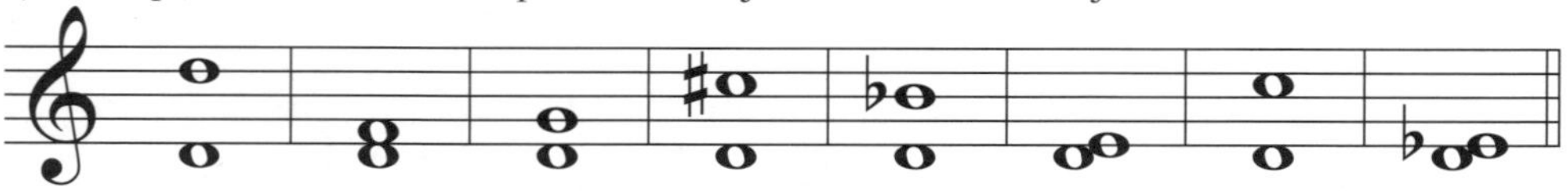

f) per 8 min 3 per 4 maj 7 min 6 maj 2 min 7 min 2

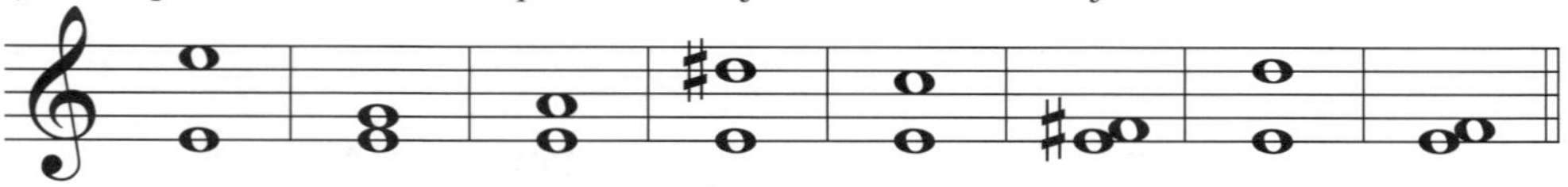

3. Name the following intervals.

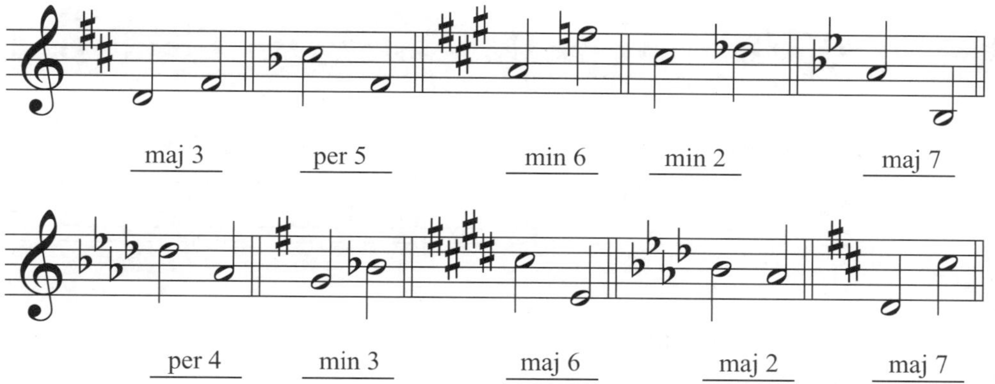

4. Name the following intervals.

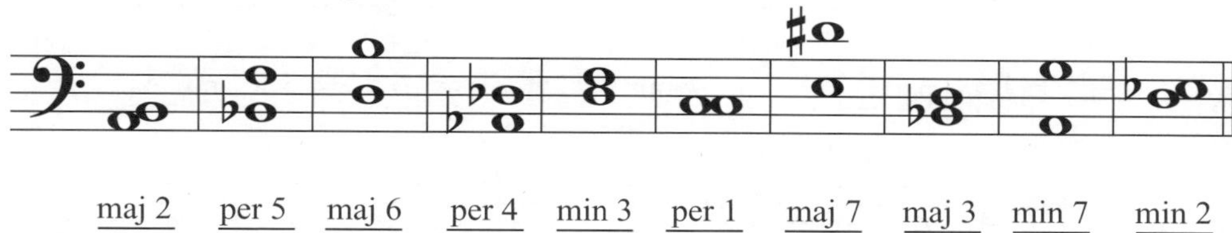

5. Write the following intervals above the given notes.

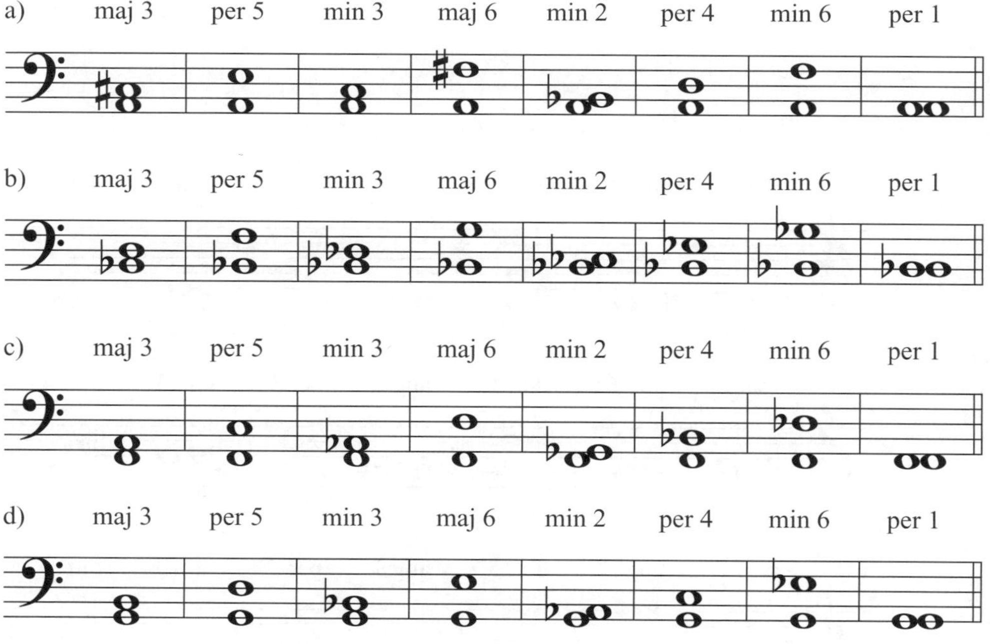

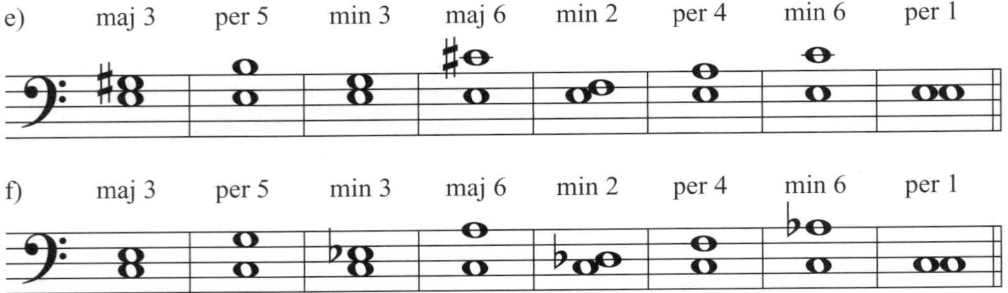

6. Name the following intervals.

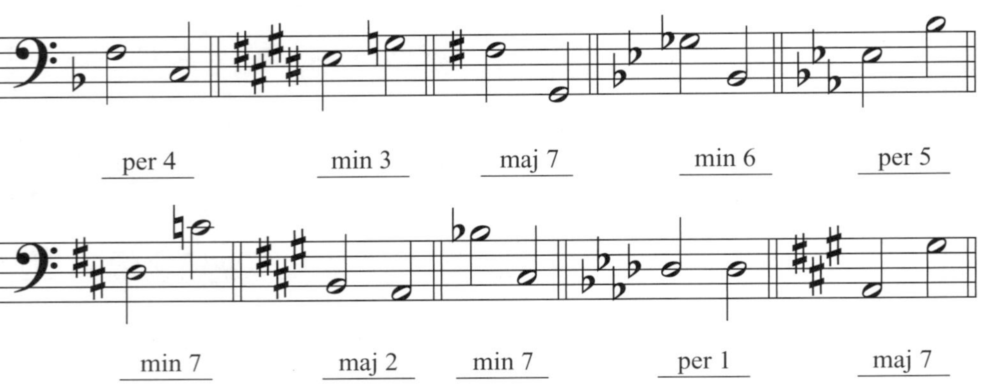

I A EXERCISES (p. 115)

1. Write the following intervals above the given notes.

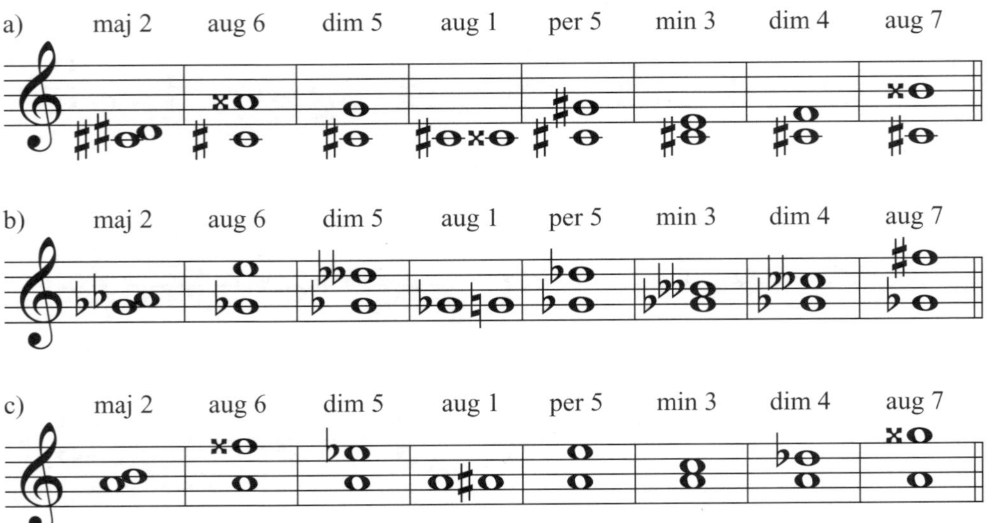

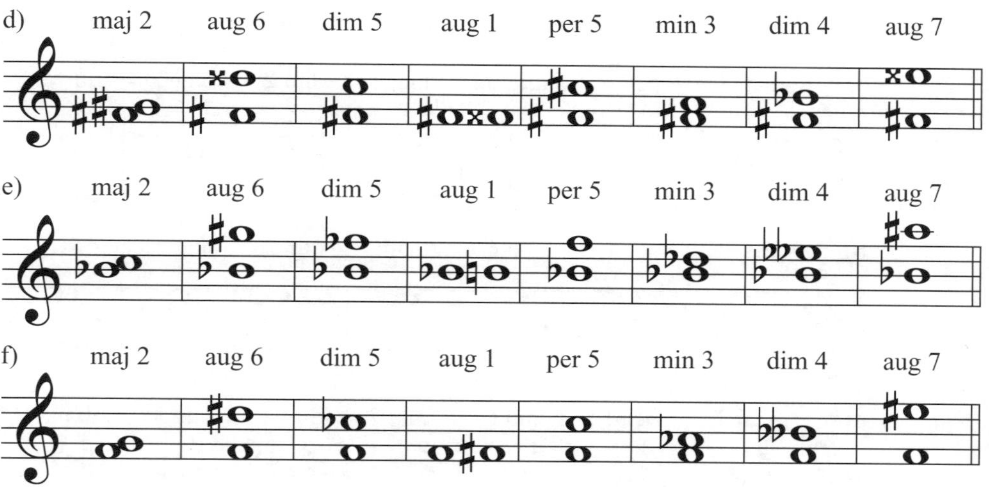

2. Write the following intervals above the given notes.

a) maj 6 aug 2 dim 3 min 7 aug 5 dim 4 min 2 per 8

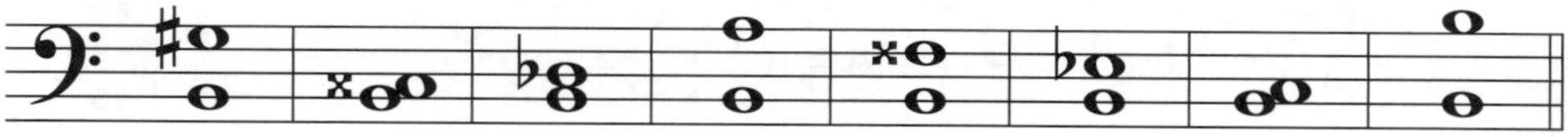

b) maj 6 aug 2 dim 3 min 7 aug 5 dim 4 min 2 per 8

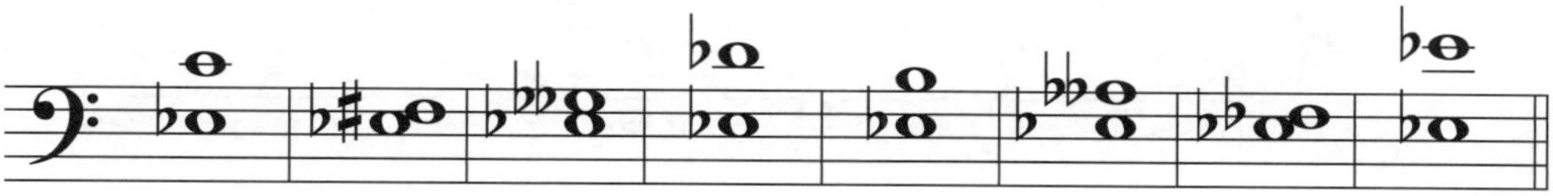

c) maj 6 aug 2 dim 3 min 7 aug 5 dim 4 min 2 per 8

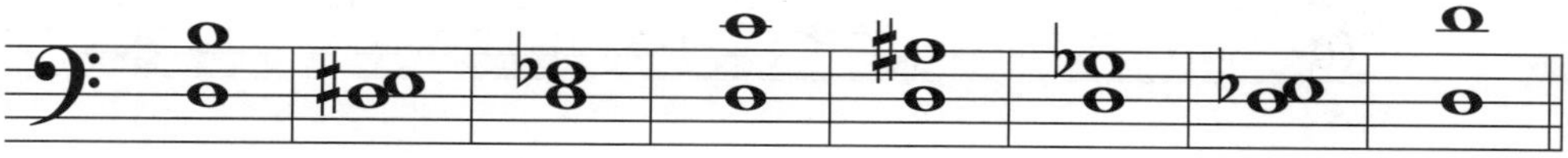

d) maj 6 aug 2 dim 3 min 7 aug 5 dim 4 min 2 per 8

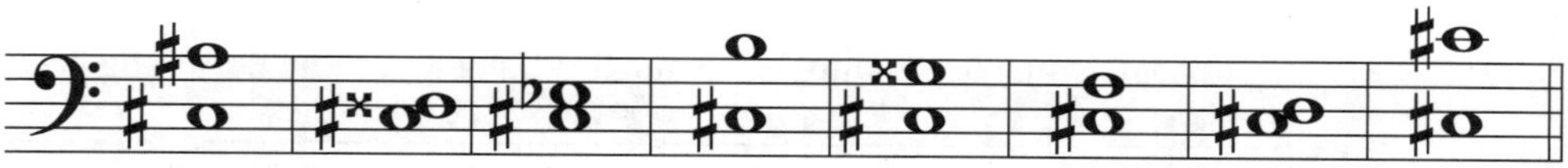

e) maj 6 aug 2 dim 3 min 7 aug 5 dim 4 min 2 per 8

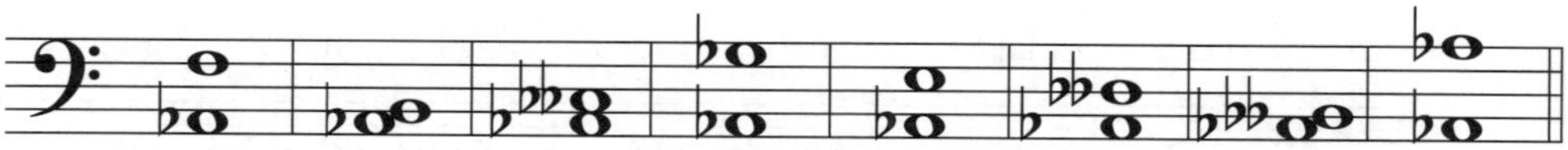

f) maj 6 aug 2 dim 3 min 7 aug 5 dim 4 min 2 per 8

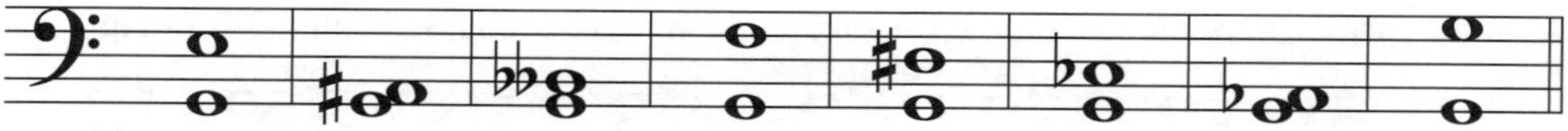

3. Write the following intervals below the given notes.

a) maj 3 per 4 min 6 maj 7 dim 2 aug 3 dim 8 aug 5

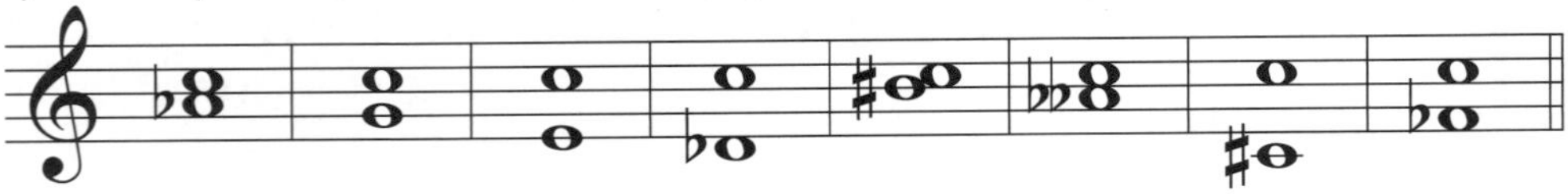

b) maj 3 per 4 min 6 maj 7 dim 2 aug 3 dim 8 aug 5

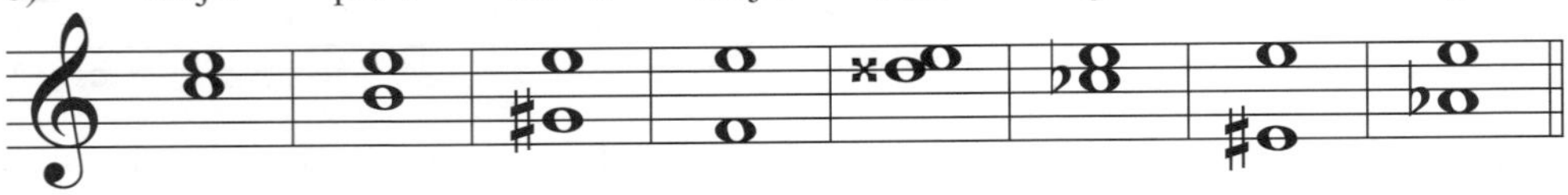

c) maj 3 per 4 min 6 maj 7 dim 2 aug 3 dim 8 aug 5

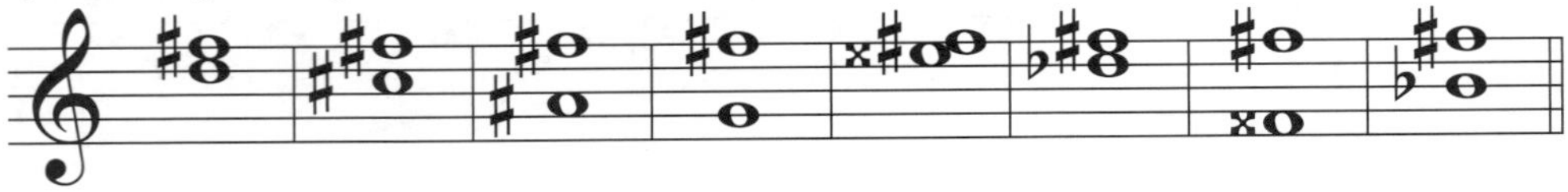

d) maj 3 per 4 min 6 maj 7 dim 2 aug 3 dim 8 aug 5

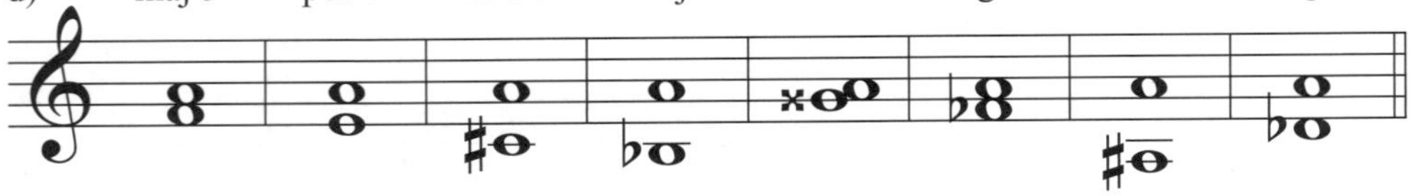

e) maj 3 per 4 min 6 maj 7 dim 2 aug 3 dim 8 aug 5

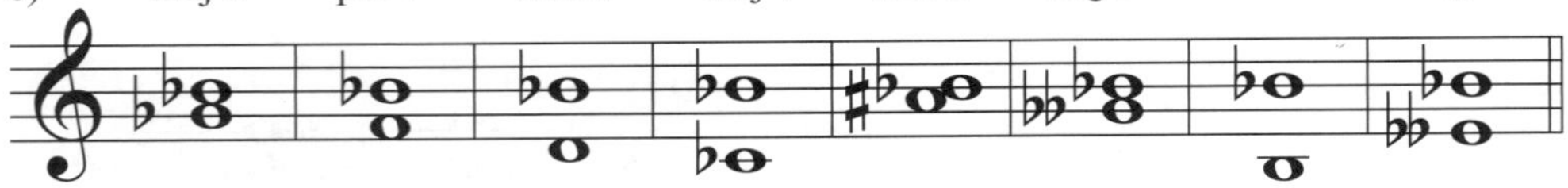

f) maj 3 per 4 min 6 maj 7 dim 2 aug 3 dim 8 aug 5

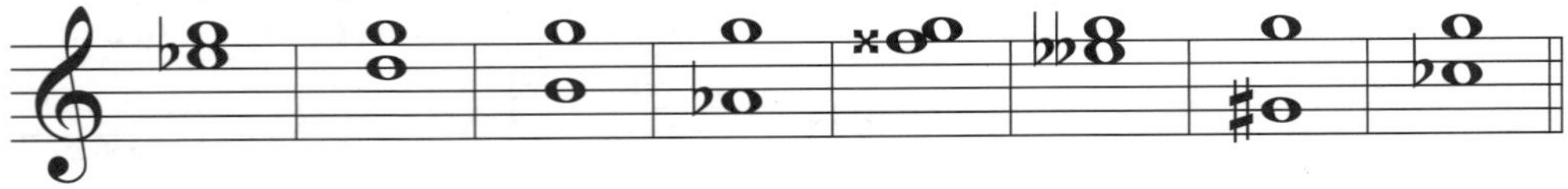

4. Write the following intervals below the given notes.

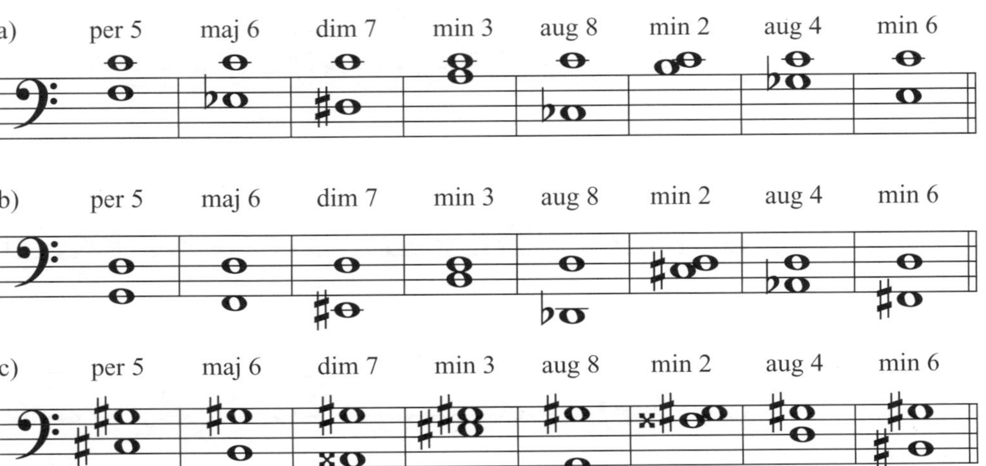

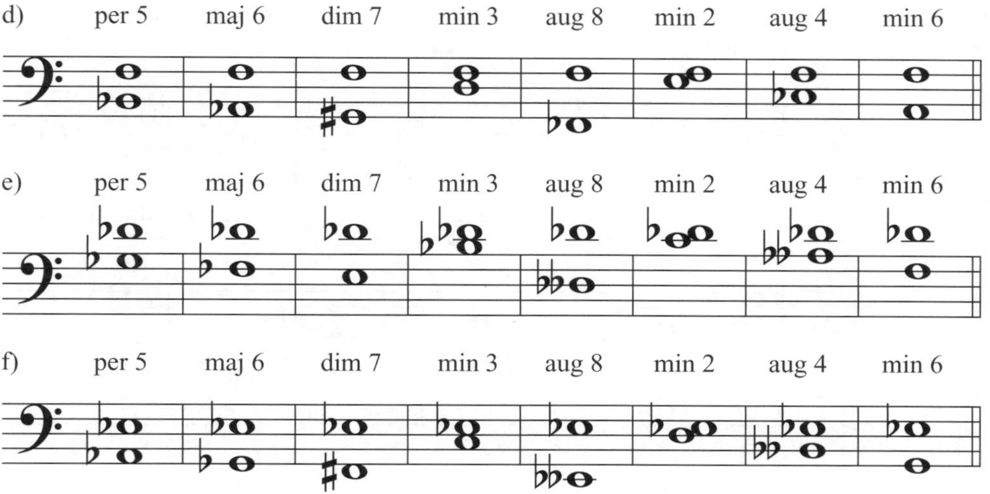

5. Name the following intervals. Invert them on the staff directly underneath and name the inversions.

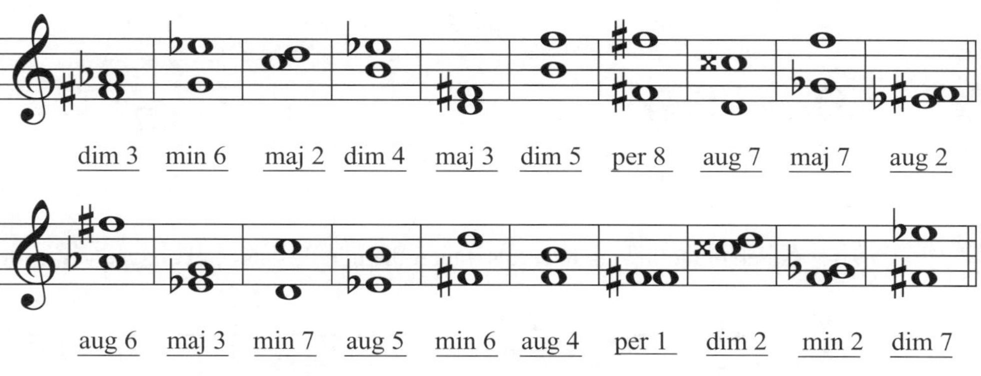

6. Name the following intervals. Invert them and name the inversions.

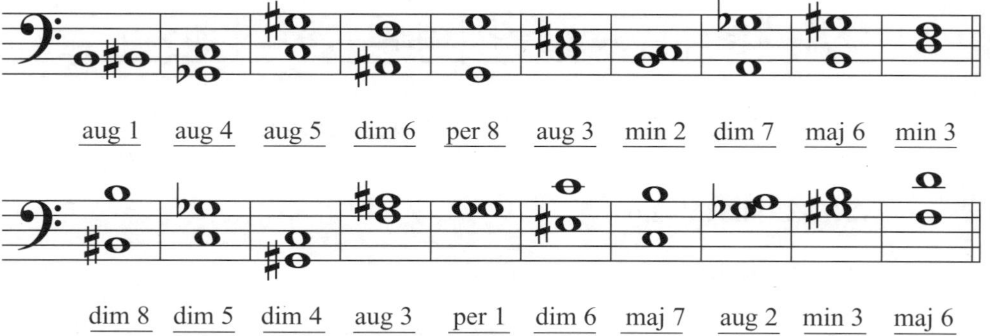

7. Write the following intervals below the given notes. Invert them and name the inversions.

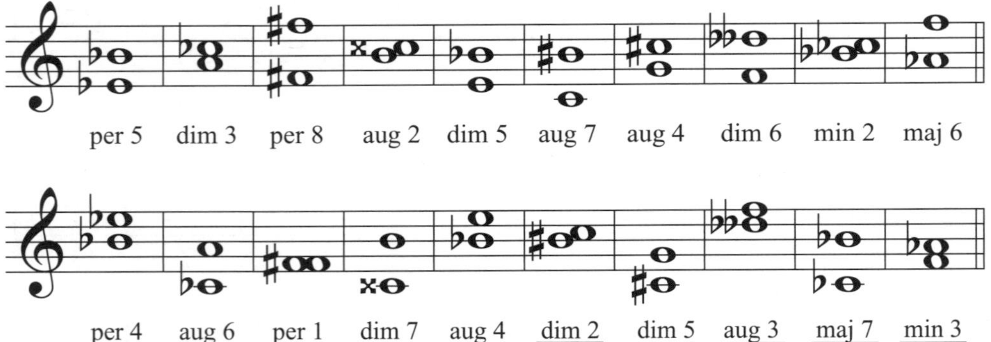

8. Write the following intervals above the given notes. Invert them and name the inversions.

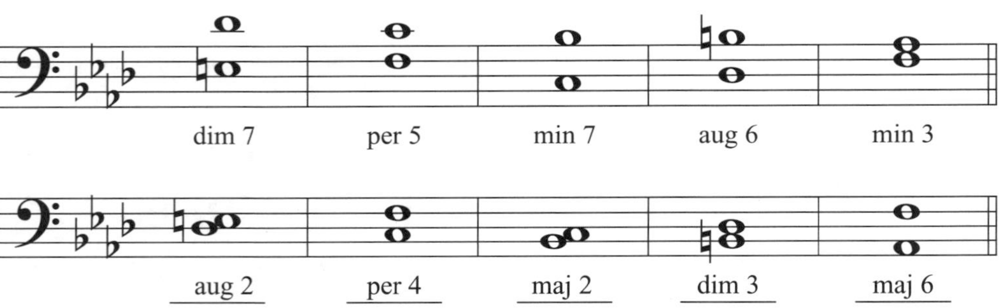

9. Name the following intervals. Invert them in the bass clef and name the inversions.

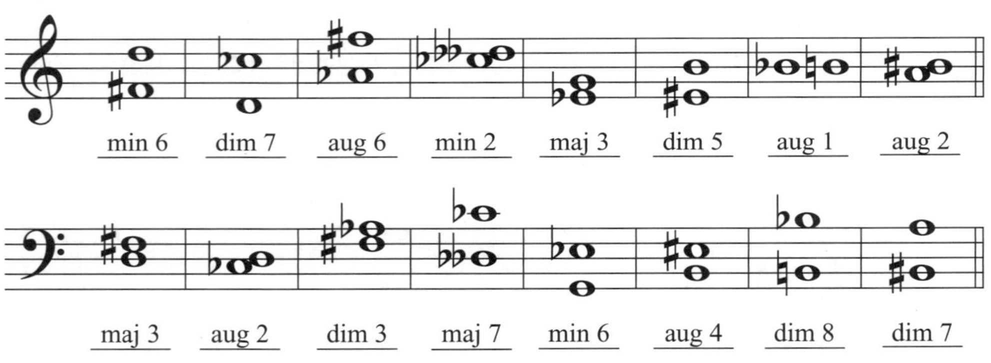

A EXERCISES (p. 120)

1. Name the following intervals.

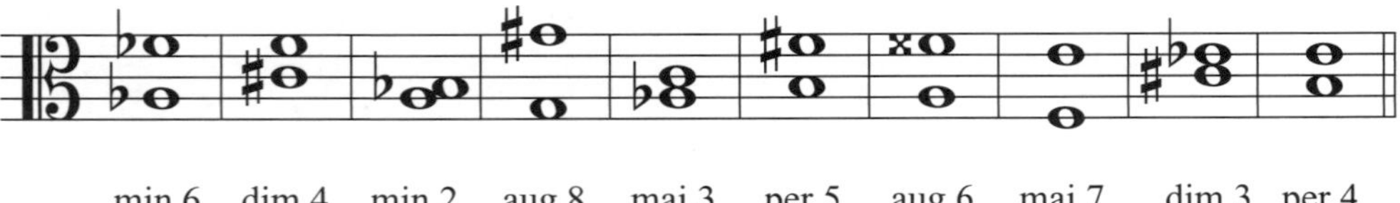

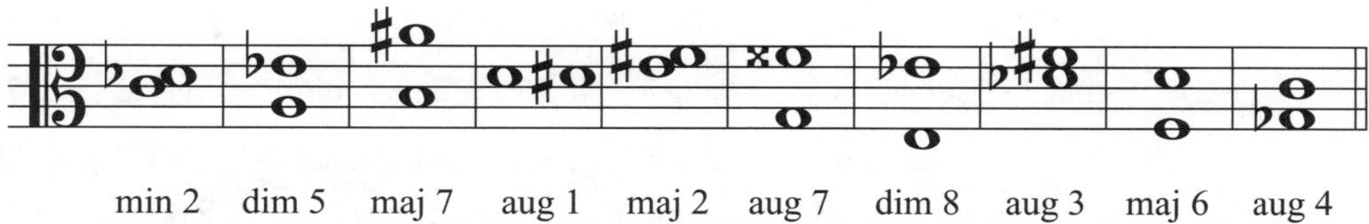

min 2 dim 5 maj 7 aug 1 maj 2 aug 7 dim 8 aug 3 maj 6 aug 4

2. Name the following intervals.

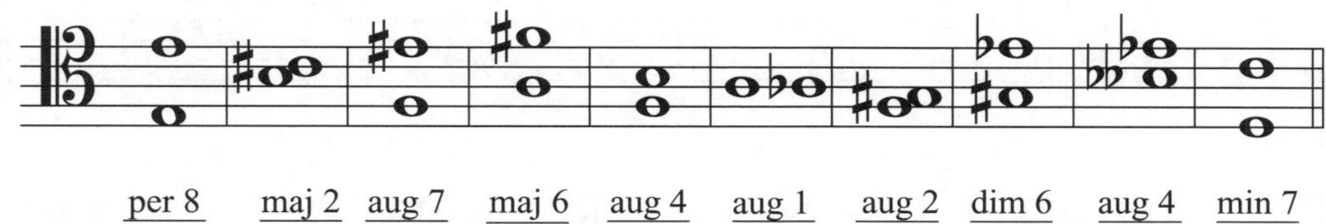

per 8 maj 2 aug 7 maj 6 aug 4 aug 1 aug 2 dim 6 aug 4 min 7

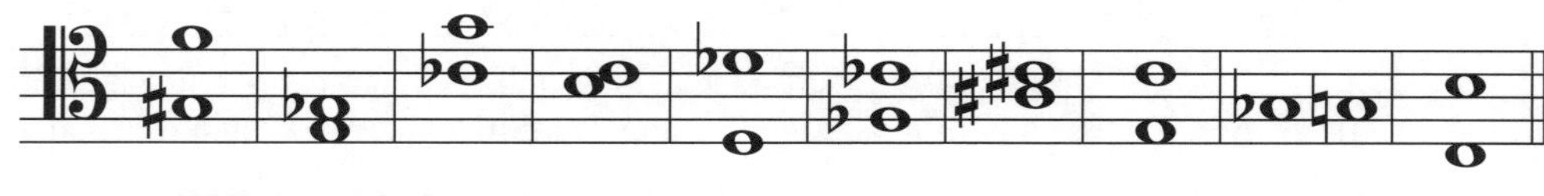

dim 7 dim 3 aug 5 min 2 dim 8 per 5 min 3 min 6 aug 1 maj 7

3. Write the following intervals above the given notes.

a) min 2 dim 7 aug 3 maj 6 dim 4 per 5 aug 2 min 7 per 1 maj 3

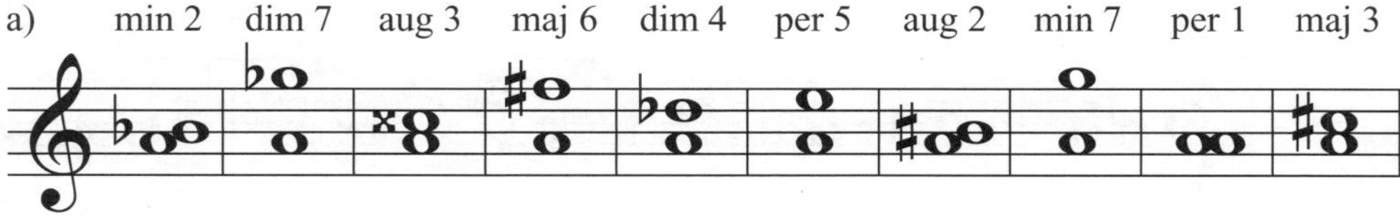

b) min 2 dim 7 aug 3 maj 6 dim 4 per 5 aug 2 min 7 per 1 maj 3

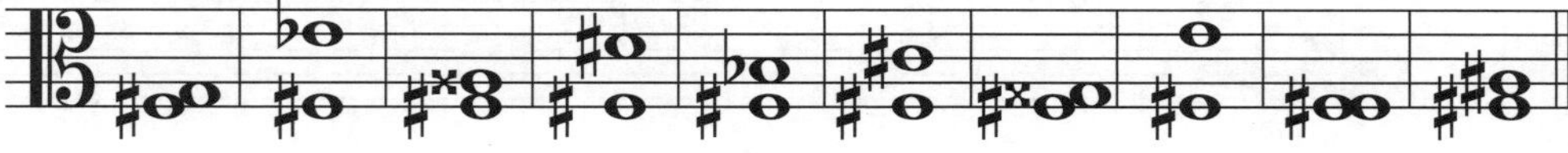

c) min 2 dim 7 aug 3 maj 6 dim 4 per 5 aug 2 min 7 per 1 maj 3

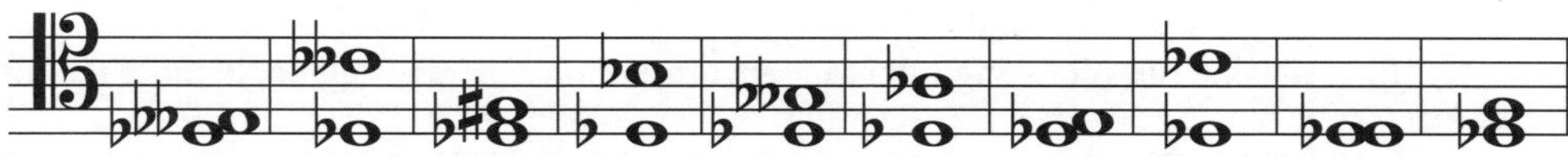

d) min 2 dim 7 aug 3 maj 6 dim 4 per 5 aug 2 min 7 per 1 maj 3

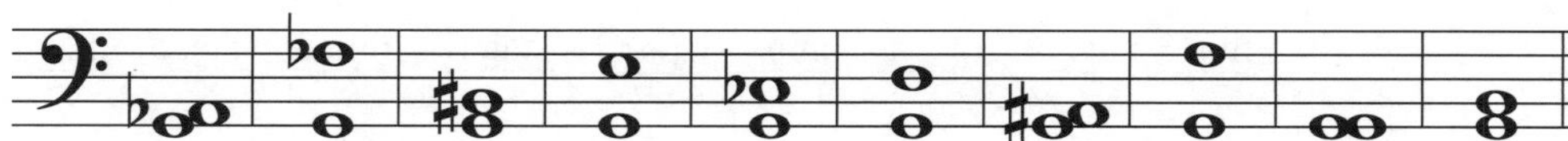

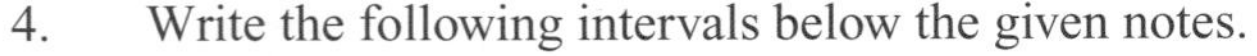

4. Write the following intervals below the given notes.

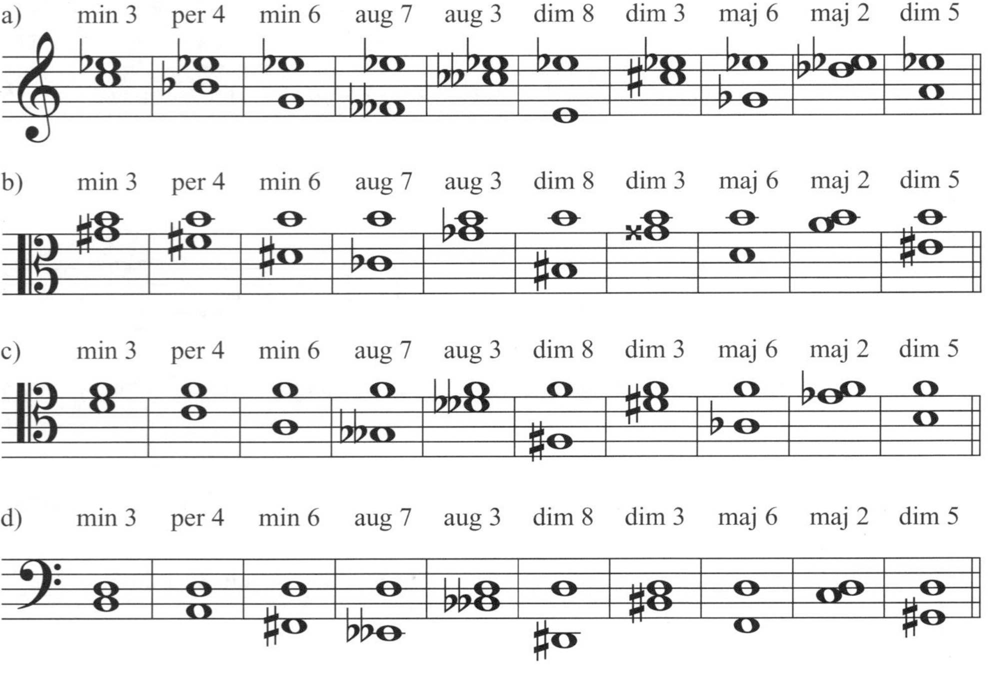

5. Name the following intervals. Invert them in the alto clef and name the inversions.

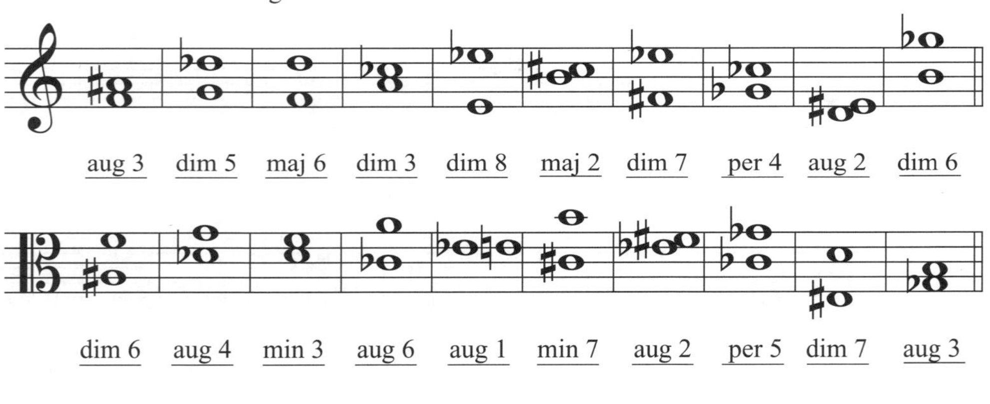

6. Name the following intervals. Invert them in the tenor clef and name the inversions.

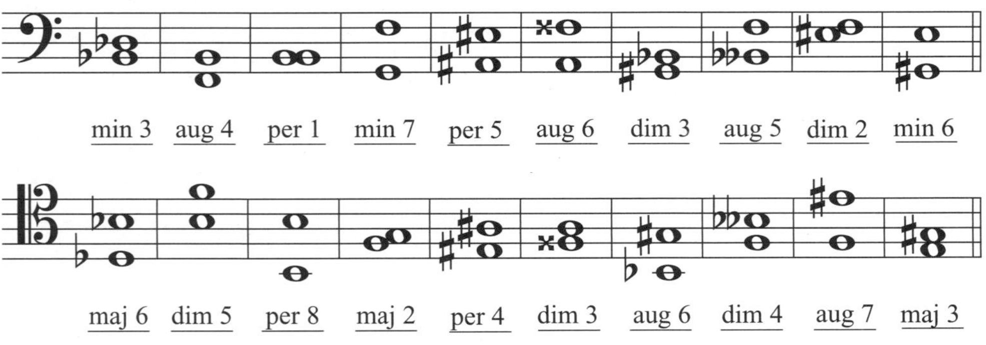

7. Name the following intervals. Change the upper note of each enharmonically and rename the intervals.

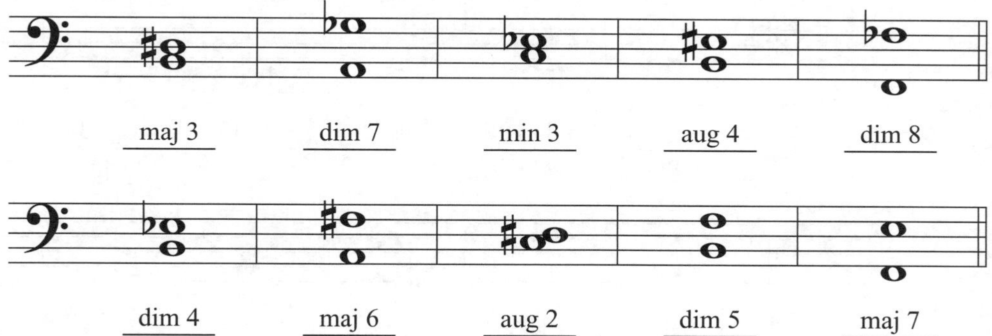

8. Name the following intervals. Change the lower note of each enharmonically and rename the intervals.

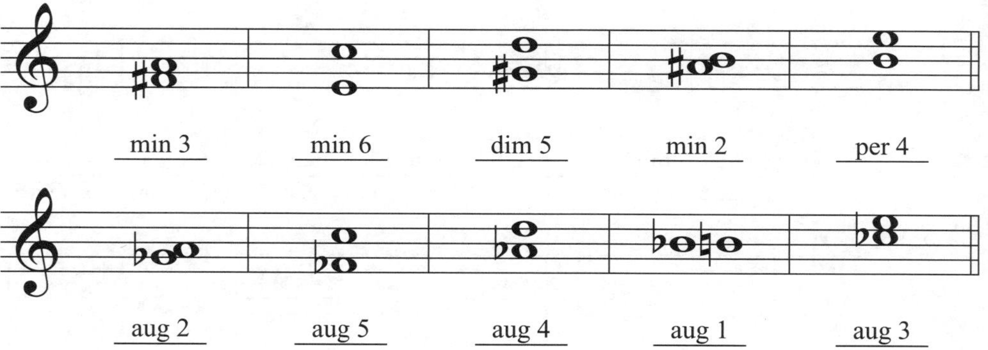

9. Name the following compound intervals. Invert them and name the inversions.

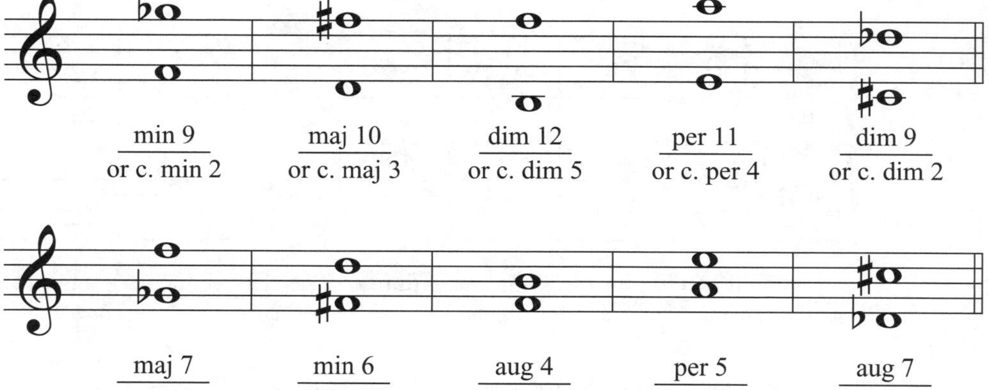

10. Name the following compound intervals. Invert them and name the inversions.

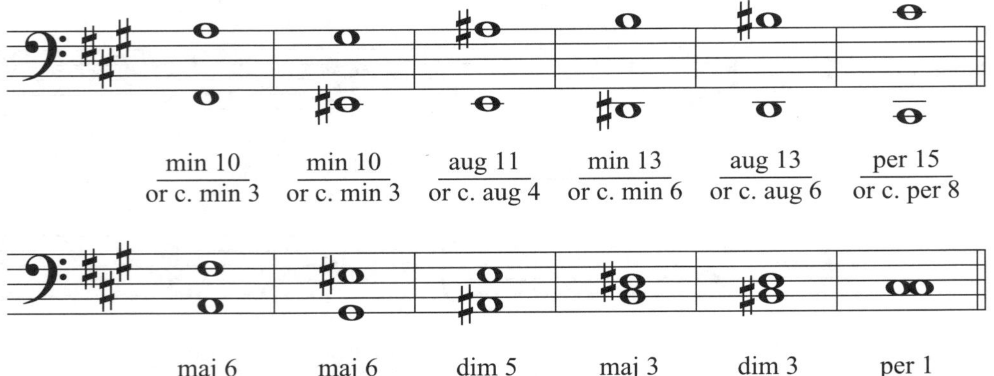

11. Name the following compound intervals. Invert them in the treble clef and name the inversions.

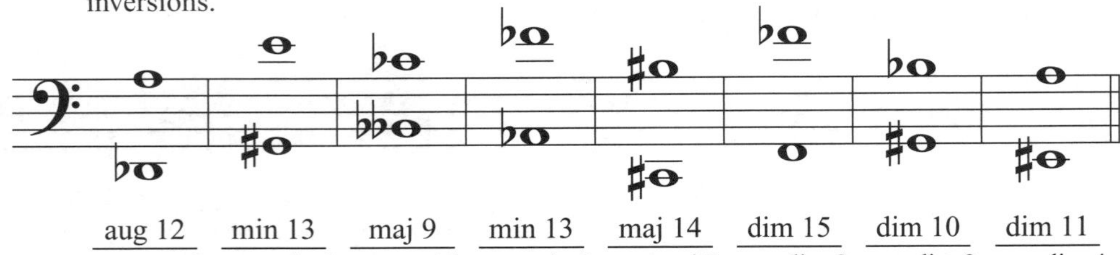

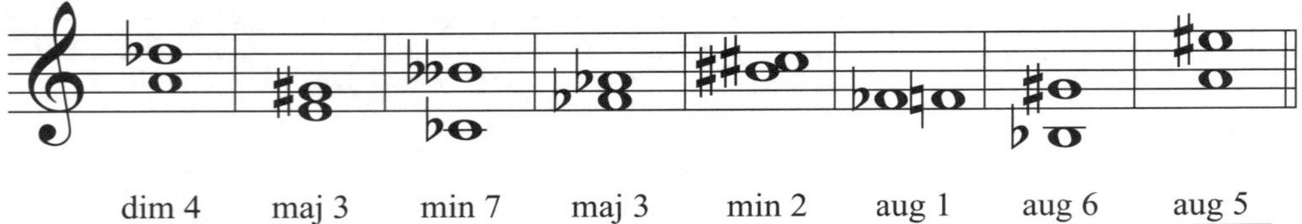

12. Name the following intervals.

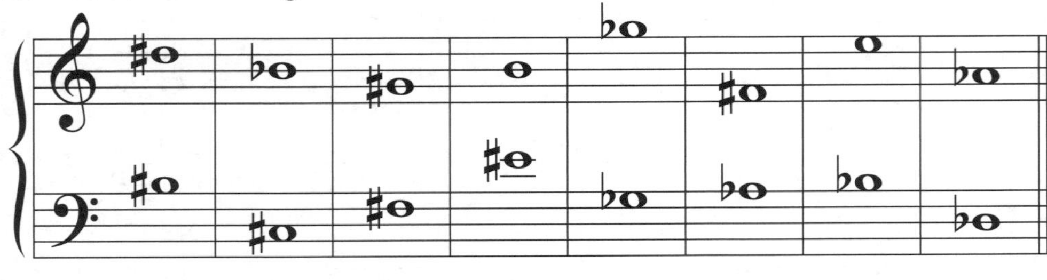

13. Name the intervals between successive notes of the following.

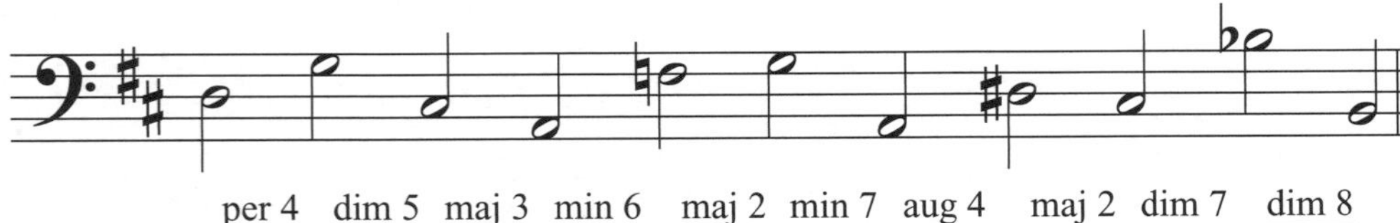

CHAPTER 5

CHORDS

B I A EXERCISES (p. 126)

1. Write the following triads in the treble clef, using the correct key signature for each.
   a) the dominant triad of A major
   b) the tonic triad of F major
   c) the subdominant triad of E♭ major
   d) the tonic triad of G major
   e) the dominant triad of E major
   f) the subdominant triad of D major

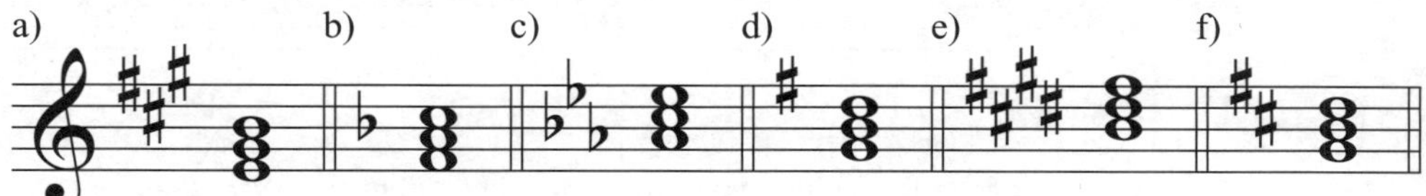

2. Write the following triads in the bass clef, using the correct key signature for each.
   a) the dominant triad of C minor
   b) the tonic triad of D minor
   c) the dominant triad of F♯ minor
   d) the subdominant triad of E minor
   e) the dominant triad of F minor
   f) the subdominant triad of C♯ minor

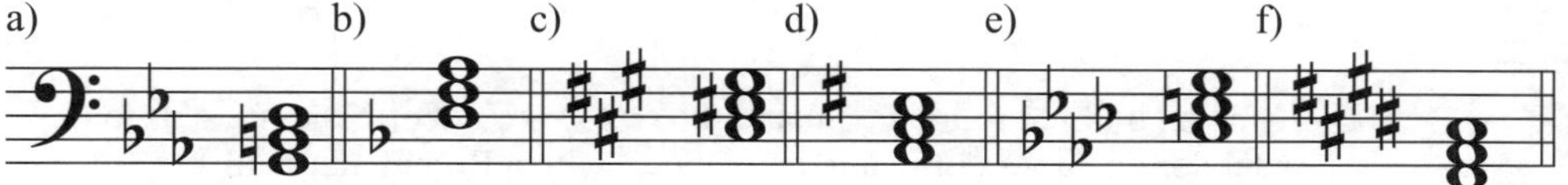

3. Write the following triads in the treble clef, using accidentals instead of a key signature.
   a) the tonic triad of B minor
   b) the dominant triad of C♯ minor
   c) the subdominant triad of F♯ minor
   d) the dominant triad of G minor
   e) the subdominant triad of A minor
   f) the dominant triad of D minor
   g) the tonic triad of C minor
   h) the dominant triad of E minor

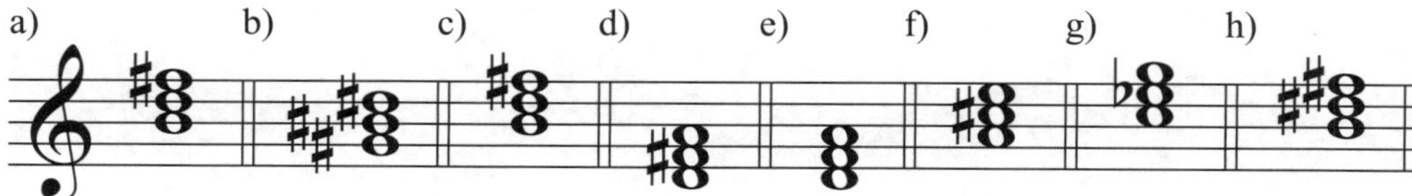

4. Write the following triads in the bass clef, using accidentals instead of a key signature.

   a) the tonic triad of A♭ major
   b) the dominant triad of C major
   c) the subdominant triad of B♭ major
   d) the dominant triad of D major
   e) the tonic triad of E♭ major
   f) the subdominant triad of A major
   g) the dominant triad of G major
   h) the subdominant triad of E major

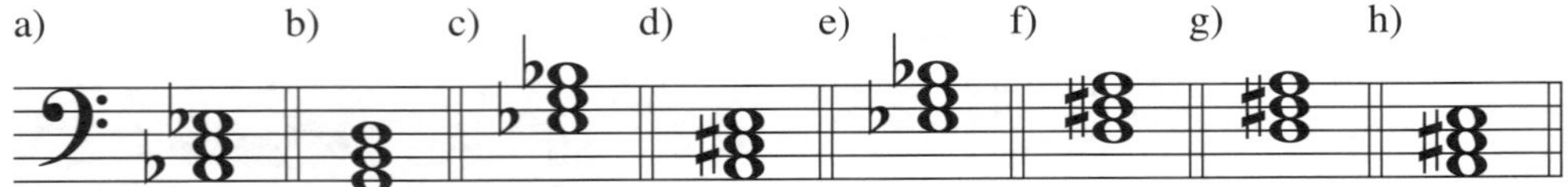

5. For each of the following, name the *major* key, identify the triad as tonic, subdominant, or dominant, and label it with a Roman numeral.

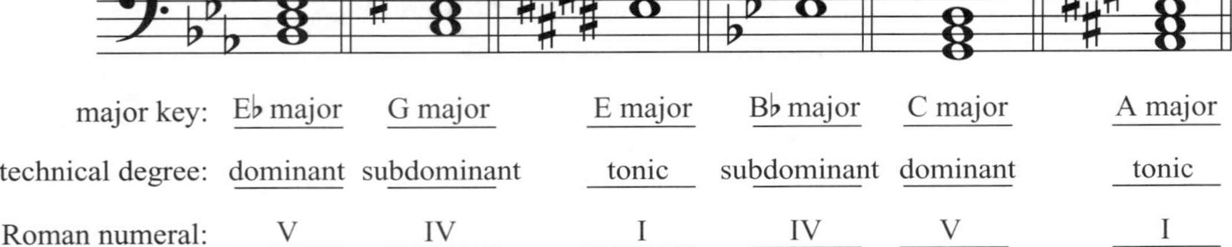

6. For each of the following, name the *minor* key, identify the triad as tonic, subdominant, or dominant, and label it with a Roman numeral.

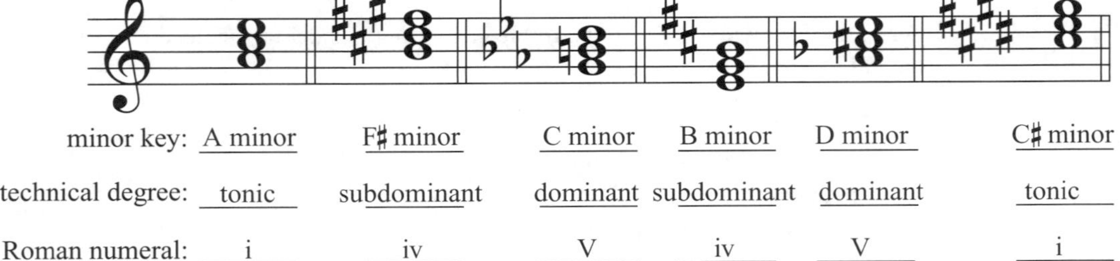

7. Fill in the blanks.

a) 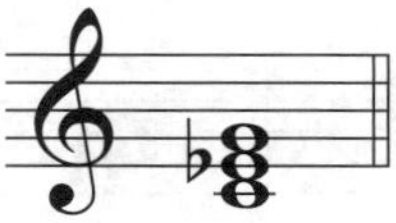 [staff] is the tonic triad of the key of C minor.

b) 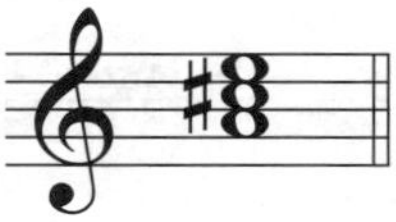 [staff] is the dominant triad of the keys of D major and D minor.

c) 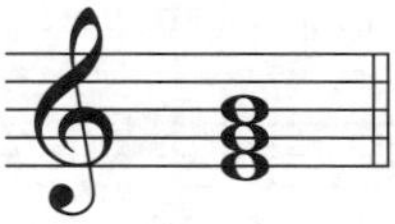 [staff] is the subdominant triad of the key of B minor.

d) 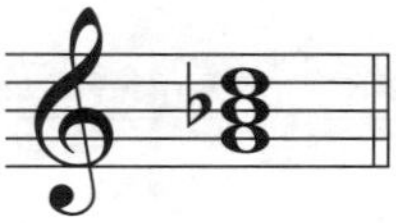 [staff] is the tonic triad of the key of G minor.

e) 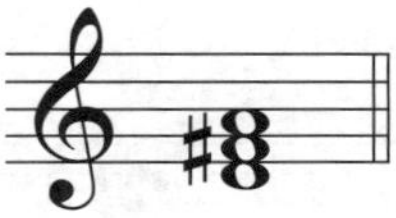 [staff] is the dominant triad of the keys of G major and G minor.

8. Fill in the blanks.

a) 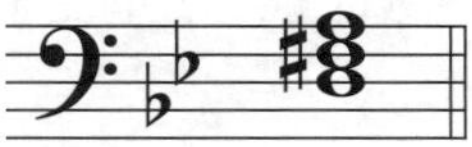 [staff] is the dominant triad in the key of G minor.

b) 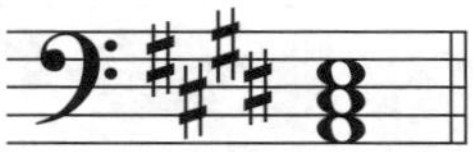 [staff] is the subdominant triad in the key of E major.

c) 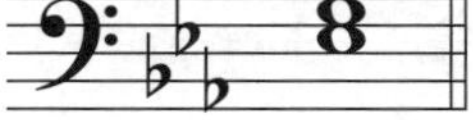 [staff] is the tonic triad in the key of E♭ major.

d) 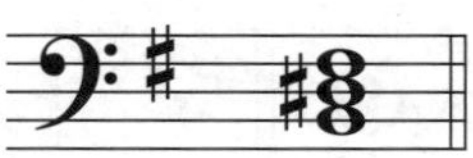 [staff] is the dominant triad in the key of E minor.

e) 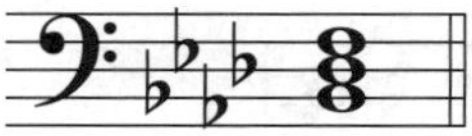 [staff] is the subdominant triad in the key of F minor.

9. Name the quality of each of the following triads as major or minor.

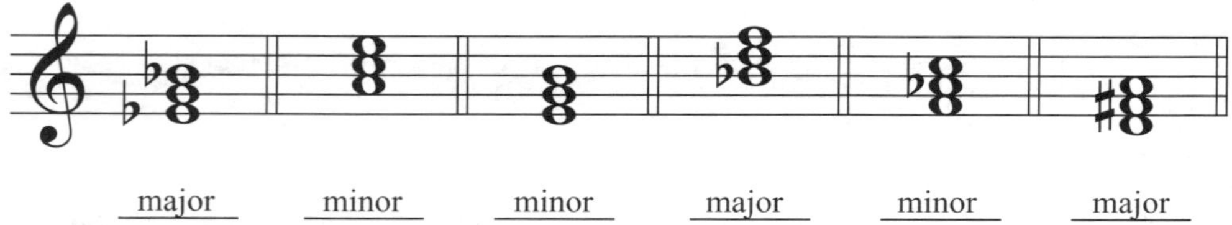

10. Name the quality of each of the following triads as major or minor.

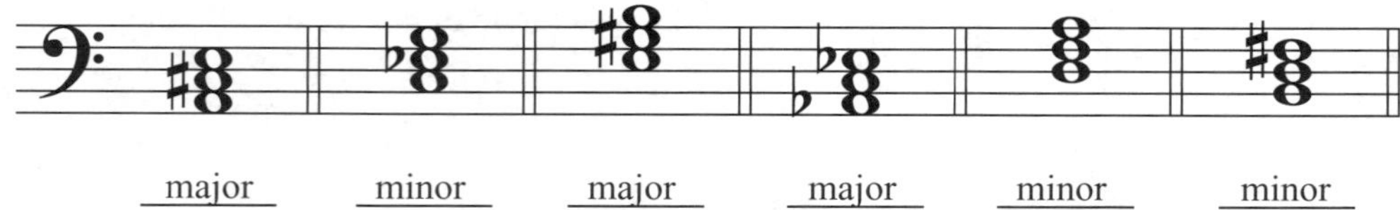

11. For each of the following notes, write a major triad using the given note as the root.

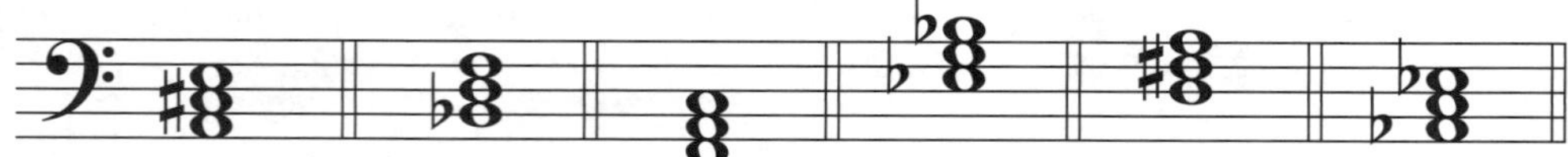

12. For each of the following notes, write a minor triad using the given note as the root.

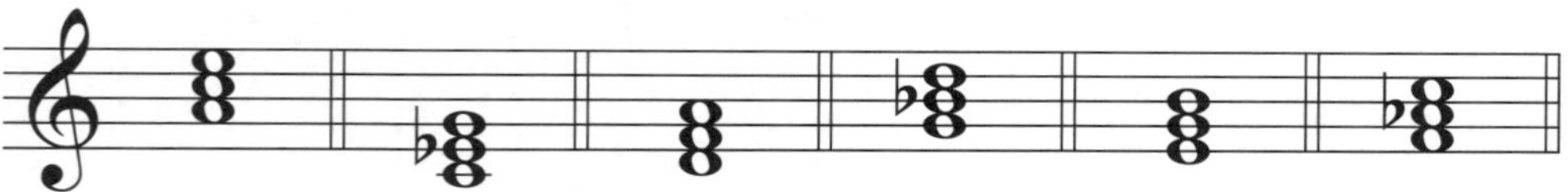

I A EXERCISES (p. 131)

1. Write a major triad and its inversions, using each of the following notes as the root. Use close position.

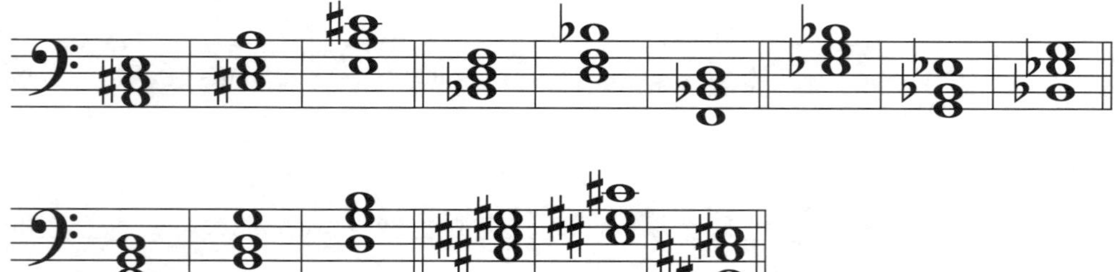

2. Write a minor triad and its inversions, using each of the following notes as the root. Use close position.

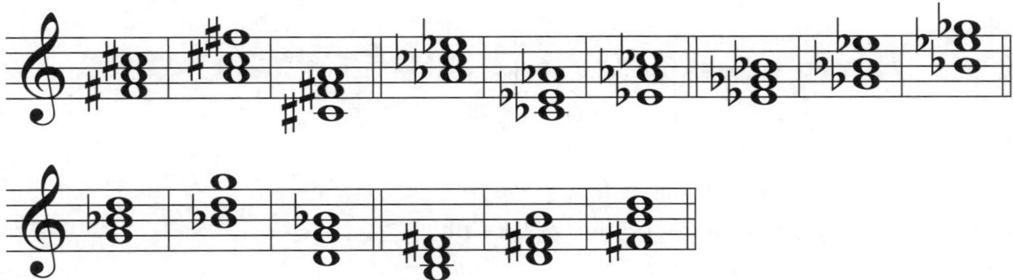

3. Solve the following triads.

Example:

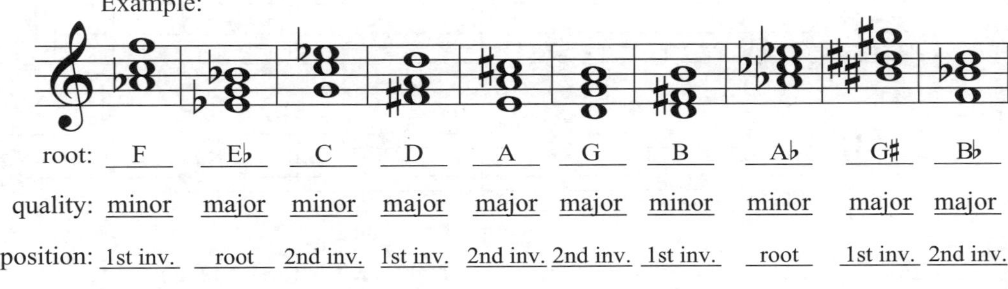

4. Write the following triads in close position in the treble clef.

a) the root position of the F major triad
b) the root position of the D minor triad
c) the first inversion of the G major triad
d) the second inversion of the E minor triad
e) the root position of the B♭ minor triad
f) the second inversion of the C major triad
g) the first inversion of the A♭ major triad
h) the second inversion of the G♯ minor triad
i) the root position of the B major triad
j) the first inversion of the D major triad

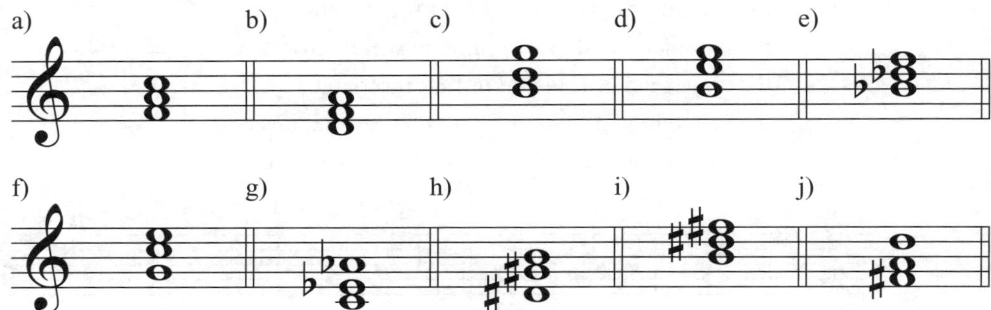

5. Write the following triads in root position in the bass clef. Use close position.

a) a major triad with F as the root
b) a minor triad with D as the fifth
c) a minor triad with C as the third
d) a major triad with G as the third
e) a major triad with A♭ as the root
f) a minor triad with A as the fifth
g) a major triad with B as the fifth
h) a minor triad with E♭ as the third
i) a minor triad with B as the root
j) a major triad with C♯ as the third

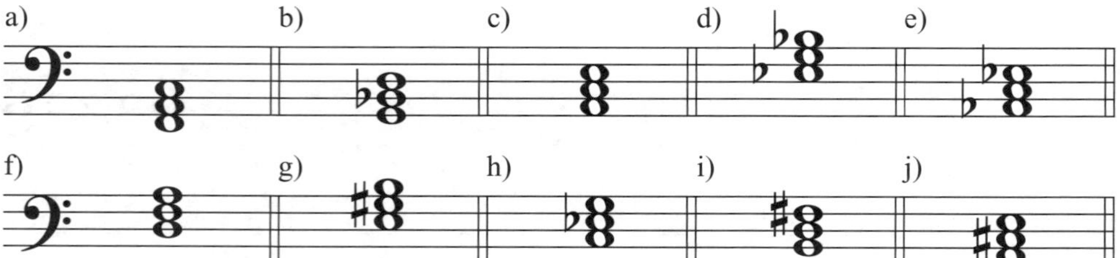

6. Add accidentals where necessary to make each of these a major triad.*

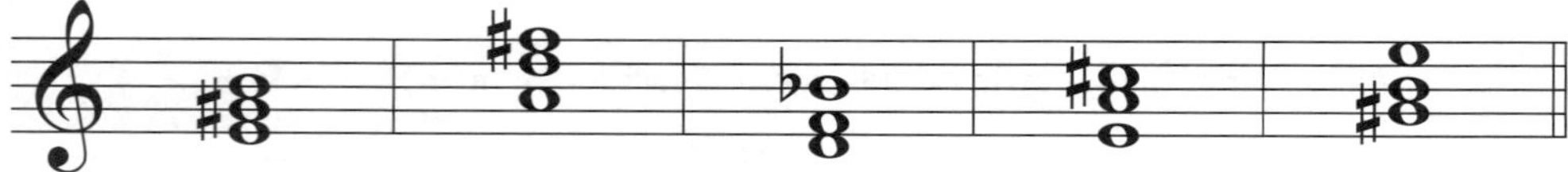

7. Add accidentals where necessary to make each of these a minor triad.*

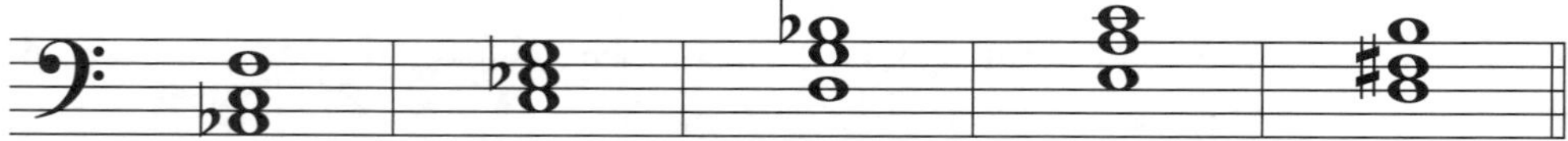

* Different accidentals from those used are also acceptable.

8. Write the following triads in the treble clef, using the correct key signature for each. Use close position.

a) the mediant triad of E♭ major, in root position
b) the dominant triad of B♭ minor, in second inversion
c) the tonic triad of E major, in first inversion
d) the subdominant triad of F minor, in second inversion
e) the supertonic triad of B major, in root position

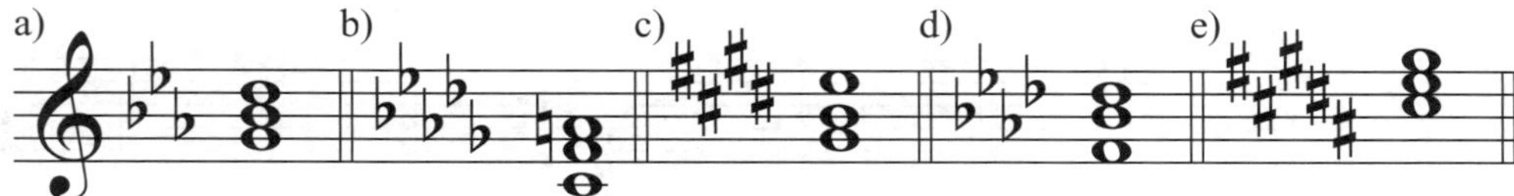

9. Write the following triads in the bass clef, using the accidentals instead of key signatures. Use close position.

   a) the tonic triad of A major, in first inversion
   b) the submediant triad of G♭ major, in root position
   c) the subdominant triad of C minor, in second inversion
   d) the dominant triad of F♯ minor, in first inversion
   e) the supertonic triad of B♭ major, in root position

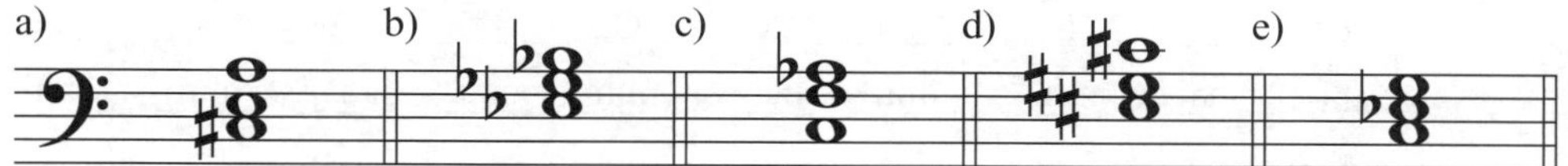

10. Identify the root, quality, and position of each of the following triads. Then name the major key of each and the technical degree of the root.

Example:

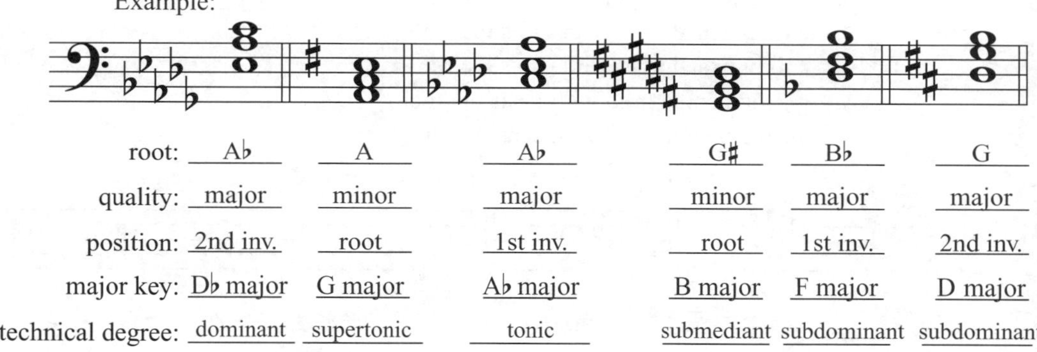

	Example					
root:	A♭	A	A♭	G♯	B♭	G
quality:	major	minor	major	minor	major	major
position:	2nd inv.	root	1st inv.	root	1st inv.	2nd inv.
major key:	D♭ major	G major	A♭ major	B major	F major	D major
technical degree:	dominant	supertonic	tonic	submediant	subdominant	subdominant

11. Identify the root, quality, and position of each of the following triads. Then name the minor key of each and the technical degree of the root.

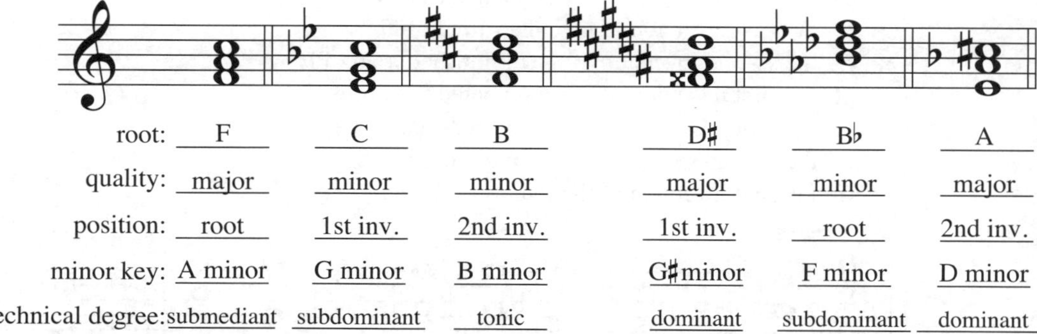

root:	F	C	B	D♯	B♭	A
quality:	major	minor	minor	major	minor	major
position:	root	1st inv.	2nd inv.	1st inv.	root	2nd inv.
minor key:	A minor	G minor	B minor	G♯minor	F minor	D minor
technical degree:	submediant	subdominant	tonic	dominant	subdominant	dominant

12. Solve the following triads.

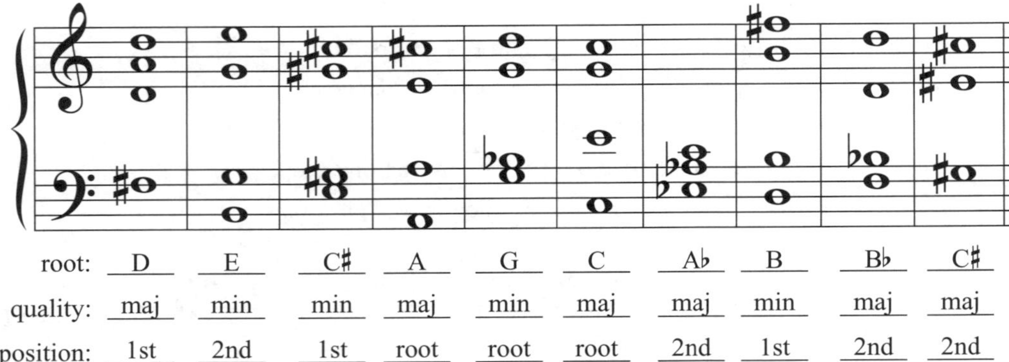

A EXERCISES (p. 136)

1. Write the following triads in root position in the treble clef. Use close position.
   a) an augmented triad with D as the third
   b) a diminished triad with C♭ as the fifth
   c) a diminished triad with C♯ as the root
   d) an augmented triad with E♭ as the root
   e) an augmented triad with D as the fifth

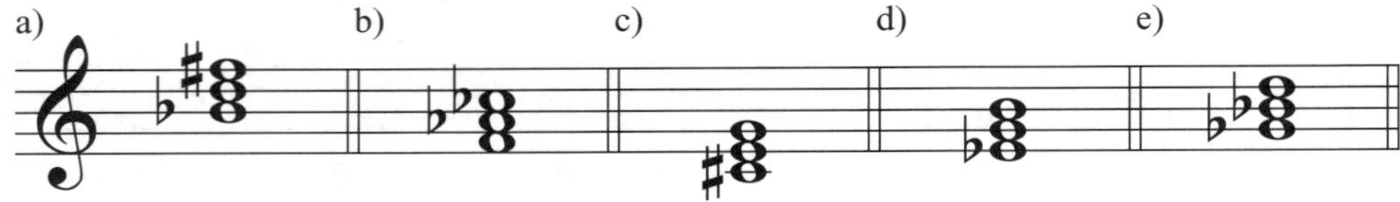

2. Write three different arrangements of each of the following triads in open position. (Sample answers. Other arrangements are possible.)
   a) the root position of the major triad of A♭
   b) the second inversion of the minor triad of F
   c) the first inversion of the minor triad of C
   d) the root position of the augmented triad of B
   e) the first inversion of the minor triad of F♯
   f) the second inversion of the diminished triad of E
   g) the first inversion of the augmented triad of A
   h) the root position of the diminished triad of C♯
   i) the second inversion of the major triad of D♭
   j) the first inversion of the minor triad of G

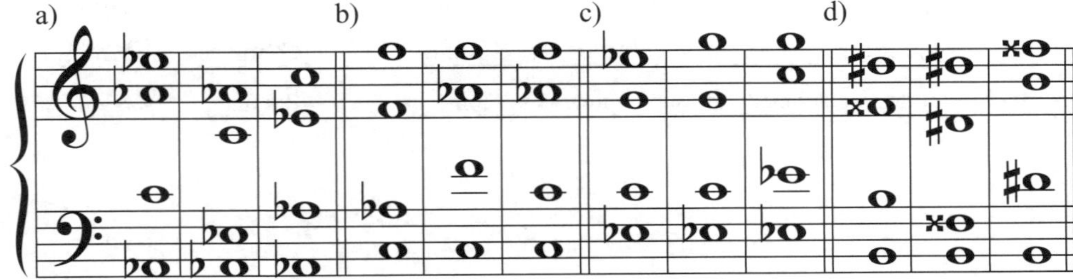

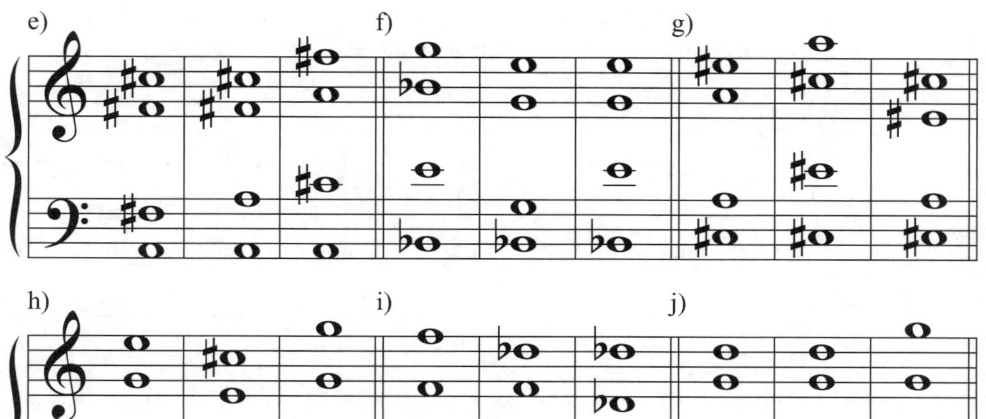

3. Write the four different kinds of triads in root position *below* each of the following notes.

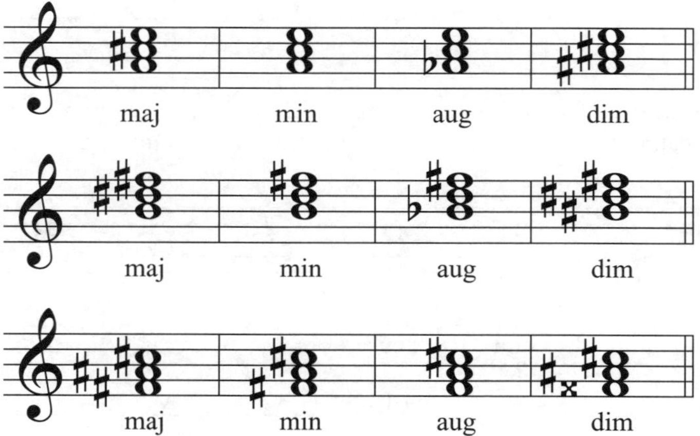

4. Write the four different kinds of triads in root position *above* each of the following notes.

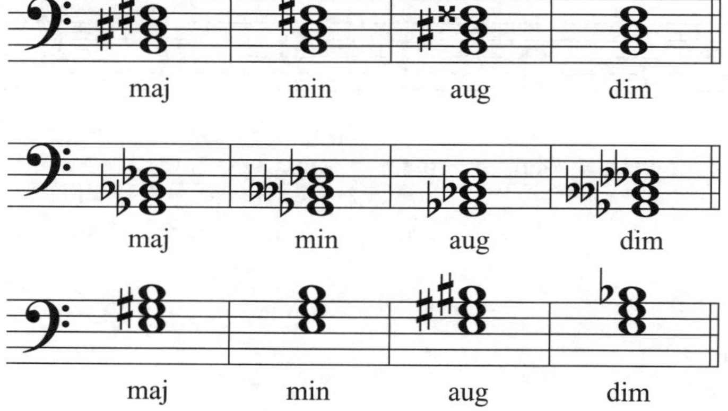

5. Write the triad found on each degree of the A major scale. For each triad, name its quality and label it with a Roman numeral.

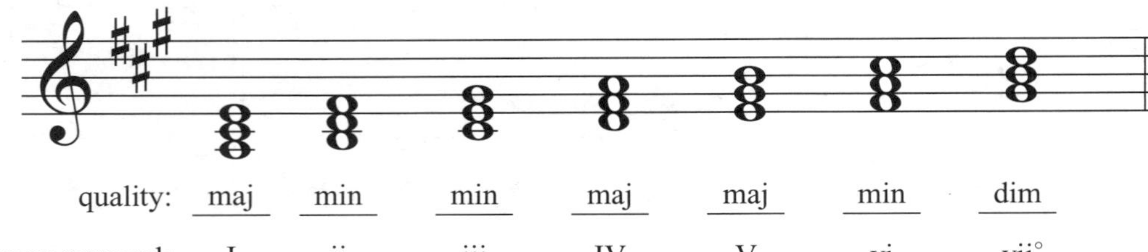

6. Write the triad found on each degree of the E♭ major scale. For each triad, name its quality and label it with a Roman numeral.

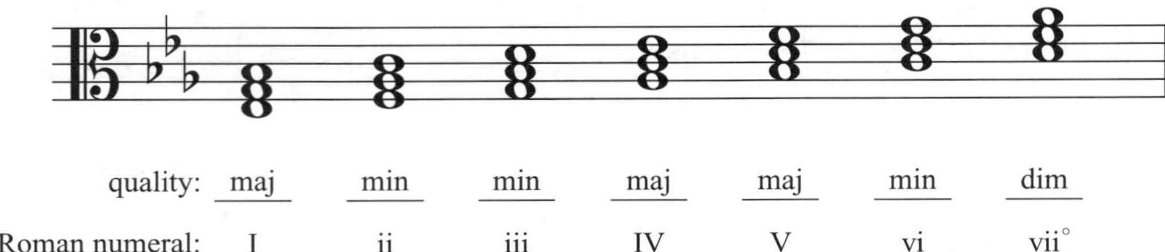

7. a) Write the triad found on each degree of the F minor scale, harmonic form. For each triad, name its quality and label it with a Roman numeral.

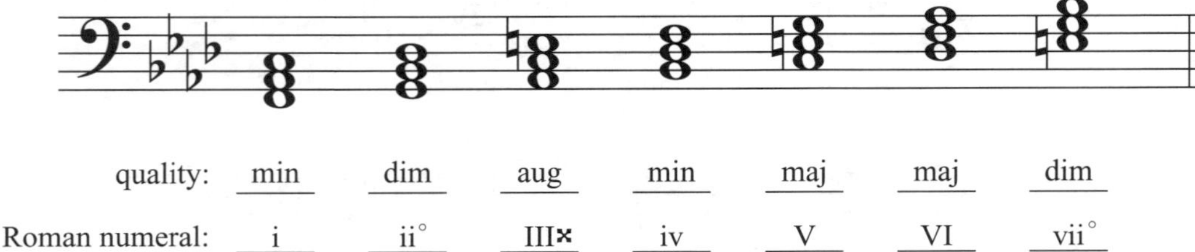

b) Write the triad found on each degree of the F minor scale, natural form. For each triad, name its quality and label it with a Roman numeral.

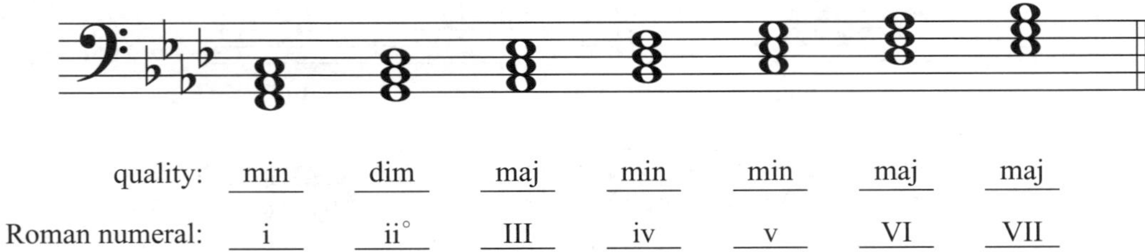

8. a) Write the triad found on each degree of the G minor scale, harmonic form. For each triad, name its quality and label it with a Roman numeral.

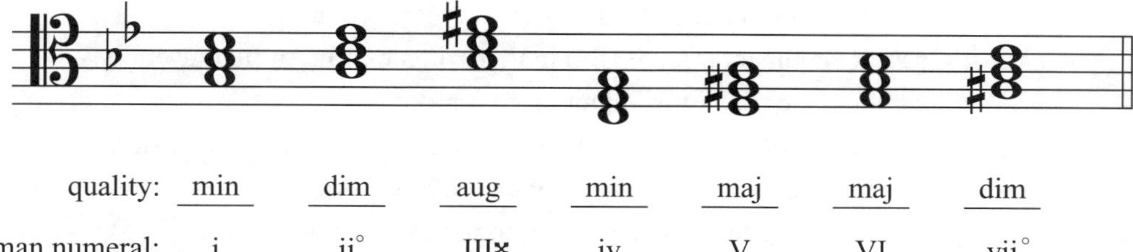

quality:	min	dim	aug	min	maj	maj	dim
Roman numeral:	i	ii°	III+	iv	V	VI	vii°

b) Write the triad found on each degree of the G minor scale, natural form. For each triad, name its quality and label it with a Roman numeral.

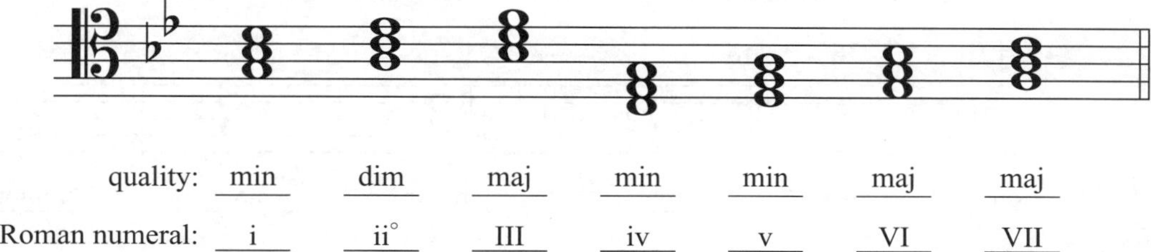

quality:	min	dim	maj	min	min	maj	maj
Roman numeral:	i	ii°	III	iv	v	VI	VII

9. Write the following triads in close position in the treble clef, using the proper key signature for each. Name the quality of each triad.

a) the mediant triad of F minor, natural form, in root position
b) the leading-note triad of G♯ minor, harmonic form, in second inversion
c) the subdominant triad of E minor, in first inversion
d) the dominant triad of B♭ minor, natural form, in first inversion
e) the tonic triad of A♭ minor, in second inversion
f) the mediant triad of C minor, harmonic form, in first inversion
g) the subtonic triad of C♯ minor, natural form, in second inversion
h) the dominant triad of D♯ minor, harmonic form, in root position

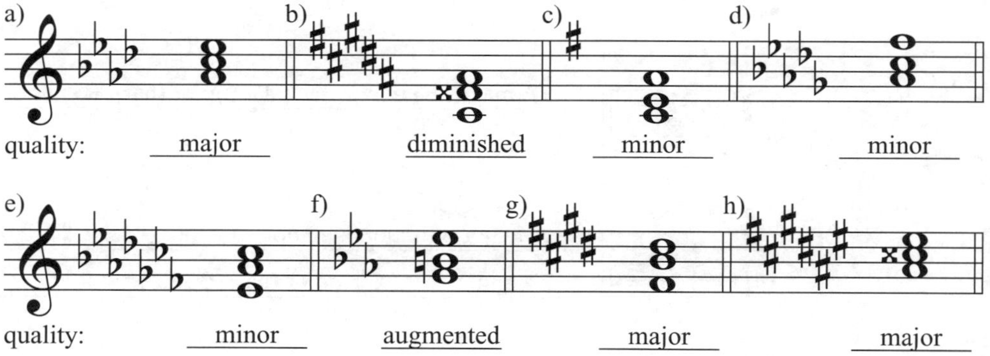

Why was the form (harmonic or natural) of the minor scale to be used in parts c) and e) not specified? The subdominant and tonic triads do not contain the 7th scale degree, so they are the same in the harmonic and natural forms of the minor scale.

10. Write the following triads in close position in the bass clef, using accidentals instead of key signatures. Name the quality of each triad.

a) the supertonic triad of F major, in root position
b) the dominant triad of B♭ minor, harmonic form, in first inversion
c) the tonic triad of F♯ minor, in first inversion
d) the subtonic triad of G minor, natural form, in second inversion
e) the mediant triad of E♭ major, in root position
f) the submediant triad of B major, in first inversion
g) the subdominant triad of C minor, in second inversion
h) the dominant triad of G♯ minor, natural form, in root position
i) the tonic triad of C♯ major, in first inversion
j) the supertonic triad of D minor, in second inversion

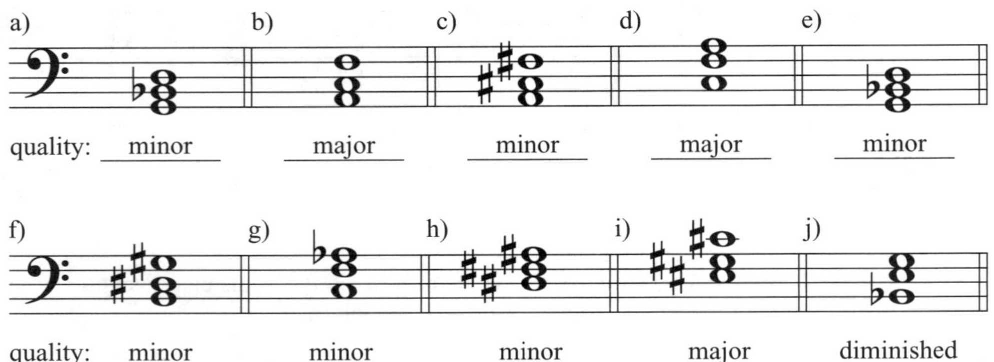

Opt. **EXERCISES** (p. 143)

1. Name all the scales (major, harmonic minor, and natural minor) in which each of the following triads is found.

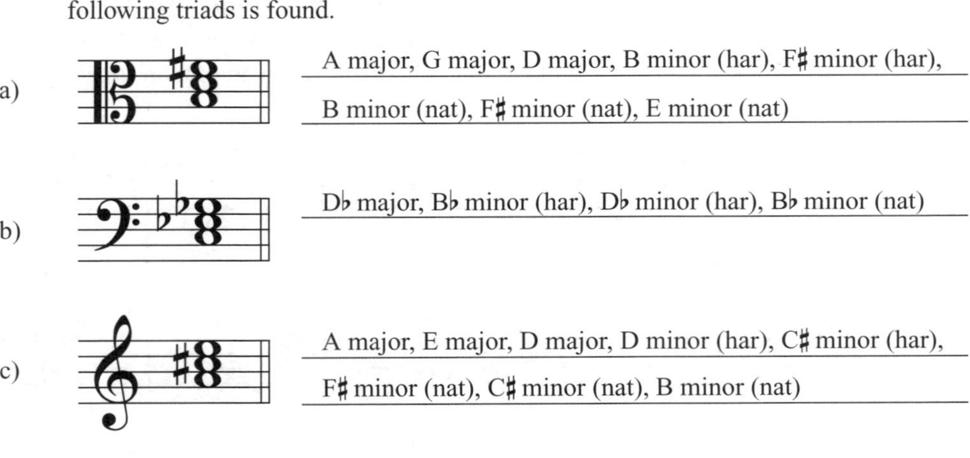

2. Write the triad that is found only in the G minor harmonic scale.

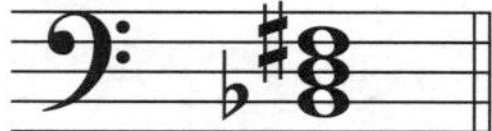

3. Write the triad that is common only to these scales: B♭ major, G minor (harmonic and natural forms), and B♭ minor (harmonic form only).

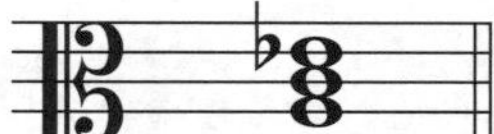

4. Name all the scales (major, harmonic minor, and natural minor) in which each of the following triads is found.

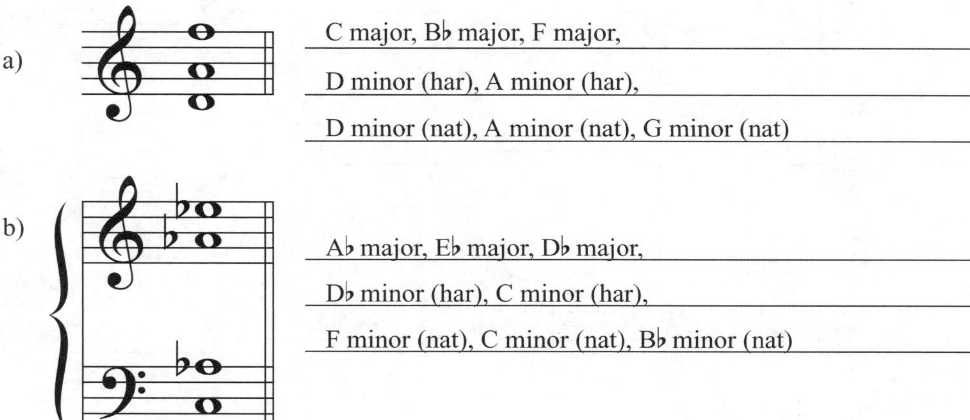

5. Write the triad that is common only to these scales: D♭ major, B♭ minor (harmonic and natural forms), G♭ major, F minor (harmonic and natural forms), A♭ major, and E♭ minor (natural form only).

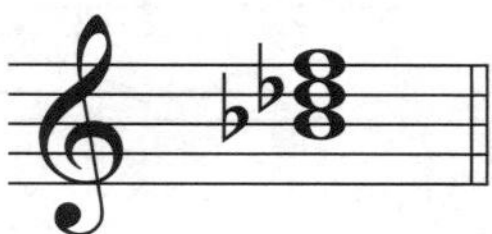

6. In the treble clef, write the diminished triads that are found in the following scales: a) D major b) A♭ major c) B major d) E major e) D♭ major.

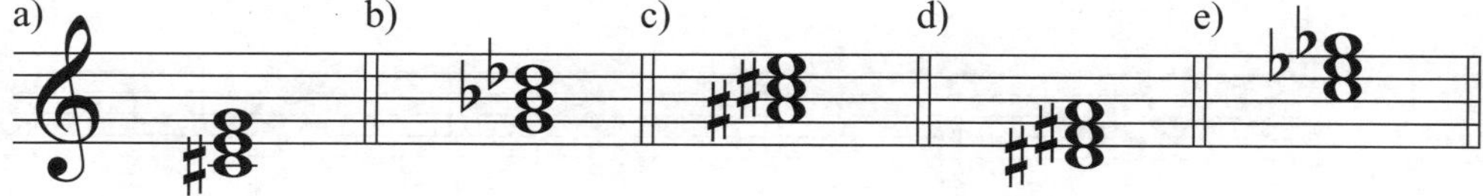

7. In the bass clef, write the augmented triads that are found in the following harmonic minor scales: a) B minor b) G♯ minor c) C minor d) F minor e) D minor

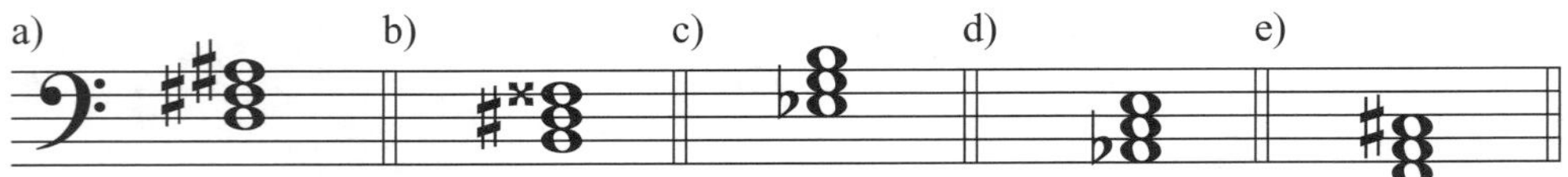

A EXERCISES (p. 147)

1. Write the dominant 7th chord and its inversions in each of the following keys, using the correct key signature for each.

a) A major

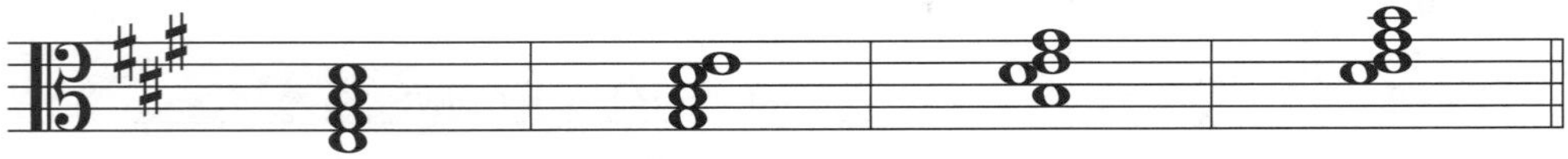

b) E♭ major

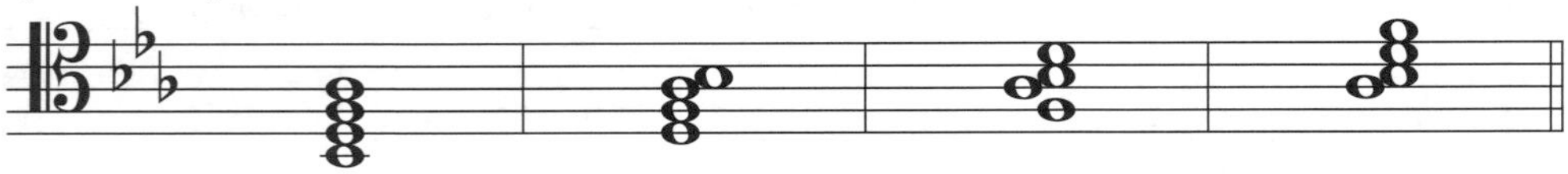

c) B minor

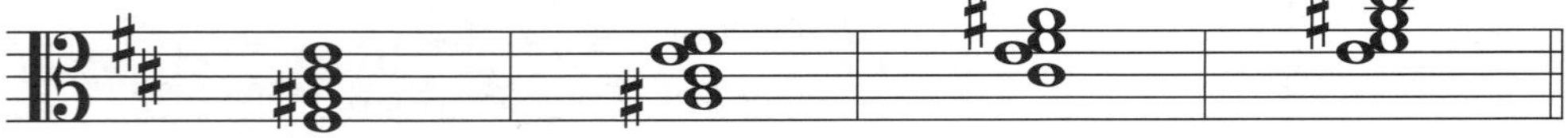

d) F minor

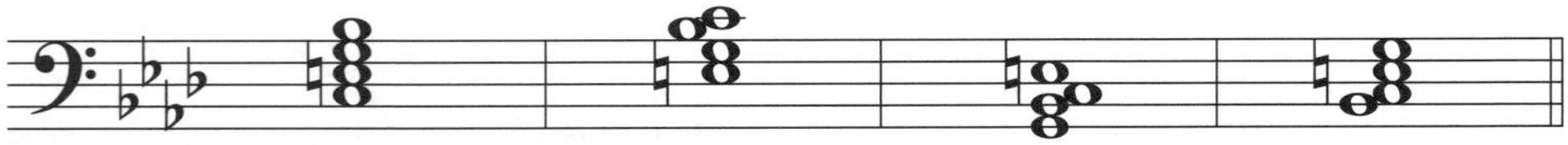

e) C♯ minor

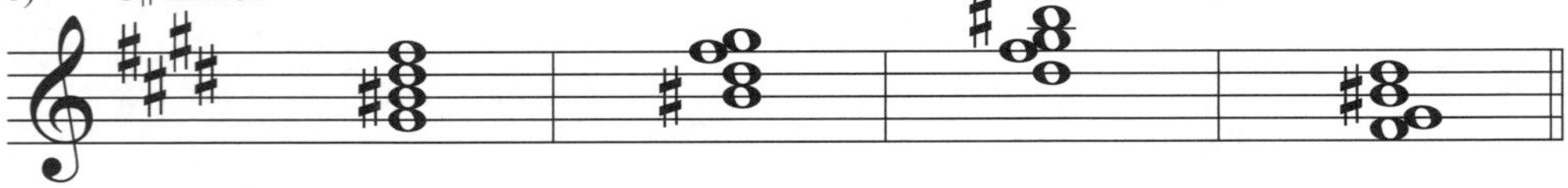

f) B♭ major

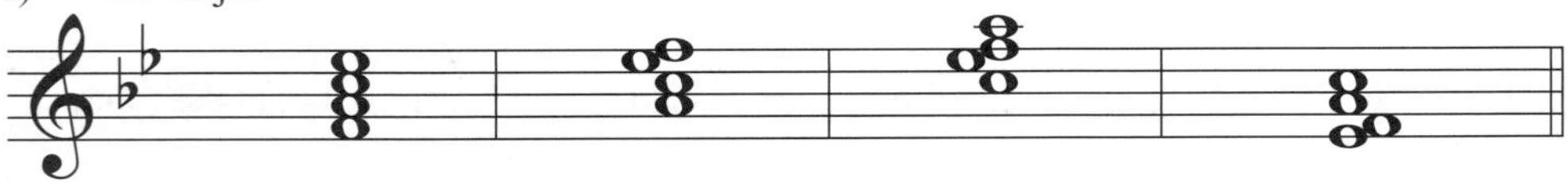

g) G♯ minor

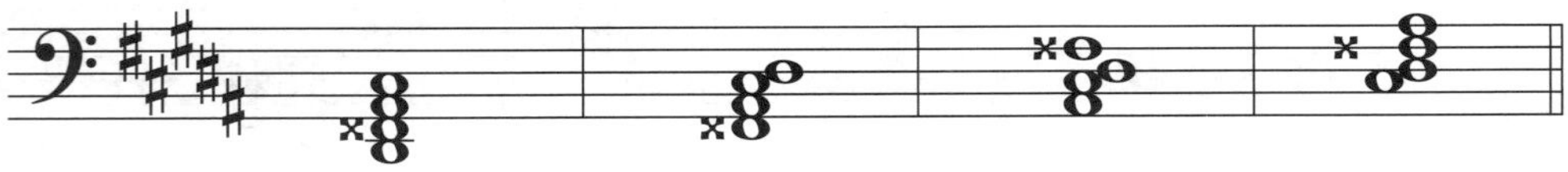

h) D major

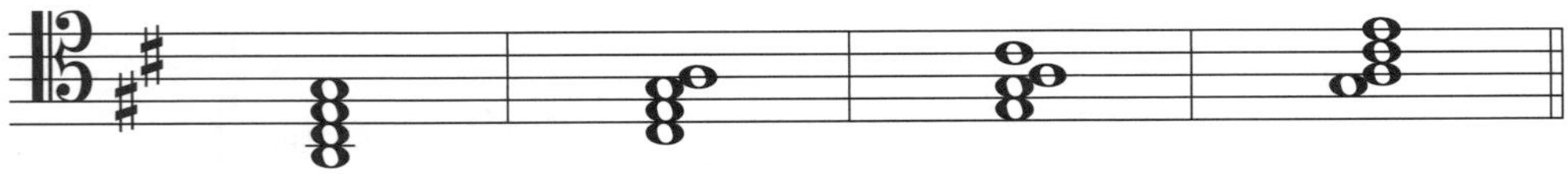

i) E minor

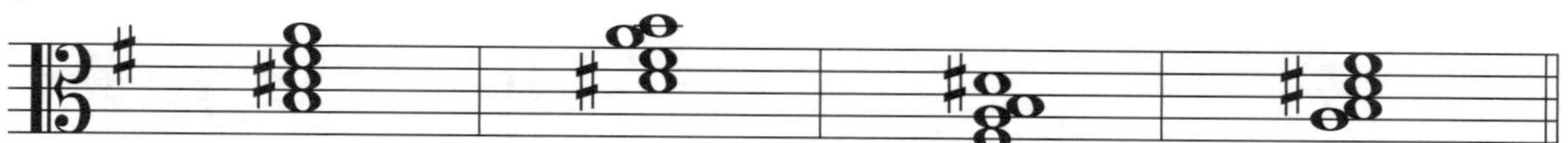

2. Solve the following dominant 7th chords.

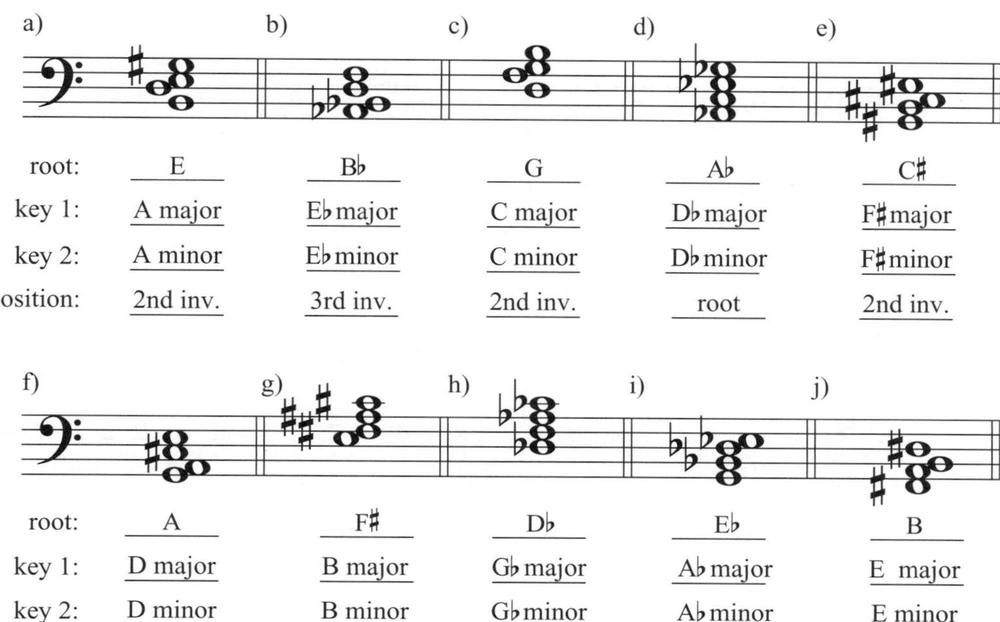

	a)	b)	c)	d)	e)
root:	E	B♭	G	A♭	C♯
key 1:	A major	E♭ major	C major	D♭ major	F♯ major
key 2:	A minor	E♭ minor	C minor	D♭ minor	F♯ minor
position:	2nd inv.	3rd inv.	2nd inv.	root	2nd inv.

	f)	g)	h)	i)	j)
root:	A	F♯	D♭	E♭	B
key 1:	D major	B major	G♭ major	A♭ major	E major
key 2:	D minor	B minor	G♭ minor	A♭ minor	E minor
position:	3rd inv.	3rd inv.	root	1st inv.	2nd inv.

3. Write the following dominant 7ths in the treble clef, using the correct key signature for each.

a) the first inversion of the dominant 7th of D minor
b) the second inversion of the dominant 7th of F♯ minor
c) the root position of the dominant 7th of B major
d) the third inversion of the dominant 7th of G minor
e) the root position of the dominant 7th of E♭ major
f) the first inversion of the dominant 7th of C♯ minor
g) the second inversion of the dominant 7th of A major
h) the root position of the dominant 7th of G♭ major
i) the third inversion of the dominant 7th of G♯ minor
j) the second inversion of the dominant 7th of D♭ major

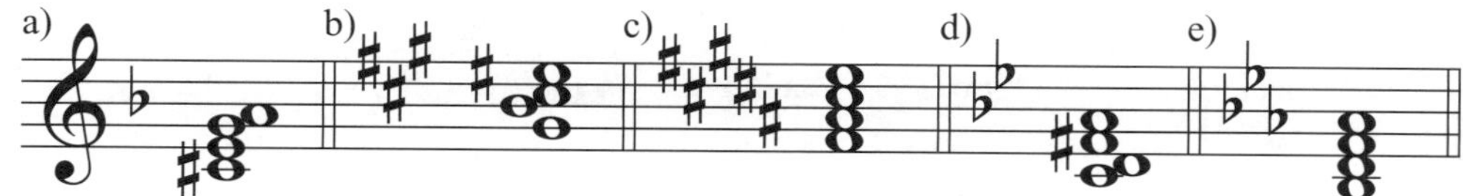

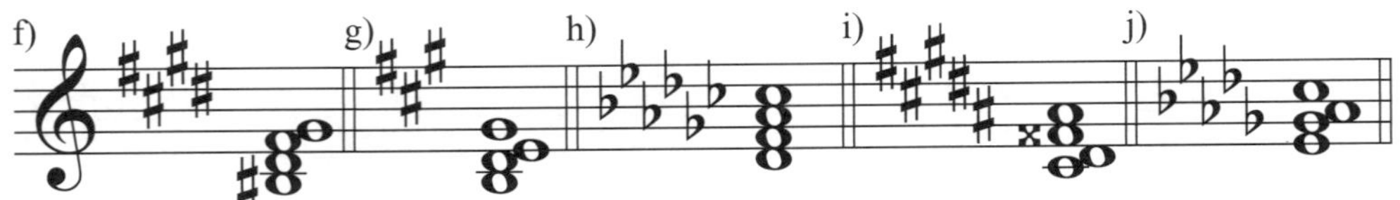

4. Write the dominant 7th and inversions of other dominant 7ths, using F as the lowest note in each case. Name the major key of each.

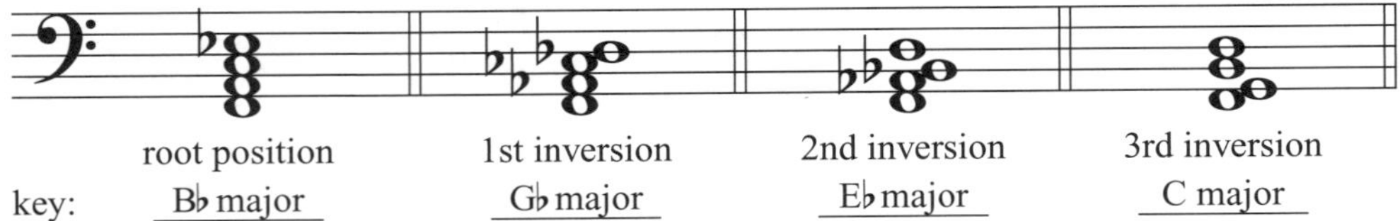

5. Add accidentals to the following to make them into dominant 7th chords. Name the minor key of each. (Alternate accidentals and keys are possible.)

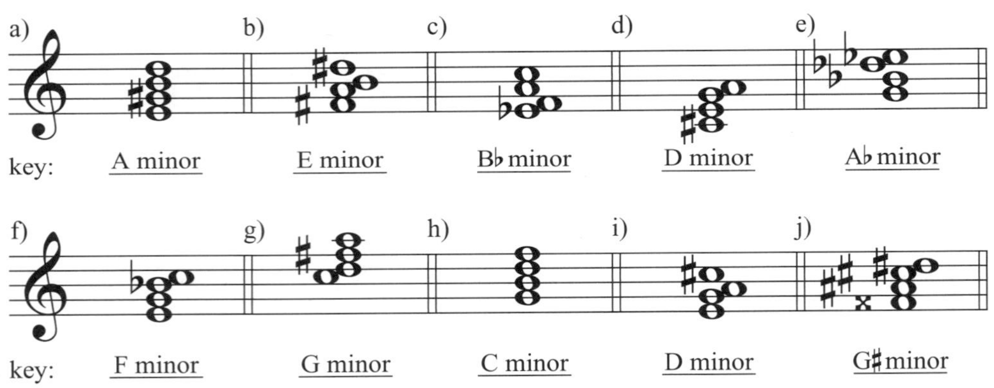

6. Solve the following dominant 7th chords.

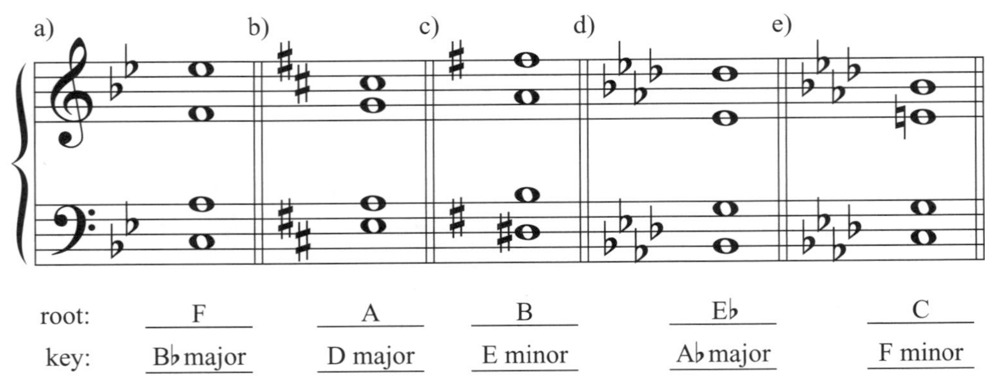

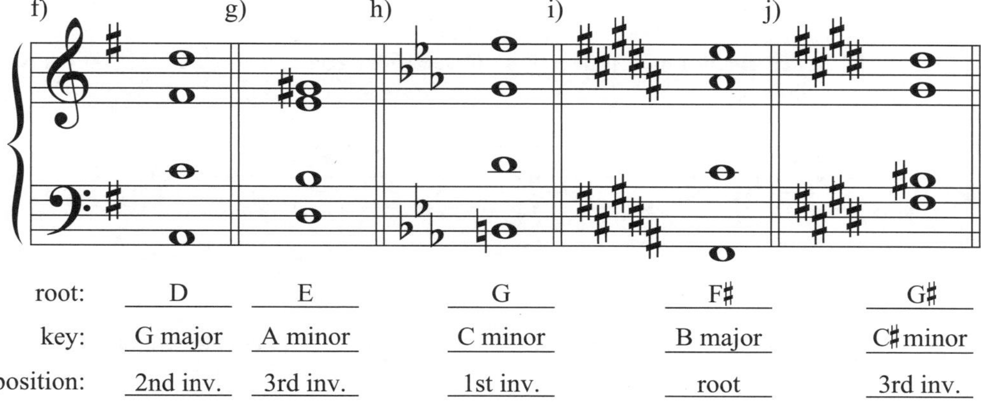

7. Write the dominant 7th and inversions of other dominant 7ths, using E as the lowest note for each. Name two keys for each.

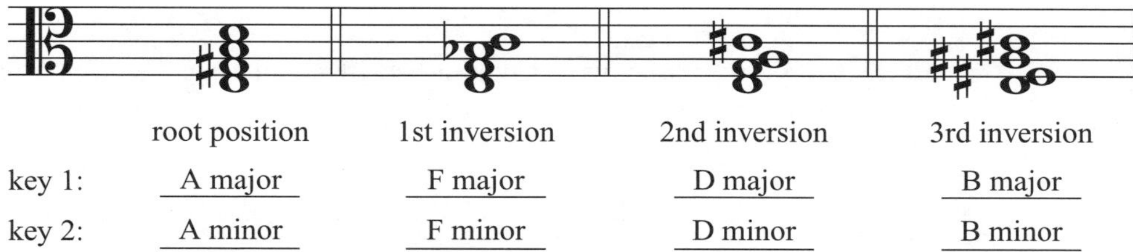

8. Write the dominant 7th and inversions of other dominant 7ths, using G as the lowest note for each. Name the minor key of each.

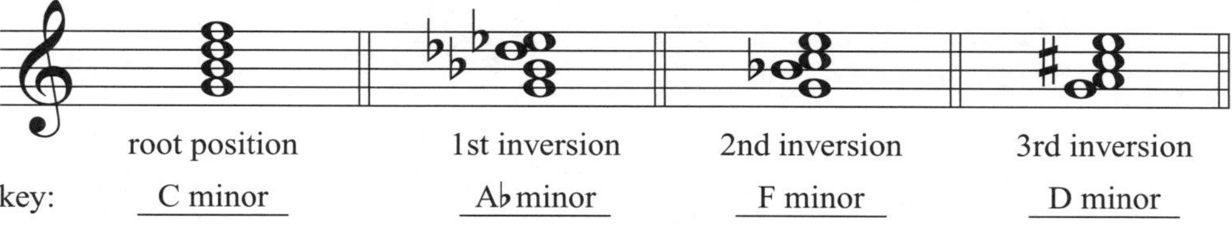

9. Write the dominant 7th and inversions of other dominant 7ths, using A as the lowest note of each. Name two keys for each.

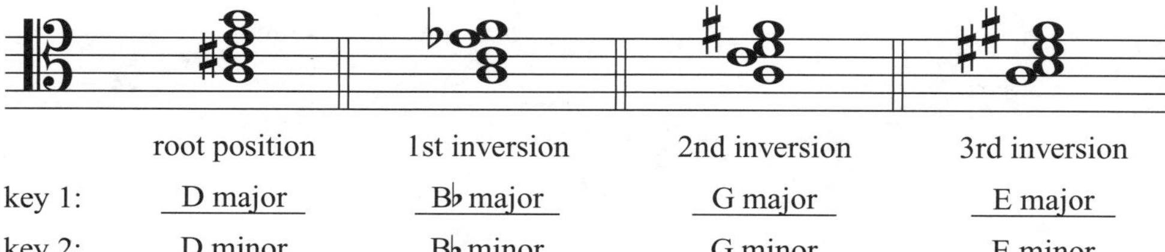

A EXERCISES (p. 151)

1. For each of the following diminished 7th chords, name the minor key to which it belongs.

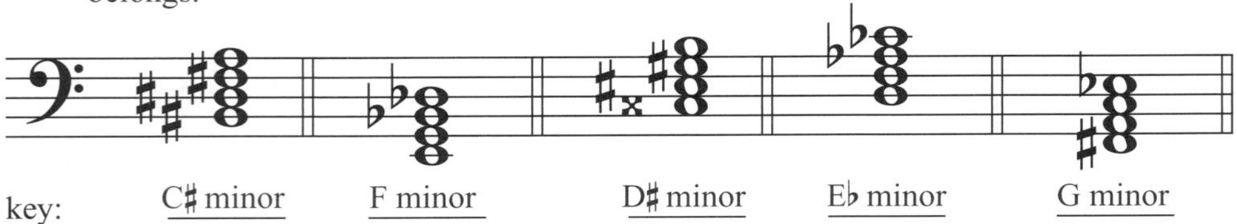

2. For each of the following diminished 7th chords, name the minor key to which it belongs.

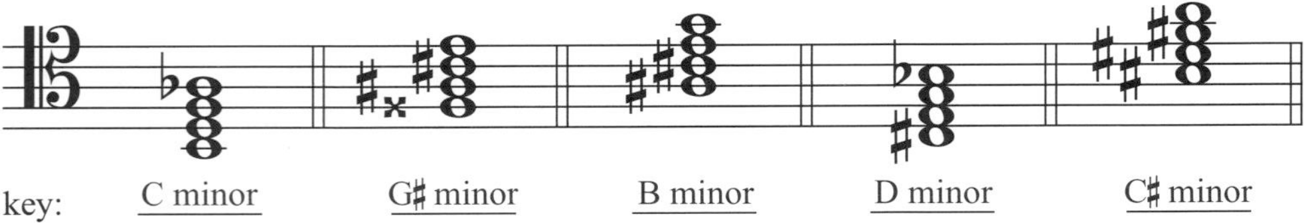

3. For each of the following, write a diminished 7th chord using the given note as the root. Write each chord in root position and in close position, using accidentals.

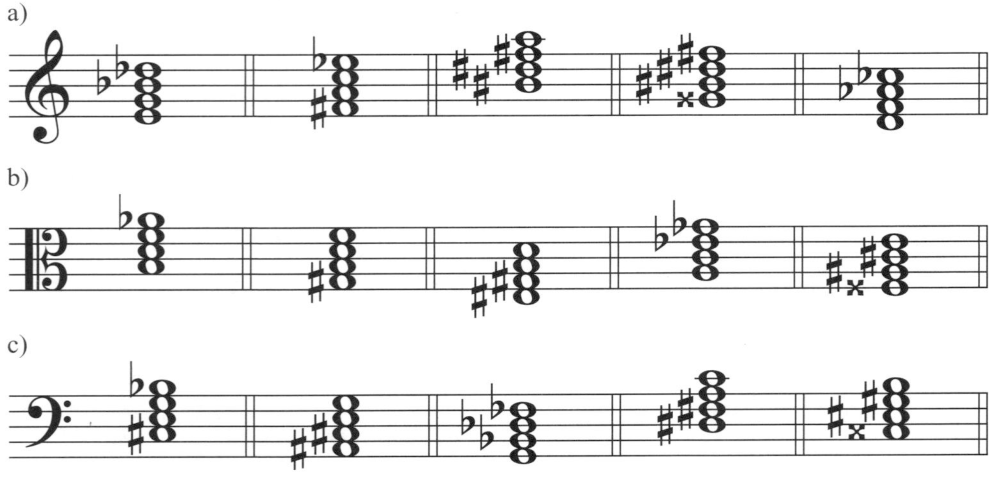

4. Write the leading-note diminished 7th chord in each of the following keys, using the correct key signature for each. Write each chord in root position and in close position.

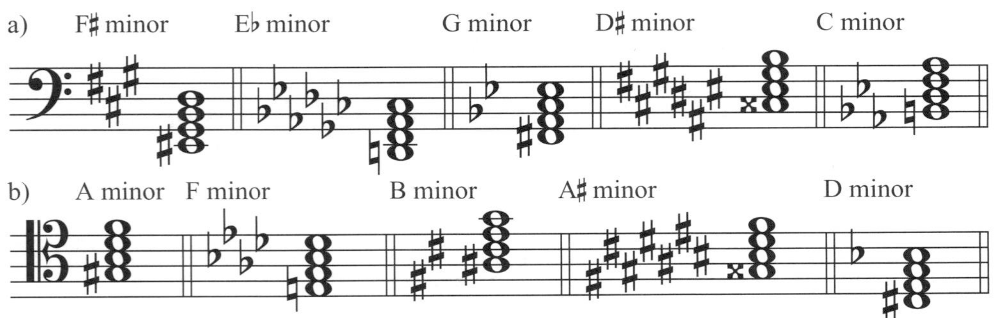

c)

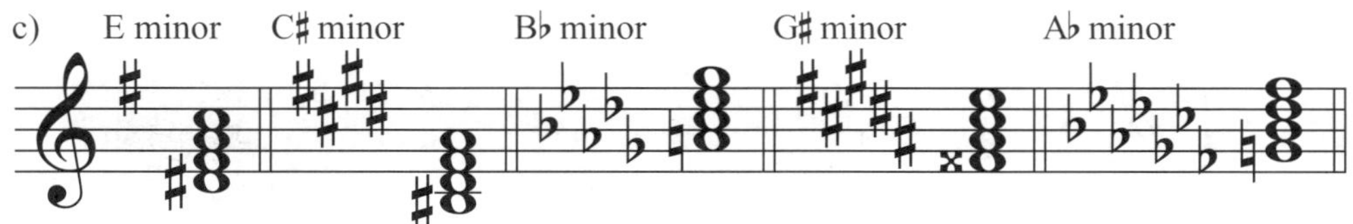

5. For each of the following 7th chords, identify the chord type as dominant 7th or diminished 7th. For each dominant 7th chord, name the two keys to which it belongs; for each diminished 7th chord, name the one key to which it belongs.

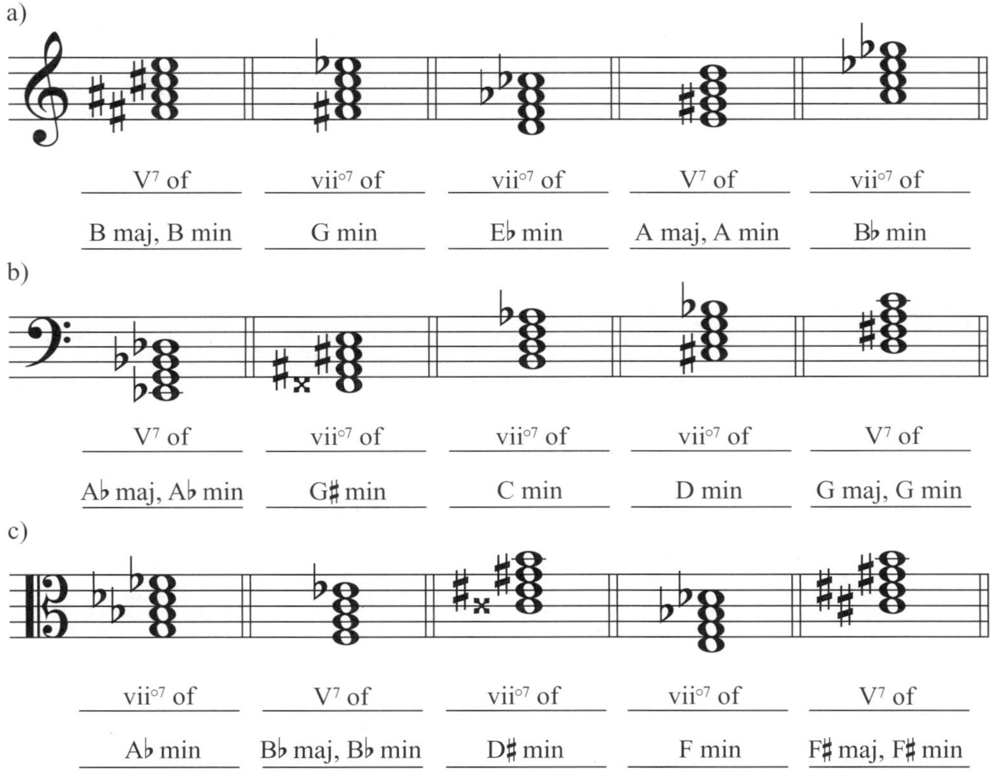

6. For each of the following 7th chords, identify the chord type as dominant 7th or diminished 7th. Name the key and name the position of each chord.

a)

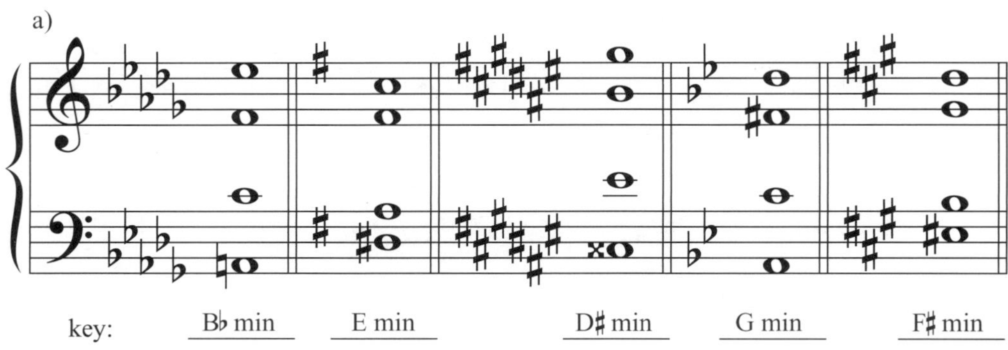

key:	B♭ min	E min	D♯ min	G min	F♯ min
chord type:	dom 7th	dim 7th	dim 7th	dom 7th	dim 7th
position:	1st	root	root	2nd	root

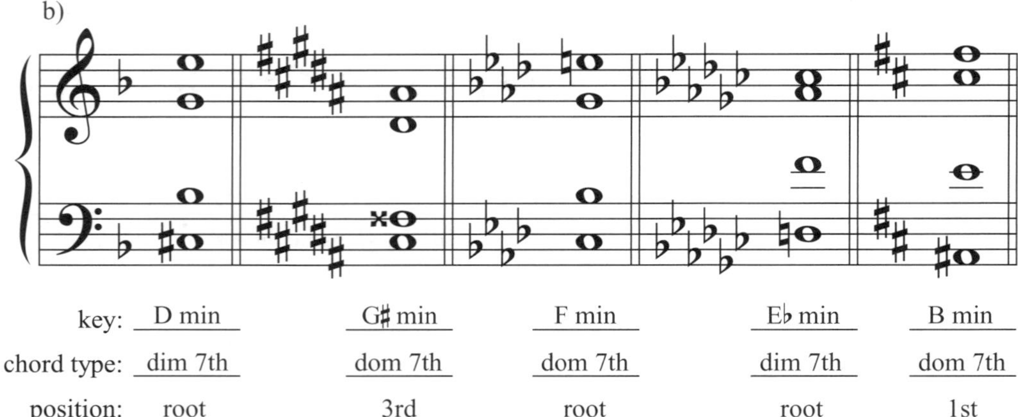

A EXERCISES (p. 158)

1. For each of the following groups of chords:
   - Identify the root, quality (major, minor, diminished, augmented, dominant 7th, or diminished 7th), and position of each chord.
   - Name the scale or scales (major, natural minor, or harmonic minor) to which all of the chords in the group belong.

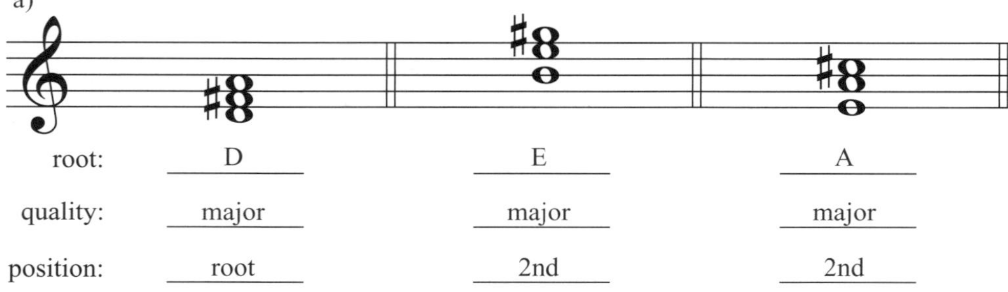

scale(s): A major and F♯ minor, natural form

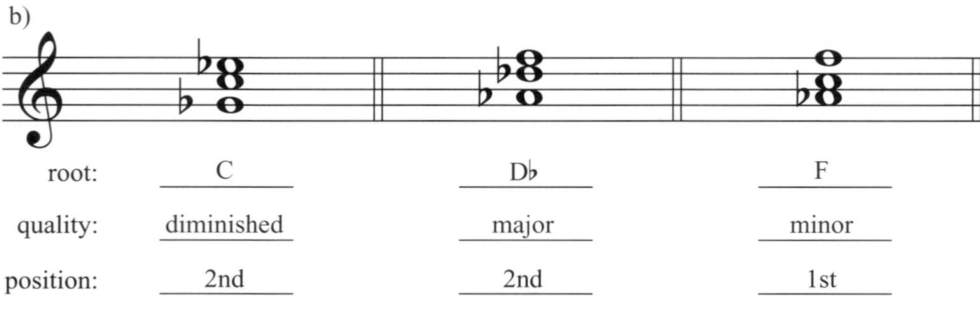

scale(s): D♭ major and B♭ minor, natural form

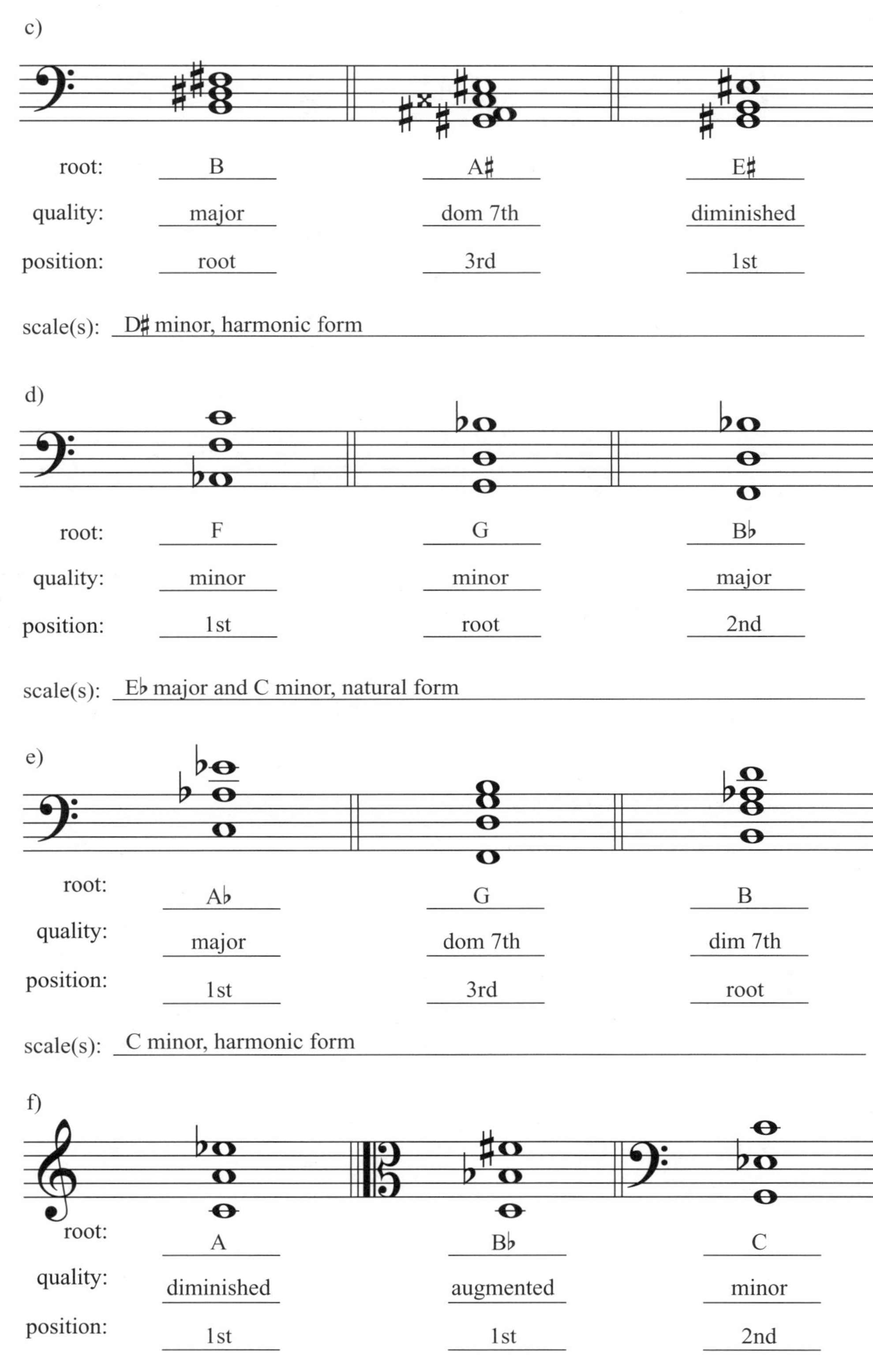
c)
root:
B
A♯
E♯
quality:
major
dom 7th
diminished
position:
root
3rd
1st
scale(s): D♯ minor, harmonic form
d)
root:
F
G
B♭
quality:
minor
minor
major
position:
1st
root
2nd
scale(s): E♭ major and C minor, natural form
e)
root:
A♭
G
B
quality:
major
dom 7th
dim 7th
position:
1st
3rd
root
scale(s): C minor, harmonic form
f)
root:
A
B♭
C
quality:
diminished
augmented
minor
position:
1st
1st
2nd
scale(s): G minor, harmonic form

g)

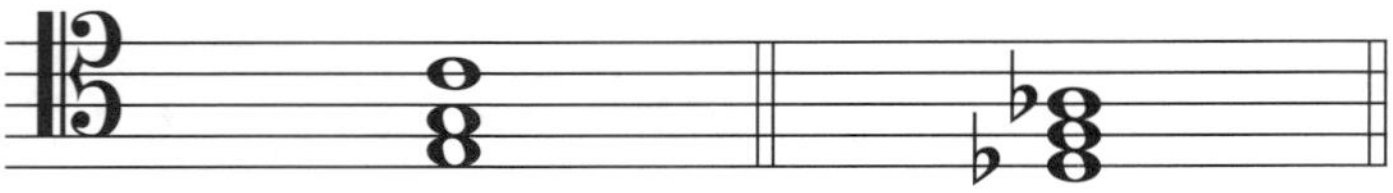

root:	C	D♭
quality:	major	major
position:	1st	root

scale(s): F minor, harmonic form

h)

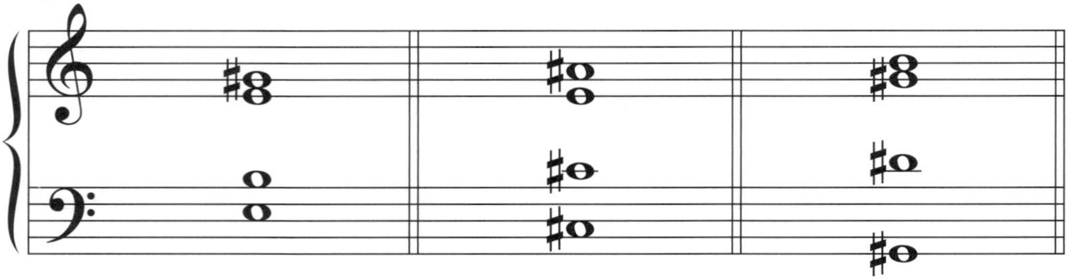

root:	E	A♯	G♯
quality:	major	diminished	minor
position:	root	1st	root

scale(s): B major, G♯ minor, natural form, and G♯ minor, harmonic form

i)

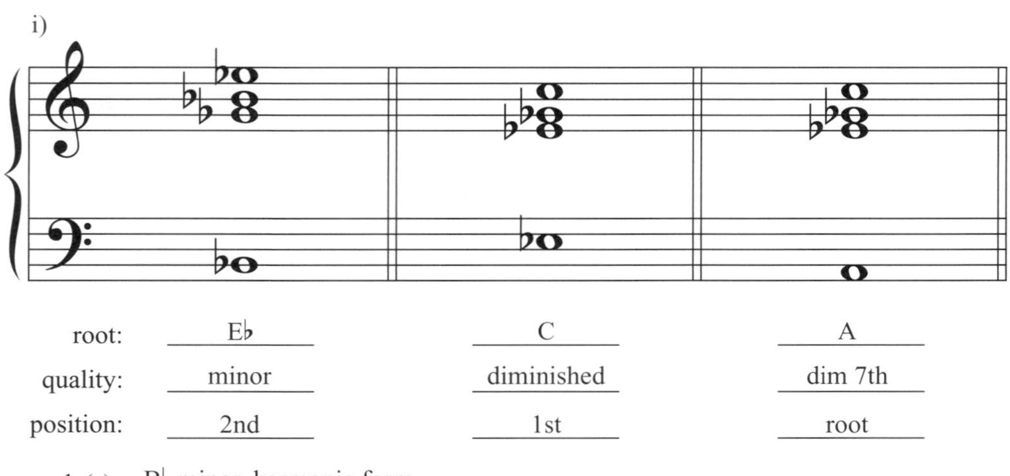

root:	E♭	C	A
quality:	minor	diminished	dim 7th
position:	2nd	1st	root

scale(s): B♭ minor, harmonic form

j)

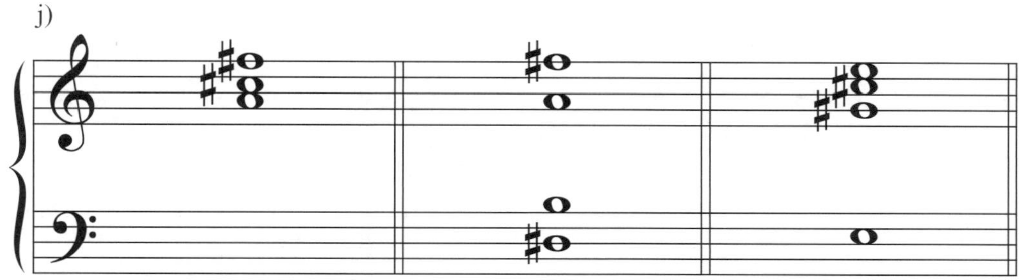

root:	F♯	B	C♯
quality:	minor	dom 7th	minor
position:	1st	1st	1st

scale(s): E major [Also C♯ minor, natural form, but this answer is not required since the ♮VII⁷ chord is not covered at this grade level.]

A EXERCISES (p. 162)

1. Name each of the following chords as:
   - triad (specify major, minor, diminished, or augmented)
   - seventh chord (specify dominant 7th, diminished 7th, or other)
   - quartal chord
   - polychord
   - cluster

   Example:

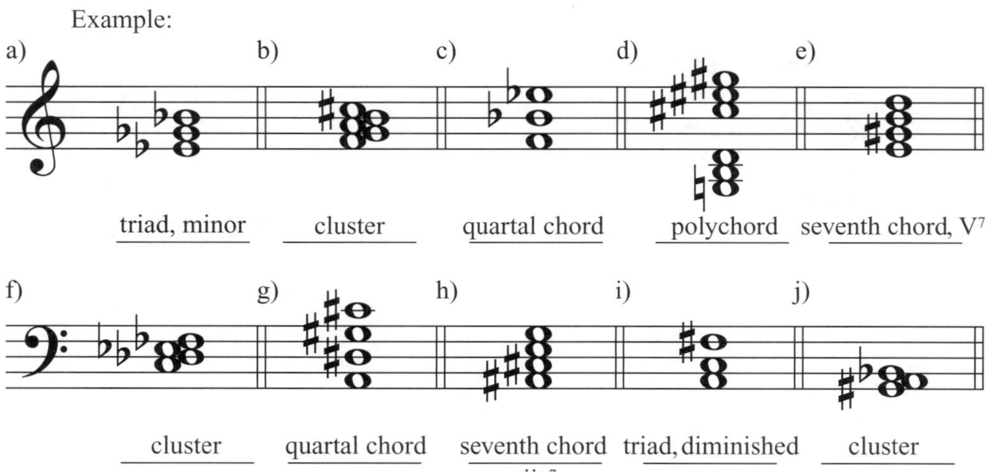

2. See instructions for Exercise 1.

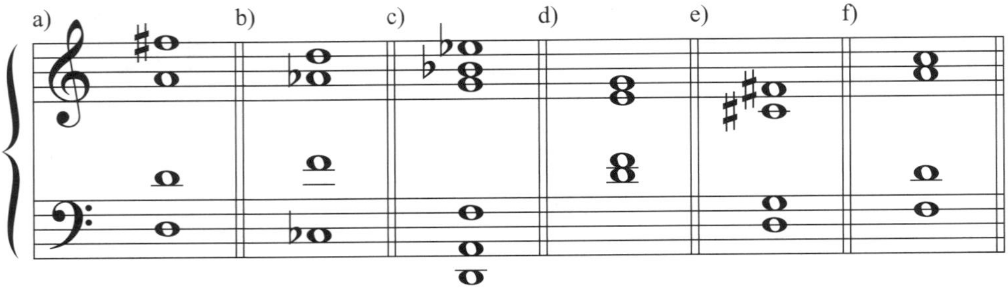

a) triad, major
b) seventh chord vii°7
c) polychord
d) cluster
e) quartal chord
f) seventh chord

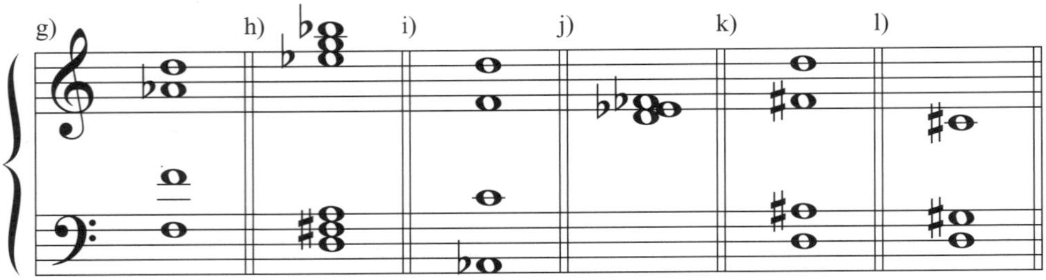

g) triad, dim
h) polychord
i) seventh chord
j) cluster
k) triad, aug.
l) quartal chord

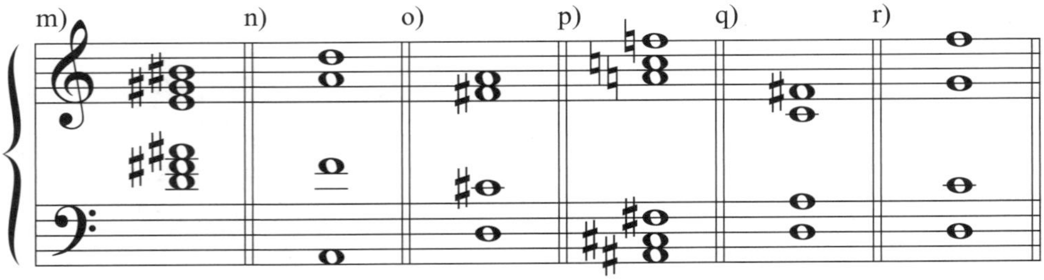

m) cluster
n) triad, minor
o) seventh chord
p) polychord
q) seventh chord V7
r) quartal chord

3. See instructions for Exercise 1.

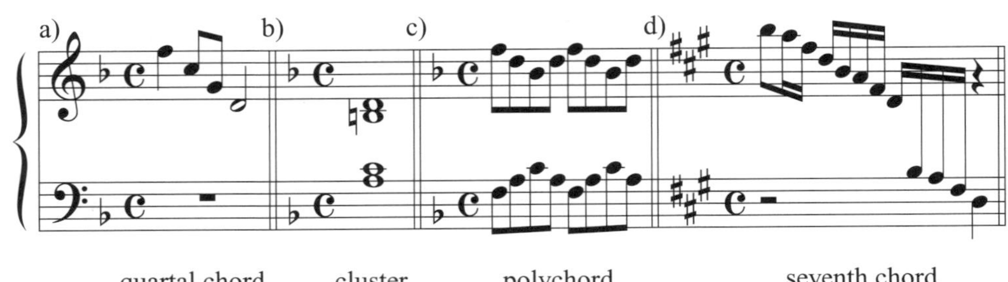

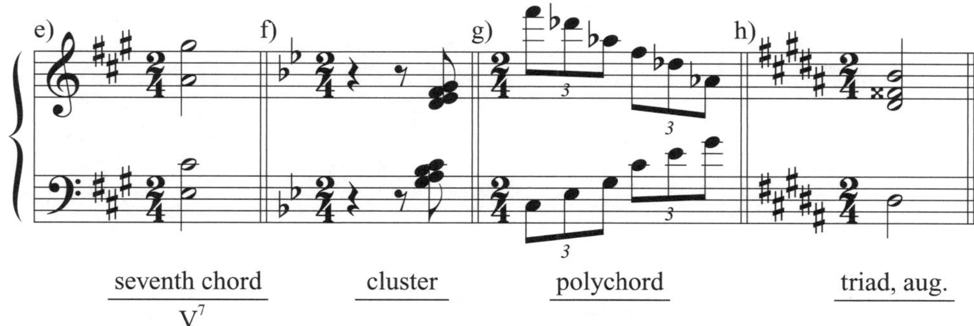

Opt. EXERCISES (p. 166)

1. Write the following scales in the treble clef, ascending only, using key signatures. Use whole notes. Build a triad on each scale degree. Above the staff, label the triads with root/quality chord symbols. Below the staff, label the triads with Roman numerals (using uppercase and lowercase numerals to indicate the qualities of the chords).

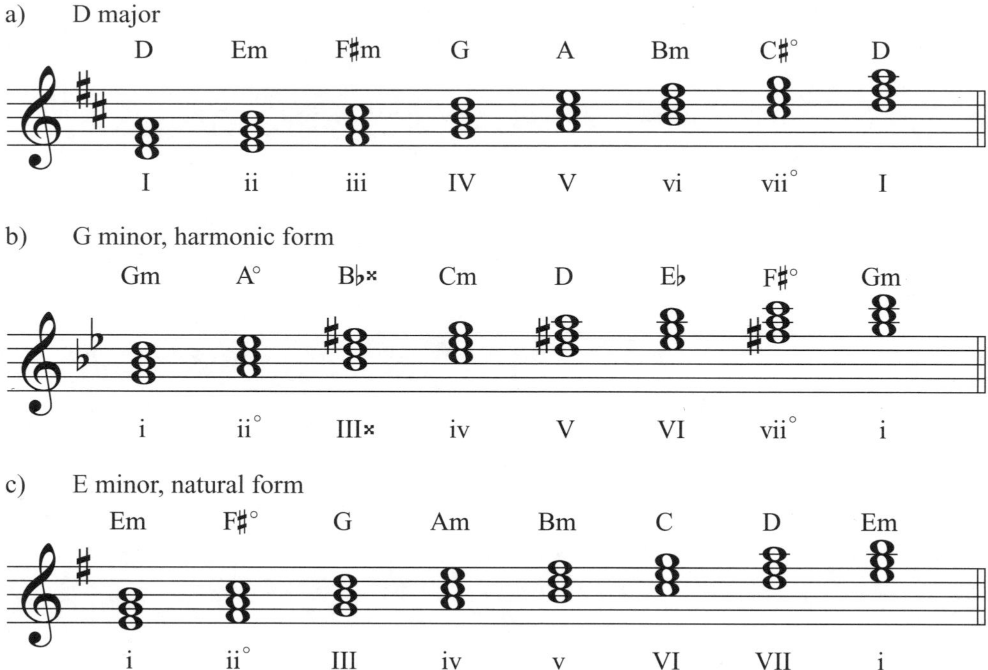

2. Write the root/quality chord symbol for each of the following.

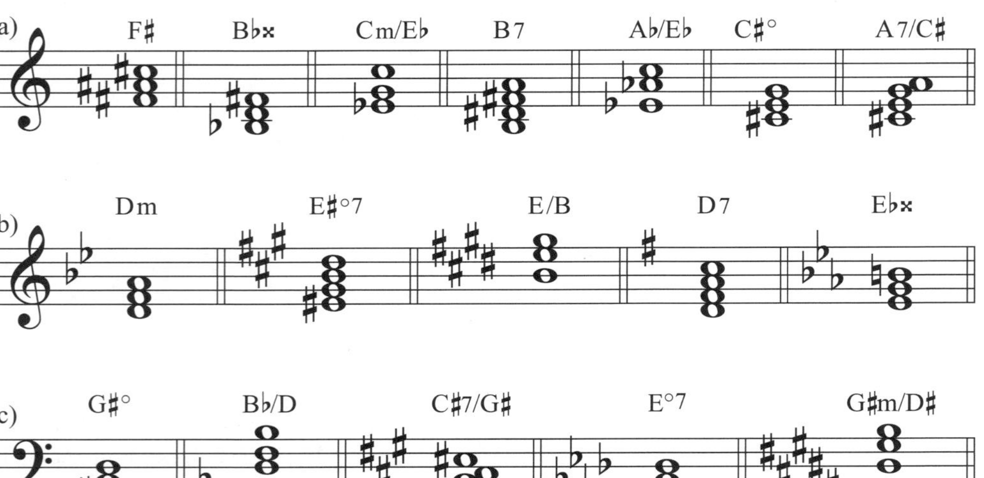

CHAPTER 6

CADENCES AND MELODY WRITING

I A EXERCISES (p. 170)

1. For each of the following, name the key, write the Roman numeral for each chord, and name the cadence.

Example:

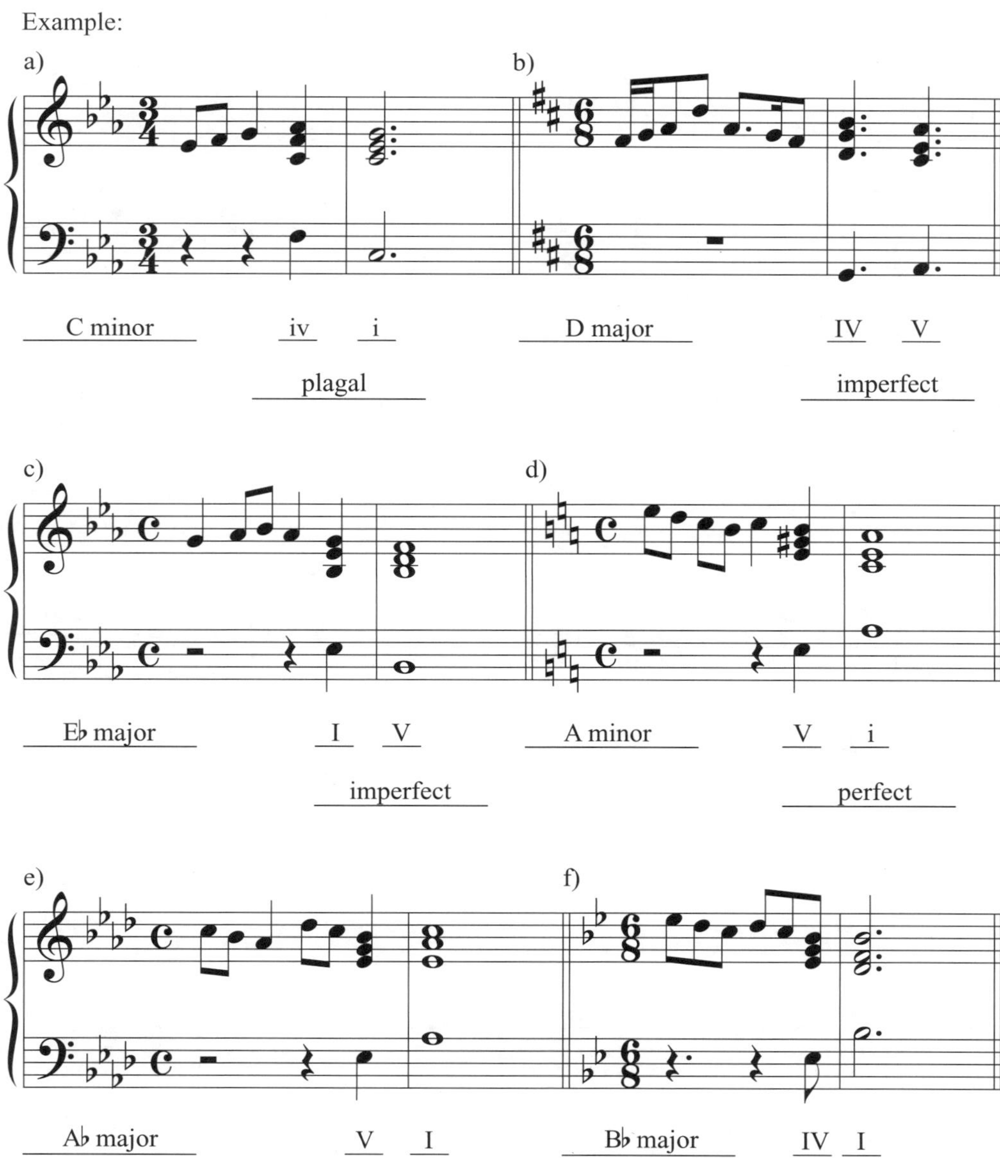

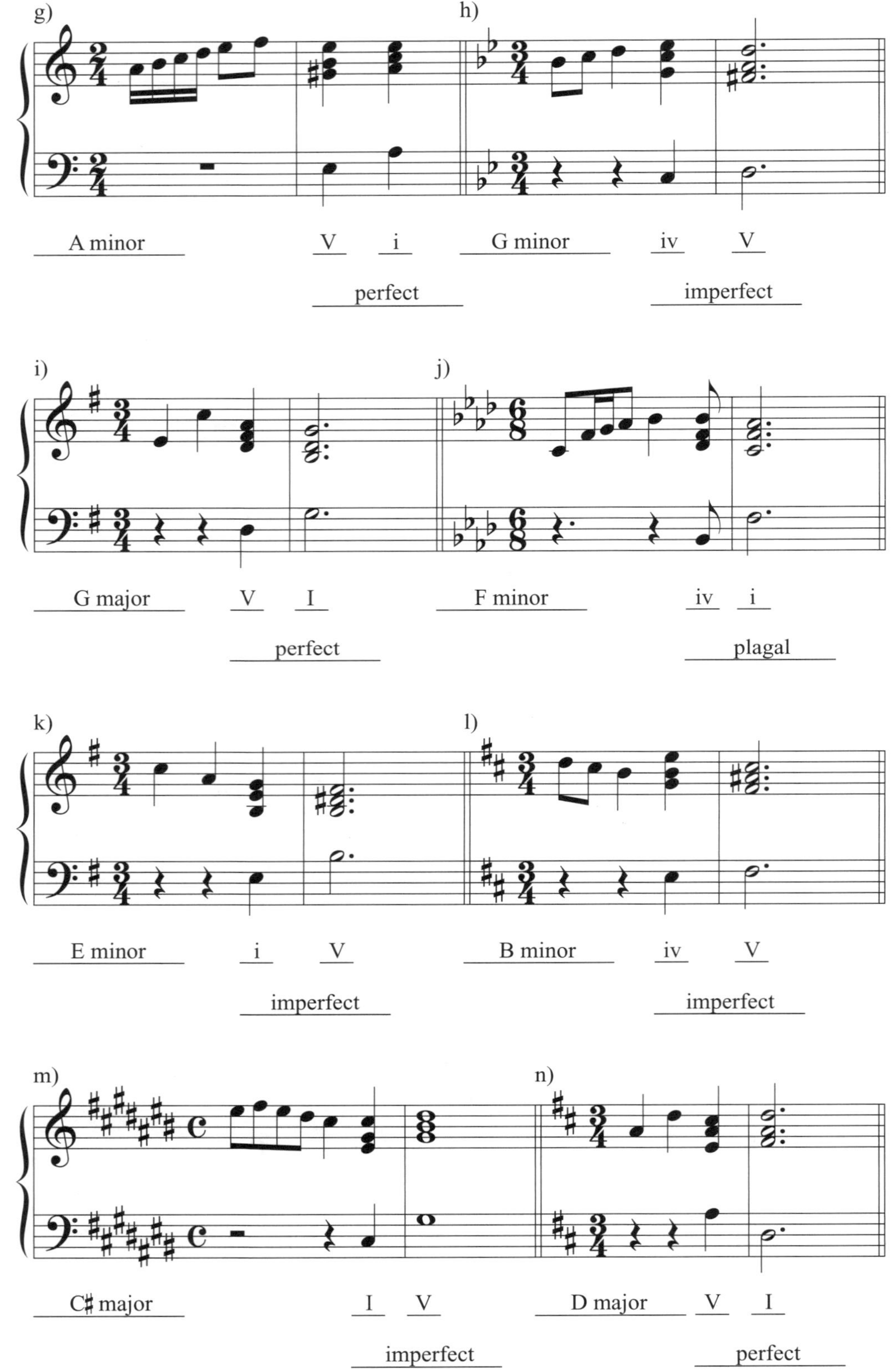
g)
h)
A minor
V
i
G minor
iv
V
perfect
imperfect
i)
j)
G major
V
I
F minor
iv
i
perfect
plagal
k)
l)
E minor
i
V
B minor
iv
V
imperfect
imperfect
m)
n)
C♯ major
I
V
D major
V
I
imperfect
perfect

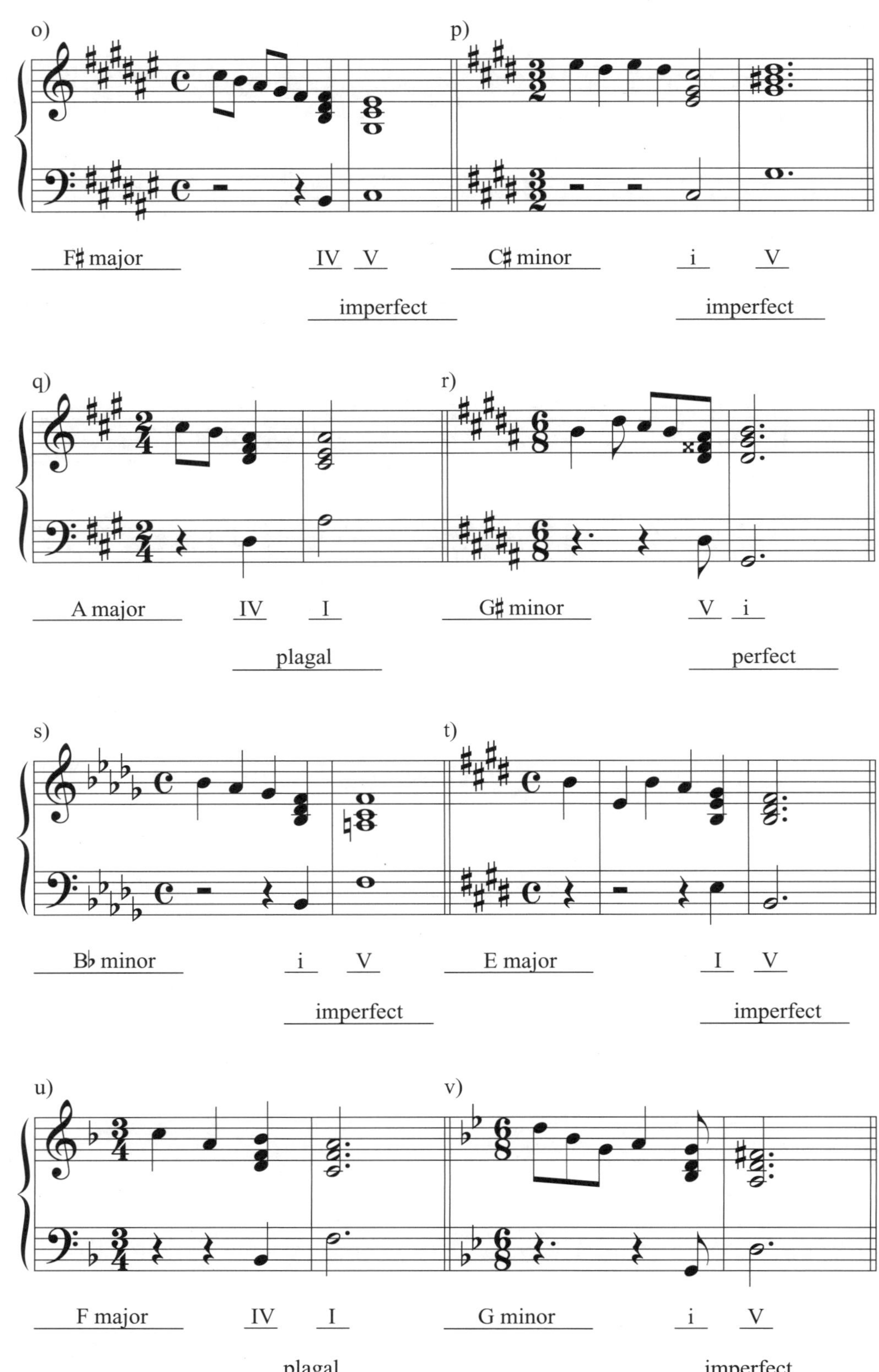
o)
F♯ major
IV
V
imperfect
p)
C♯ minor
i
V
imperfect
q)
A major
IV
I
plagal
r)
G♯ minor
V
i
perfect
s)
B♭ minor
i
V
imperfect
t)
E major
I
V
imperfect
u)
F major
IV
I
plagal
v)
G minor
i
V
imperfect

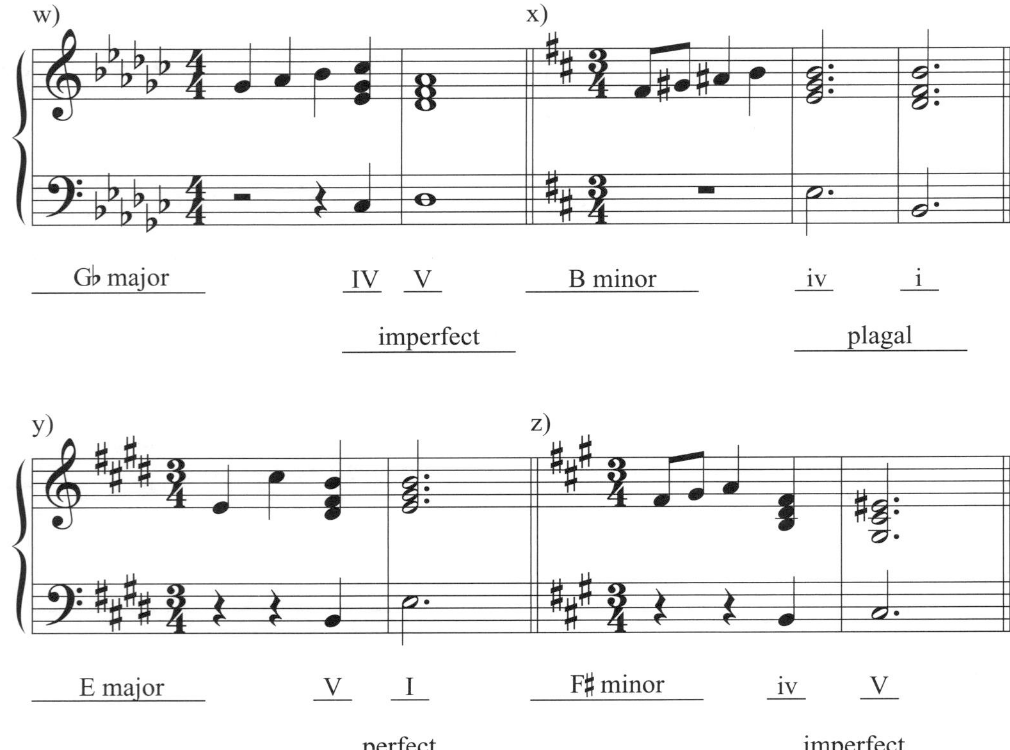
w)
x)
G♭ major
IV
V
B minor
iv
i
imperfect
plagal
y)
z)
E major
V
I
F♯ minor
iv
V
perfect
imperfect

Opt. EXERCISES (p. 177)

1. Write a two-measure example of a perfect cadence in each of the following keys. Use $\frac{3}{4}$ time. (Sample answers. Other arrangements are possible.)

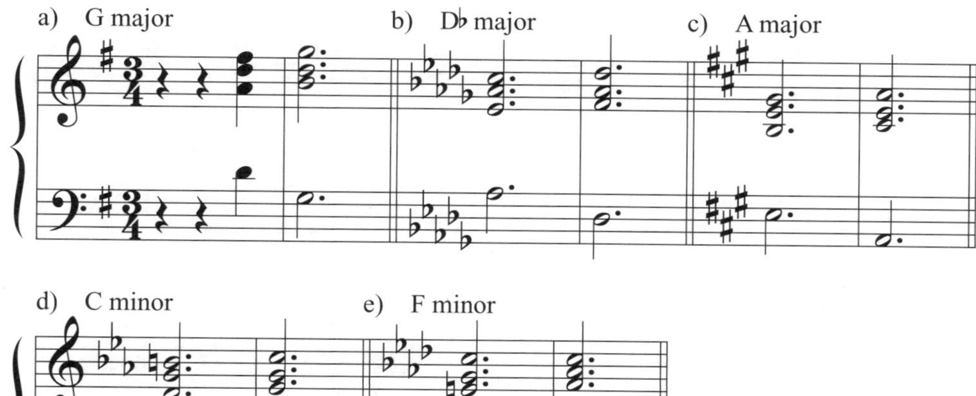

2. Write a two-measure example of a plagal cadence in each of the following keys. Use $\frac{2}{2}$ time. (Sample answers. Other arrangements are possible.)

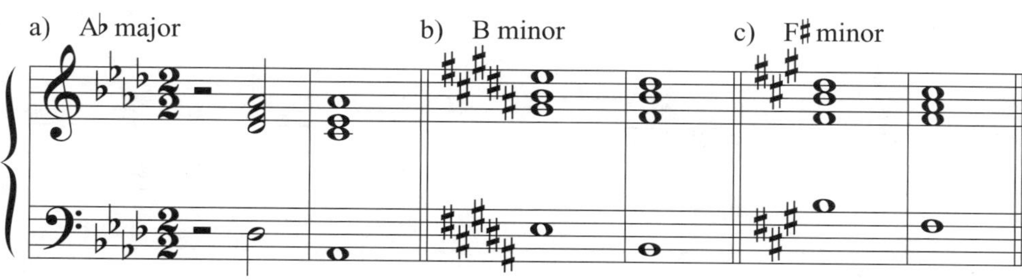

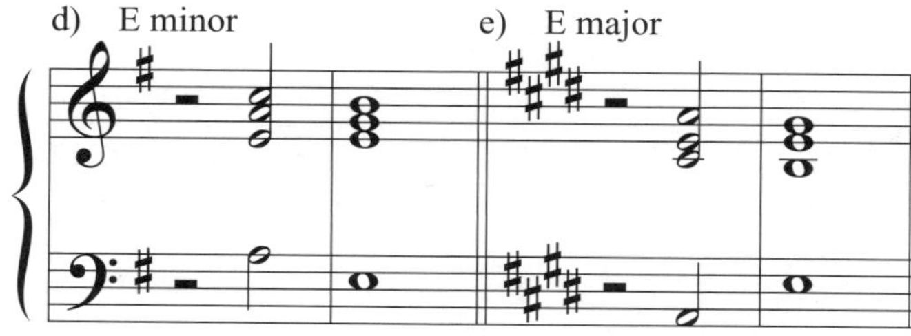

3. In each of the following keys, write one example of an imperfect cadence using tonic to dominant and one example of an imperfect cadence using subdominant to dominant. Use $\frac{2}{2}$ time. (Sample answers. Other arrangements are possible.)

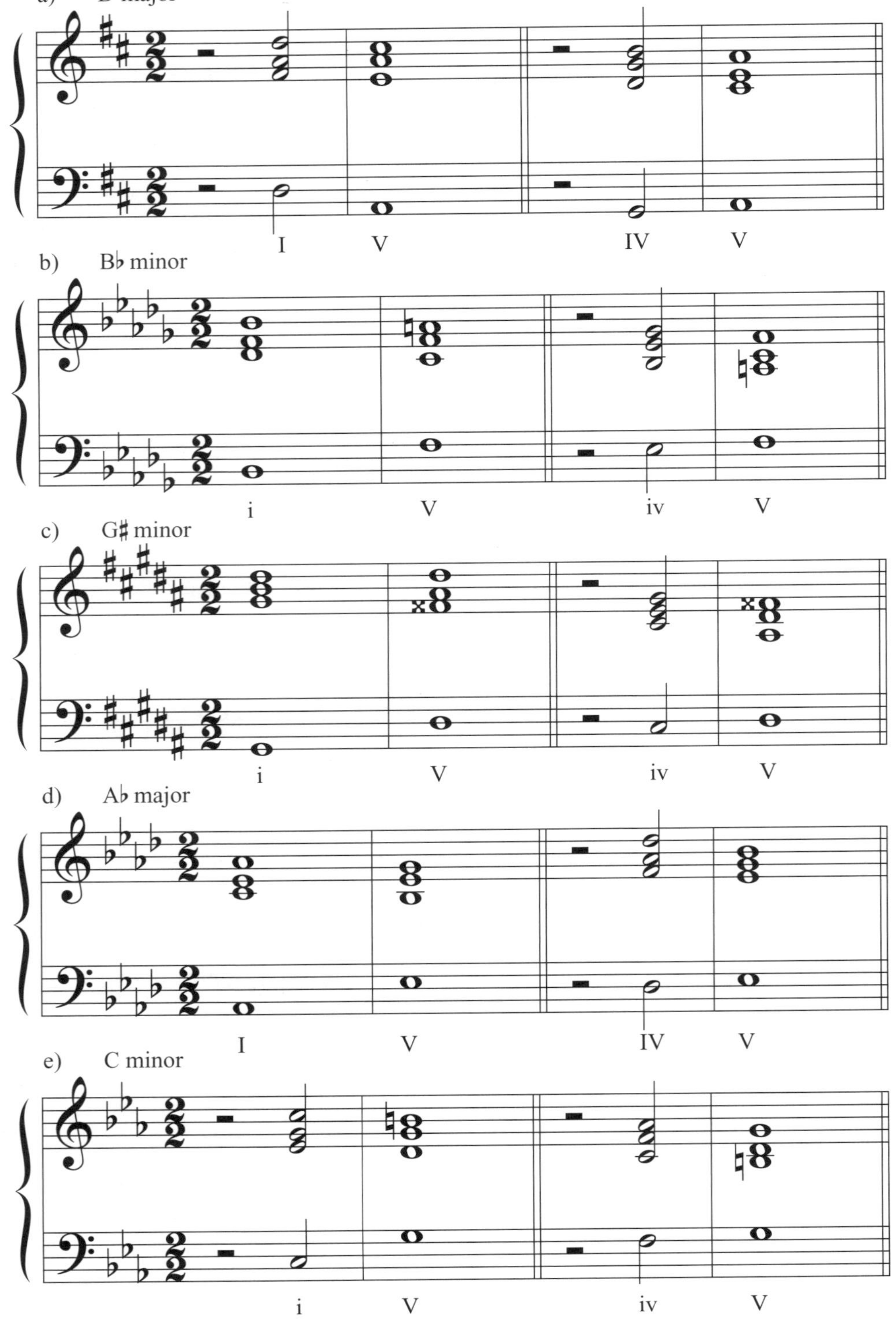

4. Write a two-measure example of each of the three kinds of cadences in each of the following keys. Use $\frac{3}{2}$ time. (Sample answers. Other arrangements are possible.)

a) A major

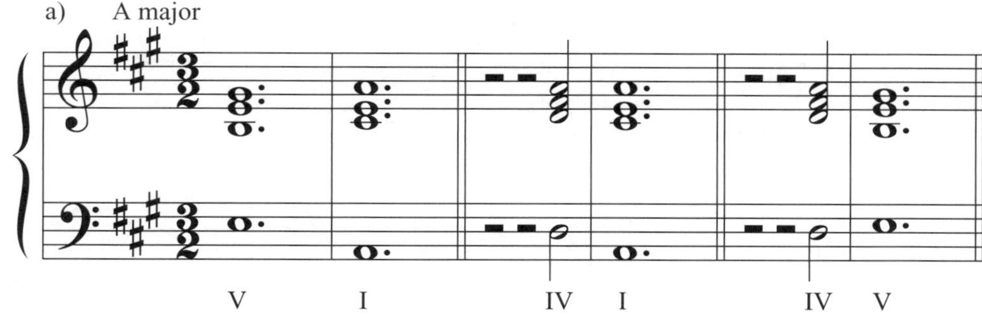

b) G minor

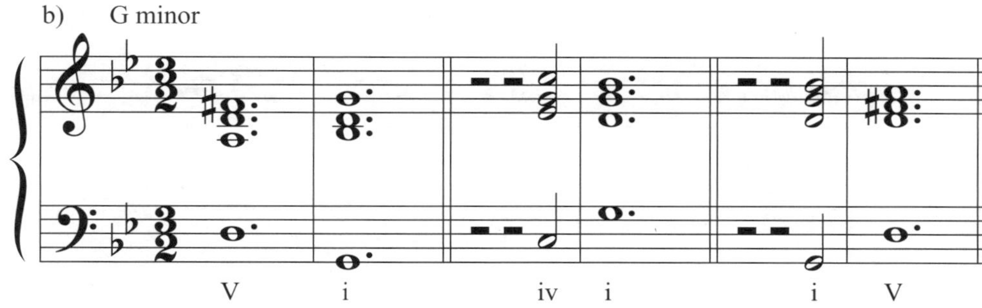

c) E minor

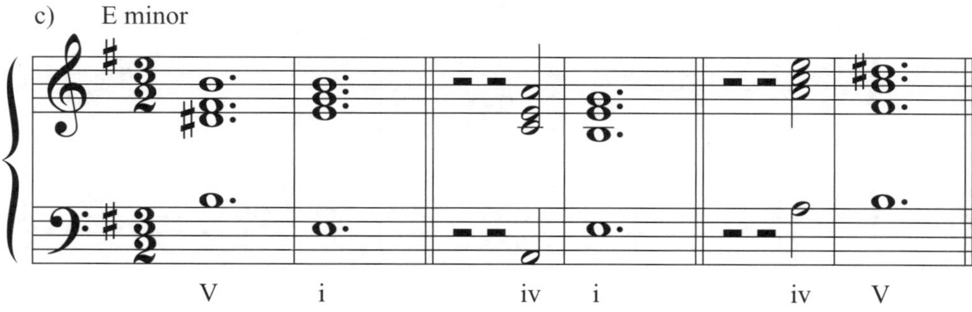

A EXERCISES (p. 183)

1. For each of the following melodic fragments:
    - Name the key.
    - Write a cadence in keyboard style at the end of the fragment.
    - Complete the unused portion of the bass staff with rests.
    - Label the chords with Roman numerals.
    - Name the cadence.

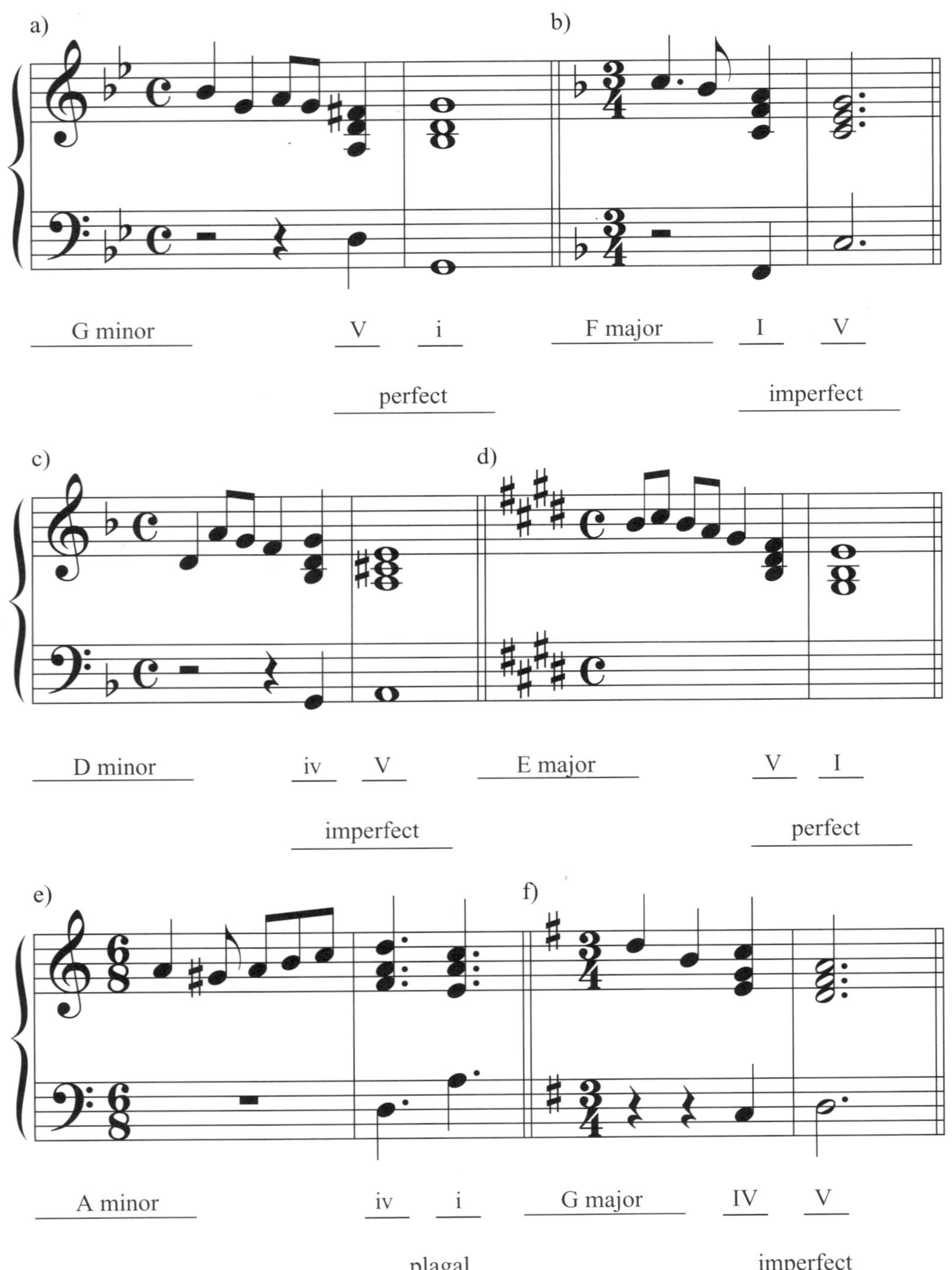

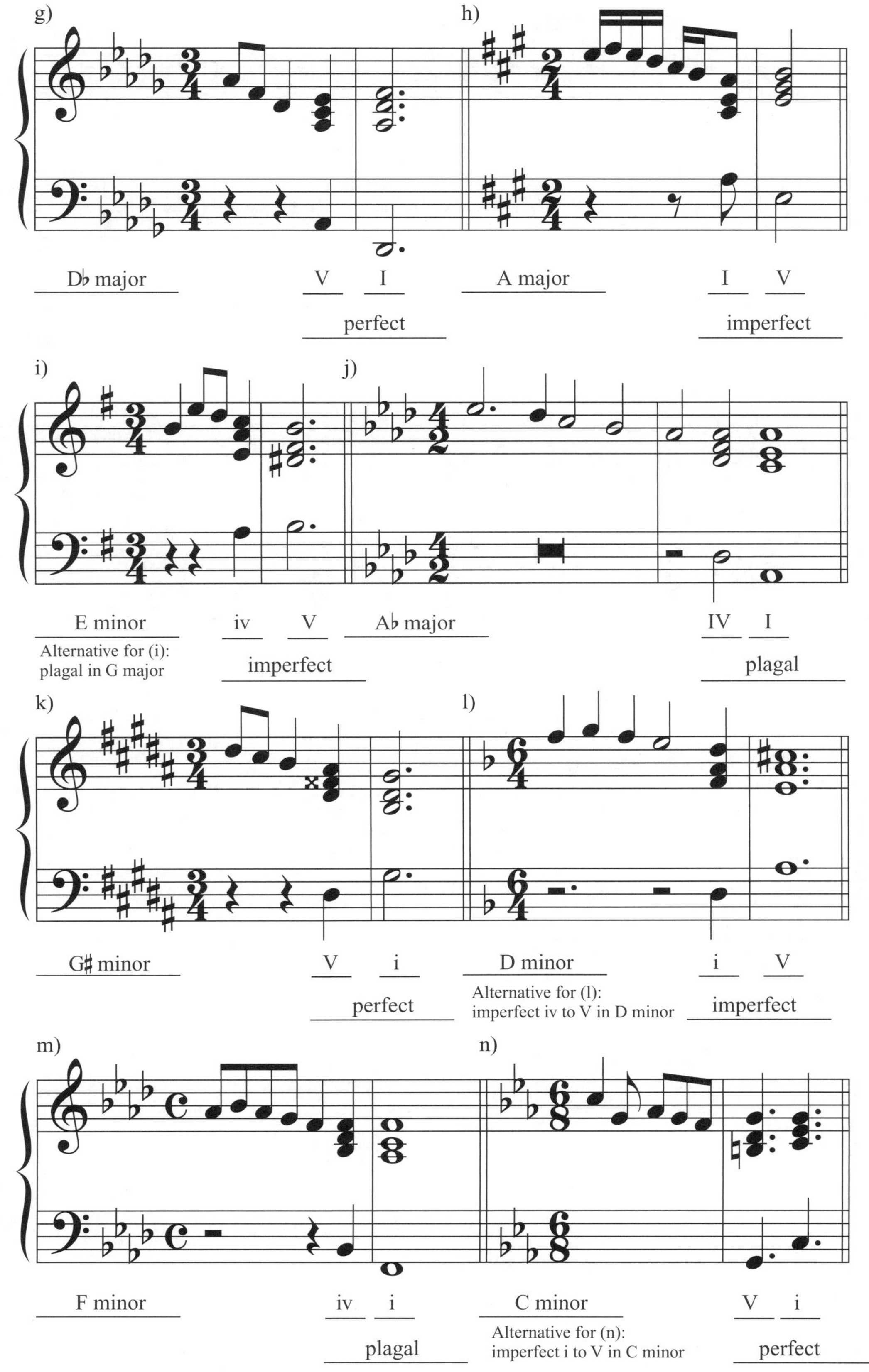

g)
D♭ major
V
I
perfect
h)
A major
I
V
imperfect
i)
E minor
iv
V
imperfect
Alternative for (i):
plagal in G major
j)
A♭ major
IV
I
plagal
k)
G♯ minor
V
i
perfect
l)
D minor
i
V
imperfect
Alternative for (l):
imperfect iv to V in D minor
m)
F minor
iv
i
plagal
n)
C minor
V
i
perfect
Alternative for (n):
imperfect i to V in C minor

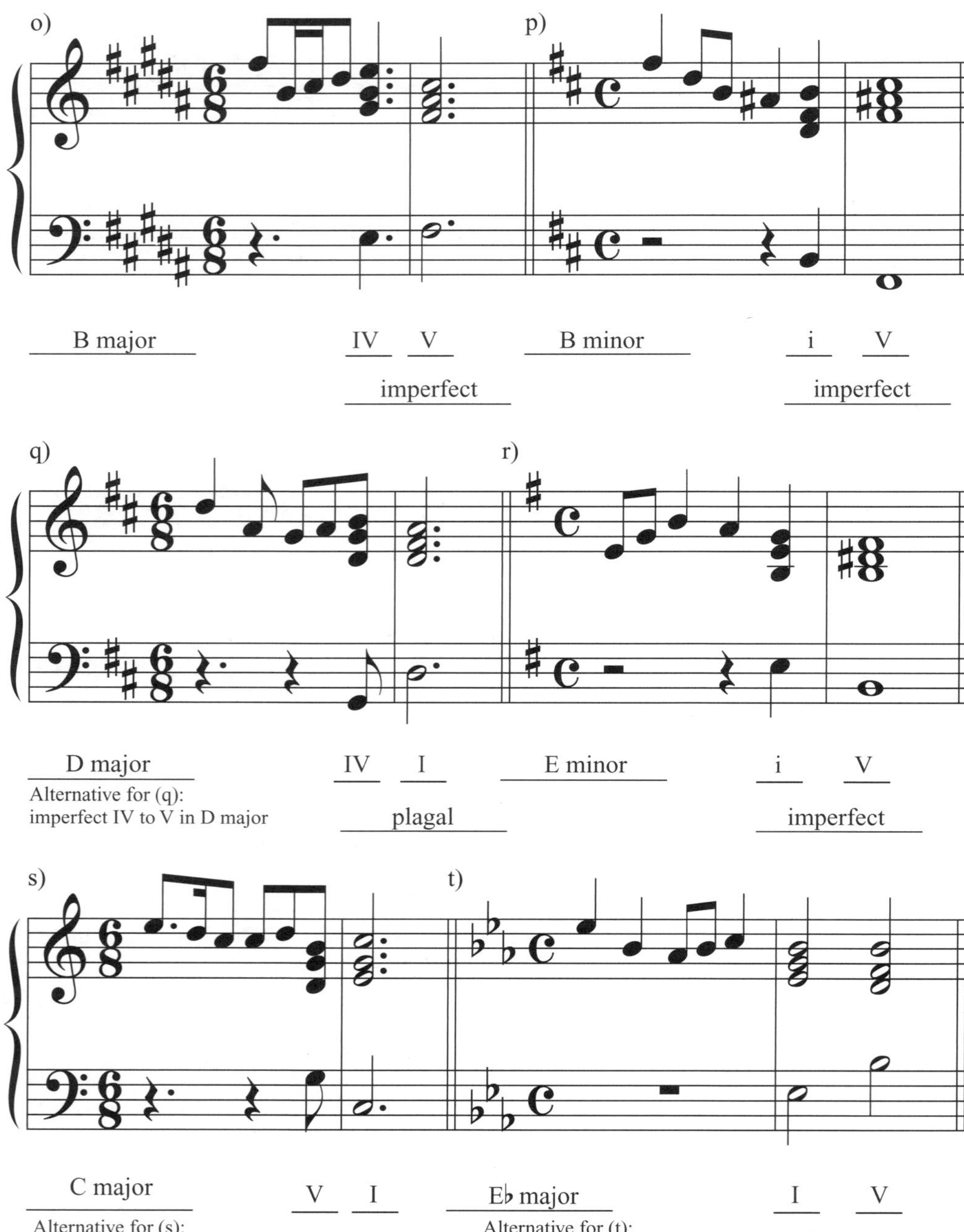
o)
p)
B major
IV
V
imperfect
B minor
i
V
imperfect
q)
r)
D major
Alternative for (q):
imperfect IV to V in D major
IV
I
plagal
E minor
i
V
imperfect
s)
t)
C major
Alternative for (s):
perfect in A minor
V
I
perfect
E♭ major
Alternative for (t):
perfect in E♭ major
I
V
imperfect

Opt. EXERCISES (p. 193)

1. For each of the following:
   - Name the key.
   - Write a cadence at the end of the given phrase and name the cadence.
   - Write an answering phrase for the melody, ending with a perfect cadence.
   - Draw the phrase mark for your answering phrase.

   (Sample answers. Other answers are possible.)

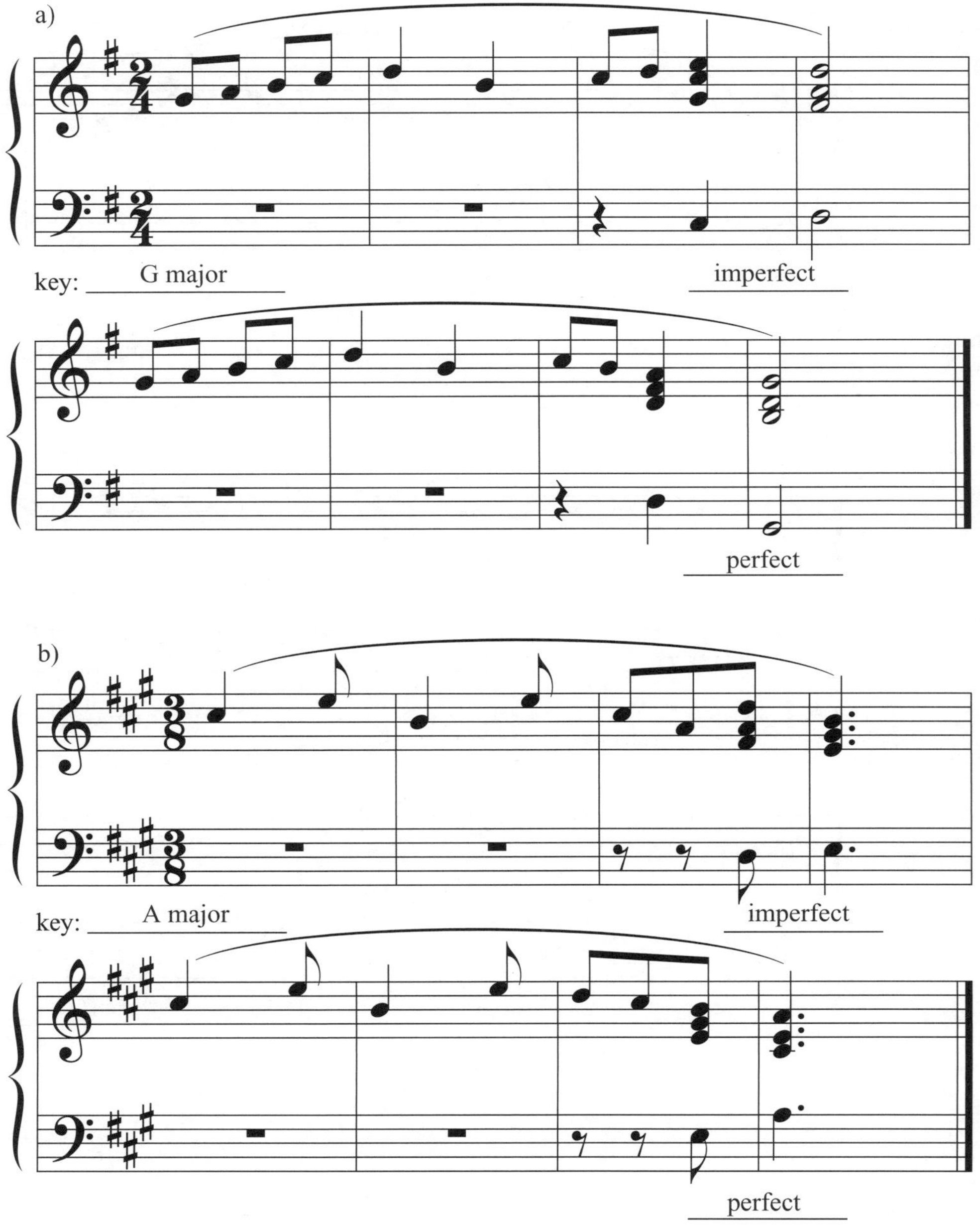

c)

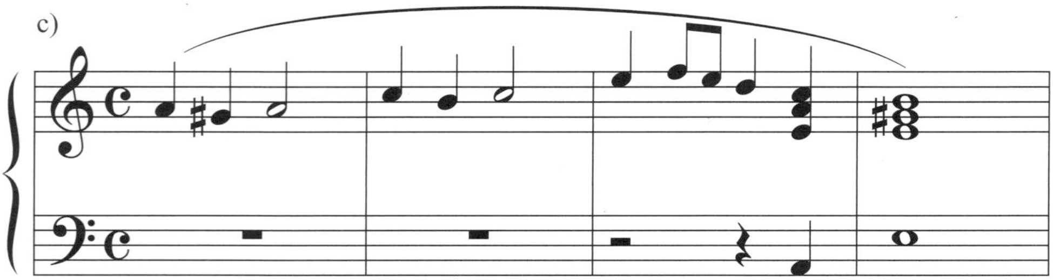

key: A minor

imperfect

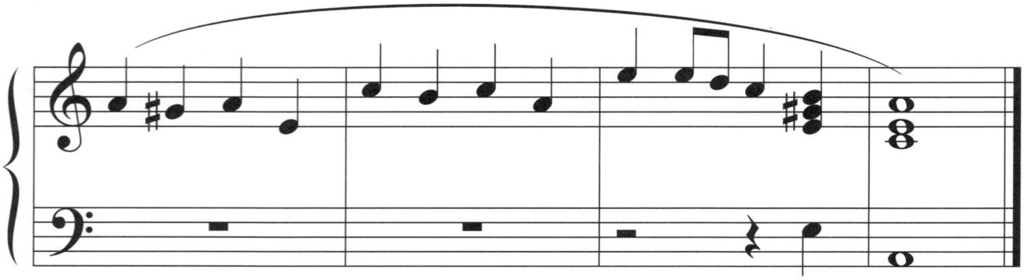

perfect

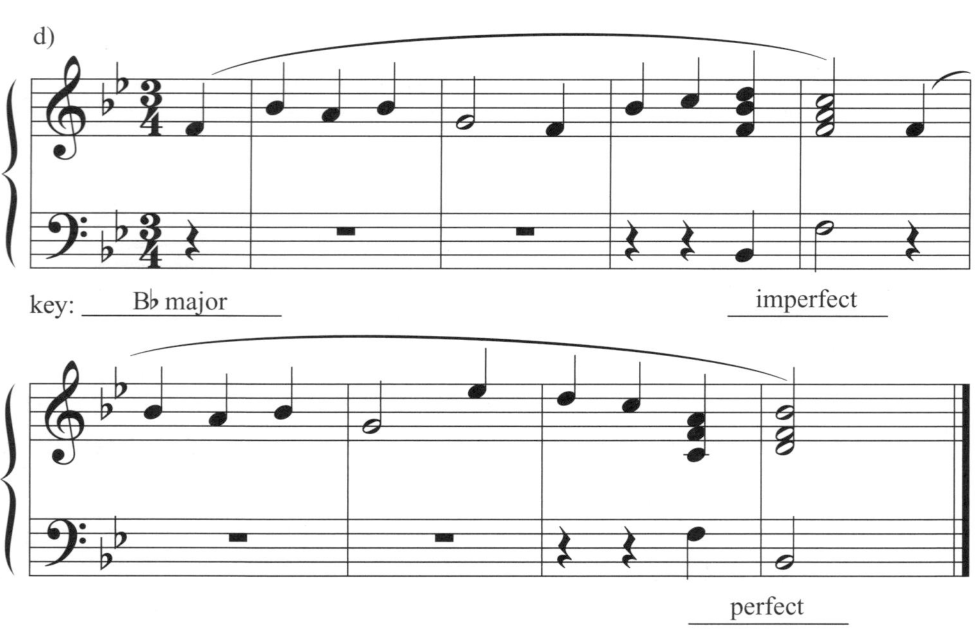

e)

key B minor
imperfect
perfect

f)

key: D minor
imperfect
perfect

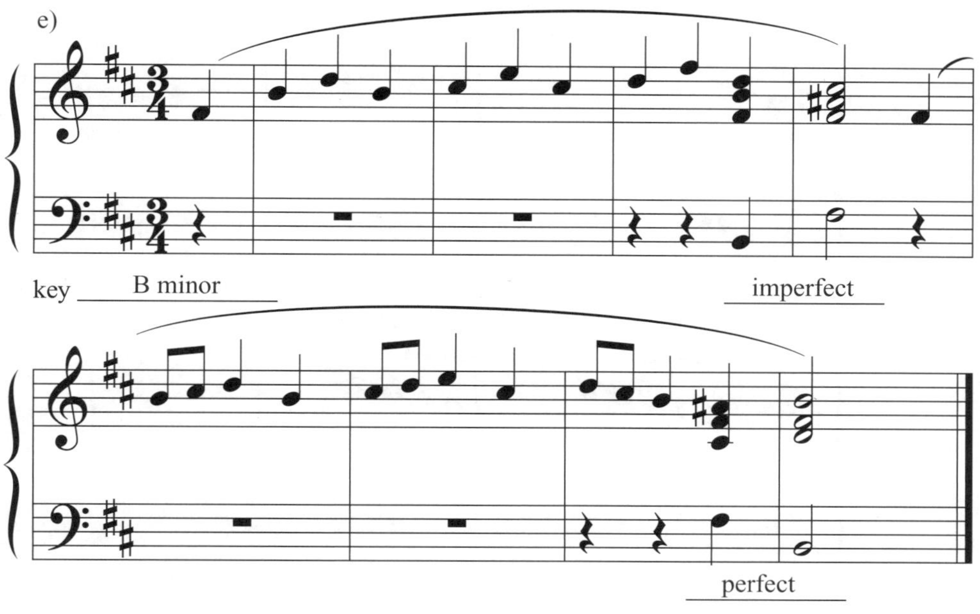

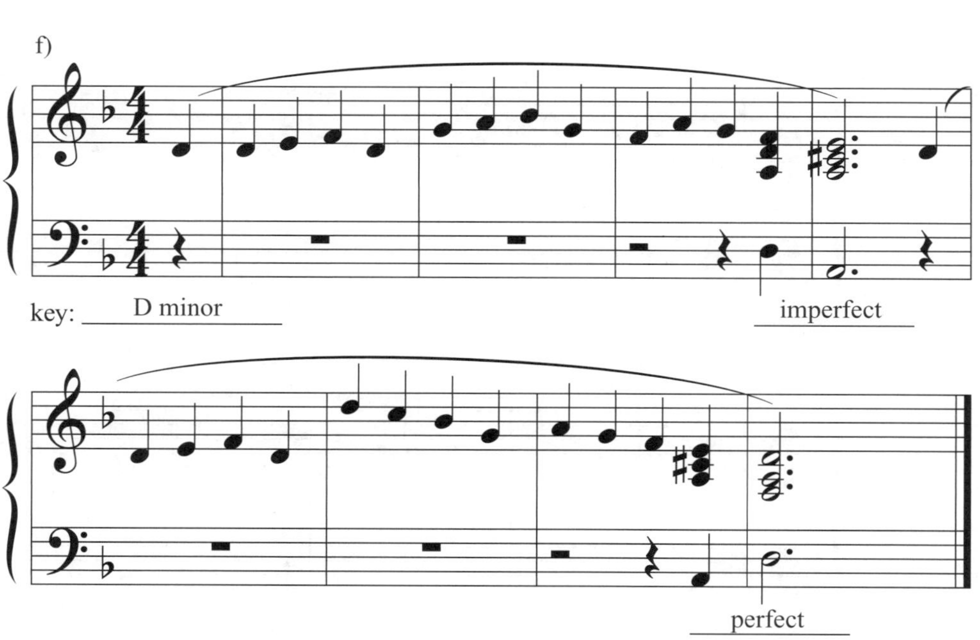

g)

key: F major
imperfect
perfect

h)

key: G major
imperfect
perfect

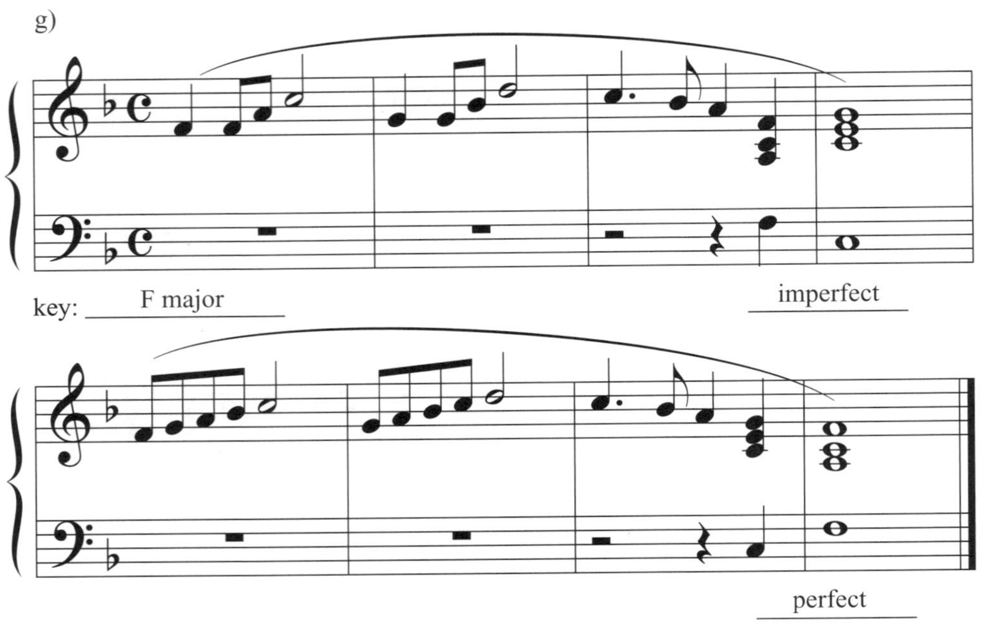

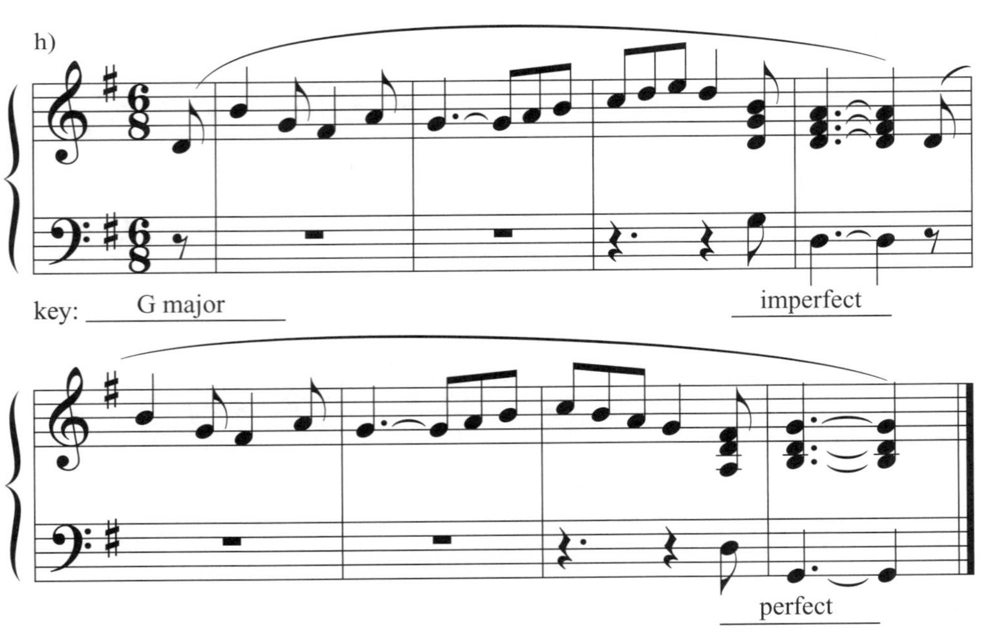

CHAPTER 7

TIME

B I A EXERCISES (p. 201)

1. Write two measures, each using a different rhythm, for each of the following time signatures. (Sample answers. Other solutions are possible.)

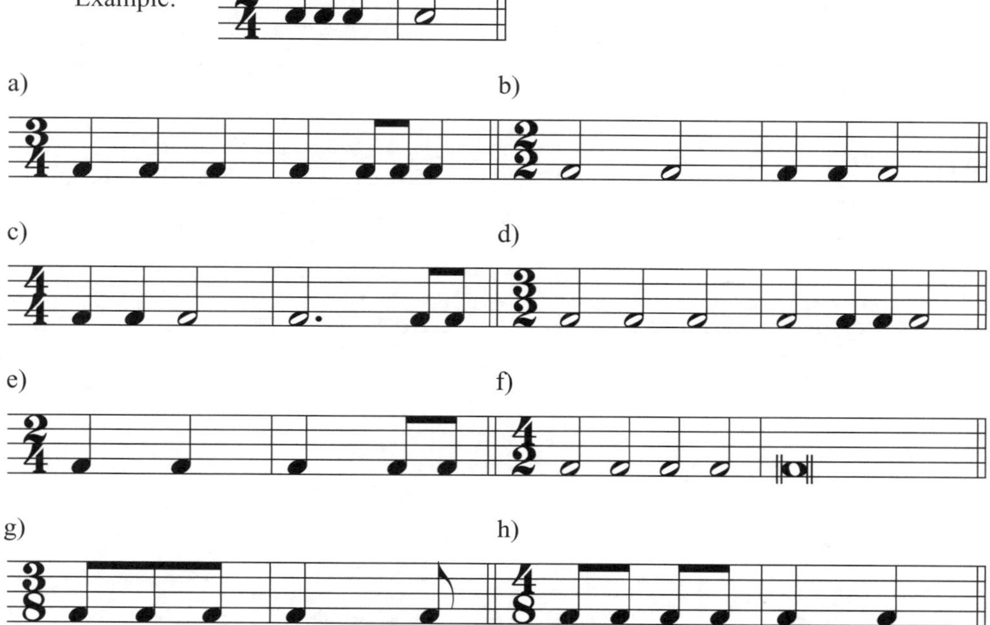

2. Add bar lines to each of the following according to the given time signature.

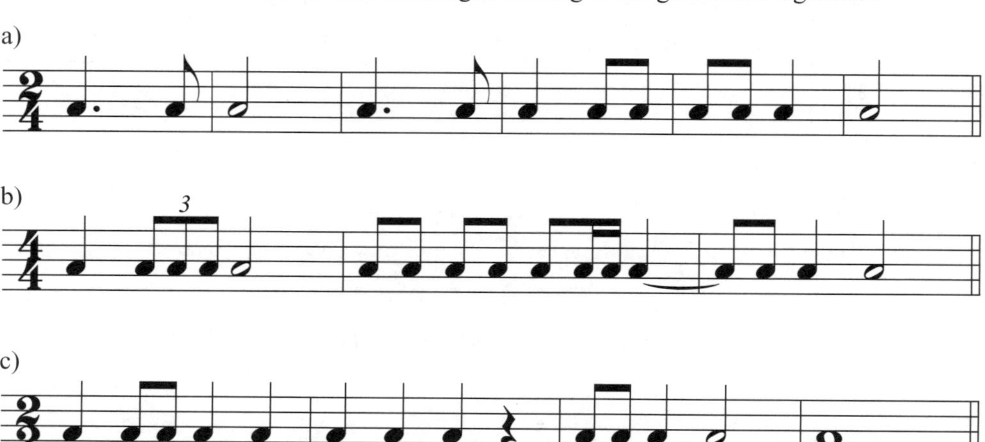

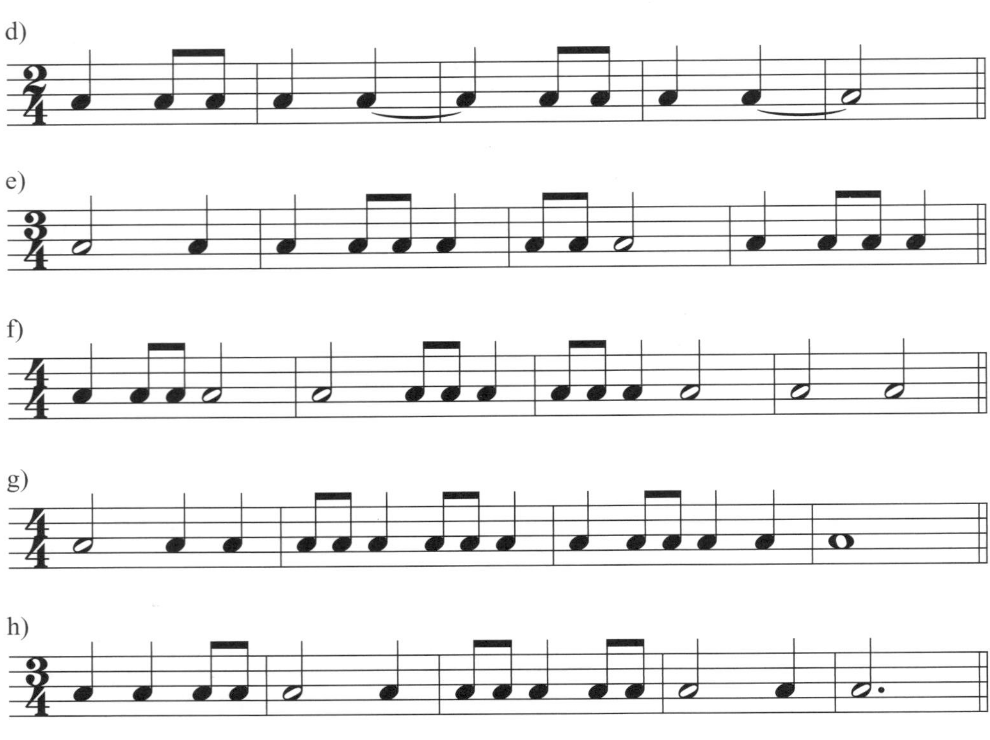

3. Add the correct time signature to each of the following rhythms.

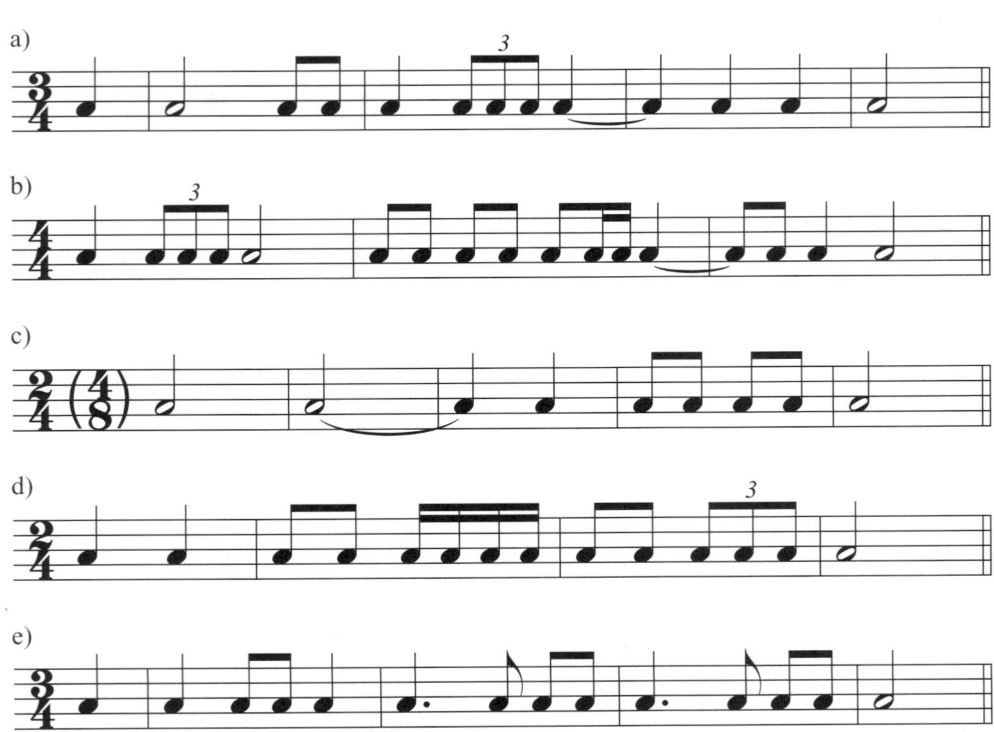

f)

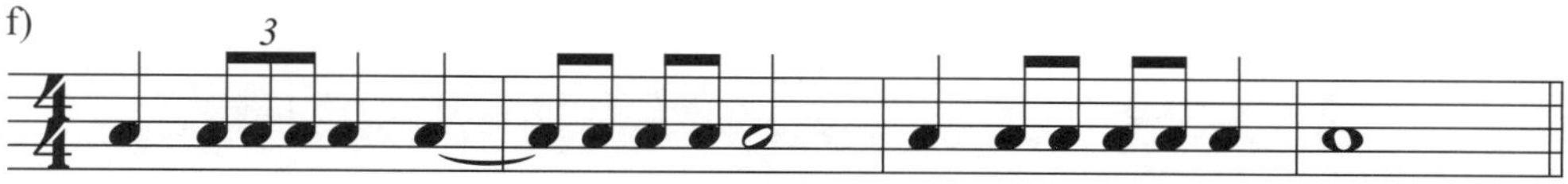

g)

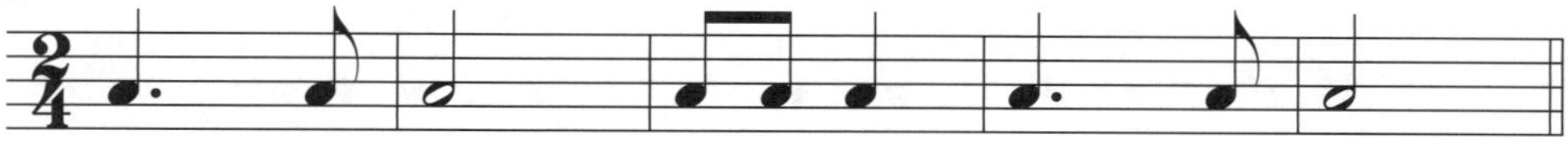

h)

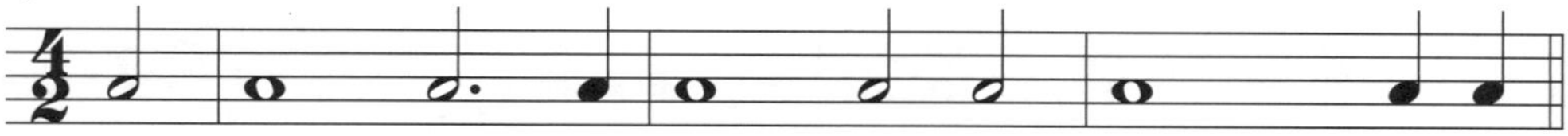

i)

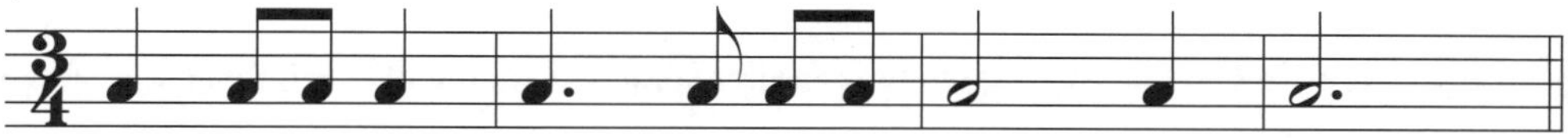

j)

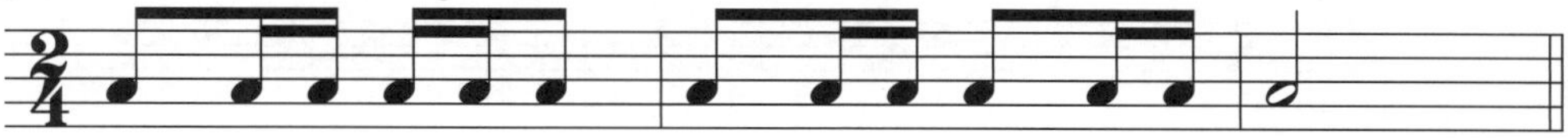

4. Add bar lines to each of the following according to the given time signature.

a)

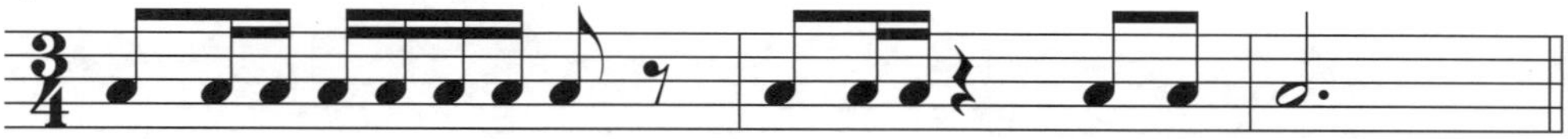

b)

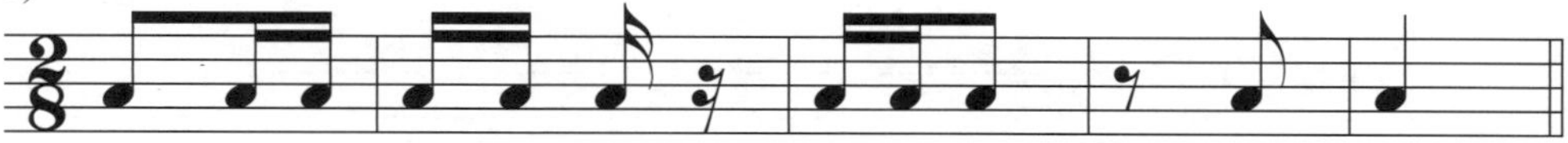

c)

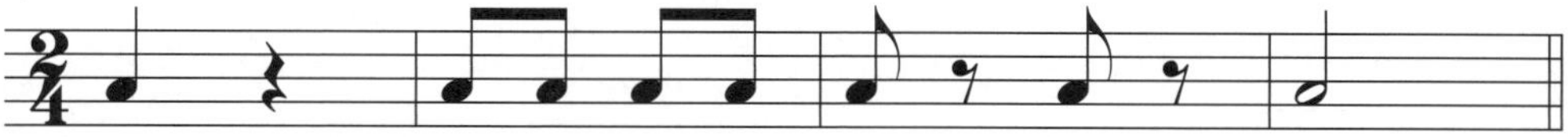

d)

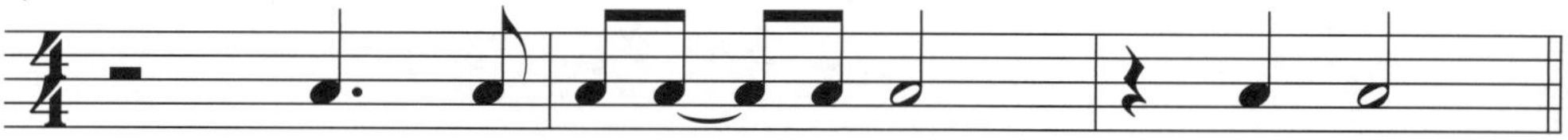

e)

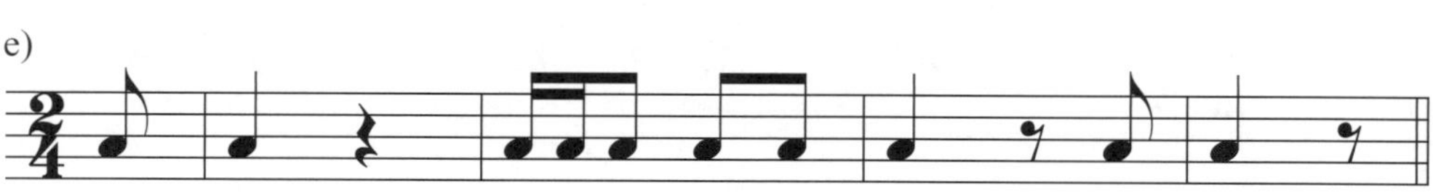

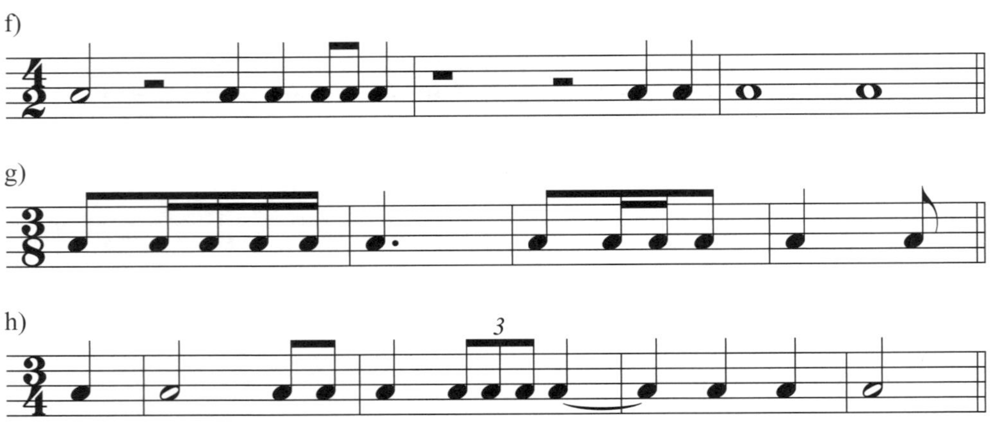

5. Complete the following measures with rests in the places indicated by the brackets.

a)

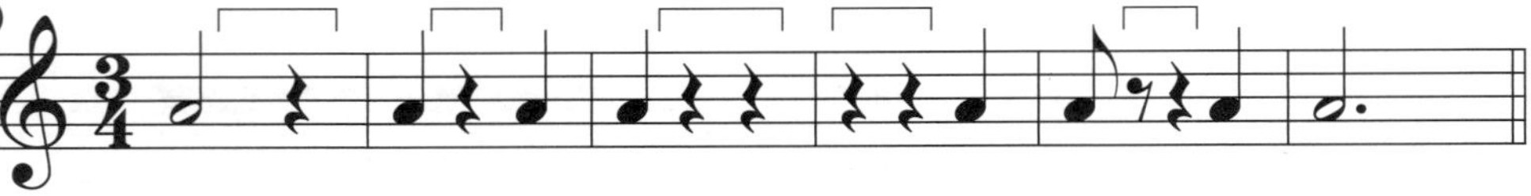

b)

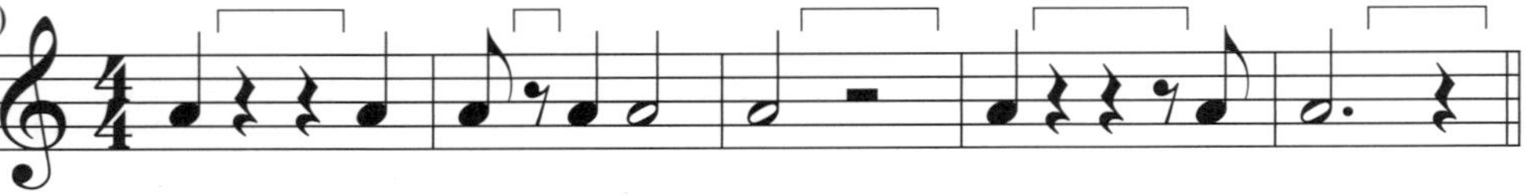

c)

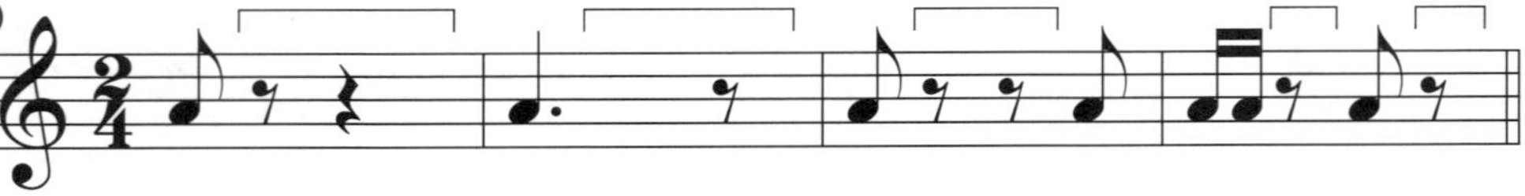

d)

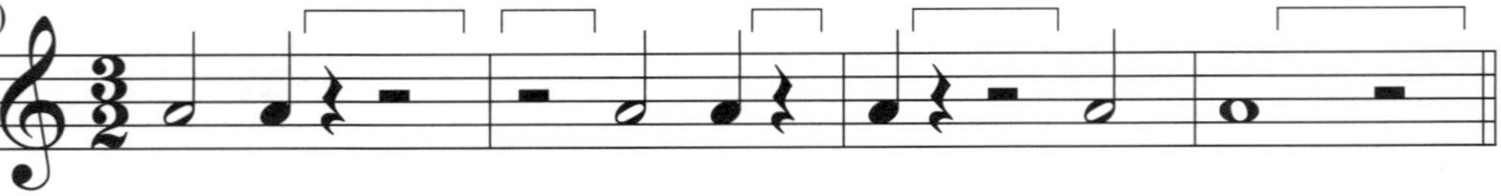

e)

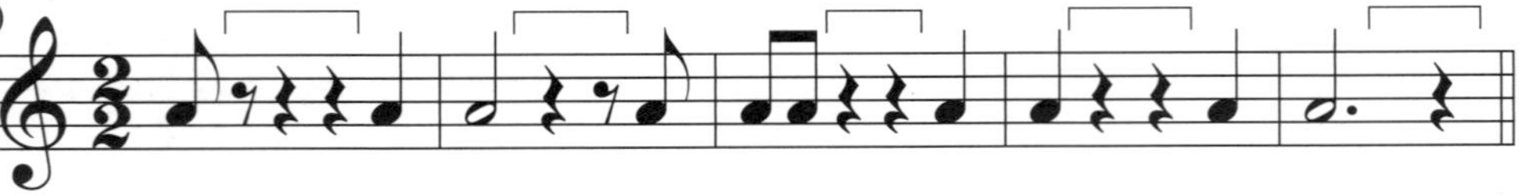

f)

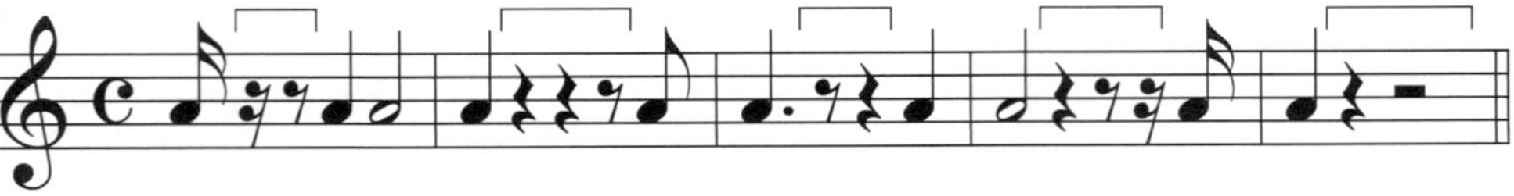

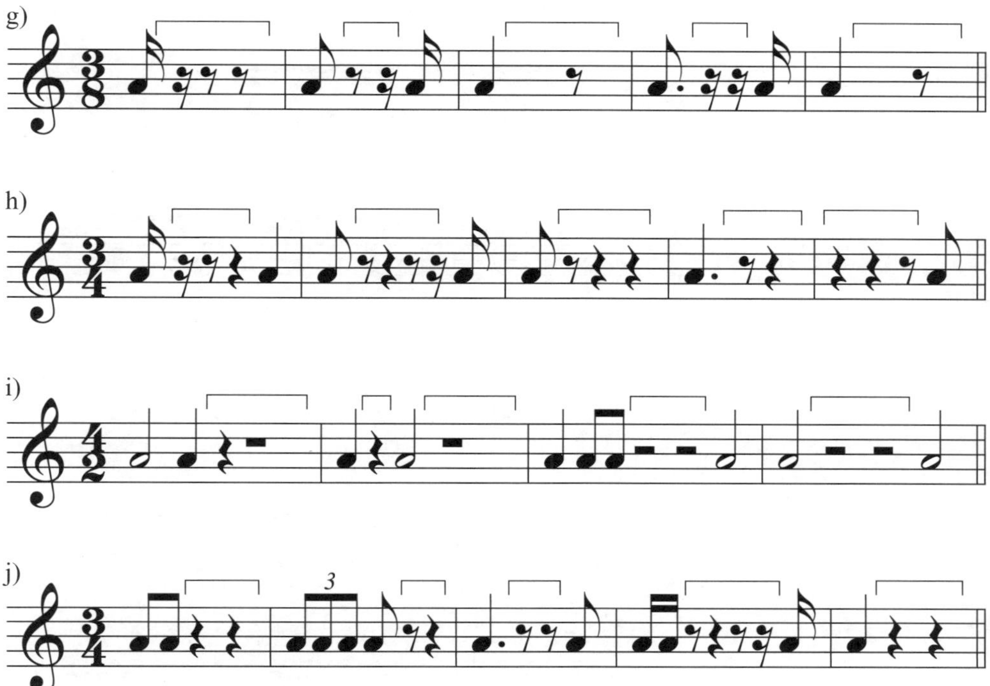

6. Add stems to the following noteheads and group them correctly to make *one* complete measure in each of the following time signatures. (Sample answers. Other groupings are possible.)

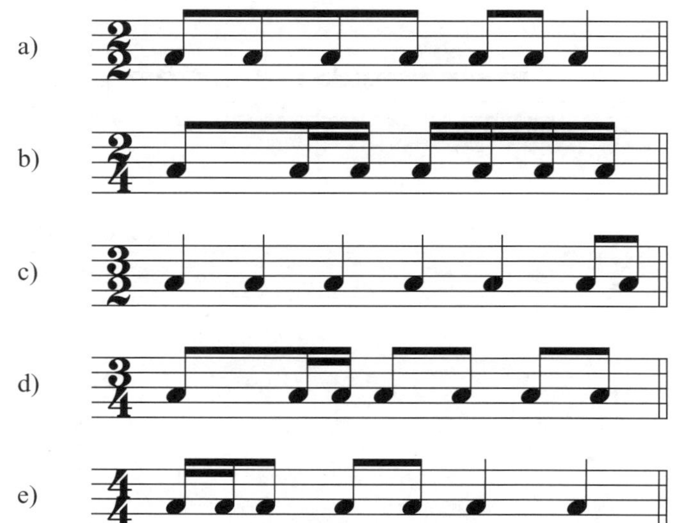

7. Add the correct time signature to each of the following measures.

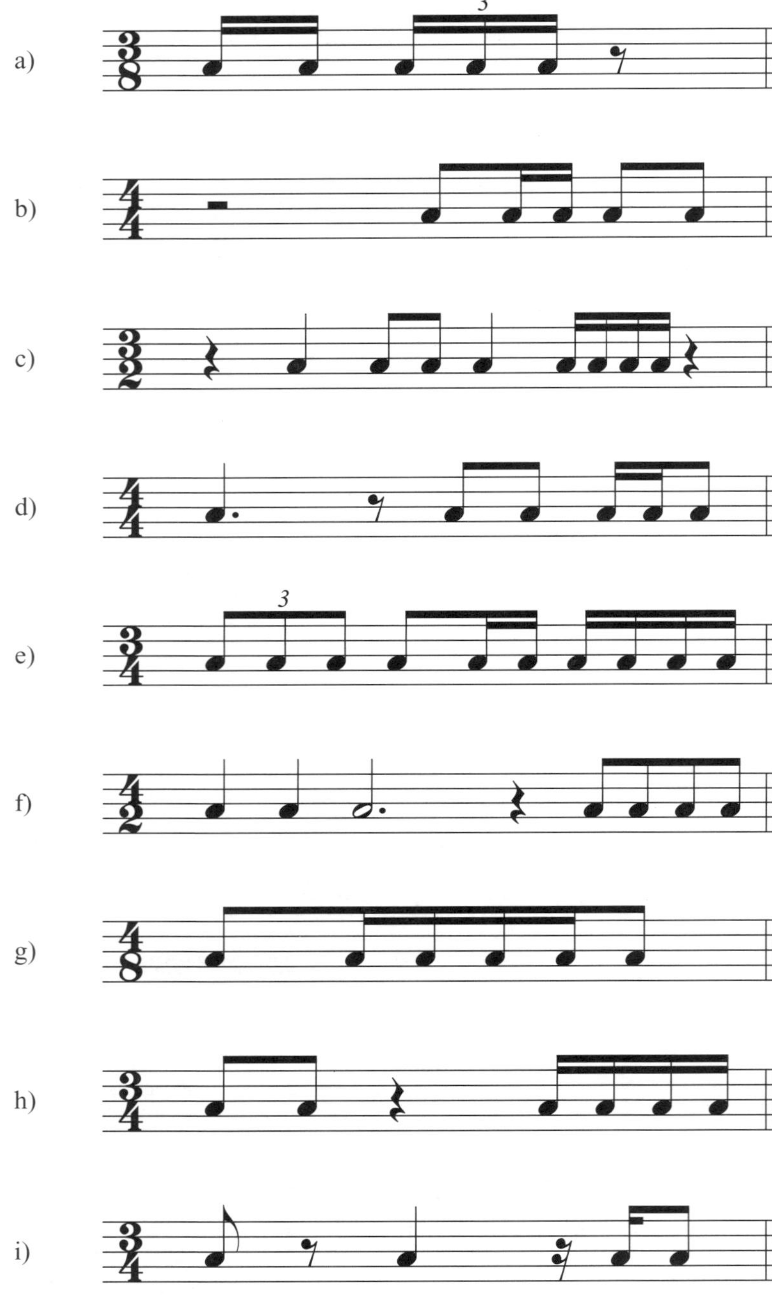

I A EXERCISES (p. 212)

1. Write three measures, each using a different rhythm, in each of the following time signatures. You may use dotted notes but not rests. (Sample answers. Other rhythms are possible.)

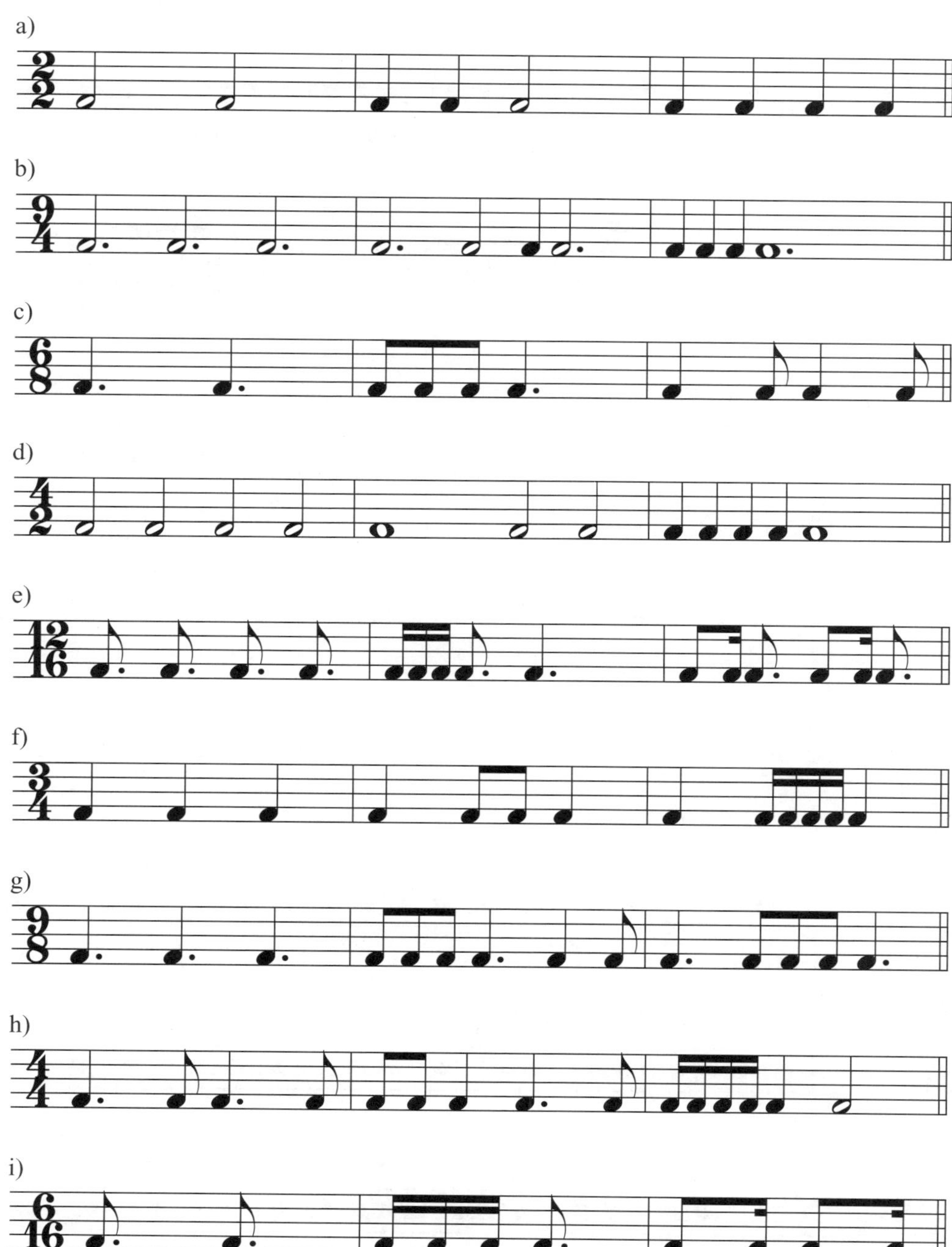

2. Add bar lines to each of the following according to the given time signatures.

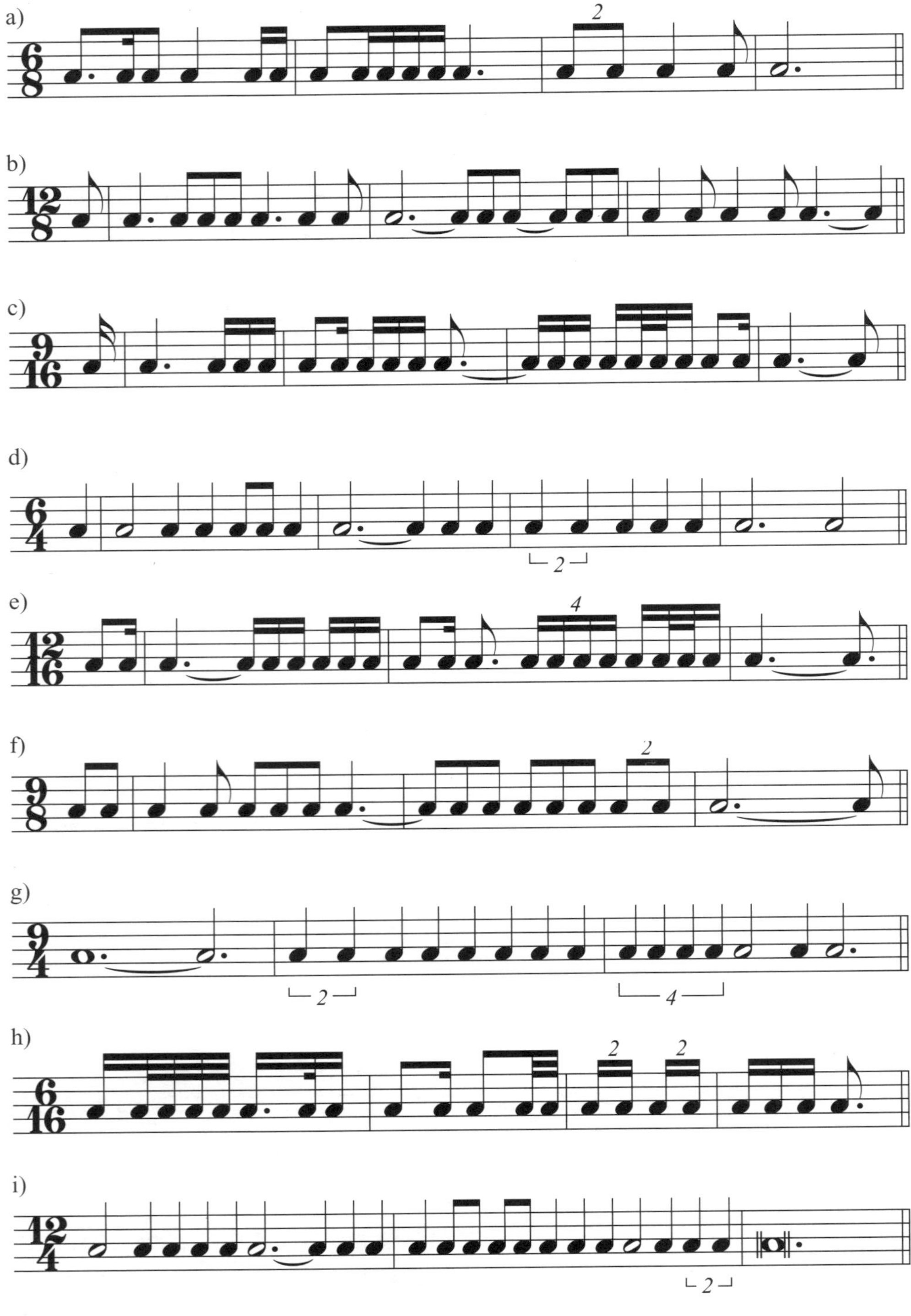

3. Add the correct time signature to each of the following measures.

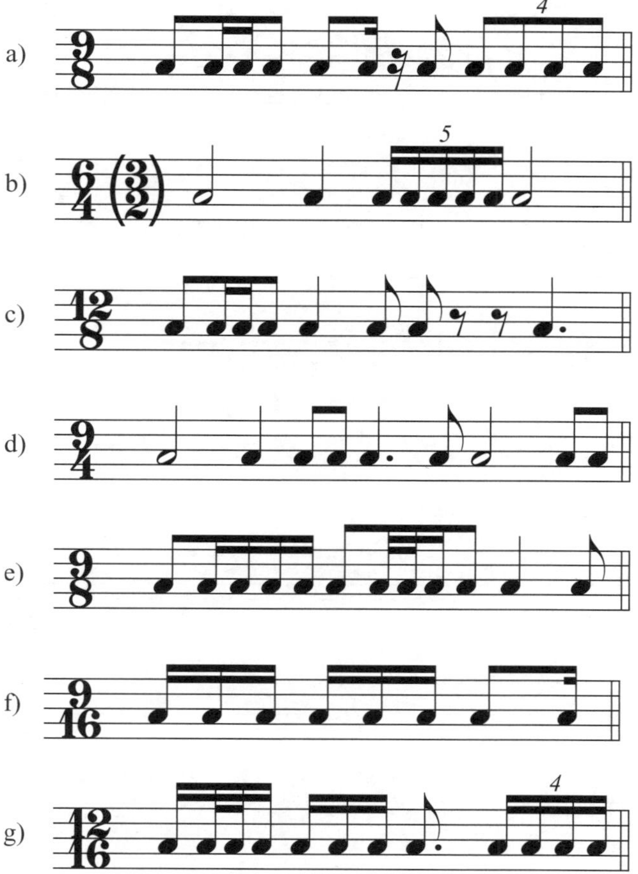

4. Add stems to the following noteheads and group them correctly to make *one* complete measure in each of the following time signatures. (Sample answers. Other groupings are possible.)

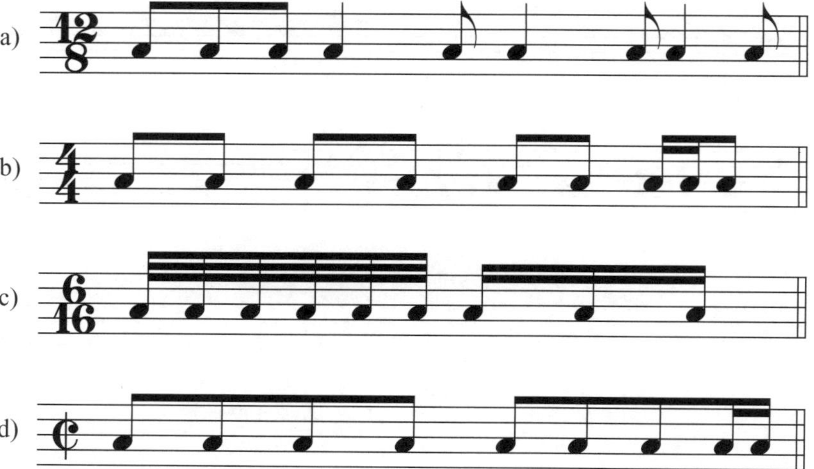

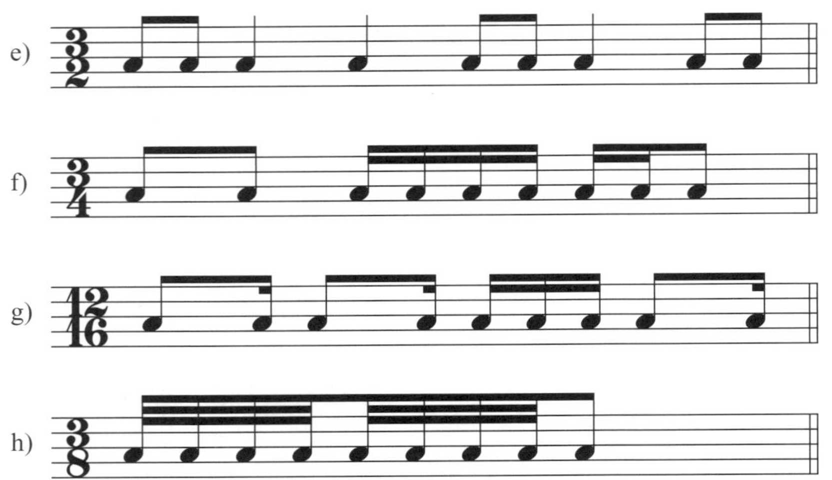

5. Complete the following measures with rests in the places indicated by the brackets.

a)

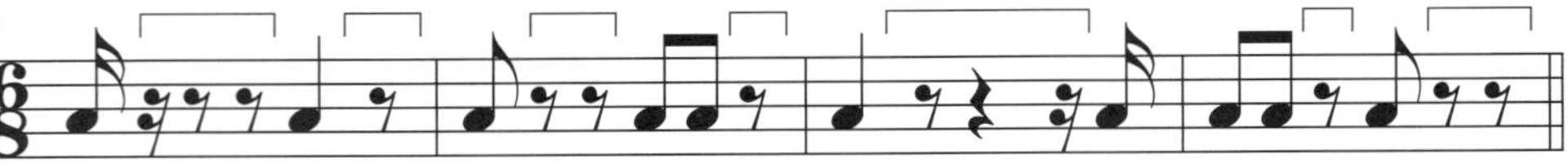

b)

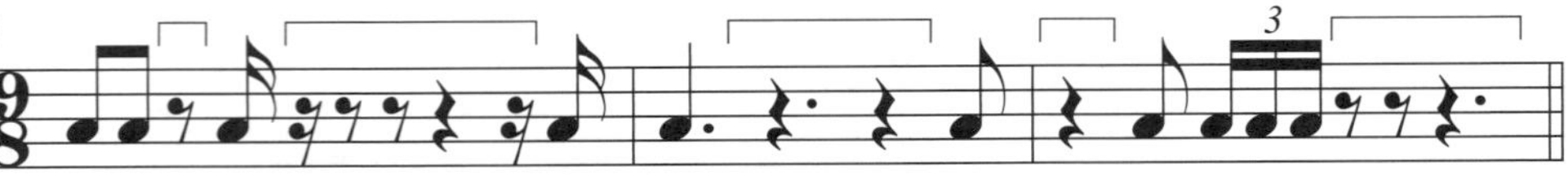

c)

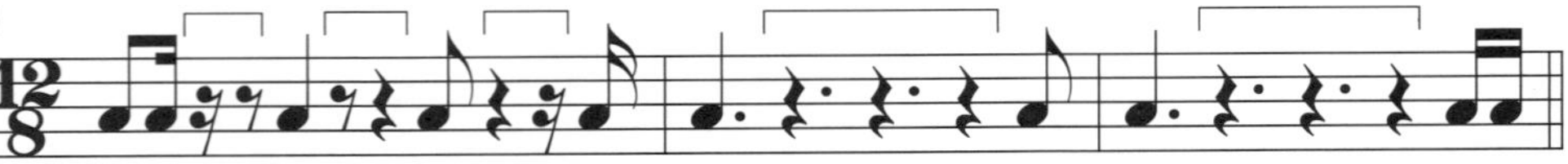

d)

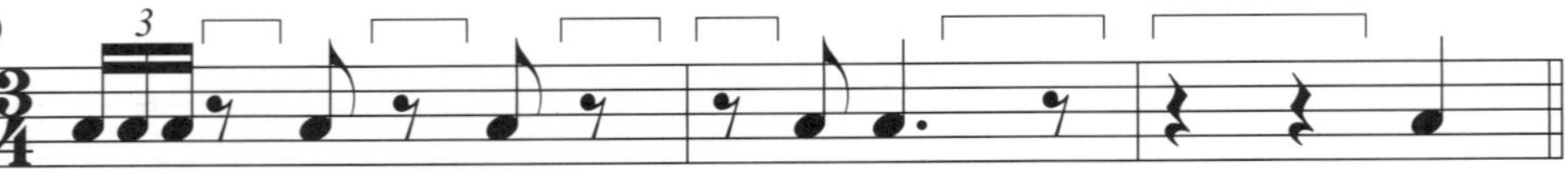

e)

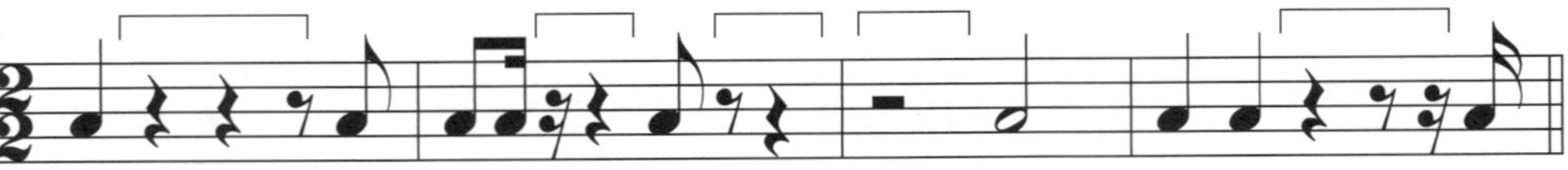

f)

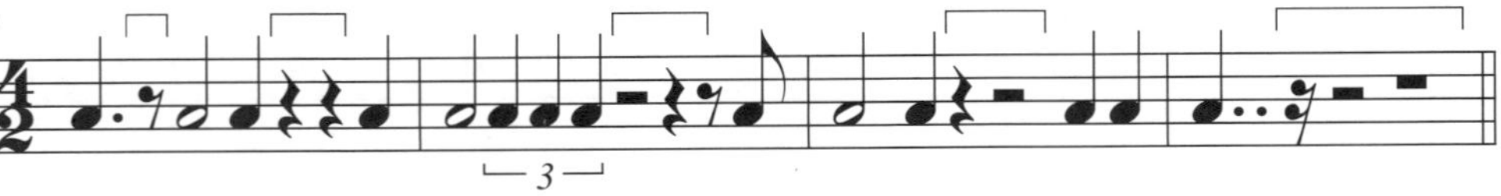

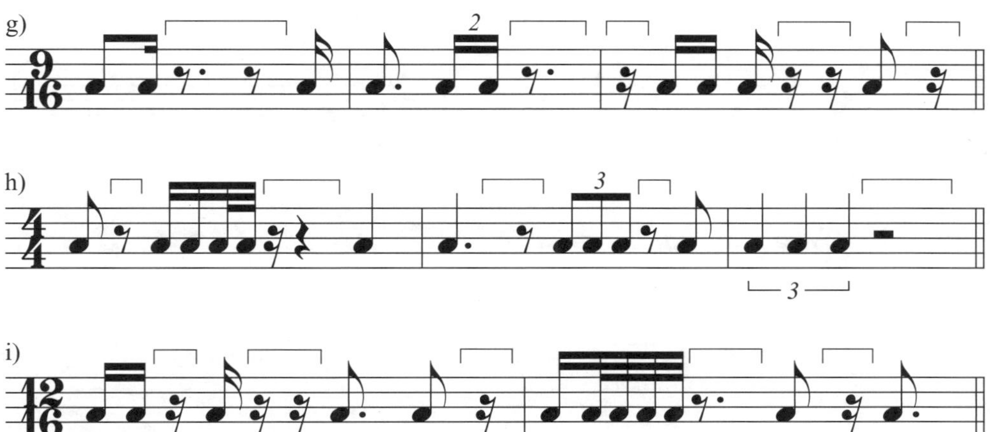

6. Re-group the following in $\frac{6}{8}$ time.

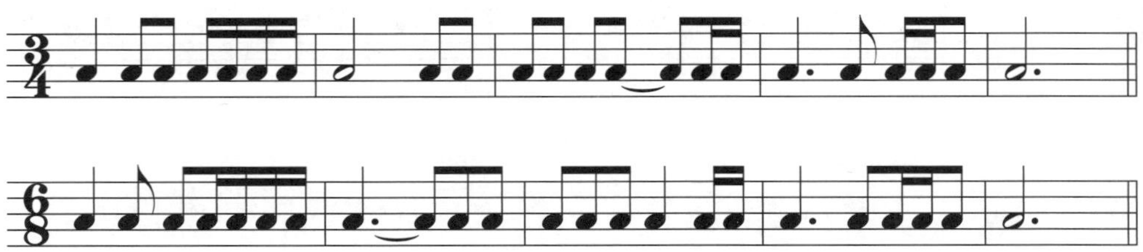

7. Re-group the following in $\frac{3}{4}$ time.

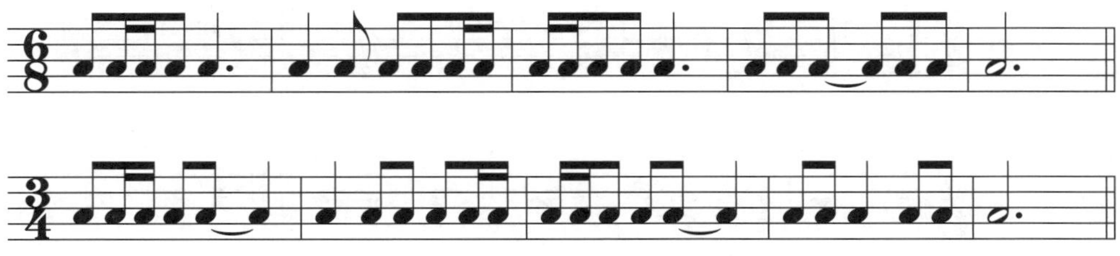

8. a) What is the difference between $\frac{6}{8}$ time and $\frac{3}{4}$ time?

The difference is: $\frac{6}{8}$ time has 2 groups of 3 eighths per measure,

$\frac{3}{4}$ time has 3 groups of 2 eighths per measure.

b) Write one measure of each, grouping the notes correctly.

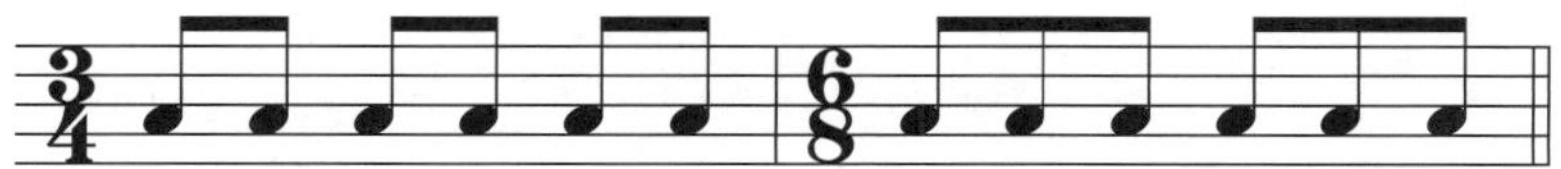

9. Complete the following measures with rests.

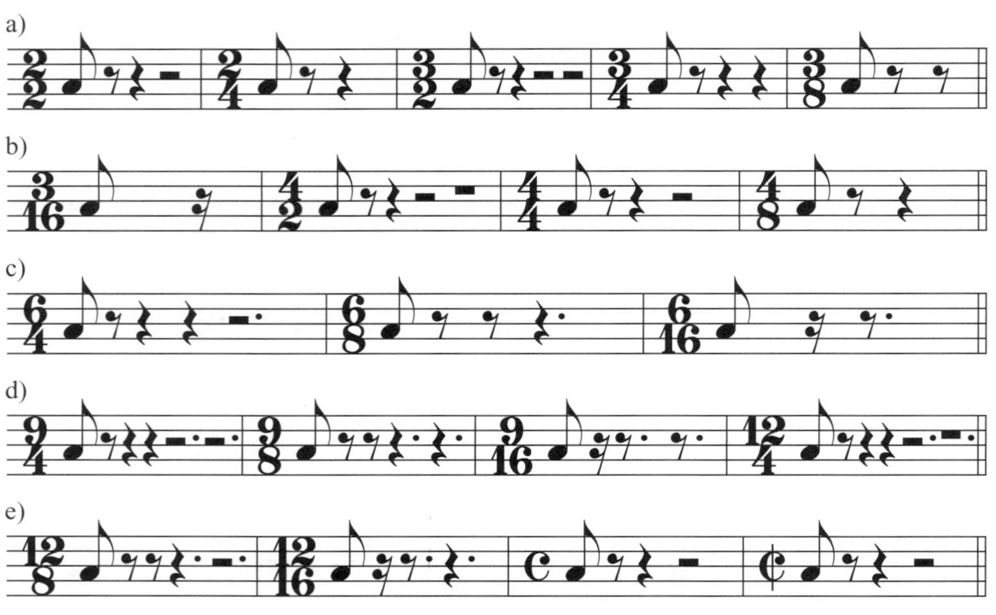

10. Complete the following measures with rests.

a)

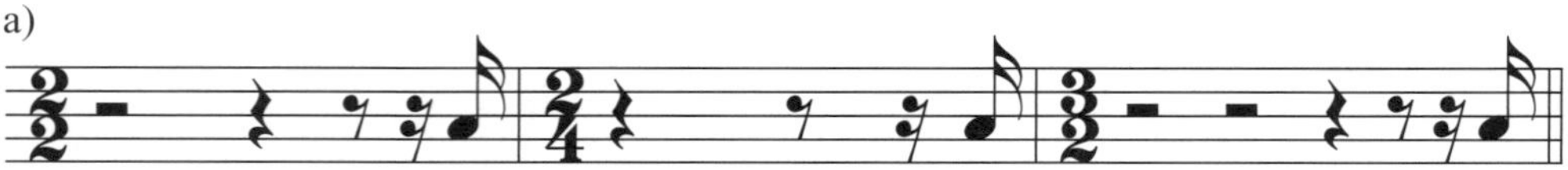

b)

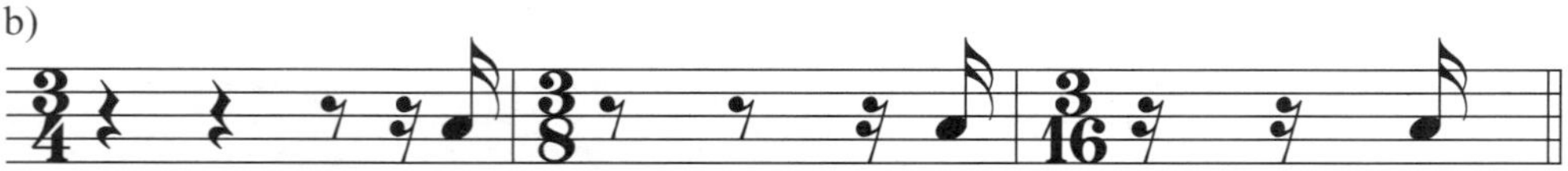

c)

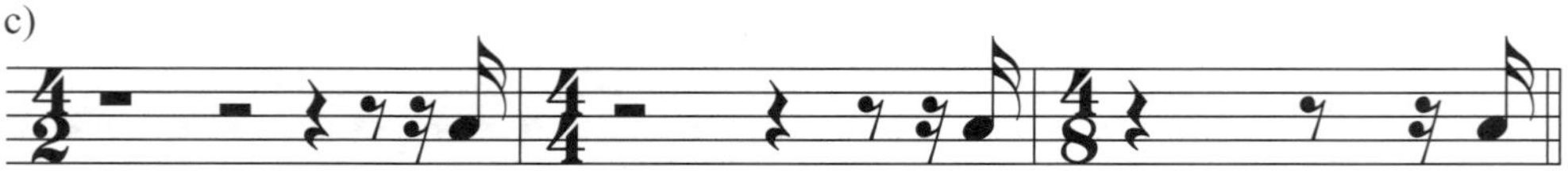

d)

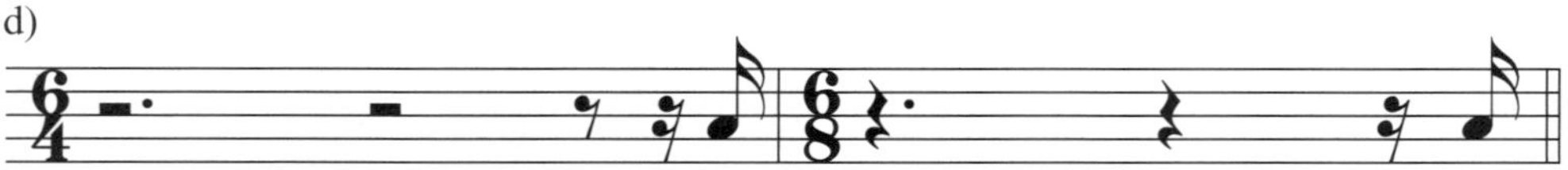

e)

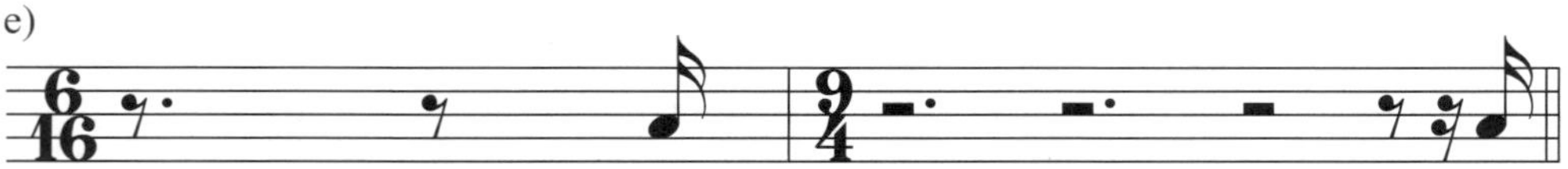

f)

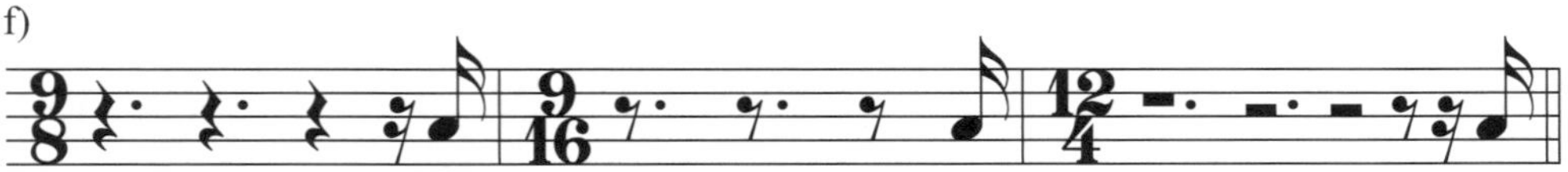

A EXERCISES (p. 221)

1. Complete the following measures with notes showing the two different ways of grouping duple meters.

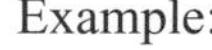
Example:

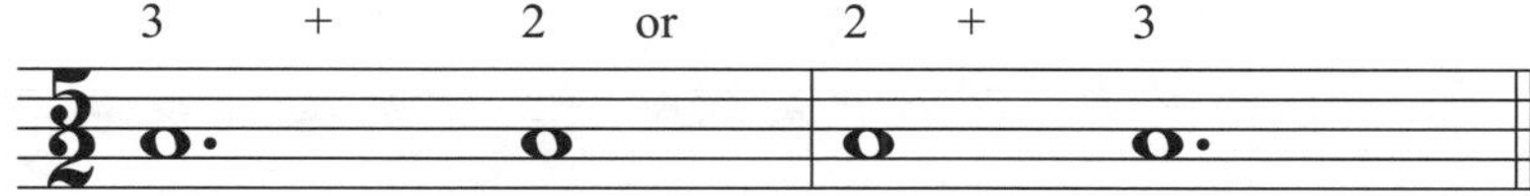

a) 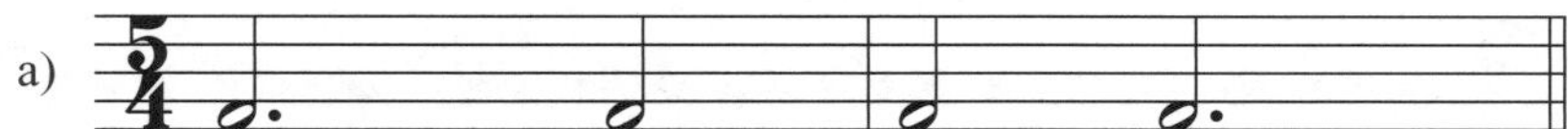

b) 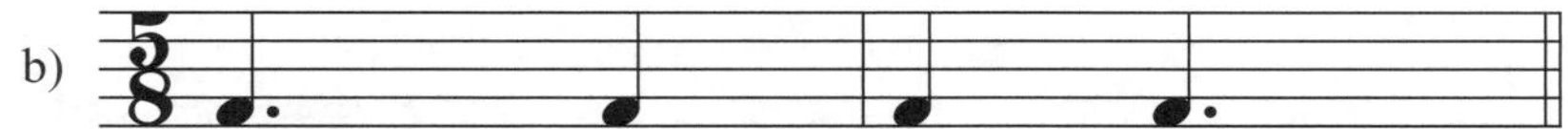

c) 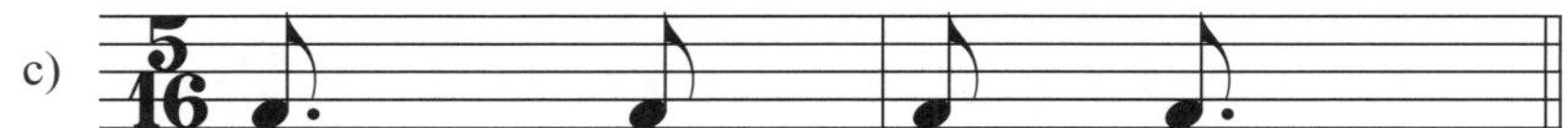

2. Complete the following measures with notes showing the five different ways of grouping hybrid triple meters.

Example:

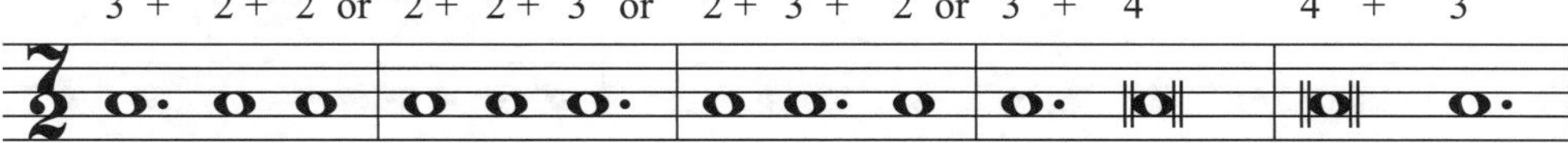

a)

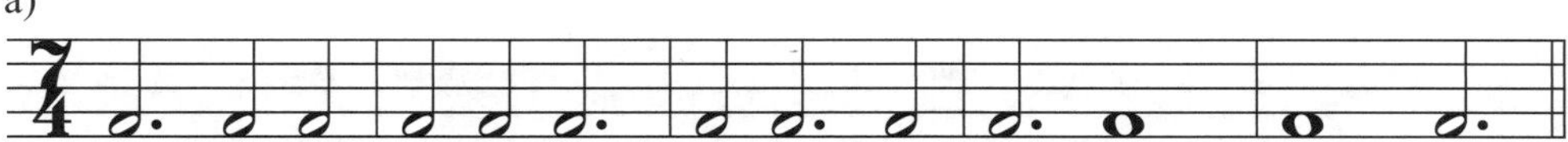

b)

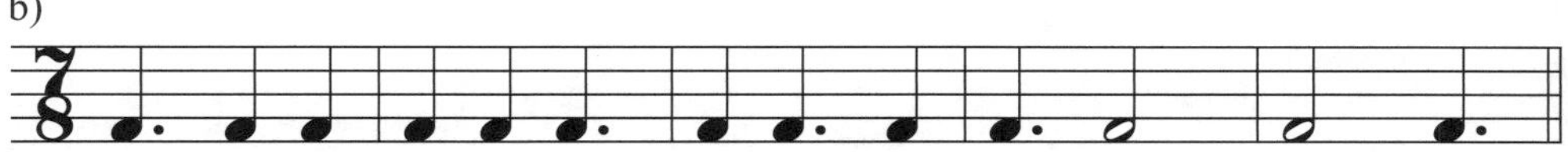

c)

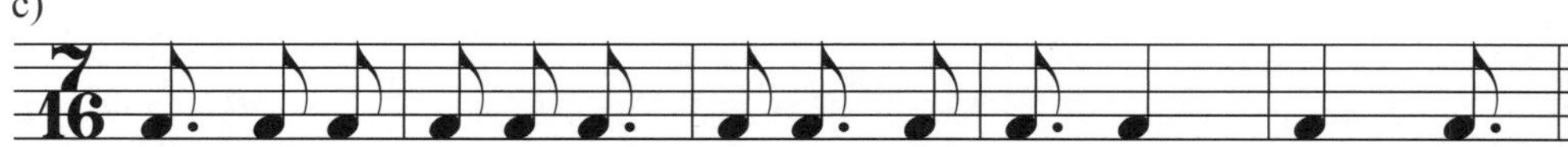

3. Add a time signature to each of the following, and indicate the grouping of the pulses into beats.

Example:

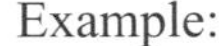

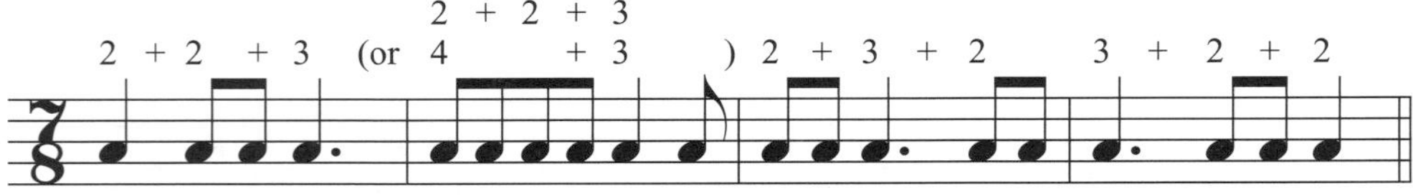

a)

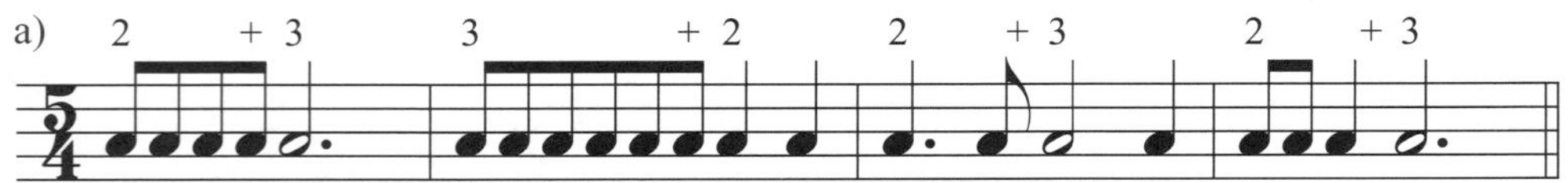

b)

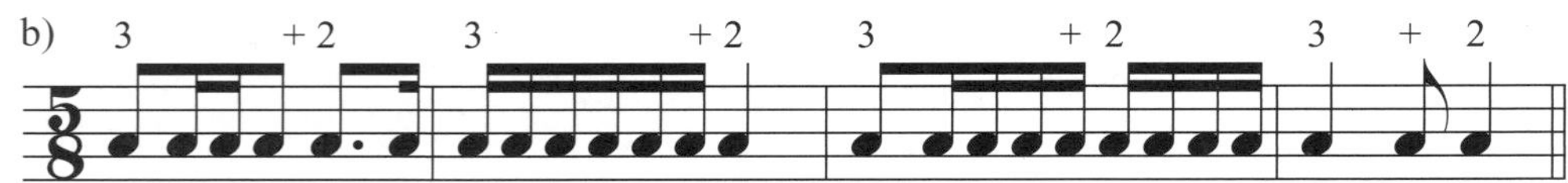

c)

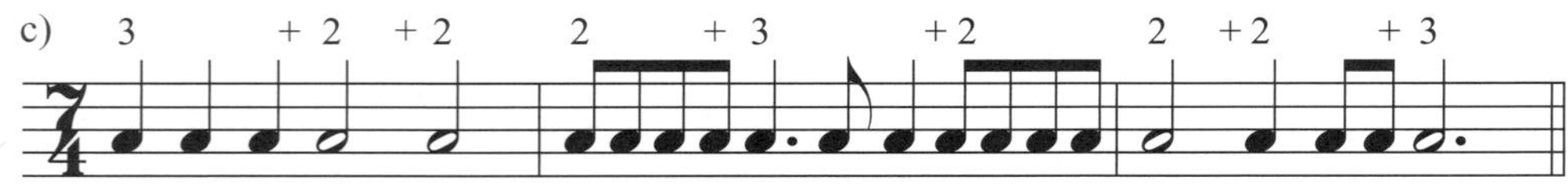

d)

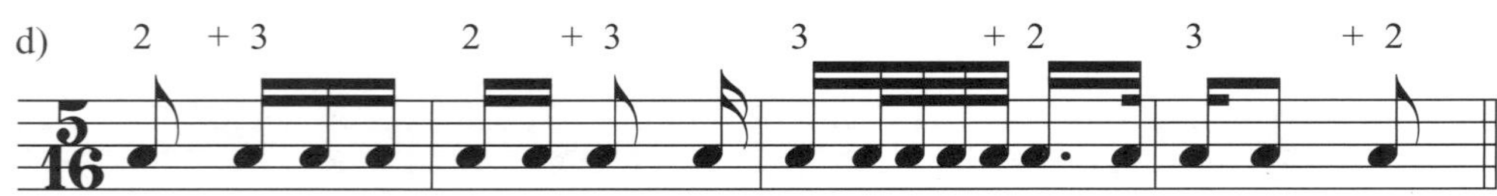

e)

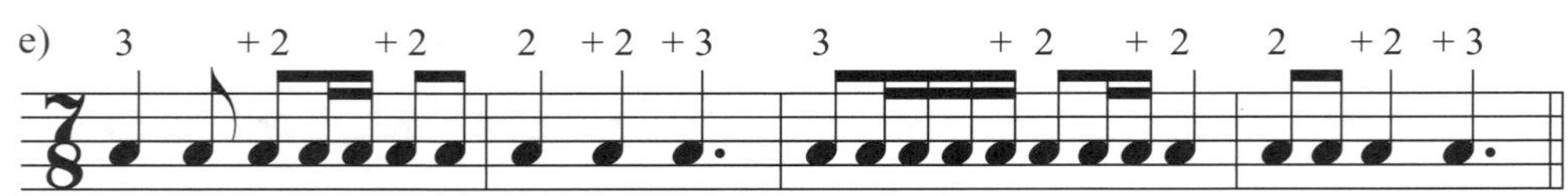

f)

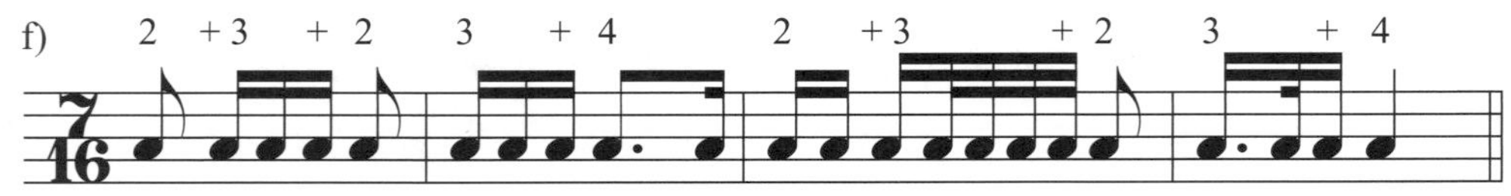

g)

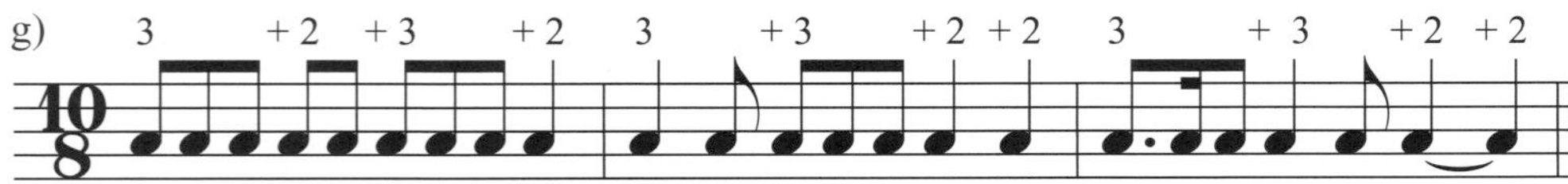

4. Complete the following measures with rests in the places indicated by the brackets. (Sample answers. Other groupings are possible.)

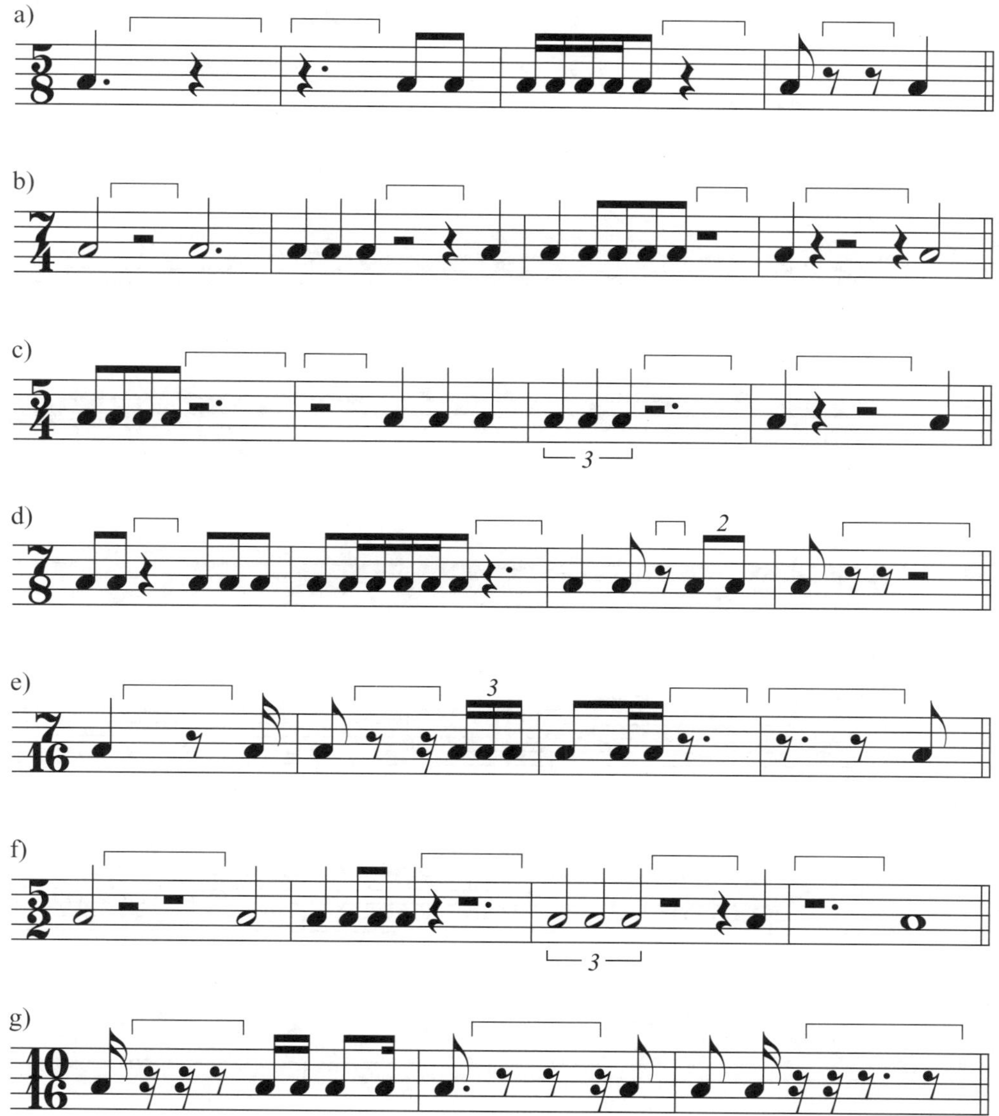

CHAPTER 8

NAMING THE KEY, TRANSPOSITION, AND DETECTING ERRORS

B I A EXERCISES (p. 226)

1. Name the key of each of the following melodies.

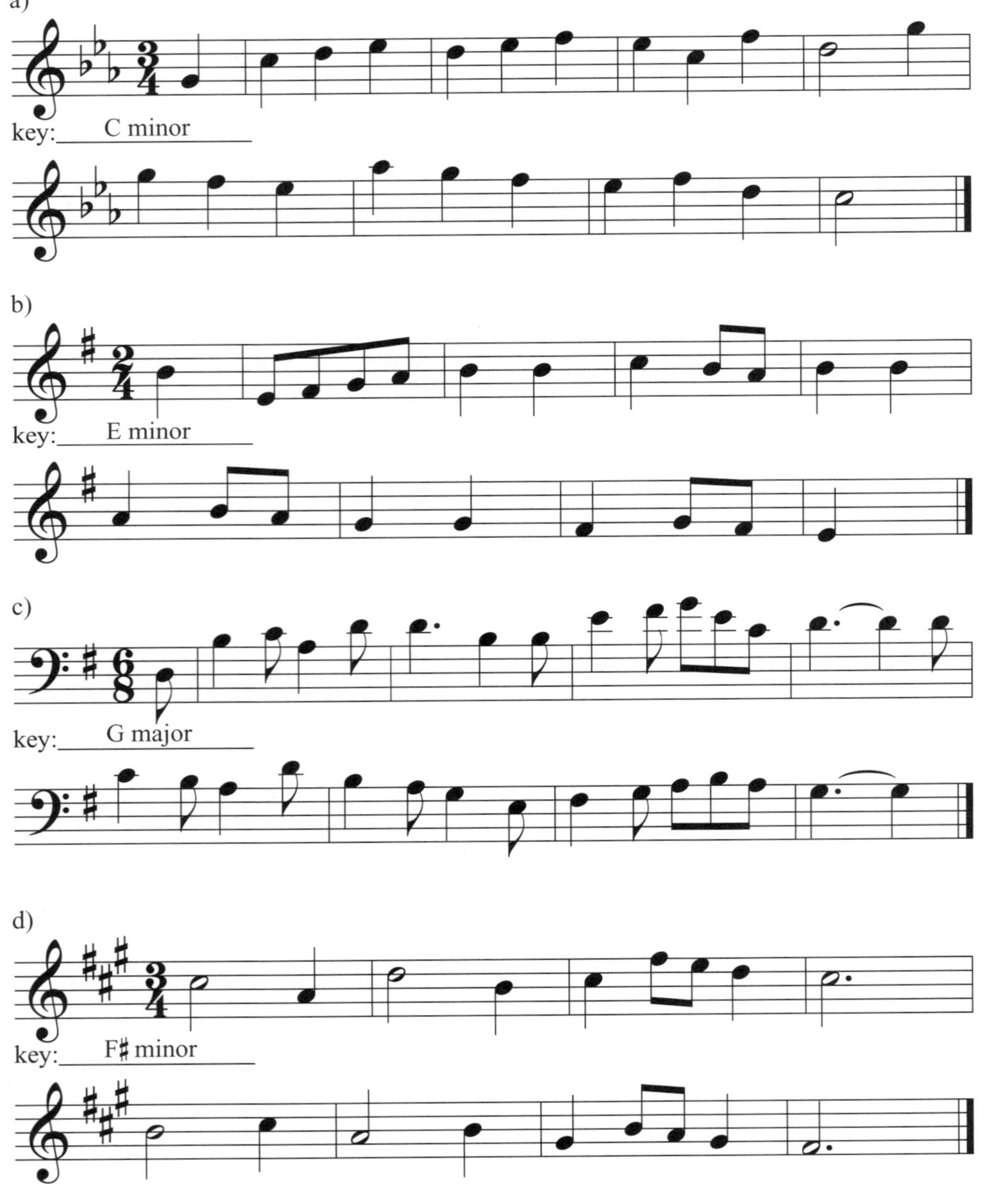

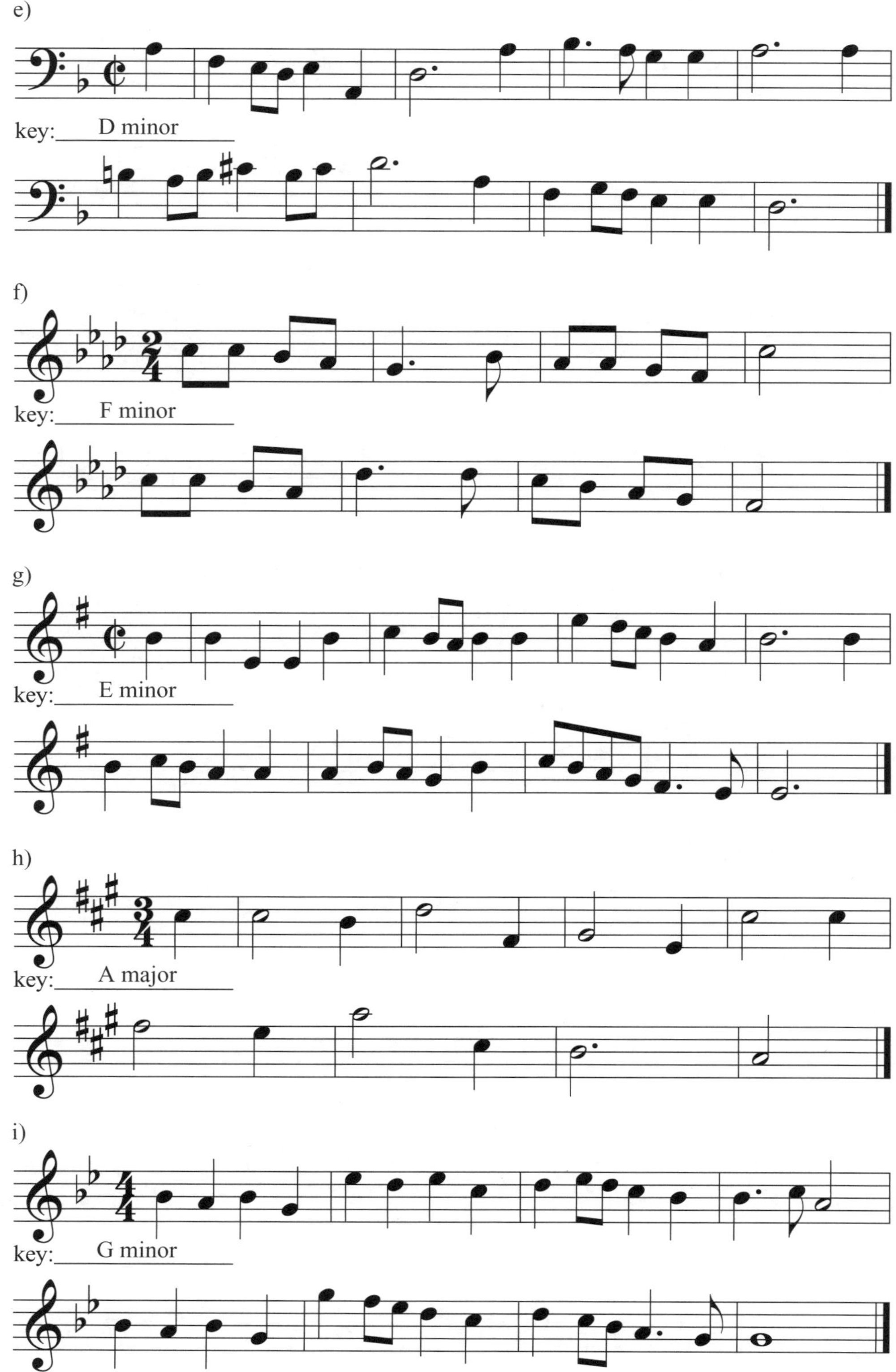
e)
key: D minor
f)
key: F minor
g)
key: E minor
h)
key: A major
i)
key: G minor

I A MORE EXERCISES (p. 228)

1. Name the key of each of the following melodies.

a)

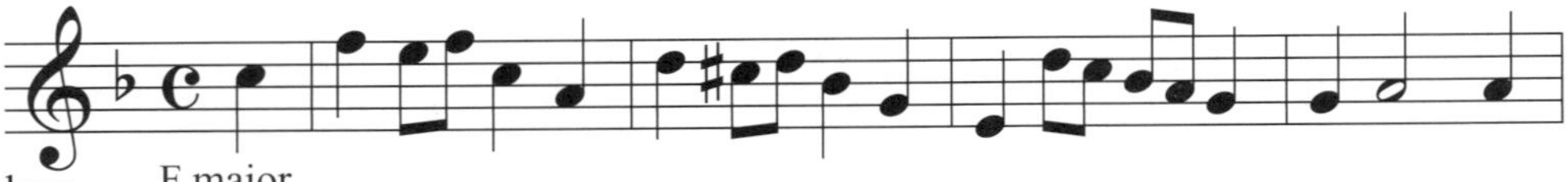

key: F major

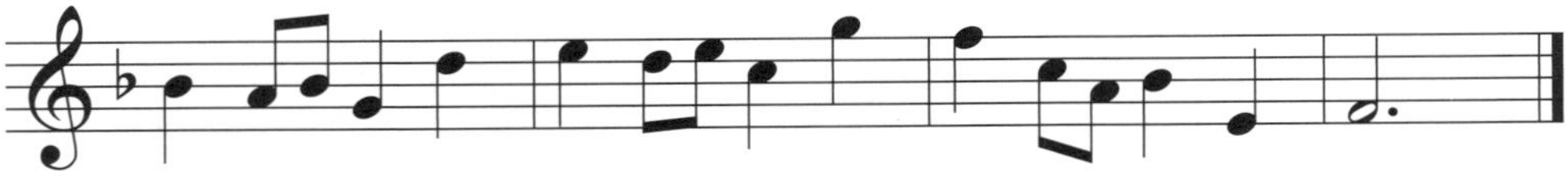

b)

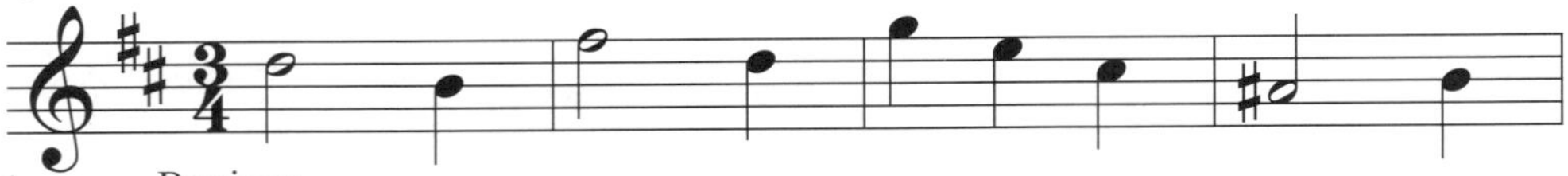

key: B minor

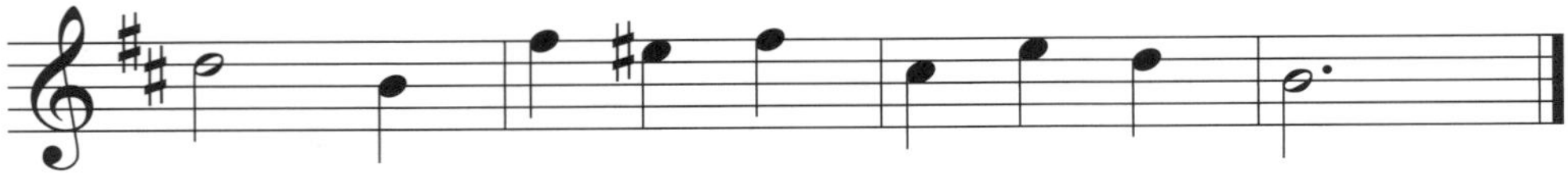

c)

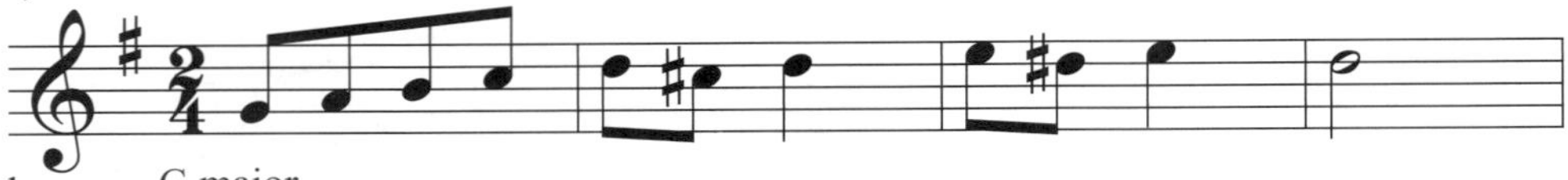

key: G major

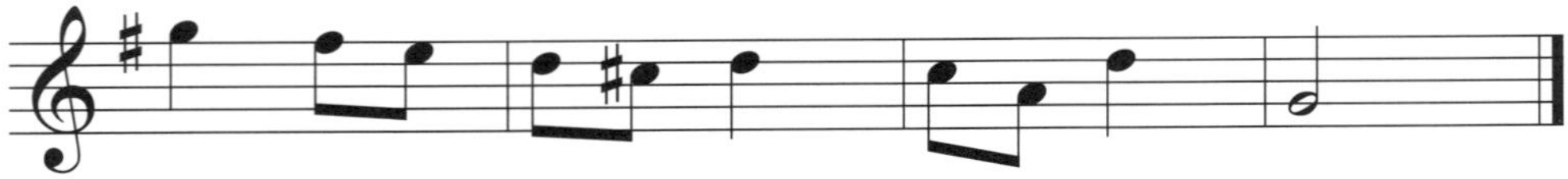

B I A EXERCISES (p. 233)

1. Name the key of the following melody. Rewrite it at the same pitch in the bass clef.

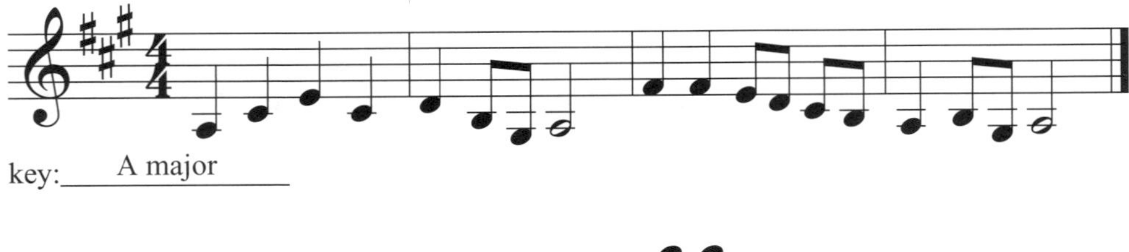

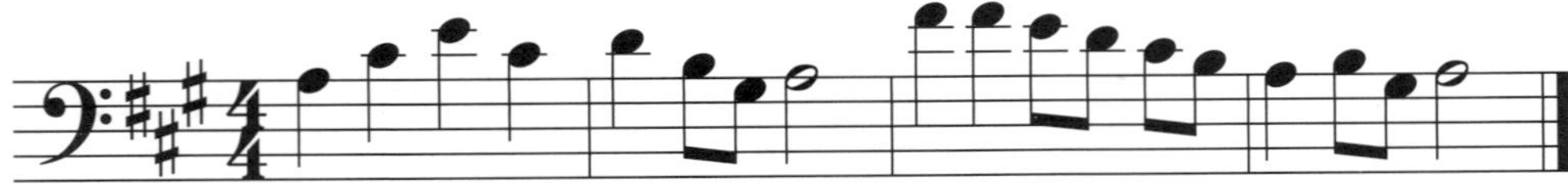

2. Name the key of the following melody. Rewrite it at the same pitch in the treble clef.

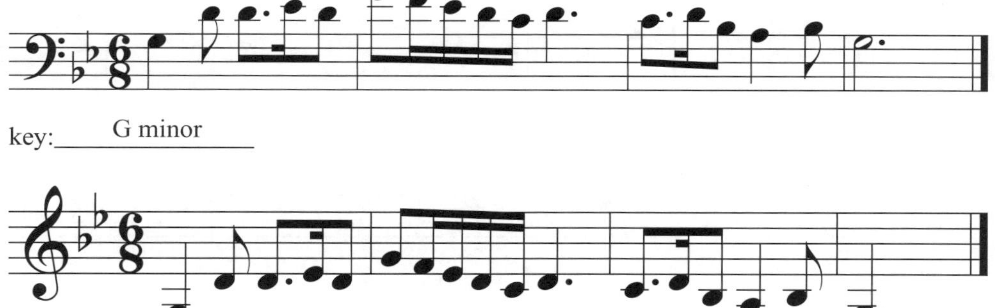

key: G minor

3. Name the key of the following melody. Rewrite it at the same pitch in the treble clef.

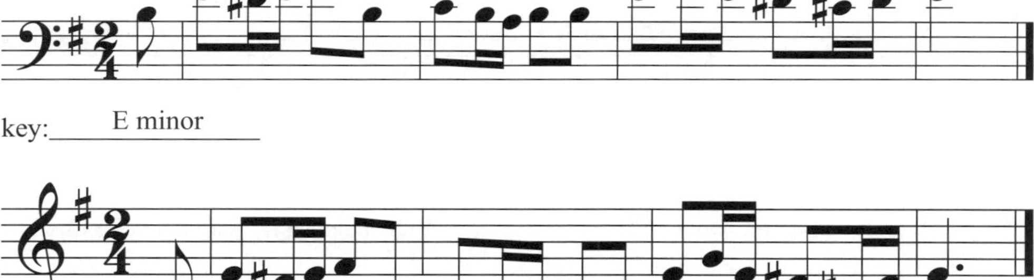

key: E minor

4. Name the key of the following melody. Rewrite it at the same pitch in the bass clef.

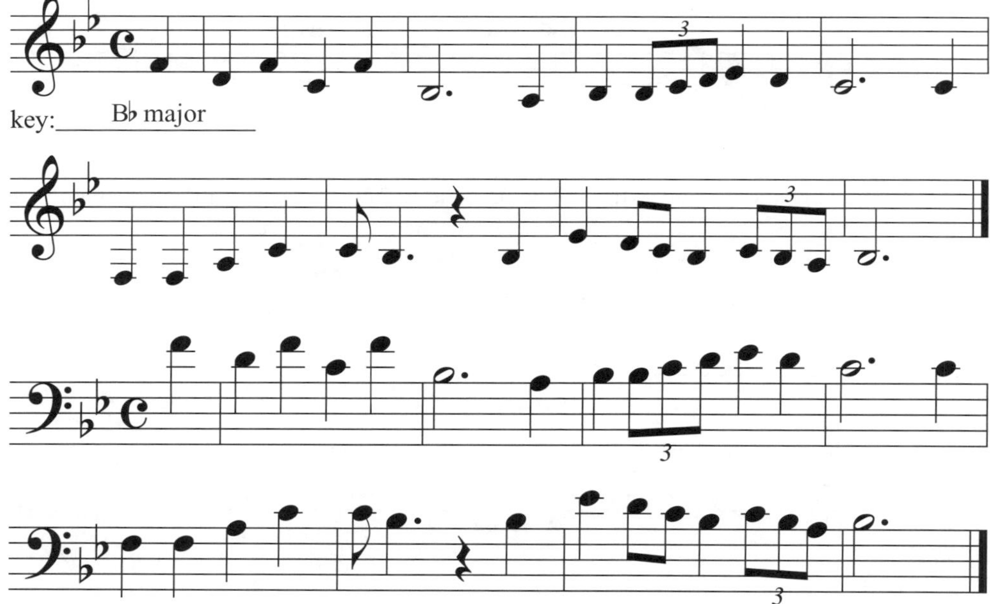

key: B♭ major

5. Name the key of the following melody. Transpose it down an octave in the treble clef.

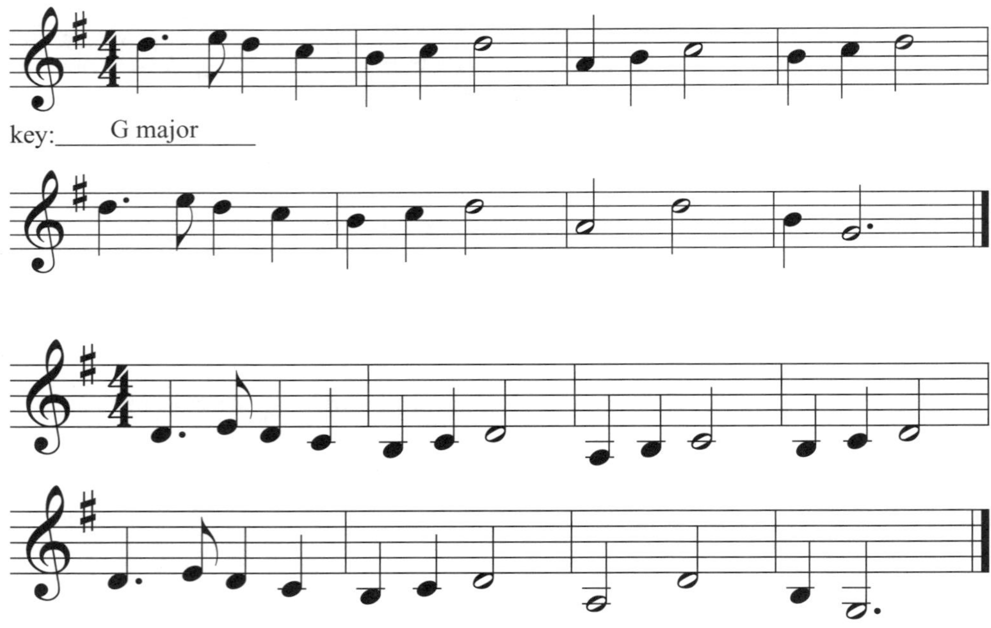

6. Name the key of the following melody. Transpose it up an octave in the bass clef.

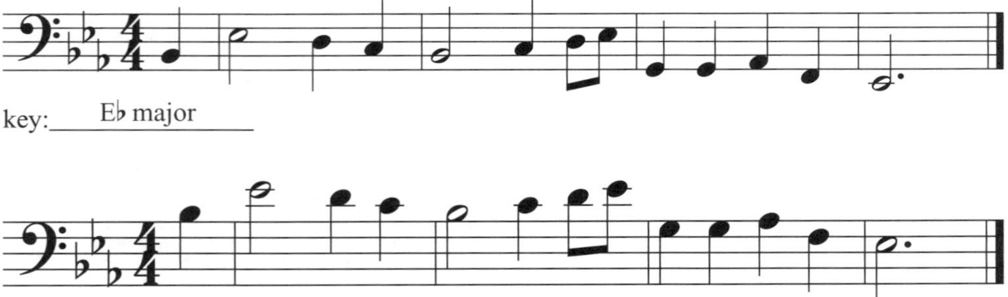

7. Name the key of the following melody. Transpose it up an octave into the treble clef.

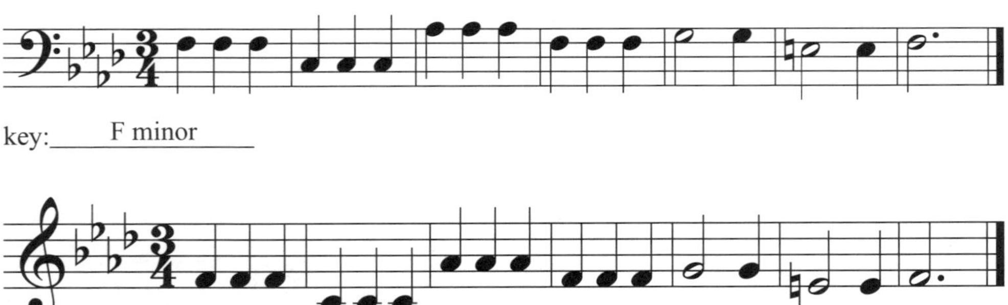

8. Name the key of the following melody. Transpose it down an octave into the bass clef.

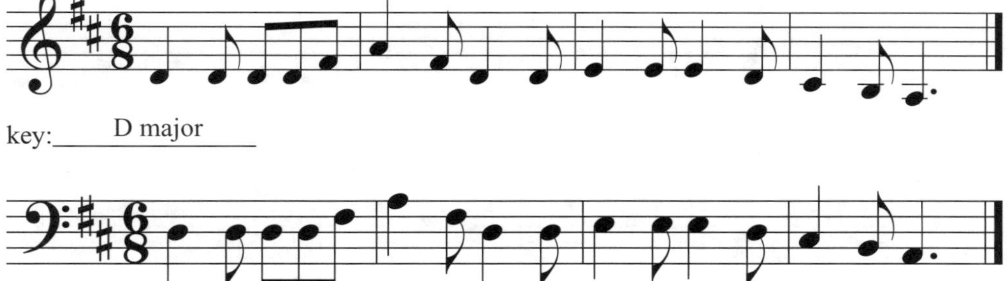

key: D major

9. Name the key of the following melody. Transpose it down an octave in the treble clef.

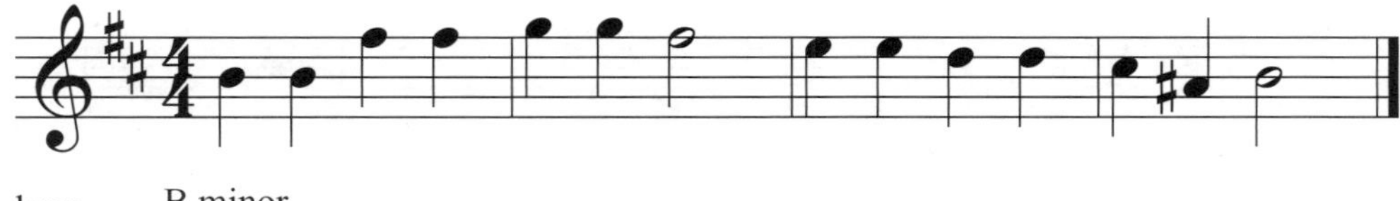

key: B minor

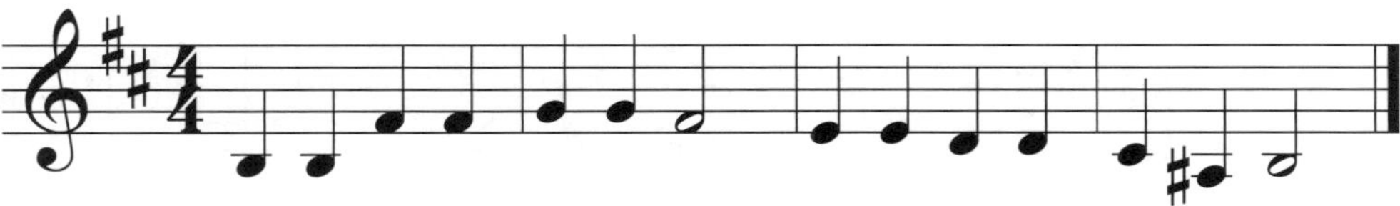

10. Name the key of the following melody. Transpose it down an octave into the bass clef.

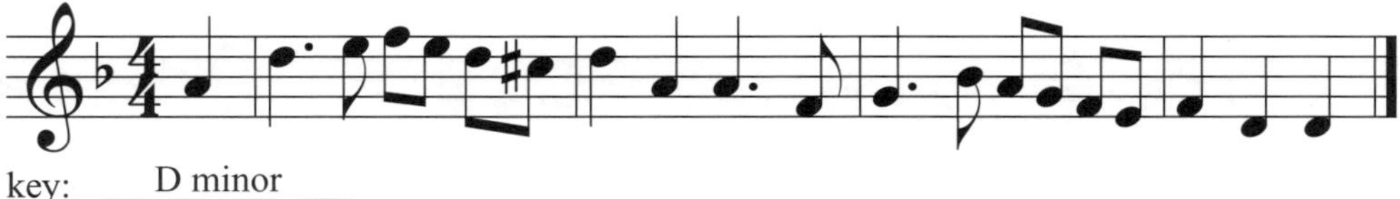

key: D minor

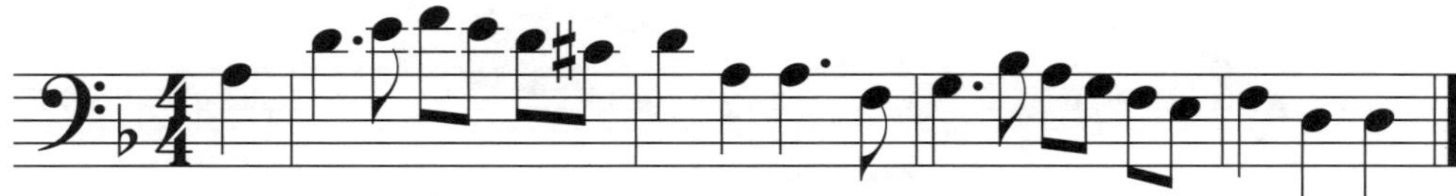

11. Name the key of the following melody. Transpose it up an octave into the treble clef.

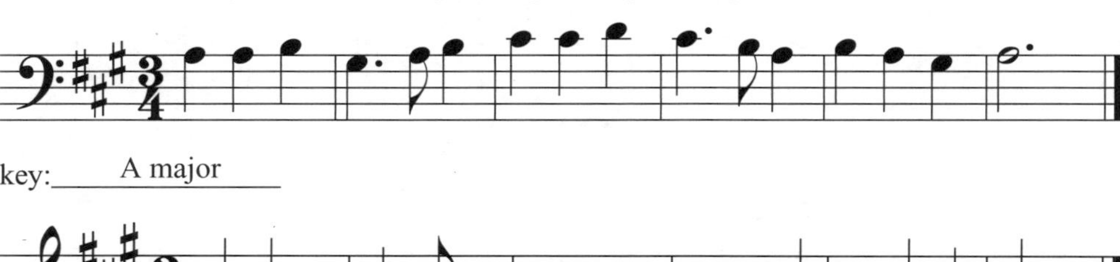

key: A major

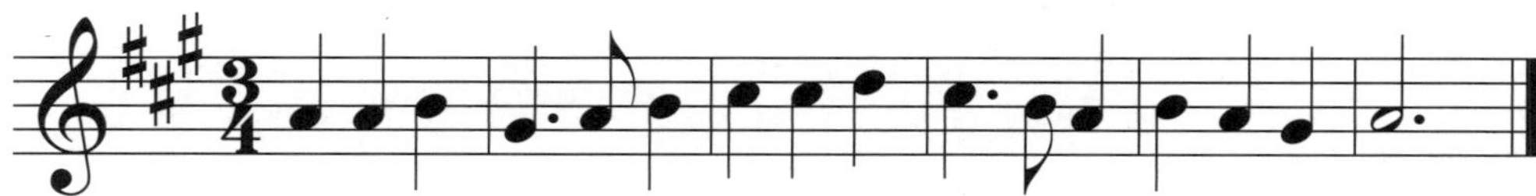

12. Name the key of the following melody. Transpose it down an octave into the bass clef.

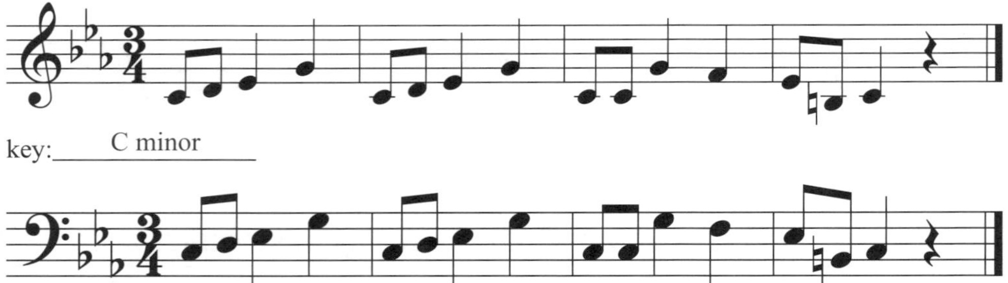

key: C minor

13. Name the key of the following melody. Transpose it down an octave into the bass clef.

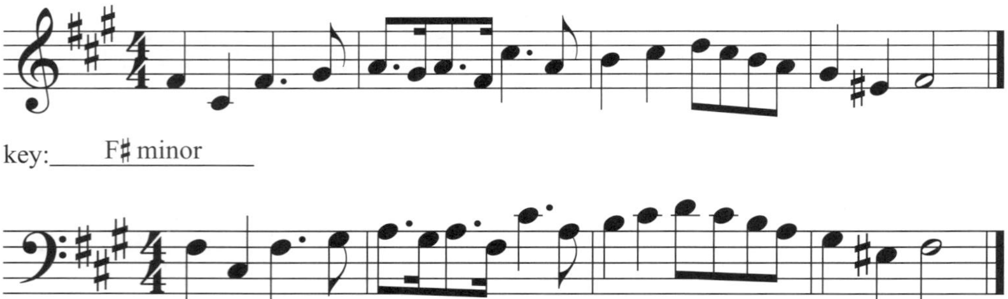

key: F♯ minor

14. Name the key of the following melody. Transpose it up an octave into the treble clef.

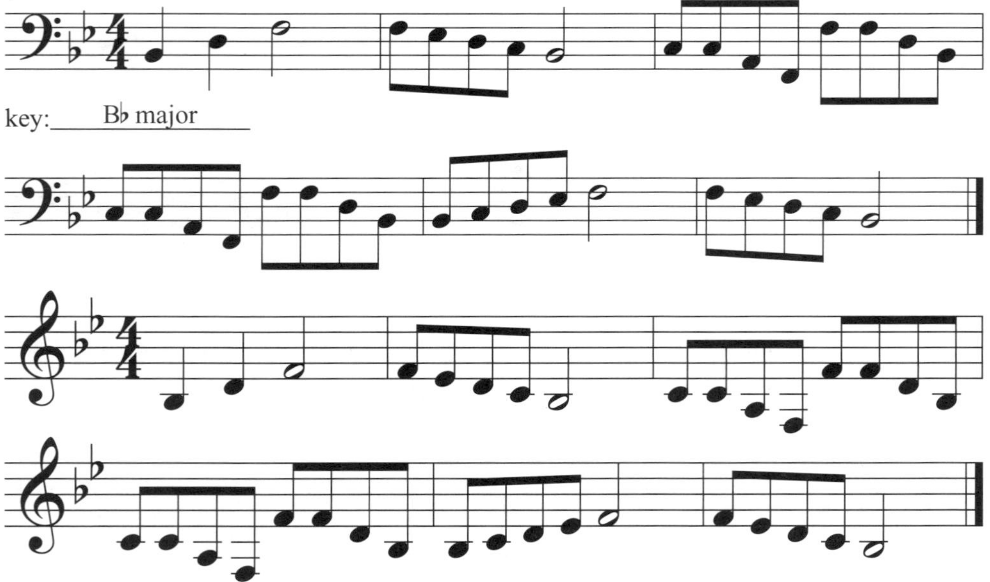

key: B♭ major

15. Name the key of the following melody. Transpose it down an octave in the bass clef.

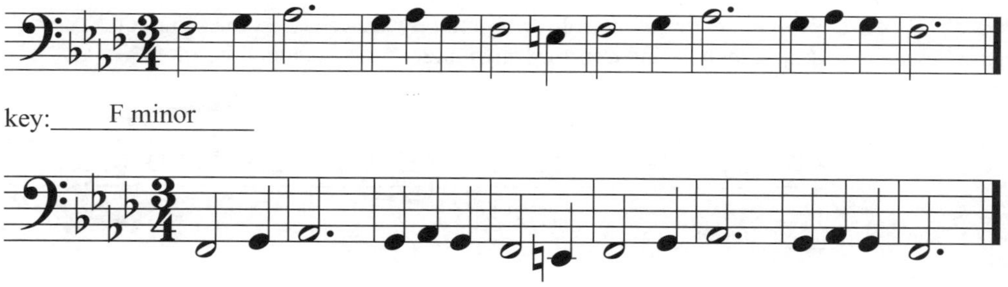

16. Name the key of the following melody. Transpose it up an octave into the treble clef.

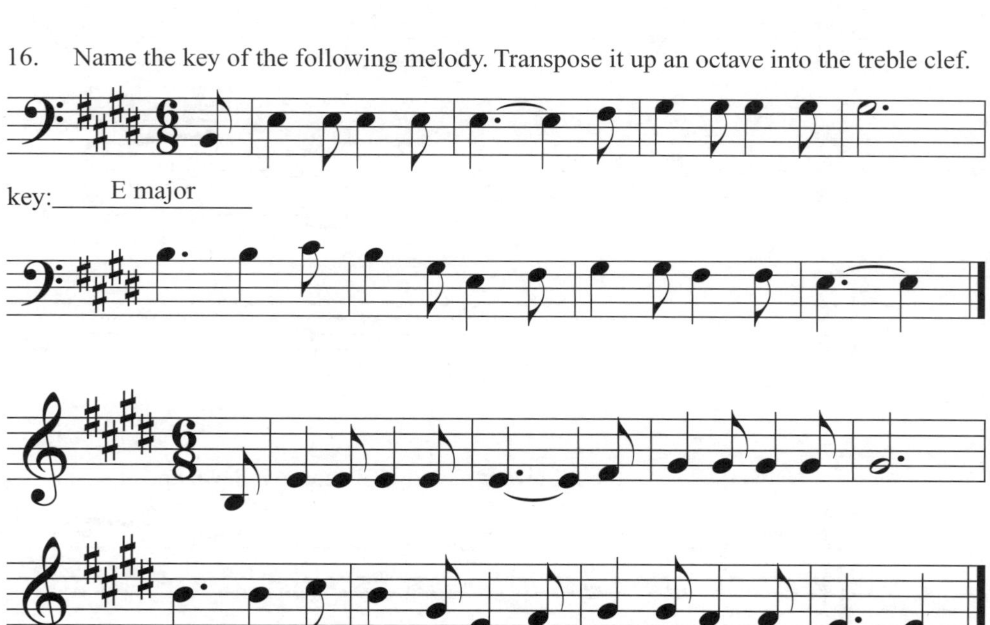

I A MORE EXERCISES (p. 238)

1. Name the key of the following melody. Rewrite it at the same pitch, using the correct key signature and omitting any unnecessary accidentals.

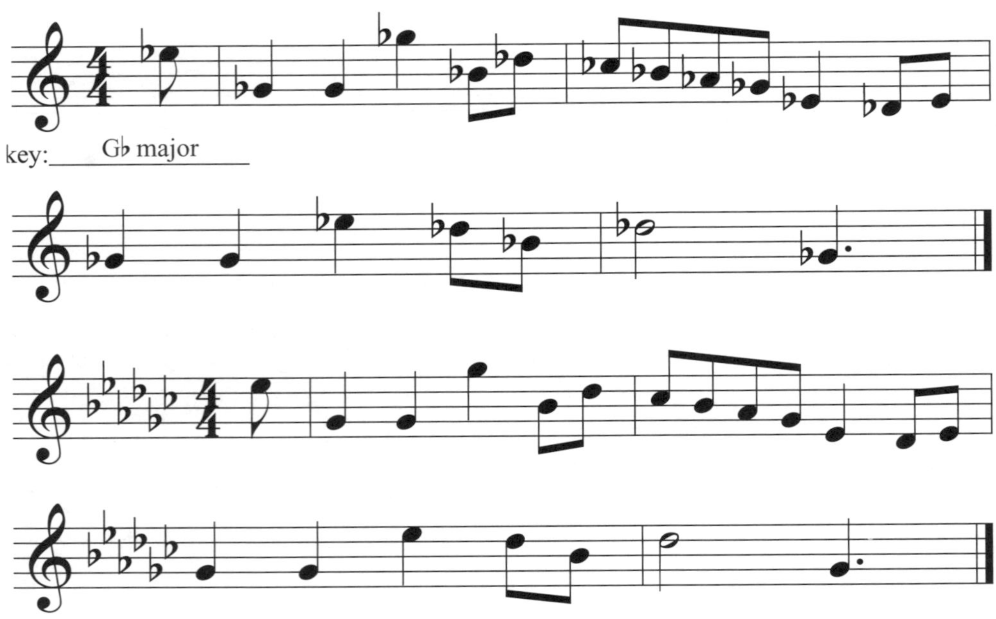

2. Name the key of the following melody. Transpose it down an octave into the bass clef.

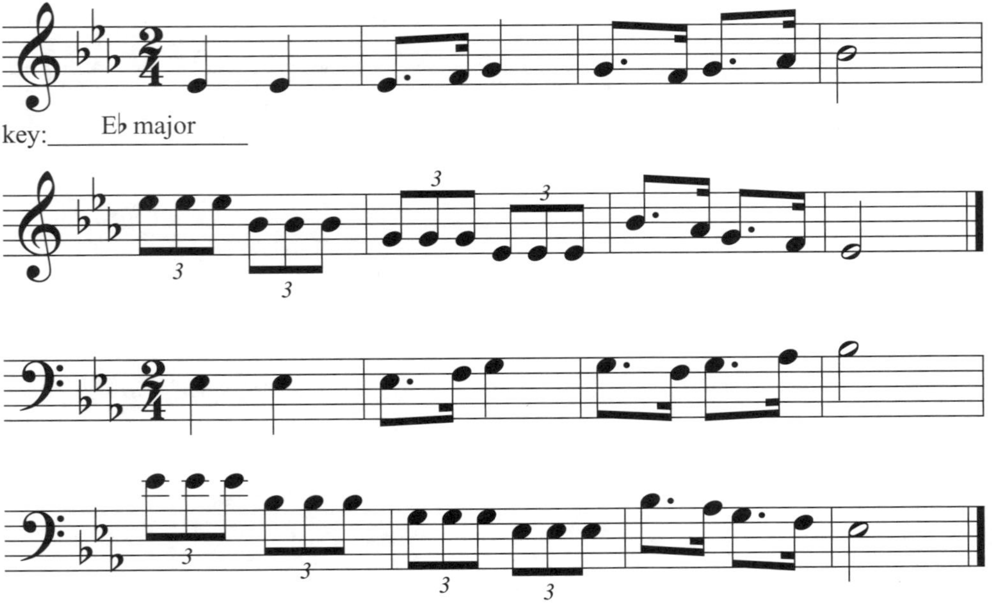

3. Name the key of the following melody. Transpose it down an octave into the bass clef.

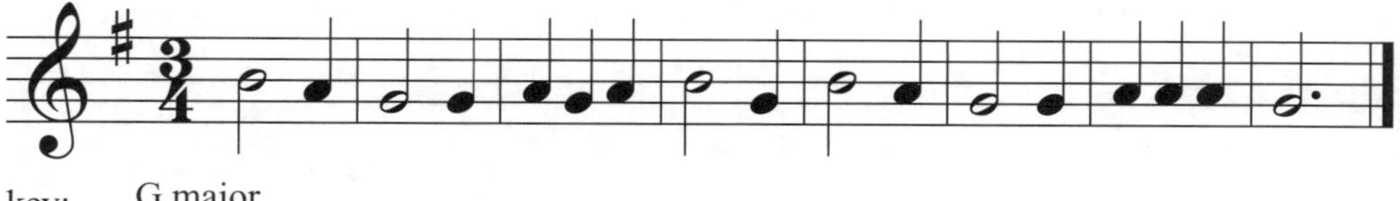

key: G major

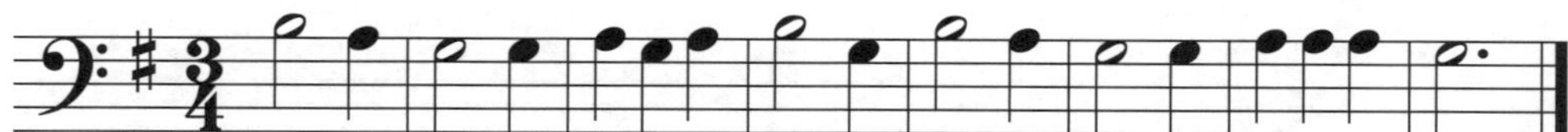

4. Name the key of the following melody. Rewrite it at the same pitch in the treble clef, using the correct key signature and omitting any unnecessary accidentals.

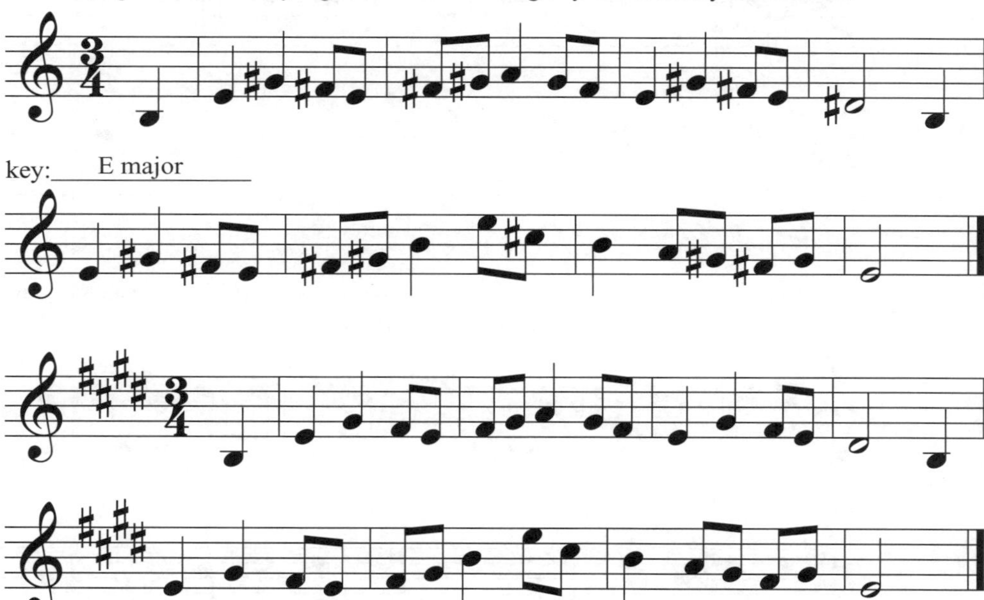

5. Name the key of the following melody. Transpose it down an octave into the bass clef, using the correct key signature and omitting any unnecessary accidentals.

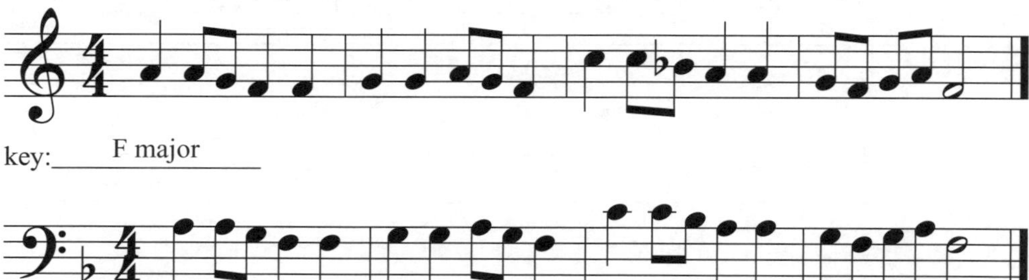

6. Name the key of the following melody. Transpose it up an octave in the bass clef, using the correct key signature and omitting any unnecessary accidentals.

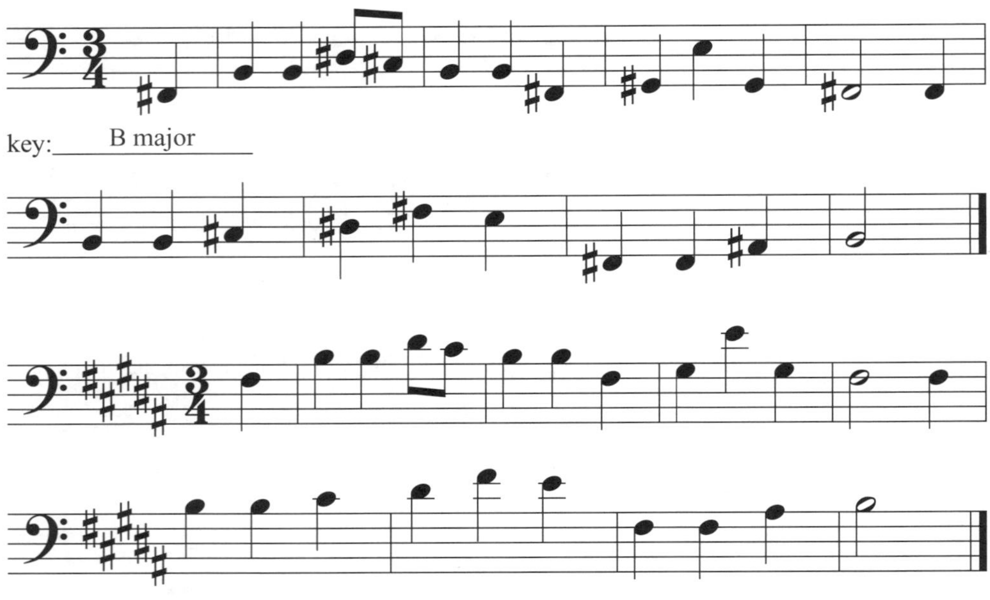

7. Name the key of the following melody. Transpose it down an octave into the bass clef, using the correct key signature and omitting any unnecessary accidentals.

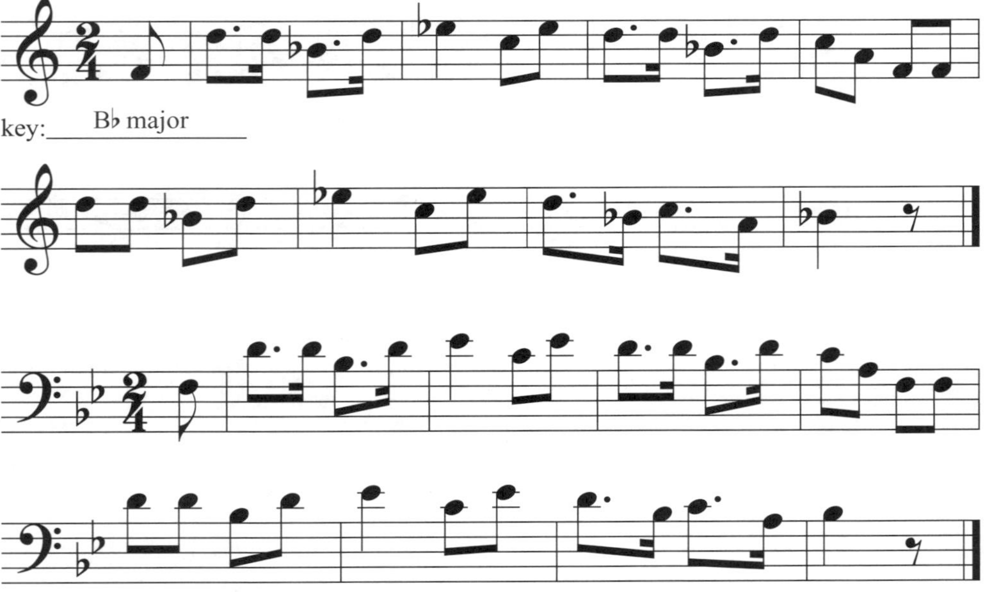

A STILL MORE EXERCISES (p. 241)

1. Name the key of the following melody. Rewrite it at the same pitch in the alto clef, using the correct key signature and omitting any unnecessary accidentals.

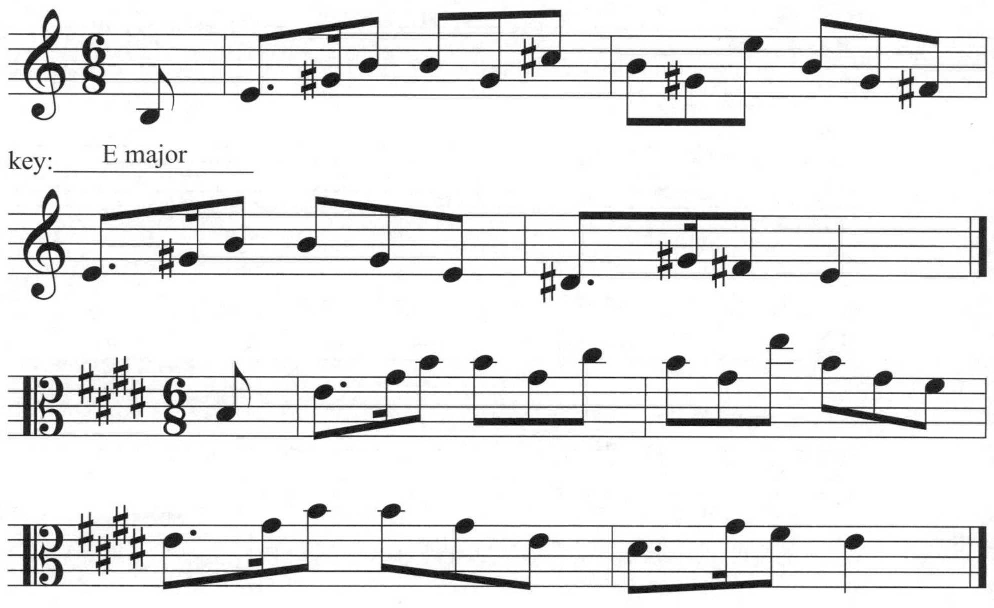

2. Name the key of the following melody. Transpose it up an octave into the treble clef.

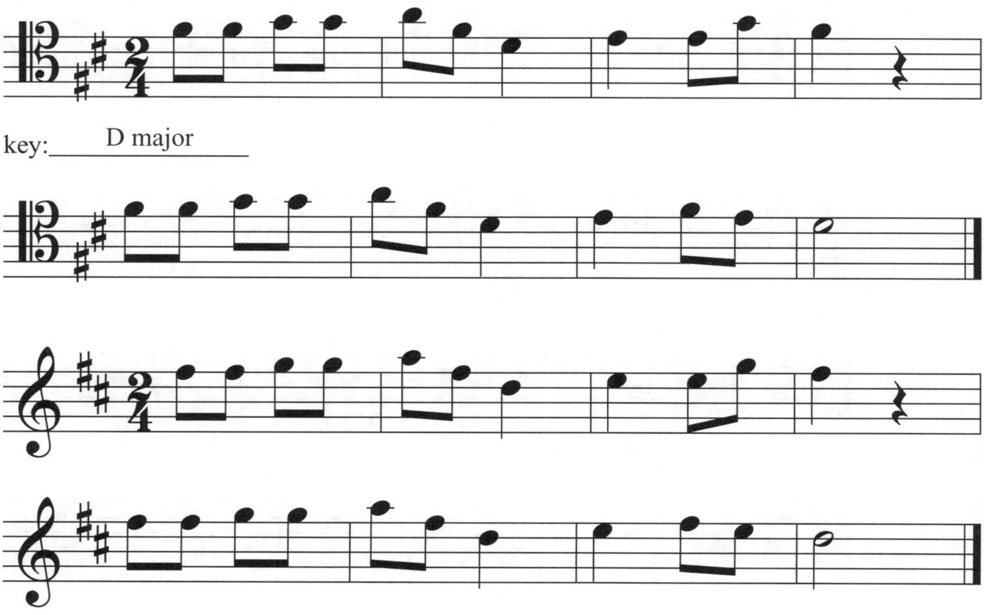

3. Name the key of the following melody. Rewrite it at the same pitch in the alto clef, using the correct key signature and omitting any unnecessary accidentals.

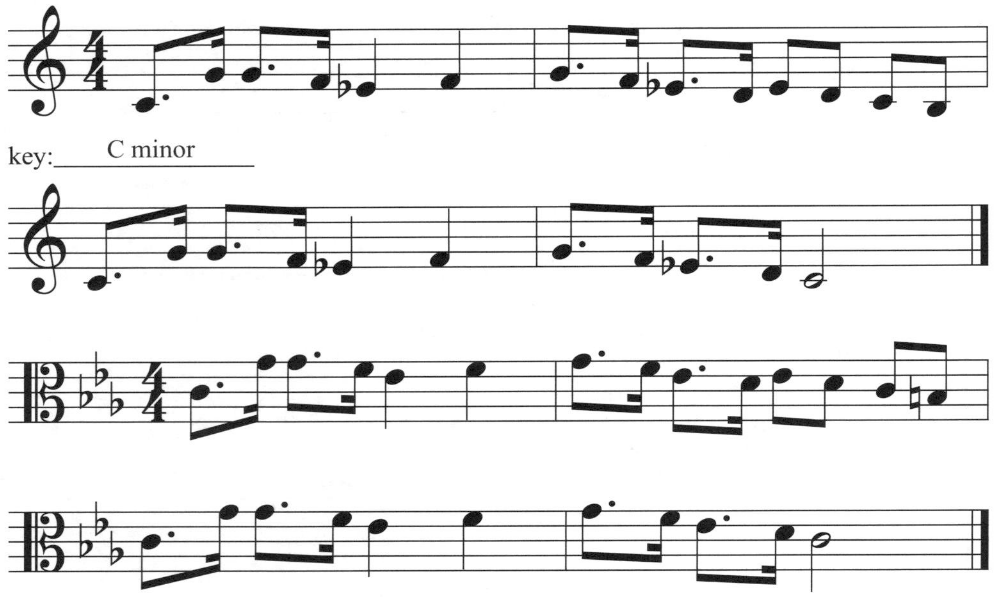

4. Name the key of the following melody. Rewrite it an octave lower in the alto clef, using the correct key signature and omitting any unnecessary accidentals.

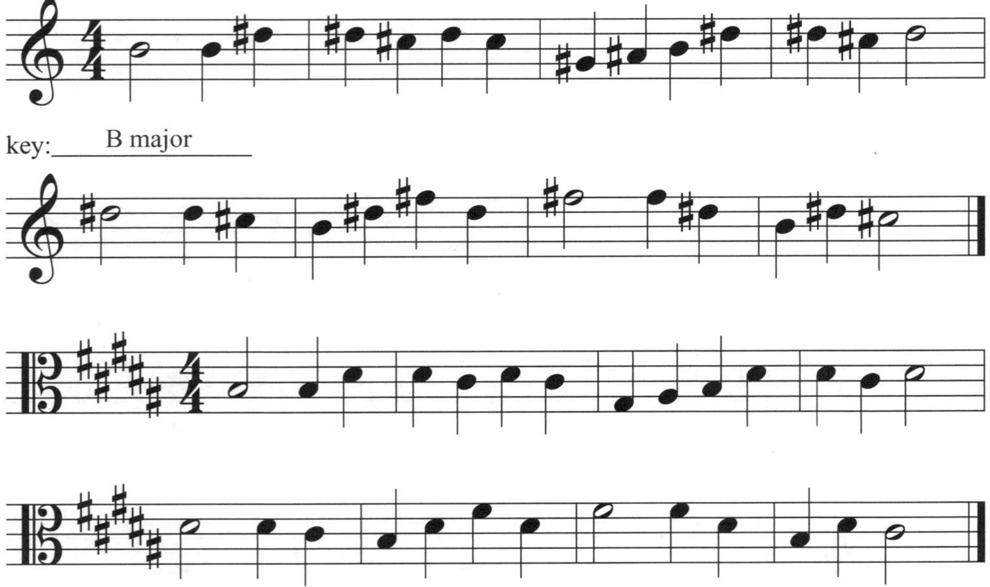

I A EXERCISES (p. 245)

1. Transpose the following melody into A major.

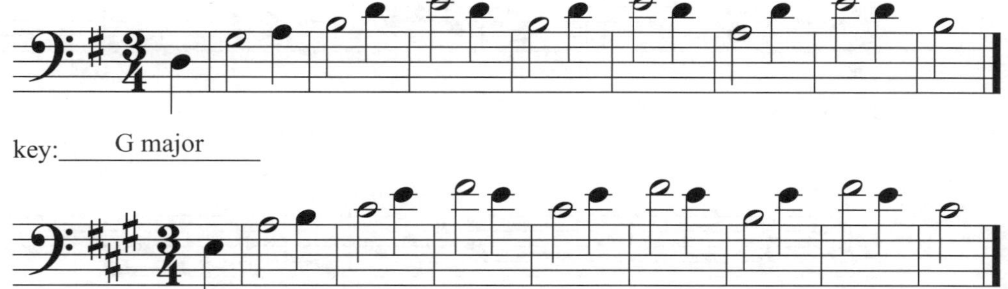

key: G major

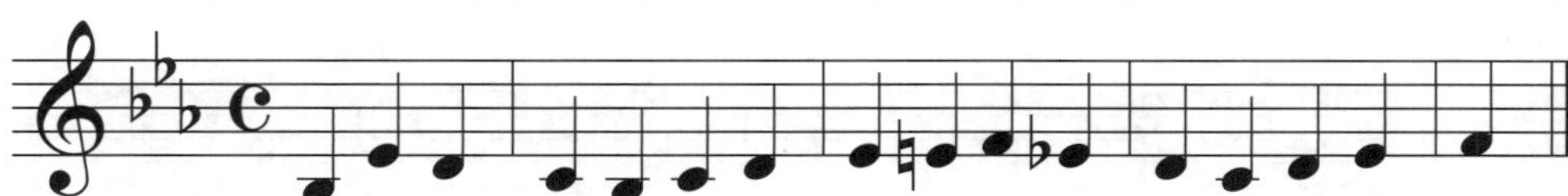

2. Transpose the following melody a) into F major b) up a major 3rd. Name the new key.

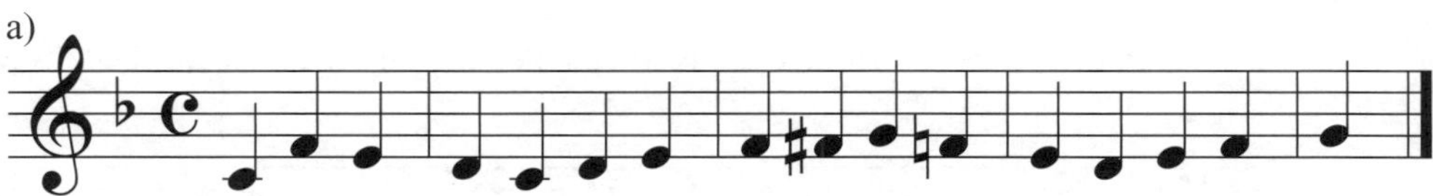

key: E♭ major

a)

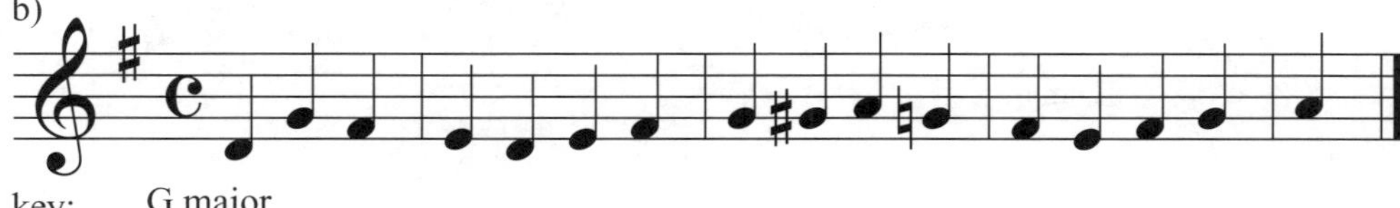

b)

key: G major

3. Transpose the following melody a) into G major b) up a perfect 4th. Name the new key.

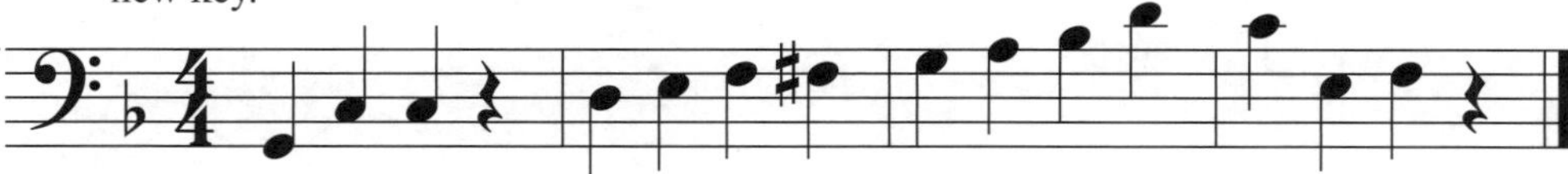

key: F major

a)

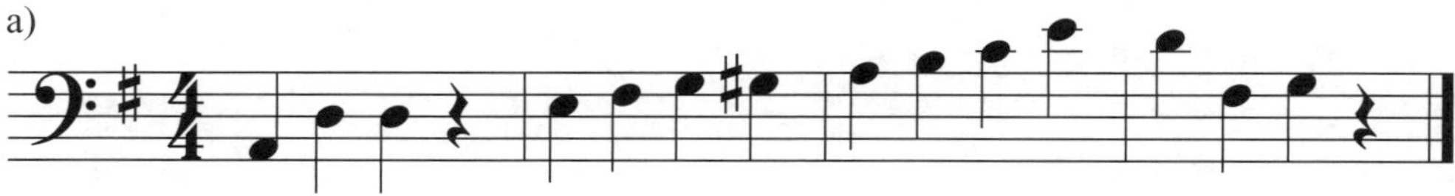

b)

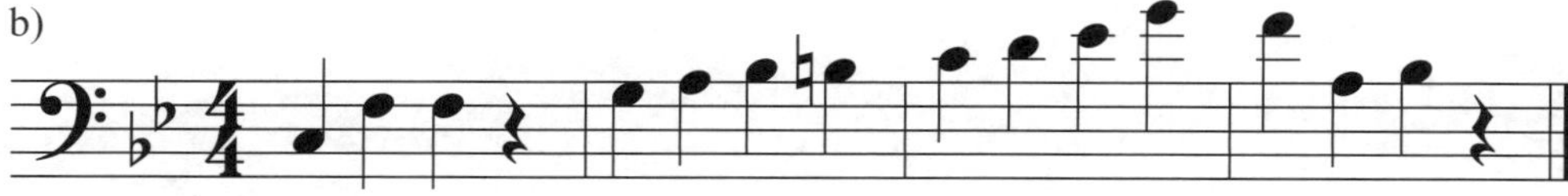

key: B♭ major

4. Transpose the following melody a) up a major 2nd and name the new key b) into A major.

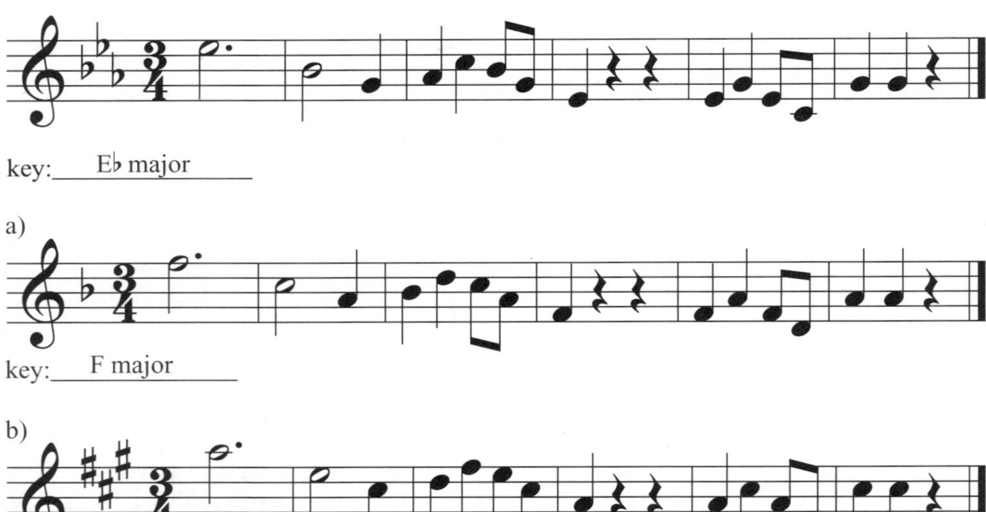

5. Transpose the following melody a) up a perfect 4th b) up a major 2nd. In each case, name the new key.

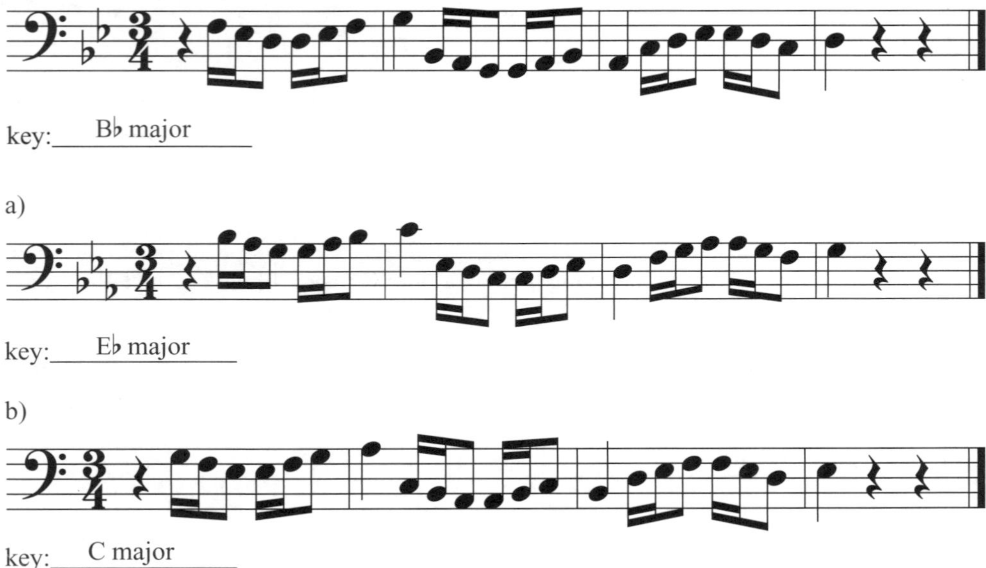

6. Transpose the following melody a) up a major 3rd and name the new key b) into G major.

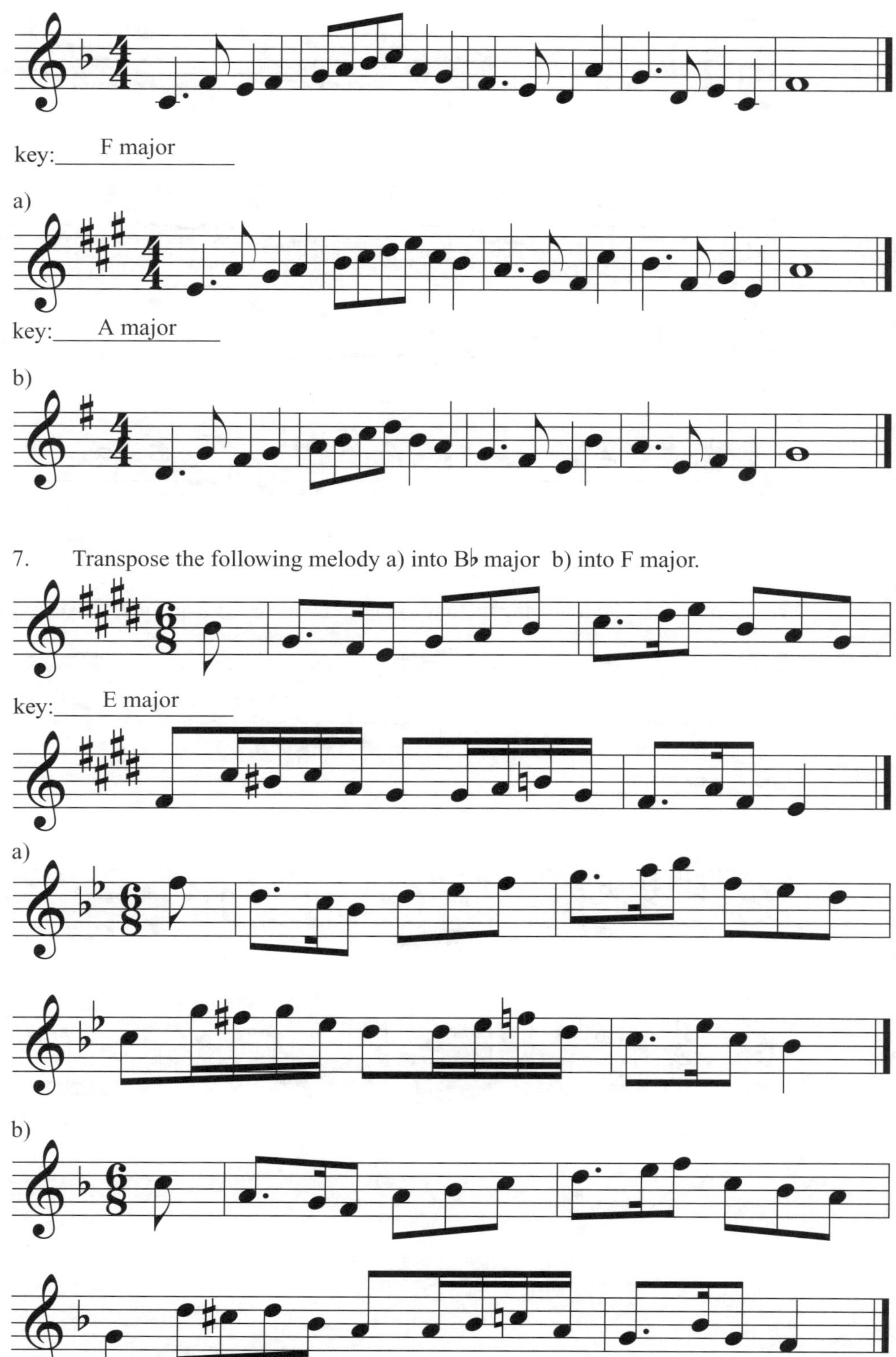

8. In what key is the following melody written? Transpose it into D major, using the correct key signature.

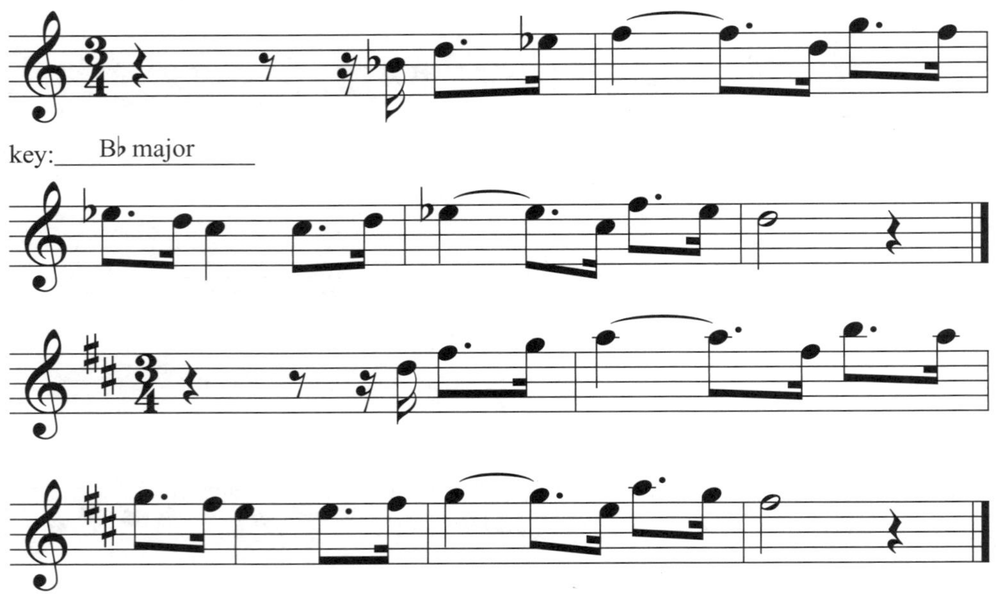

9. Transpose the following melody a) into A major b) up a major 3rd. Name the new key.

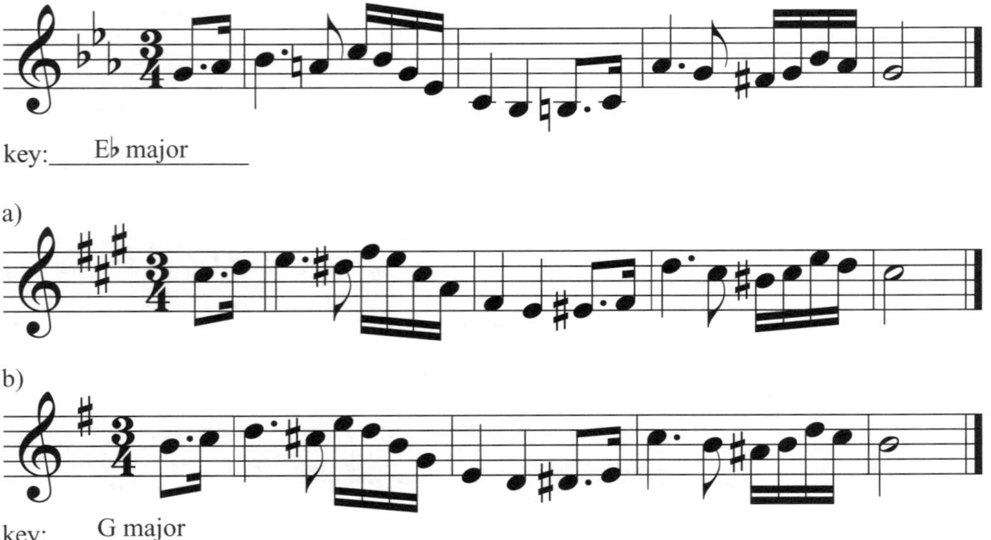

10. Transpose the following melody a) into D♭ major b) up a minor 3rd. Name the new key.

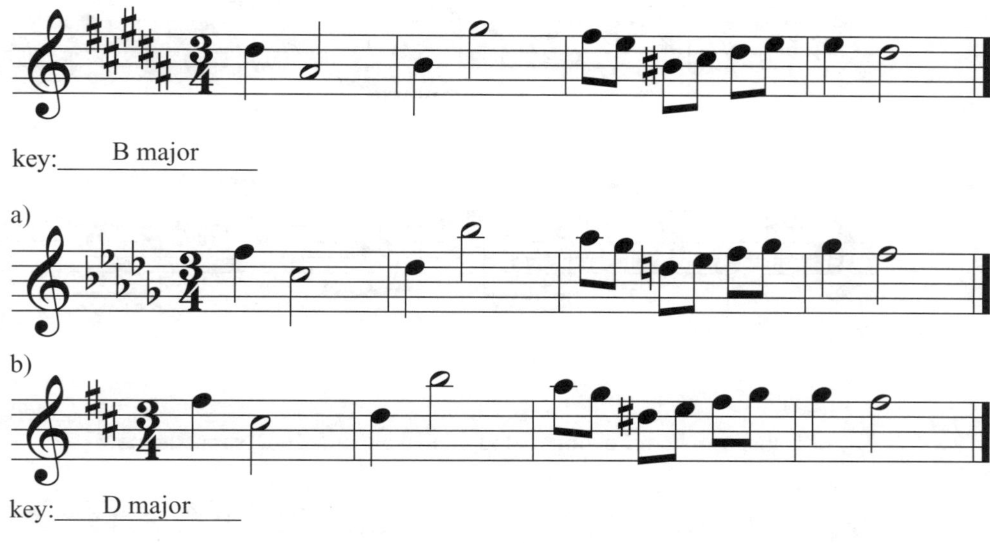

A MORE EXERCISES (p. 250)

1. Transpose the following melody down a major 2nd. Name the new key.

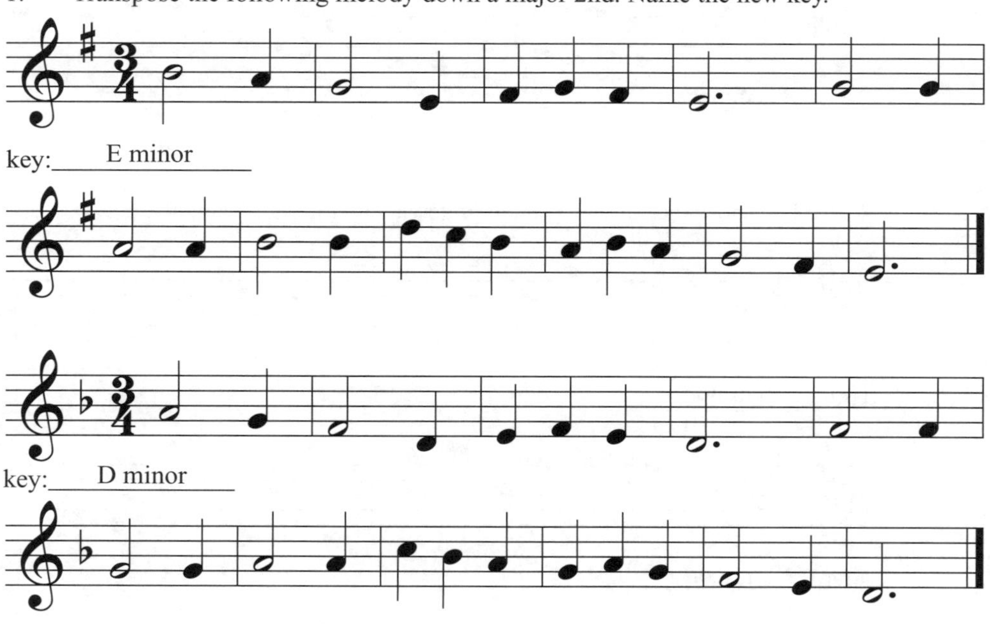

2. Transpose the following melody up a major 2nd. Name the new key.

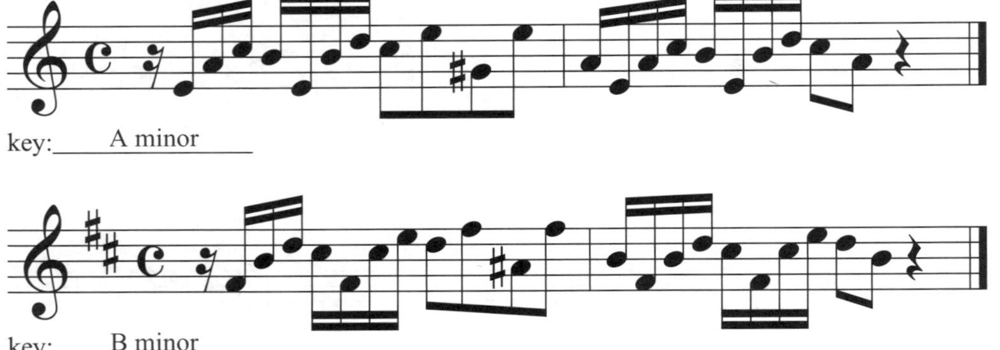

3. Transpose the following melody down a major 2nd. Name the new key.

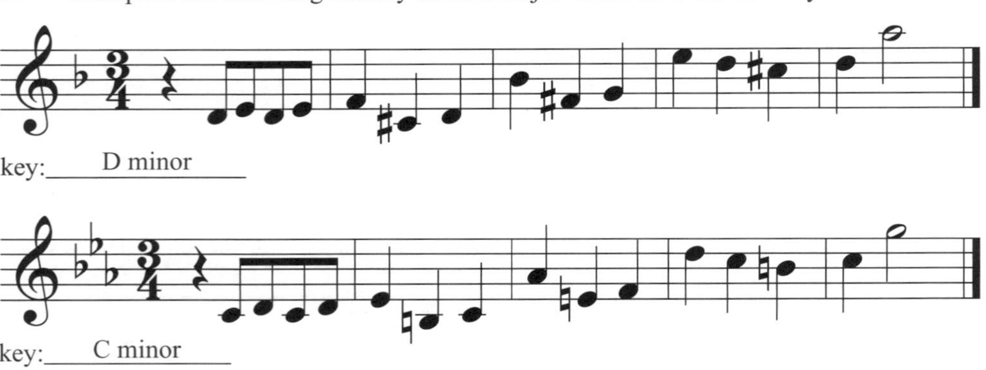

4. Transpose the following melody down a major 2nd. Name the new key.

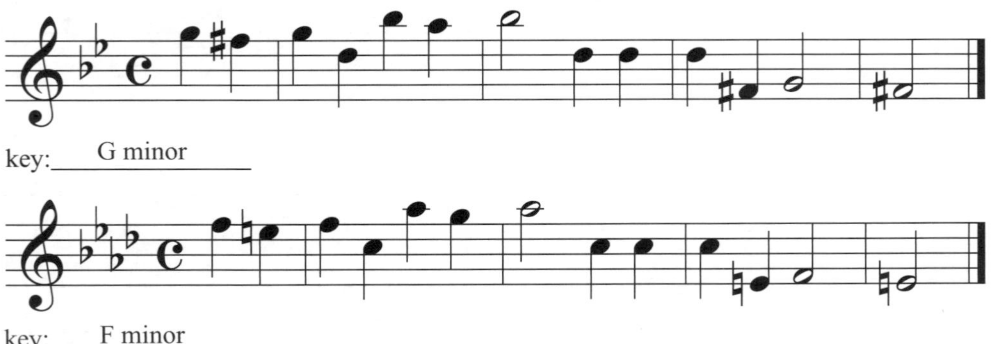

5. Transpose the following melody up a minor 3rd into the alto clef. Name the new key.

key: E minor

key: G minor

6. In what key is the following melody written? Transpose it into G minor, using the correct key signature and omitting any unnecessary accidentals.

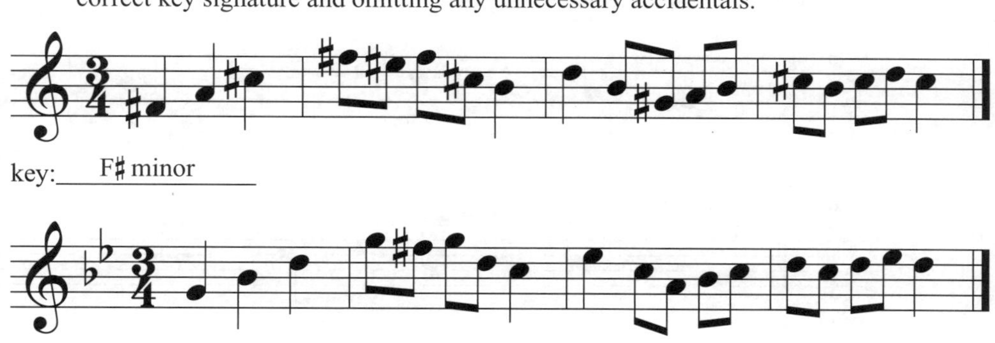

7. In what key is the following melody written? Transpose it down a major 3rd, using the correct key signature and omitting any unnecessary accidentals. Name the new key.

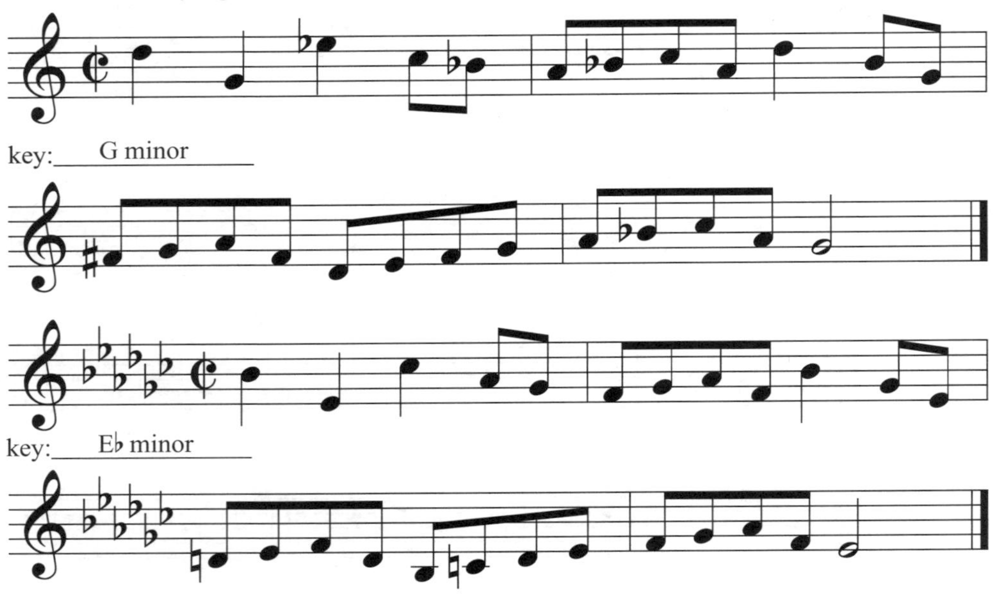

8. In what key is the following melody written? Transpose it a) into G minor b) into B♭ minor, using the correct key signature and omitting any unnecessary accidentals.

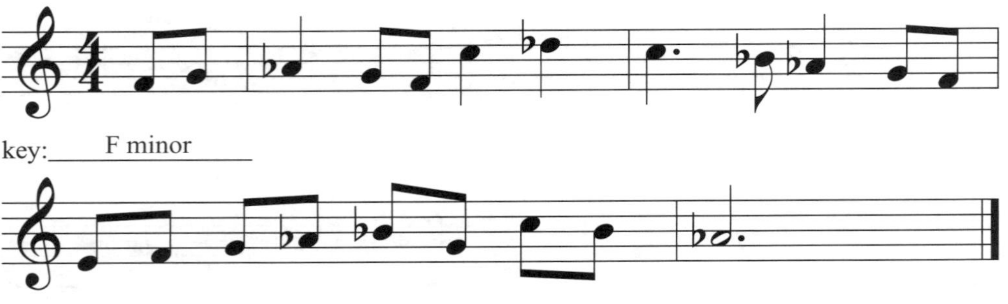

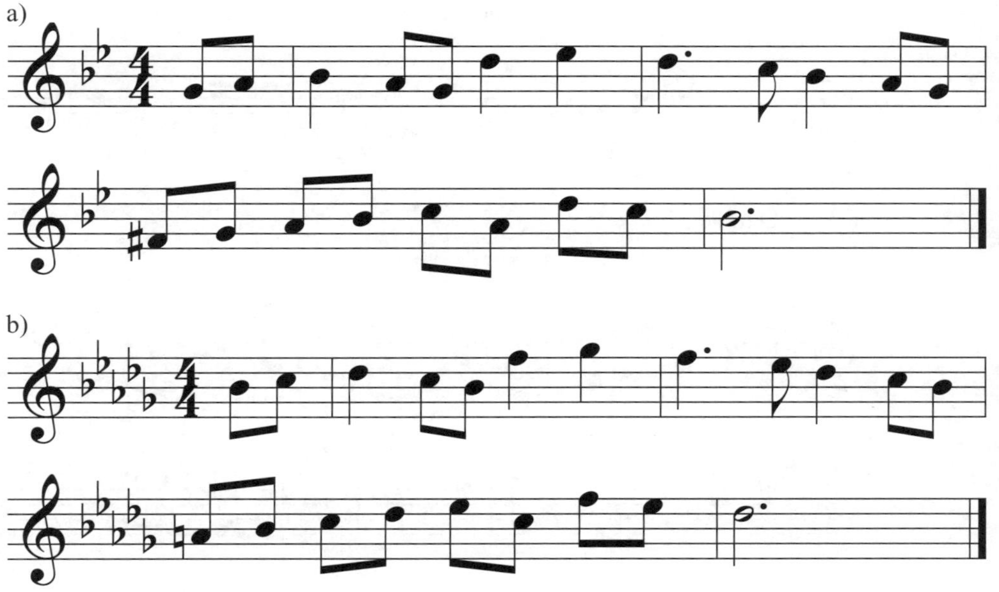

9. In what key is the following melody written? Transpose it into E minor, using the correct key signature and omitting any unnecessary accidentals.

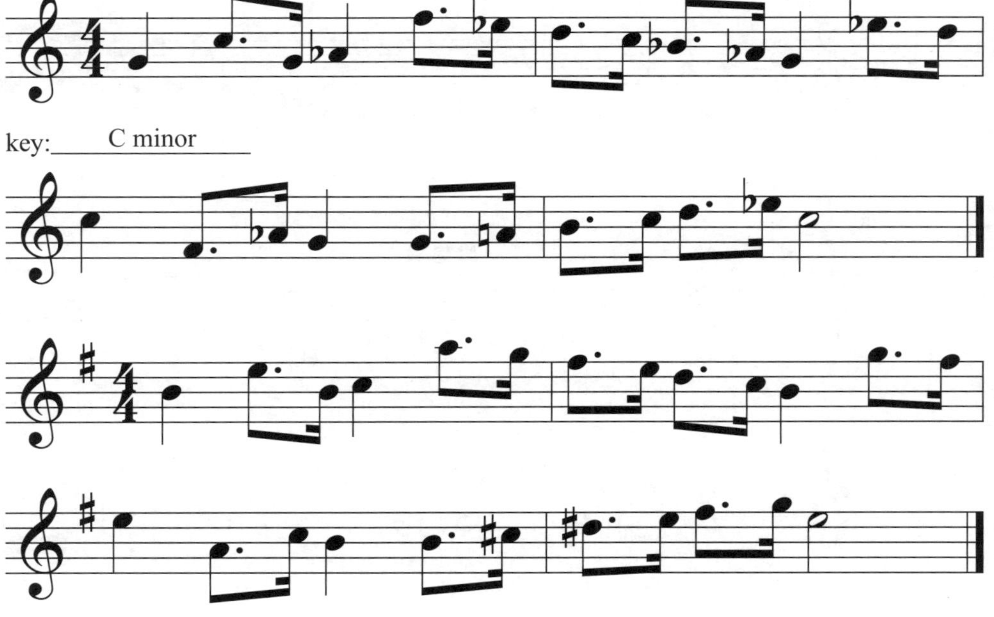

10. Transpose the following melody a) into B minor b) up a major 3rd. Name the new key.

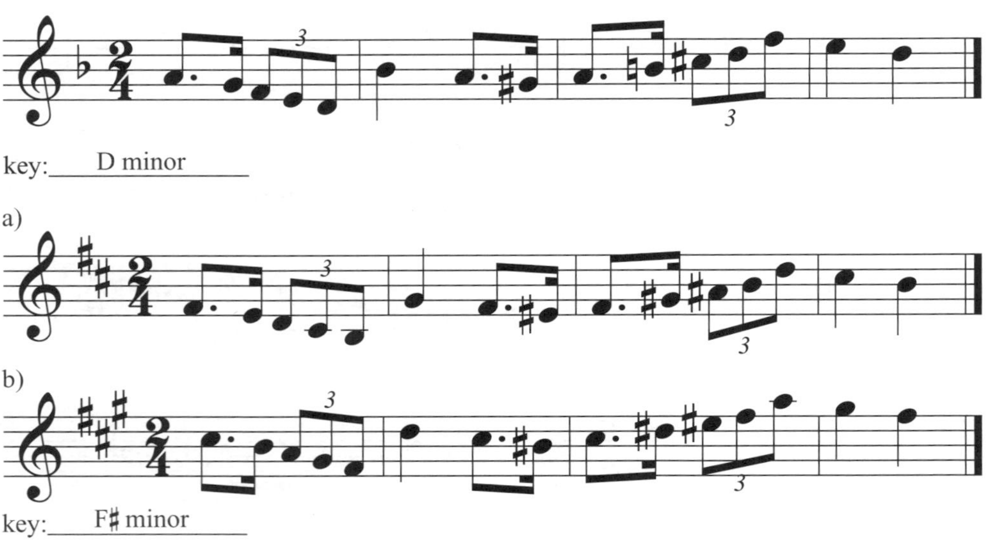

11. In what key is the following melody written? Transpose it a) down a minor 3rd b) up a minor 2nd, using the correct key signature and omitting any unnecessary accidentals. In each case, name the new key.

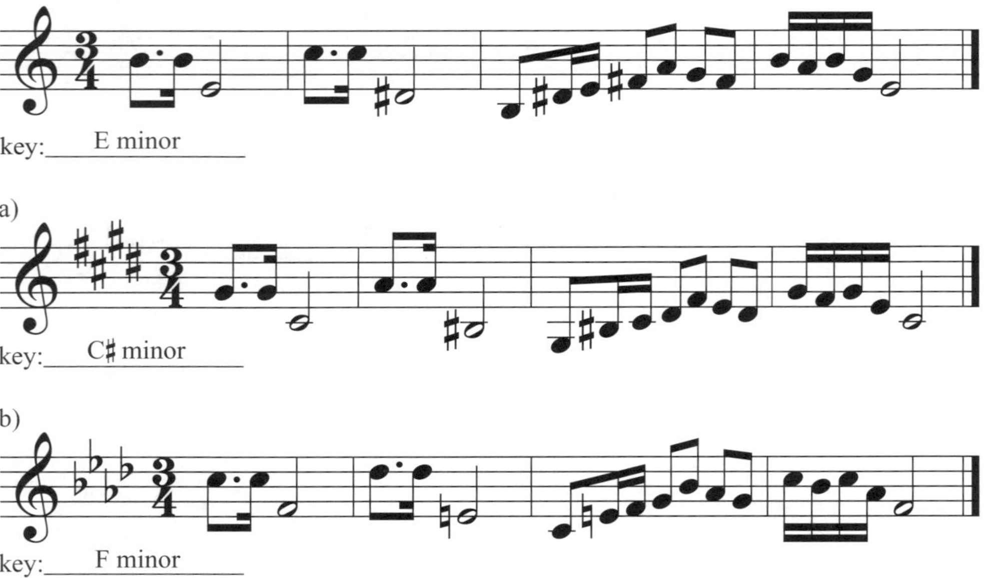

12. Transpose the following melody a) into E♭ major b) into B♭ major.

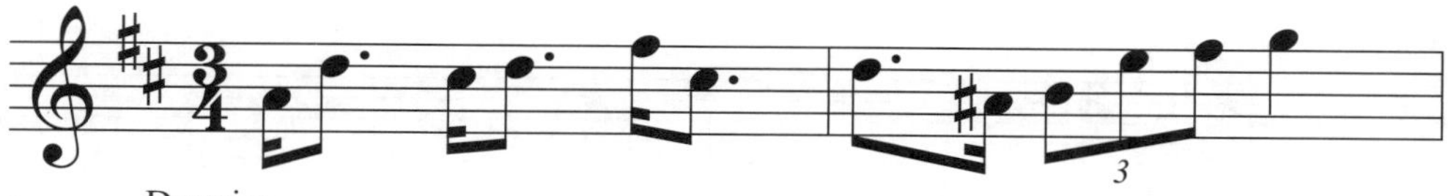

key: D major

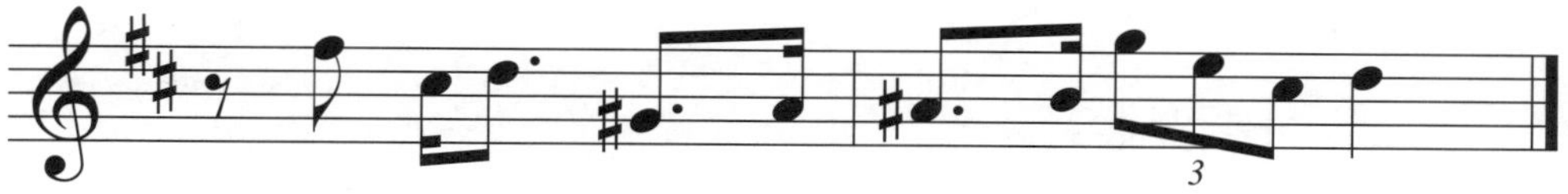

a)

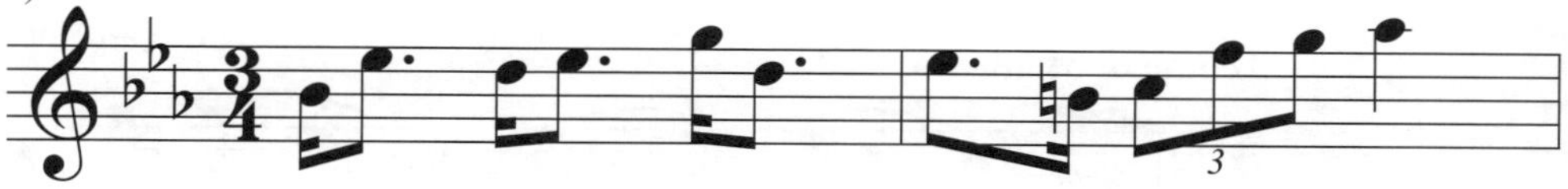

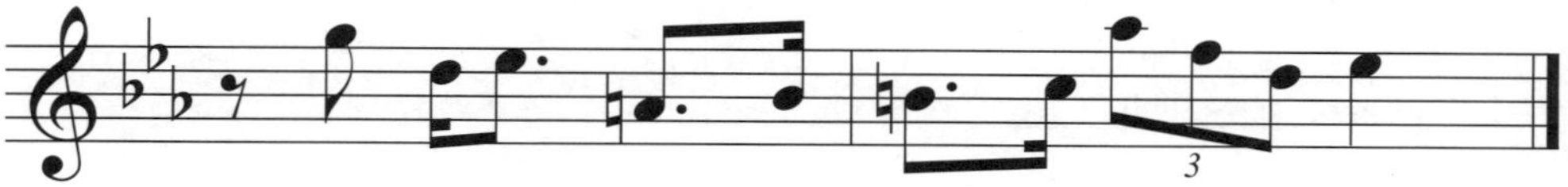

b)

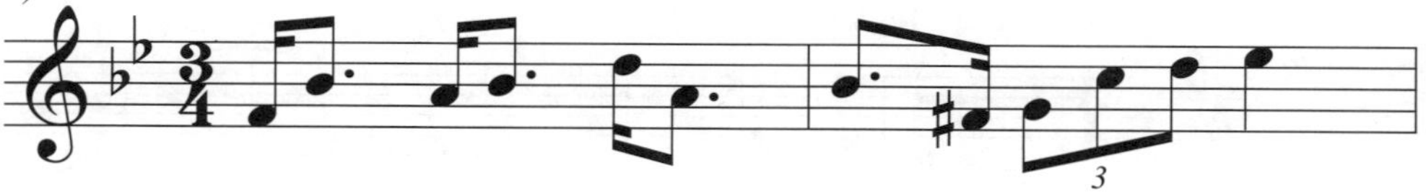

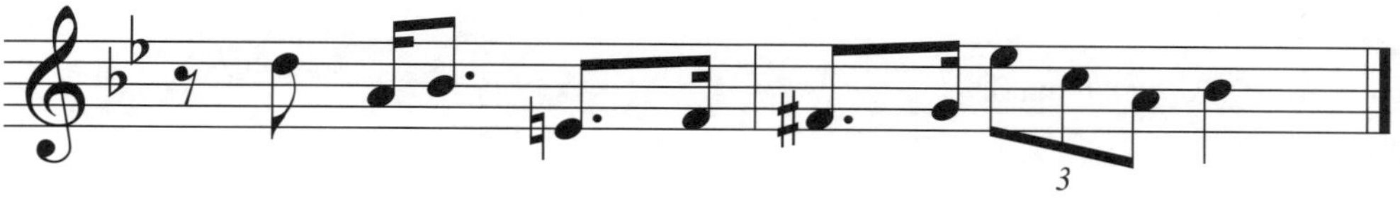

A EXERCISES (p. 258)

1. For each of the following excerpts, name the key in which it is written. Transpose it to concert pitch, using the appropriate new key signature. Name the new key.

a) Trumpet in B♭

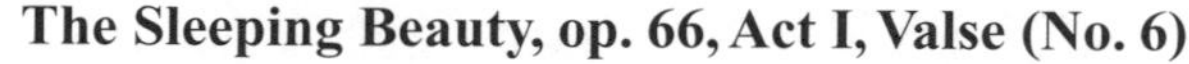

The Sleeping Beauty, op. 66, Act I, Valse (No. 6)

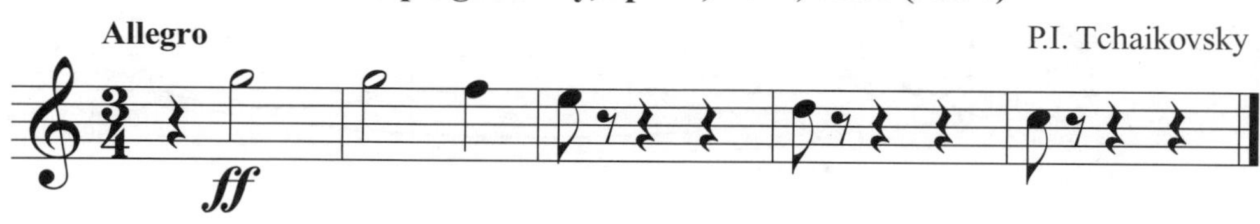

key: C major

The Sleeping Beauty, op. 66, Act I, Valse (No. 6)

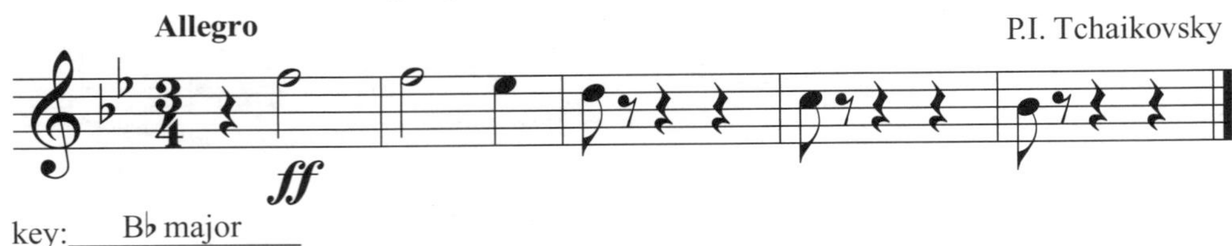

key: B♭ major

b) French horn in F

Symphony No. 8, op. 93, 3rd movement

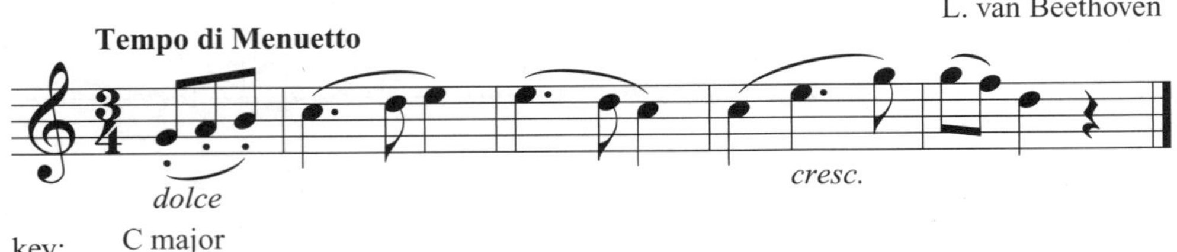

key: C major

Symphony No. 8, op. 93, 3rd movement

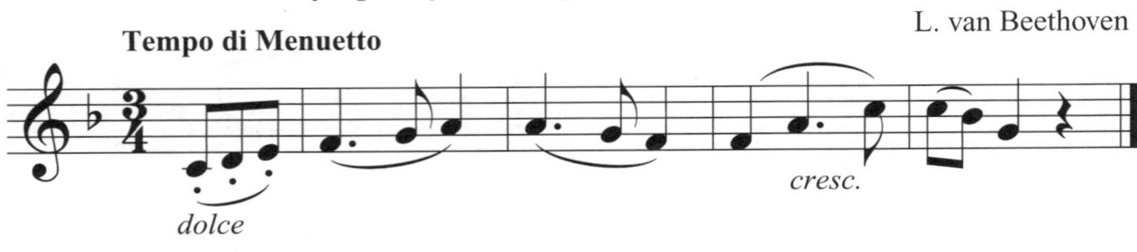

key: F major

c) English horn

Harold in Italy ("Serenade"), op. 16, 3rd movement

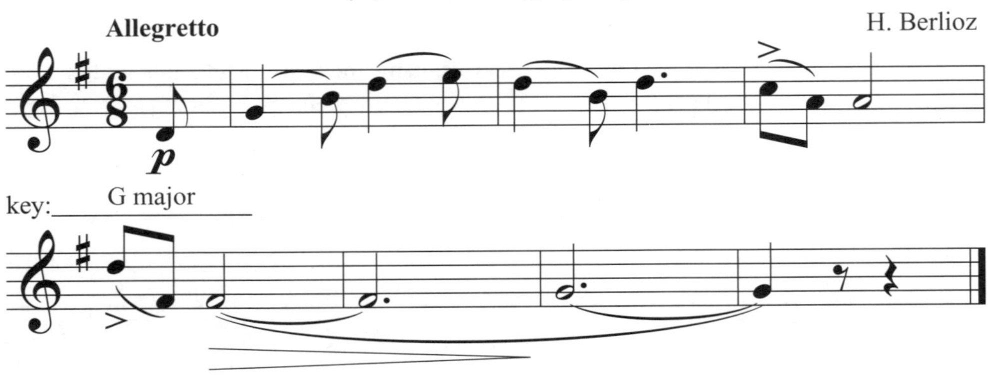

key: G major

Harold in Italy ("Serenade"), op. 16, 3rd movement

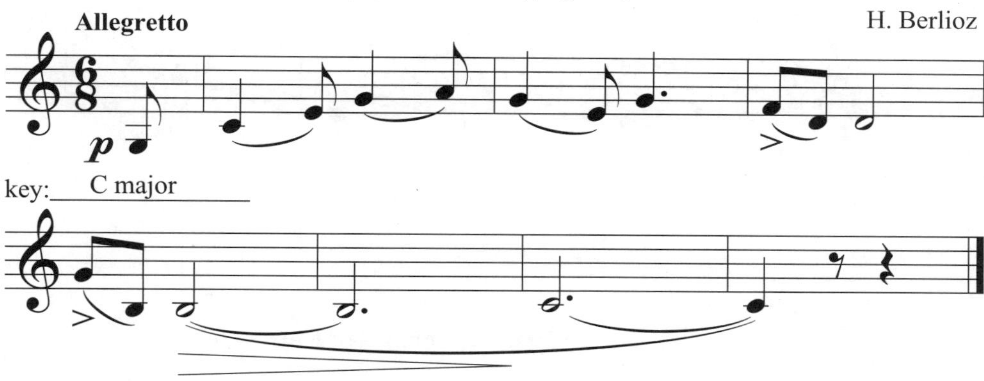

key: C major

d) Clarinet in B♭

Symphony No. 3, op. 90, 2nd movement

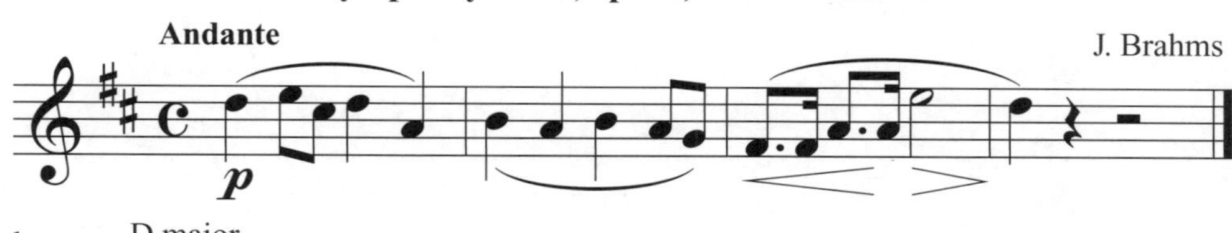

key: D major

Symphony No. 3, op. 90, 2nd movement

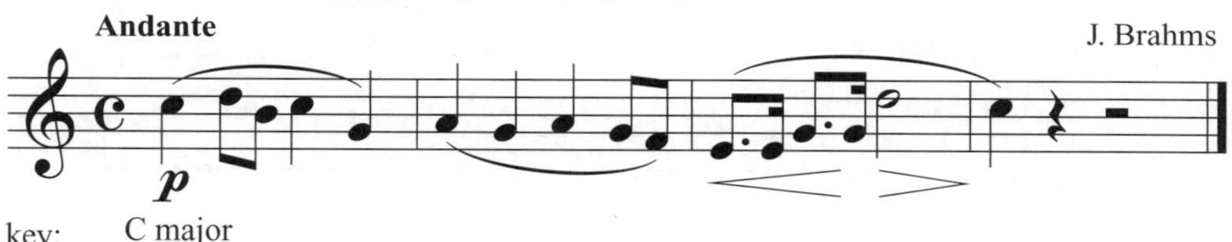

key: C major

e) English horn

Trio, op. 87

L. van Beethoven

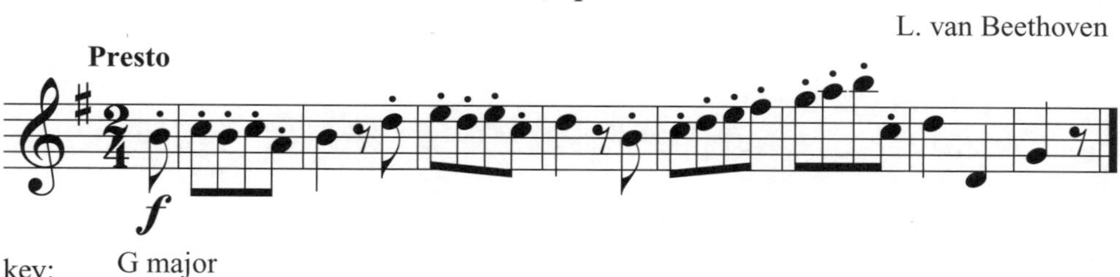

key: G major

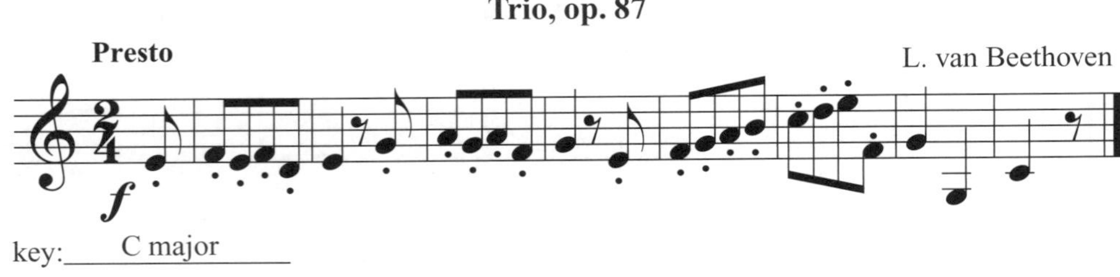

f) Clarinet in B♭

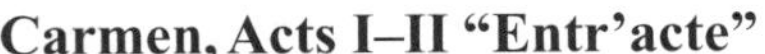

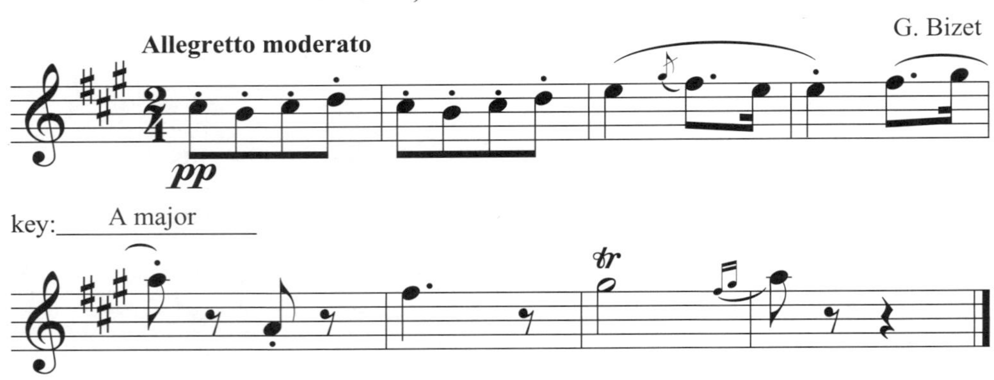

Carmen, Acts I–II "Entr'acte"

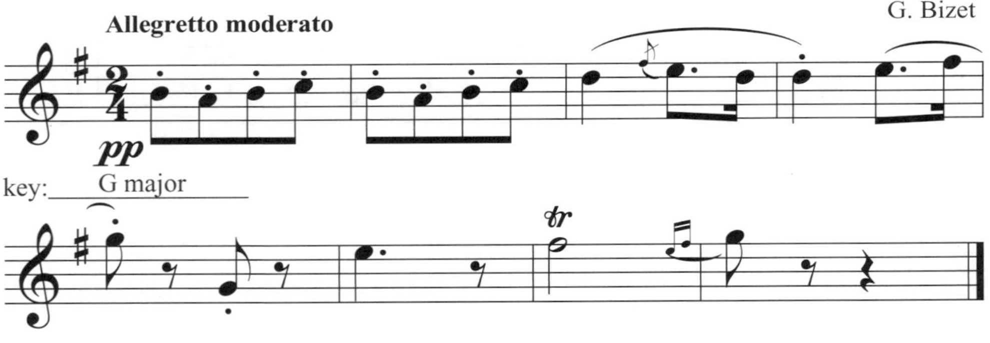

g) English horn

Fantasy Overture, Romeo and Juliet

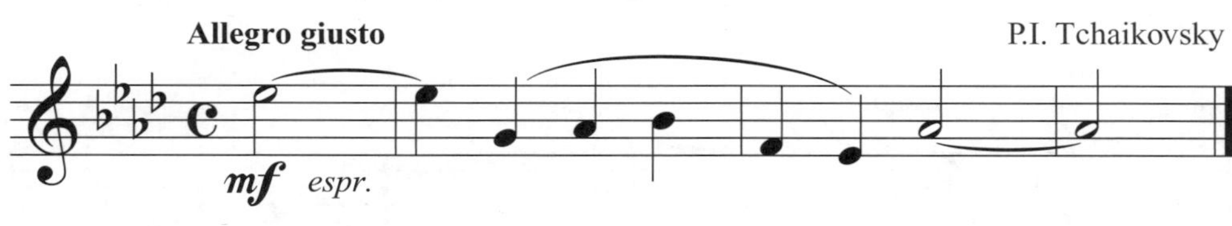

key: A♭ major

Fantasy Overture, Romeo and Juliet

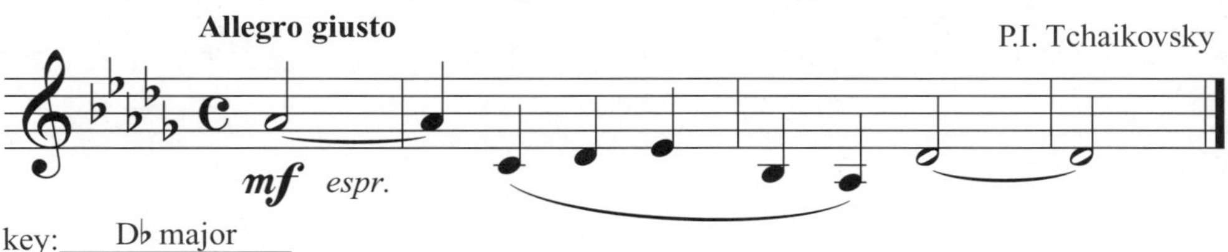

key: D♭ major

h) Clarinet in B♭

A Midsummer Night's Dream, op. 61, "Scherzo"

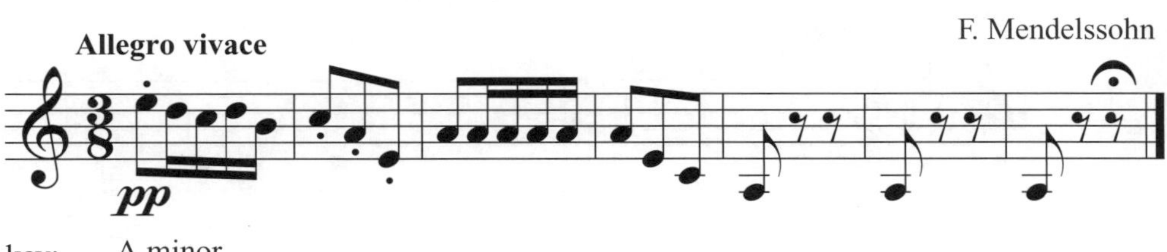

key: A minor

A Midsummer Night's Dream, op. 61, "Scherzo"

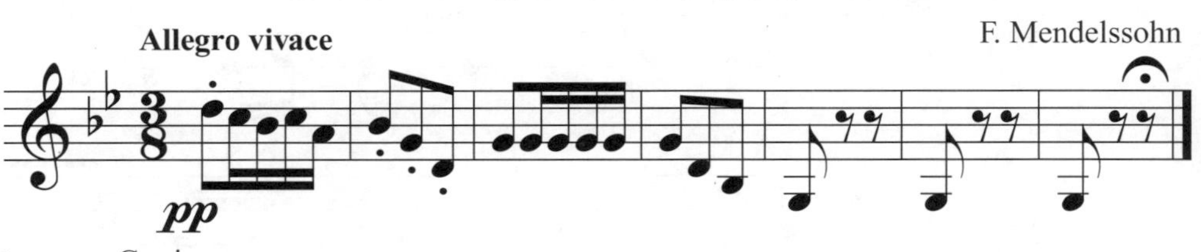

key: G minor

Opt. **EXERCISES** (p. 262)

1. Rewrite the following passages of music, correcting the mistakes.

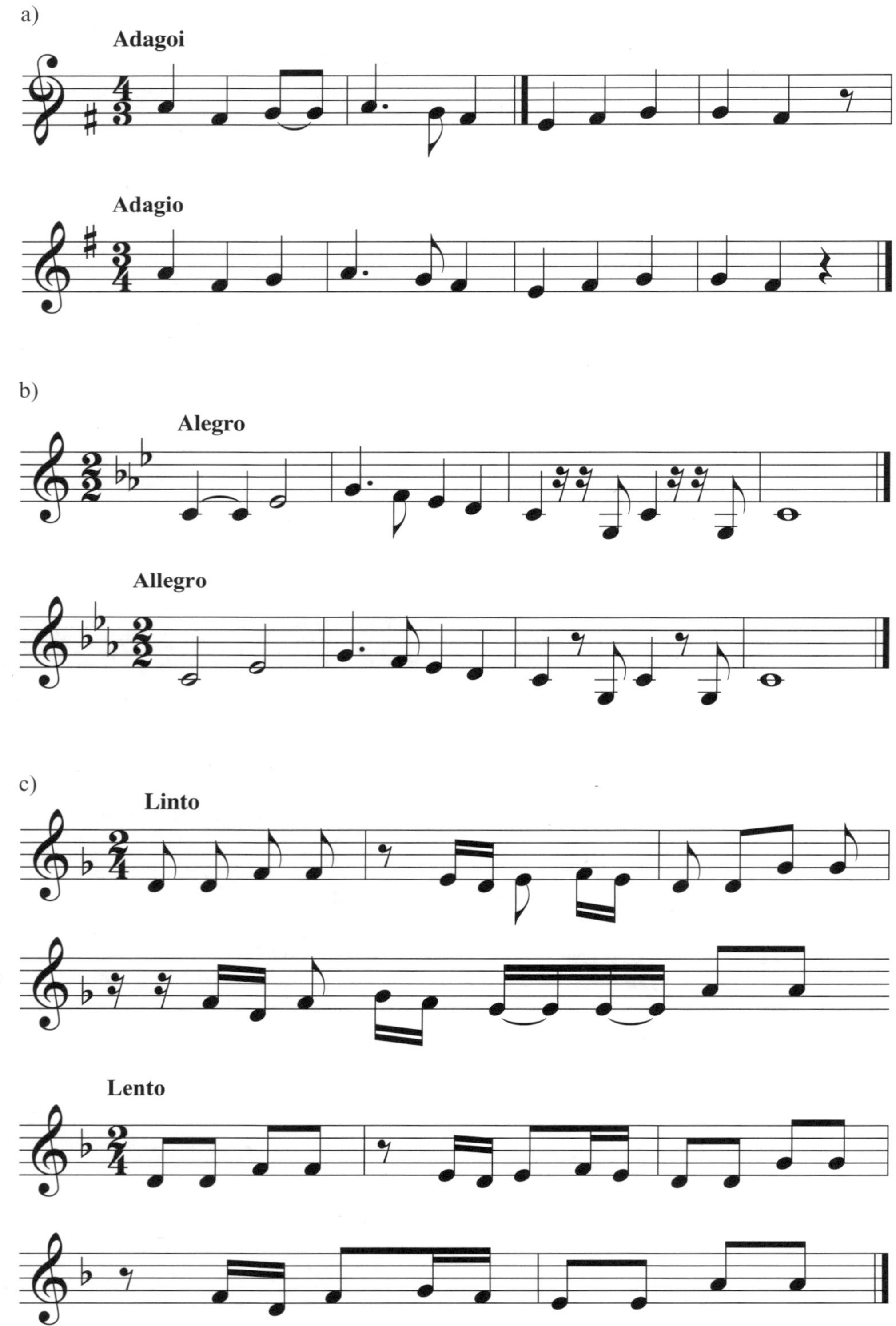

d)

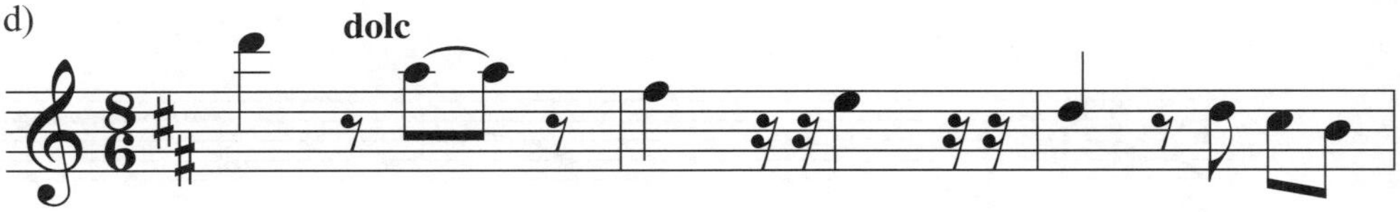

dolc

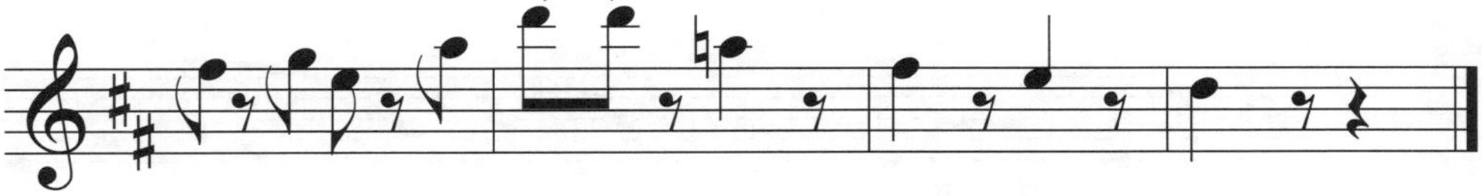

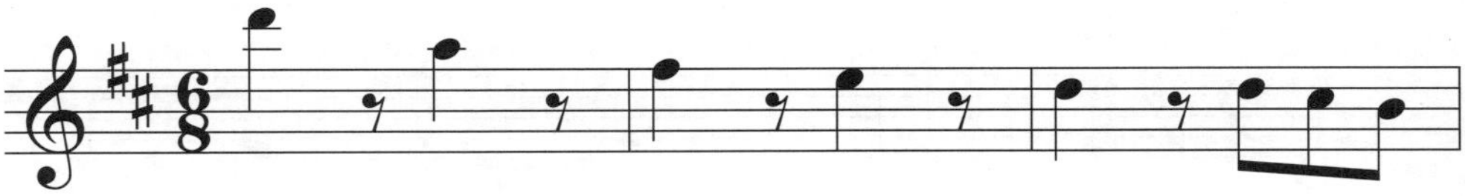

Dolce

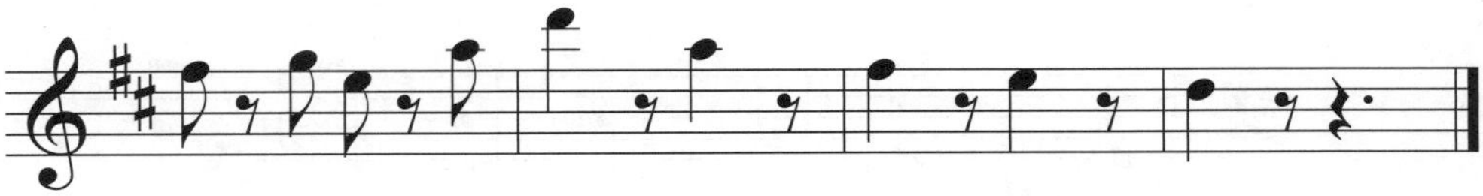

e)

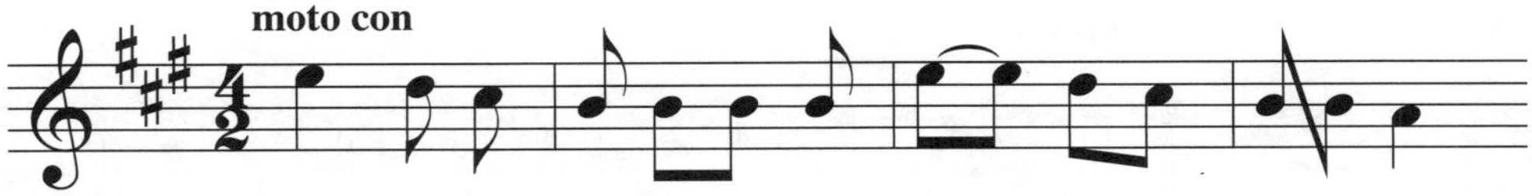

moto con

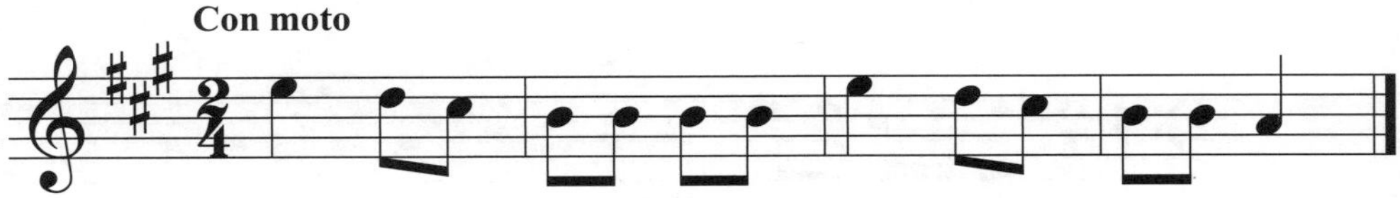

Con moto

Opt. **MORE EXERCISES** (p. 264)

1. Rewrite the following passages of music, correcting the mistakes.

a)

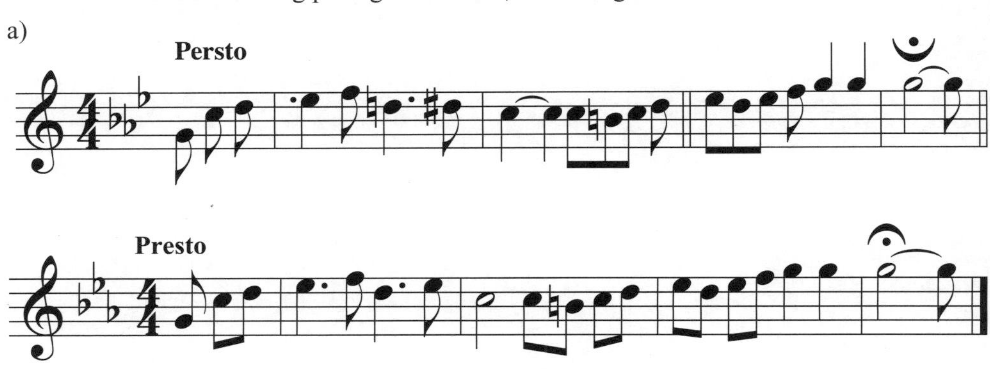

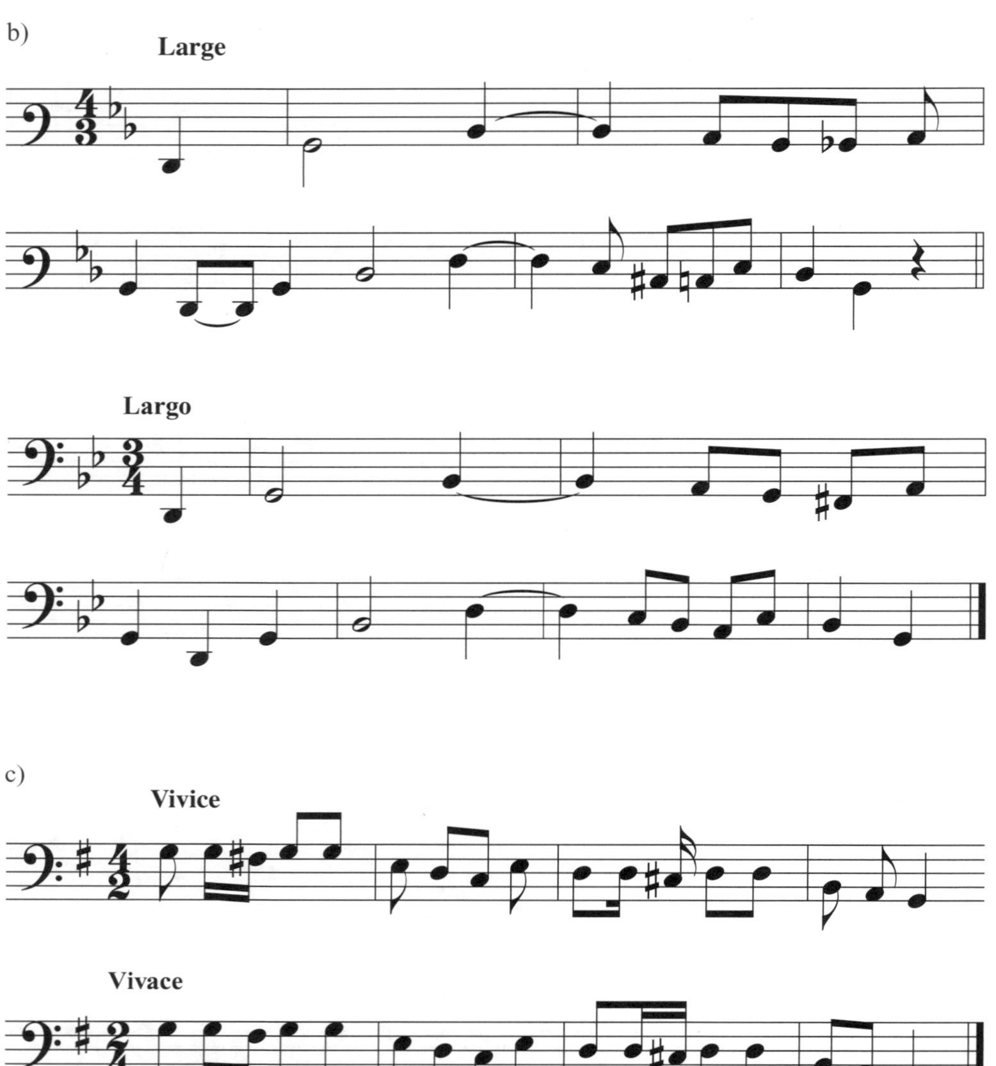
b)
Large
Largo
c)
Vivice
Vivace

d)

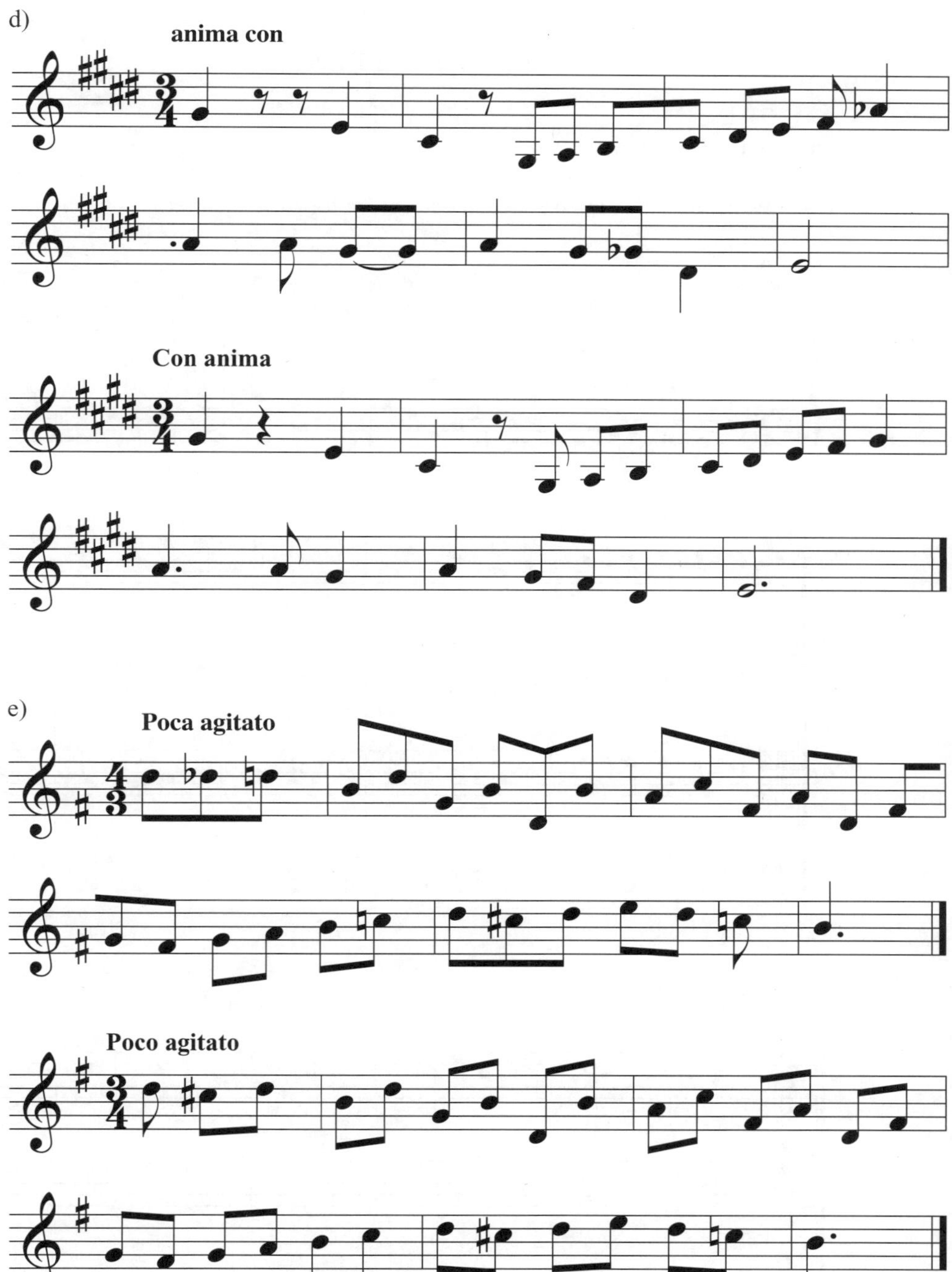

CHAPTER 9

SCORE TYPES

A EXERCISES (p. 270)

1. Write the following passage in open score for string quartet.

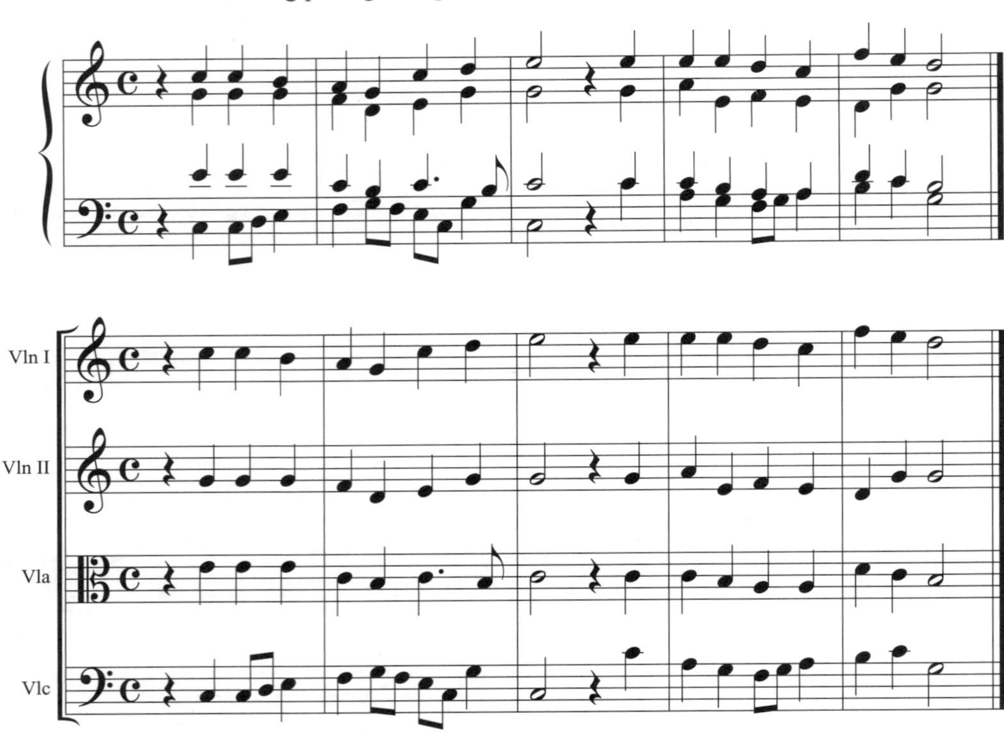

2. Write the following passage in short (condensed) score.

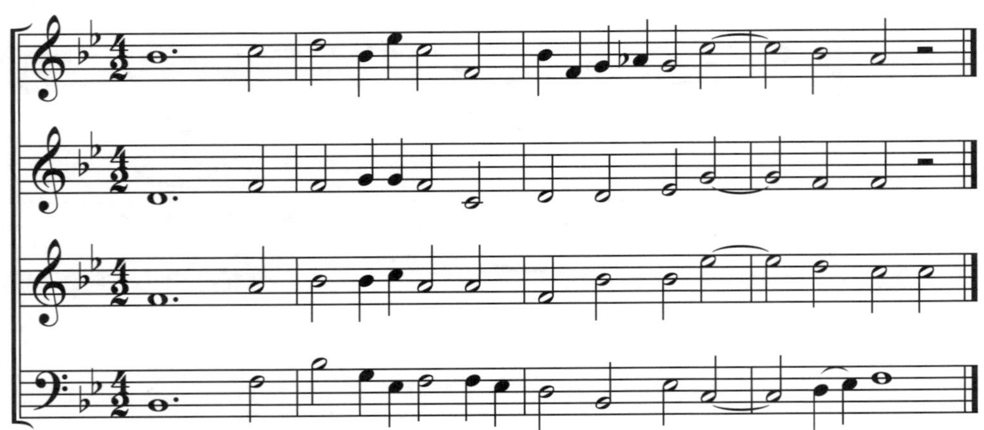

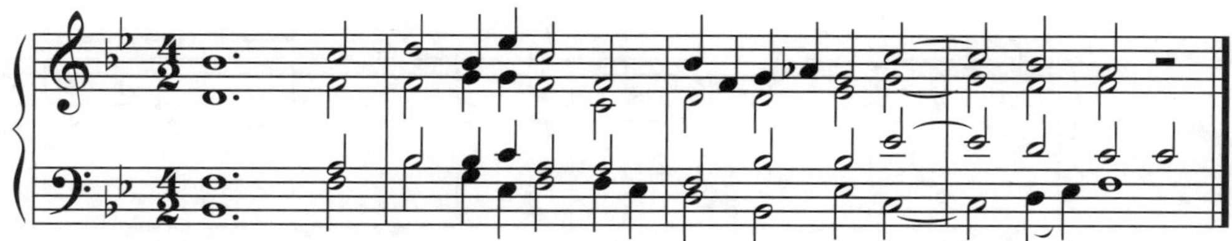

3. Write the following passage in modern vocal score.

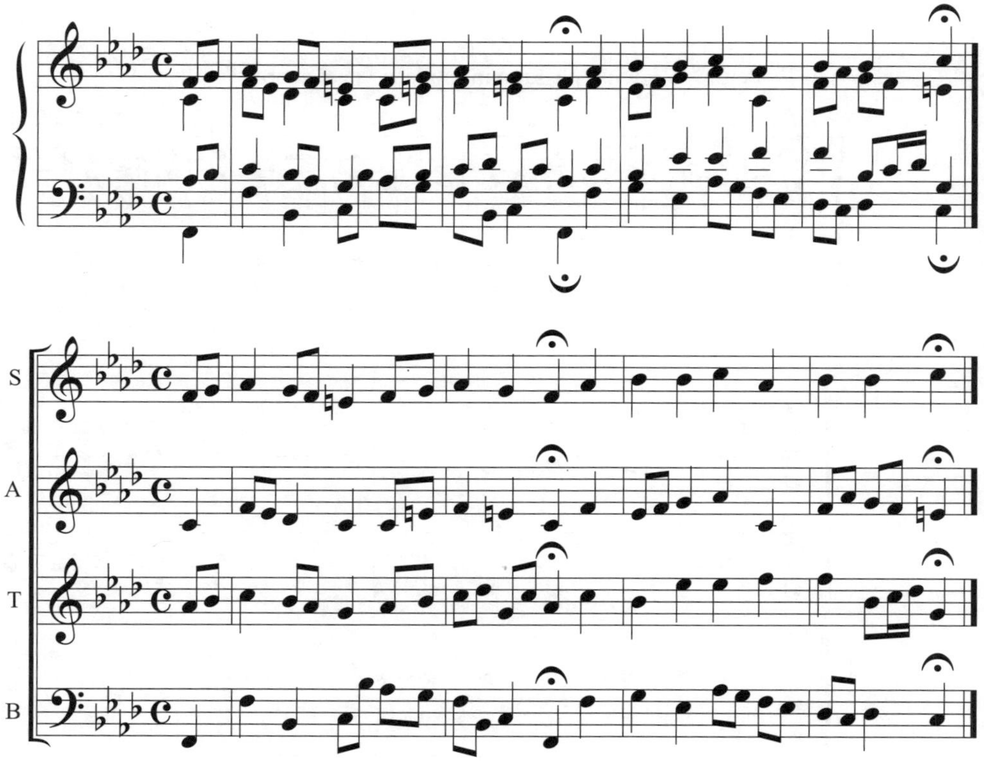

4. Write the following passage in short (condensed) score.

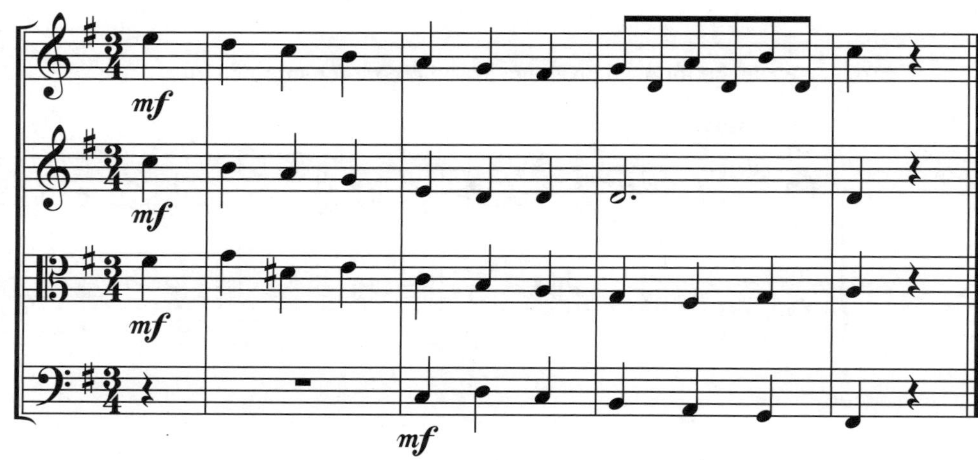

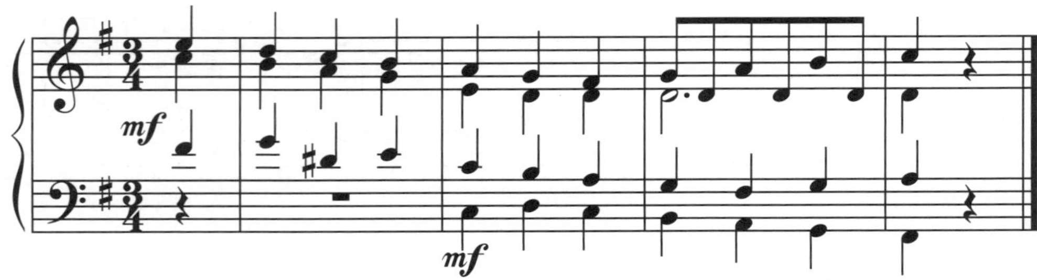

5. Write the following passage in modern vocal score.

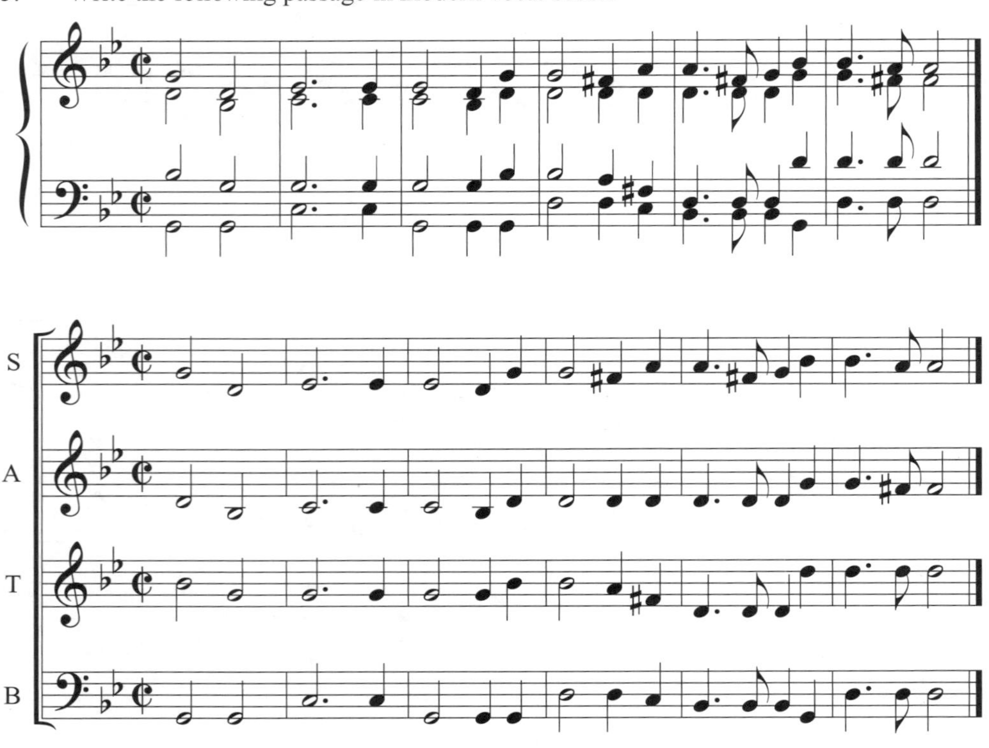

6. Write the following passage in open score for string quartet.

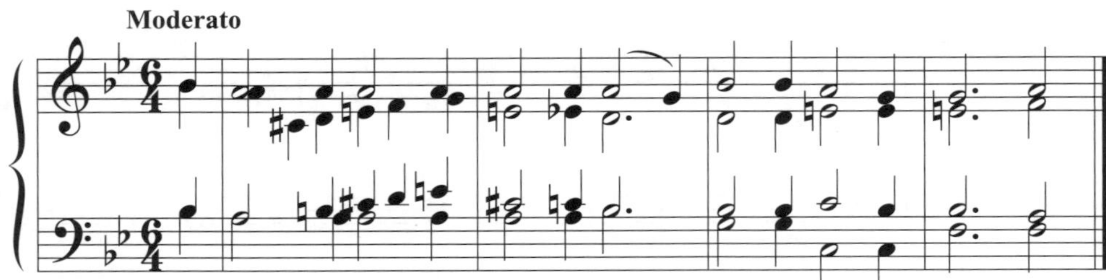

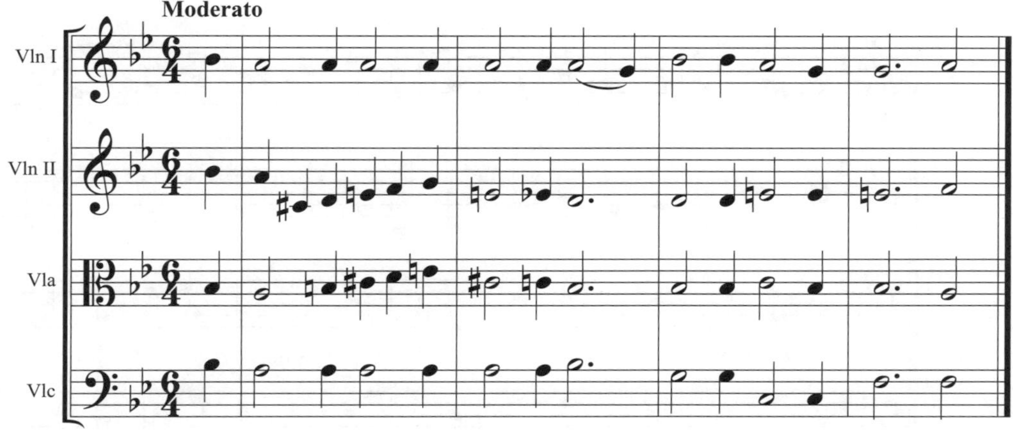

7. Write the following passage in short (condensed) score.

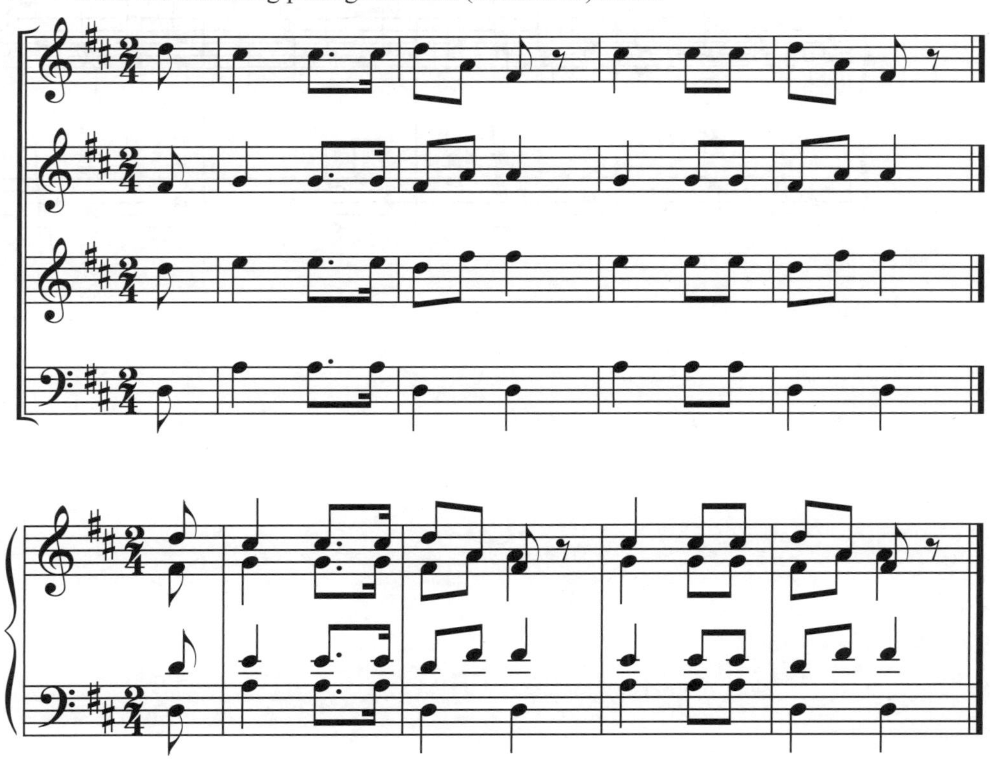

8. Write the following passage in short (condensed) score.

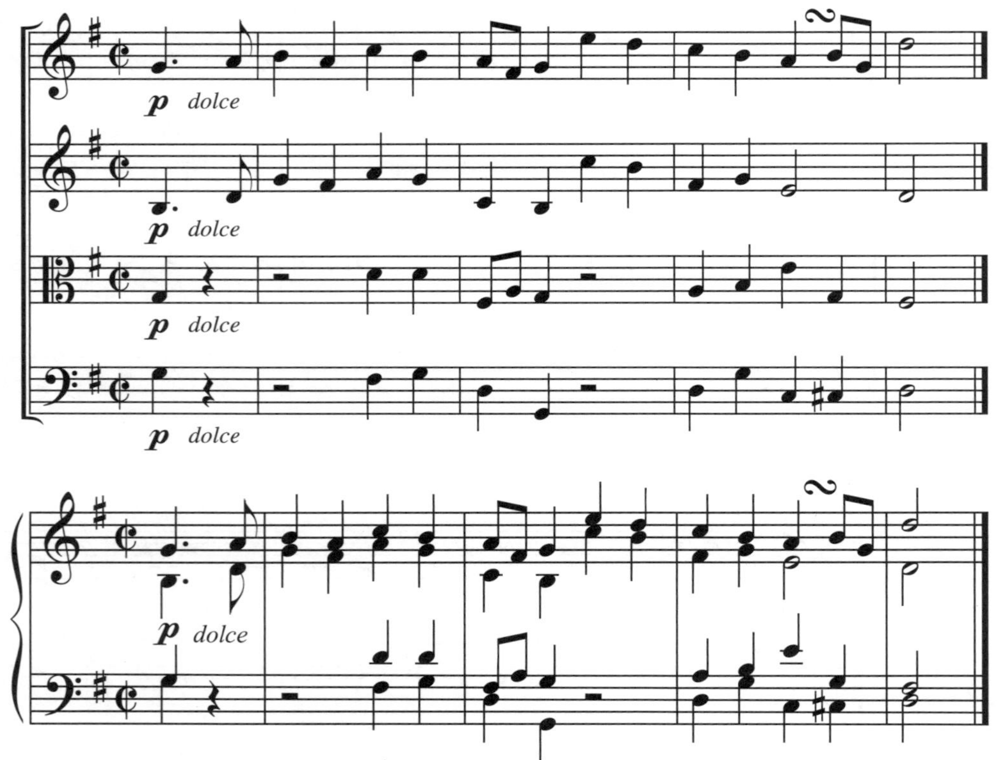

Opt. **EXERCISES** (p. 274)

1. Write the following in short (condensed) score.

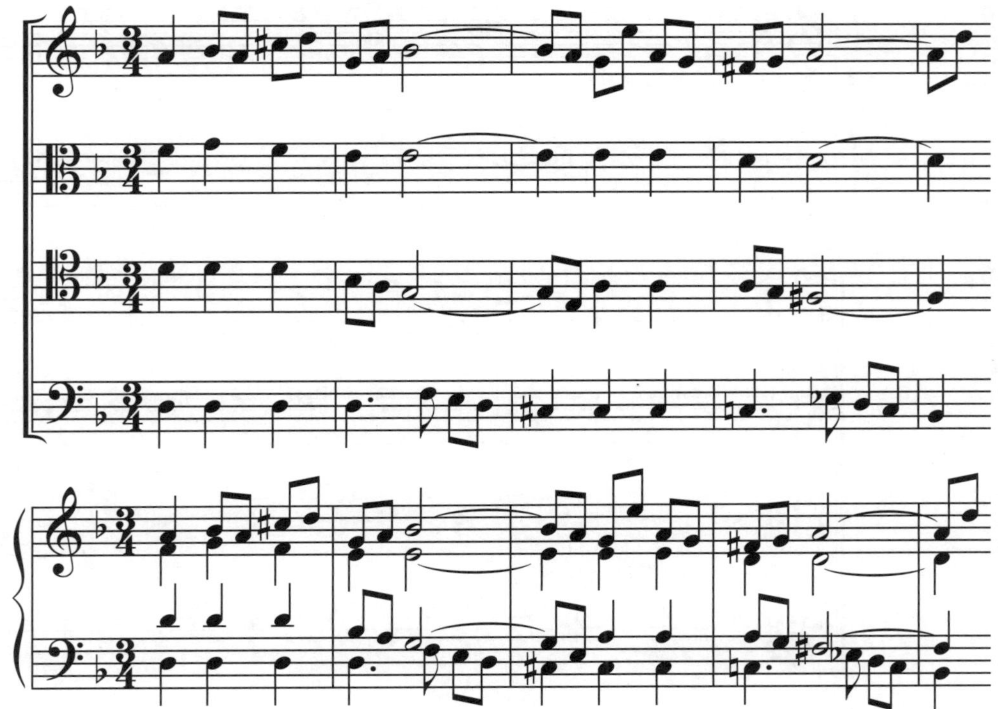

2. Write the following passage in open score, using C clefs for alto and tenor.

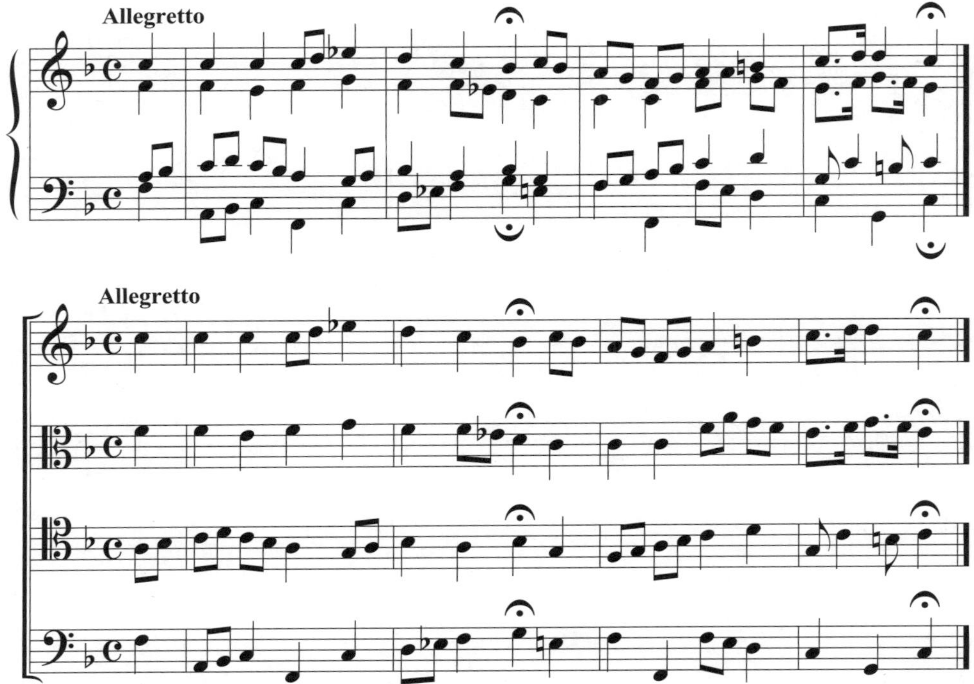

3. Write the following passage in open score, using C clefs for alto and tenor.

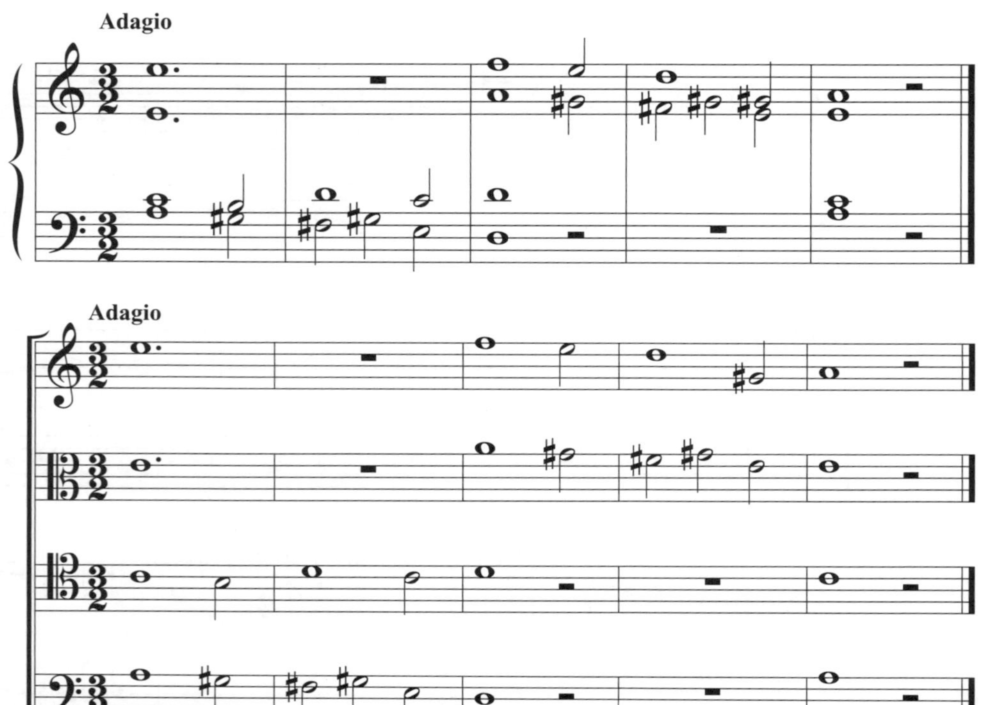

Adagio

CHAPTER 11

ANALYSIS

B I A EXERCISES (p. 289)

1. Analyze the following music excerpt by answering the questions below.

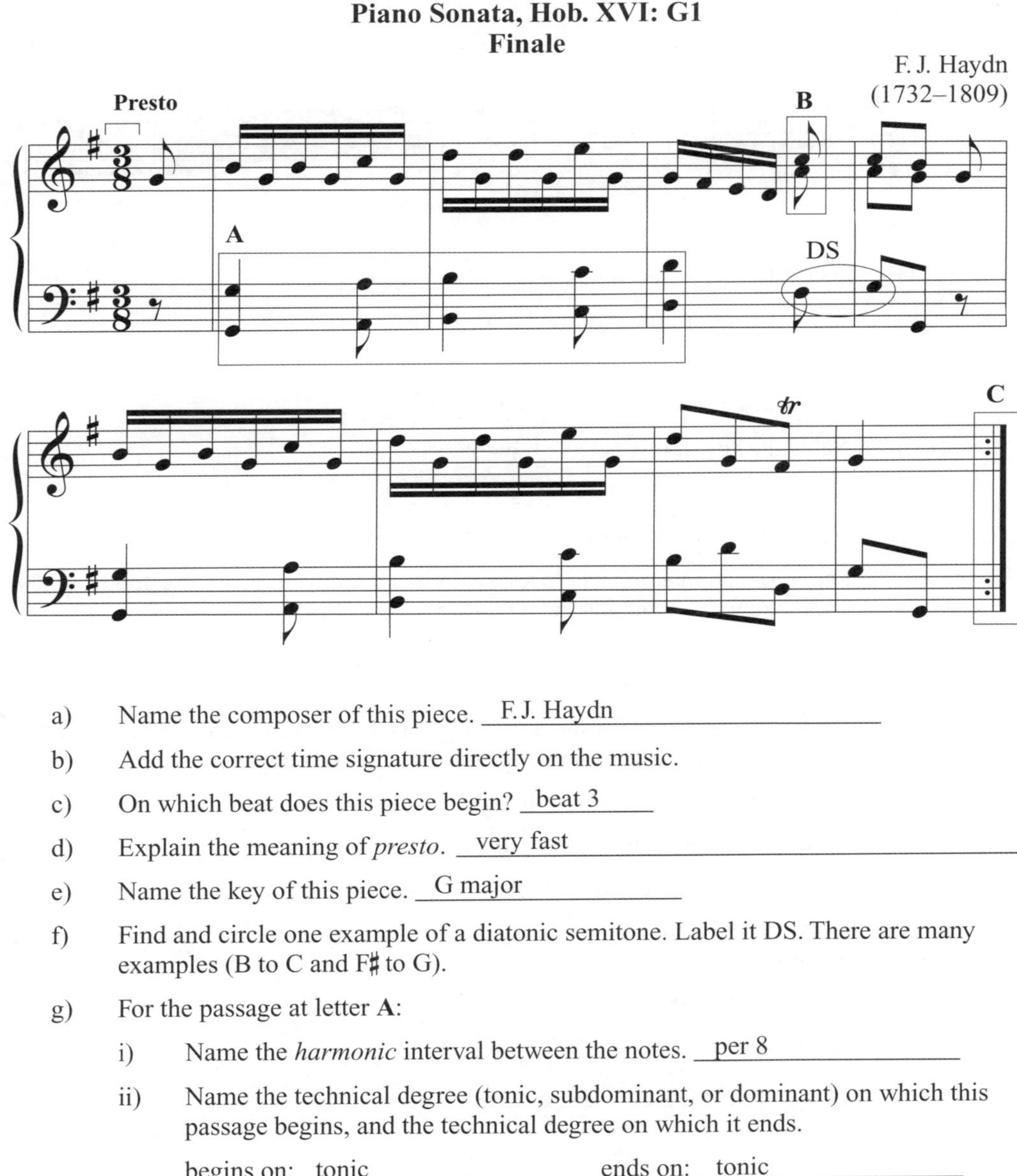

a) Name the composer of this piece. F.J. Haydn

b) Add the correct time signature directly on the music.

c) On which beat does this piece begin? beat 3

d) Explain the meaning of *presto*. very fast

e) Name the key of this piece. G major

f) Find and circle one example of a diatonic semitone. Label it DS. There are many examples (B to C and F♯ to G).

g) For the passage at letter **A**:

   i) Name the *harmonic* interval between the notes. per 8

   ii) Name the technical degree (tonic, subdominant, or dominant) on which this passage begins, and the technical degree on which it ends.

   begins on: tonic ends on: tonic

h) Name the interval at letter **B**. min 3

i) Explain the sign at letter **C**. repeat sign – repeat from the beginning

2. Analyze the following music excerpt by answering the questions below.

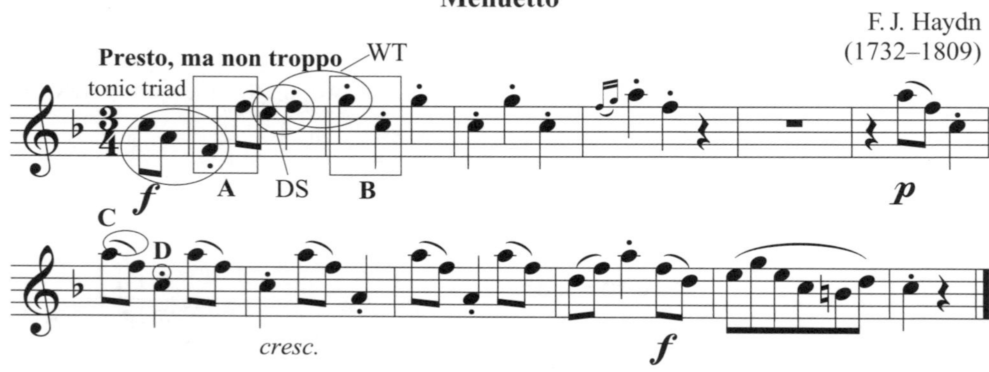

a) Name the composer of this piece. F.J. Haydn

b) Add the correct time signature directly on the music.

c) Name the type of rest in measure 5. whole rest

How many beats are in measure 5? 3 beats

d) Name the key of this piece. F major

e) Name the interval at letter **A**. per 8

f) Name the interval at letter **B**. per 5

g) Find one example of a whole tone. Circle it directly on the music and label it WT. There are many examples (F to G, G to A, D to E, D to C).

h) Find one example of a diatonic semitone. Circle it directly on the music and label it DS. There are two examples (E to F, also C to B in m. 11).

i) Find one example of the tonic triad in broken form and circle it directly on the music. There are many more examples of this triad in inversion.

j) Name and explain the sign at letter **C**.

slur–the notes within the slur are to be played *legato*

k) Name and explain the sign at letter **D**. *staccato*–detached

l) For each of the following abbreviations, give the complete Italian term, then explain its meaning:

f *forte*–loud

p *piano*–soft

cresc. *crescendo*–becoming louder

I A 3. Analyze the following music excerpt by answering the questions below.

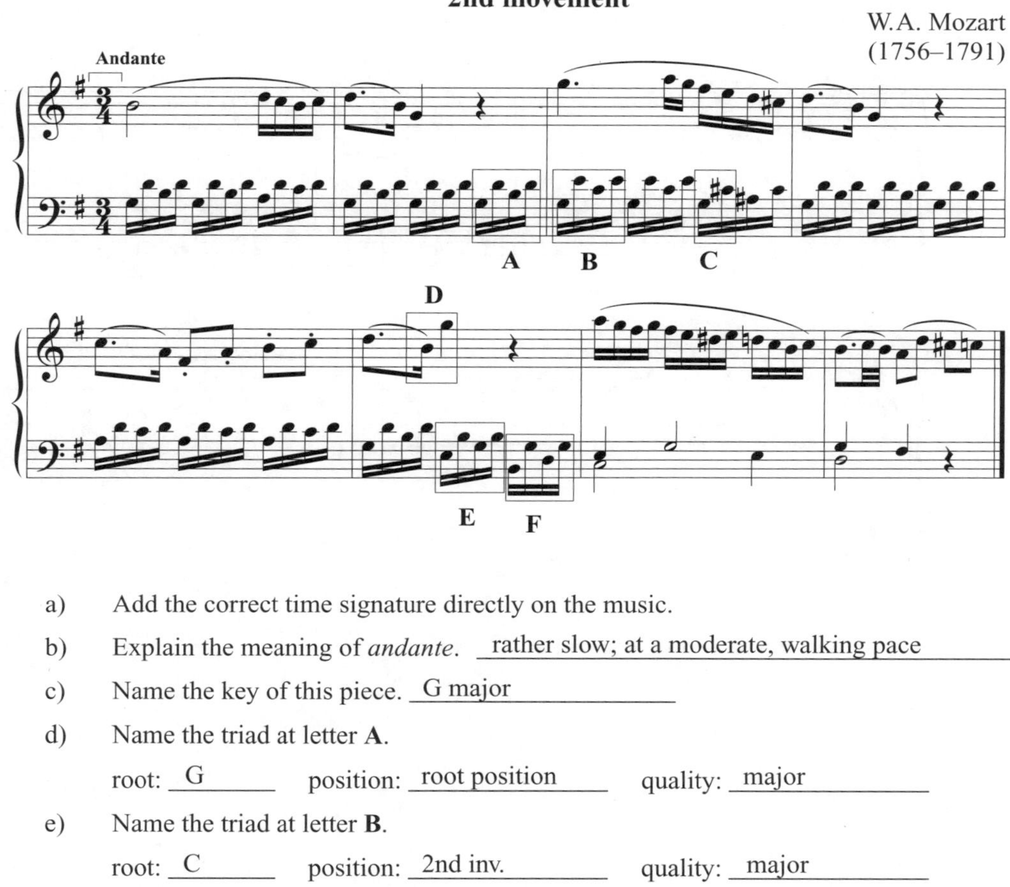

a) Add the correct time signature directly on the music.

b) Explain the meaning of *andante*. rather slow; at a moderate, walking pace

c) Name the key of this piece. G major

d) Name the triad at letter **A**.

root: G position: root position quality: major

e) Name the triad at letter **B**.

root: C position: 2nd inv. quality: major

f) Name the interval at letter **C**. aug 4

g) Name the interval at letter **D**. min 6

h) Name the triad at letter **E**.

root: E position: root position quality: minor

i) Name the triad at letter **F**.

root: G position: 1st inv. quality: major

j) Name the harmonic interval on beat 2 of measure 8 of the left-hand part.

maj 3

A 4. Analyze the following music excerpt by answering the questions below.

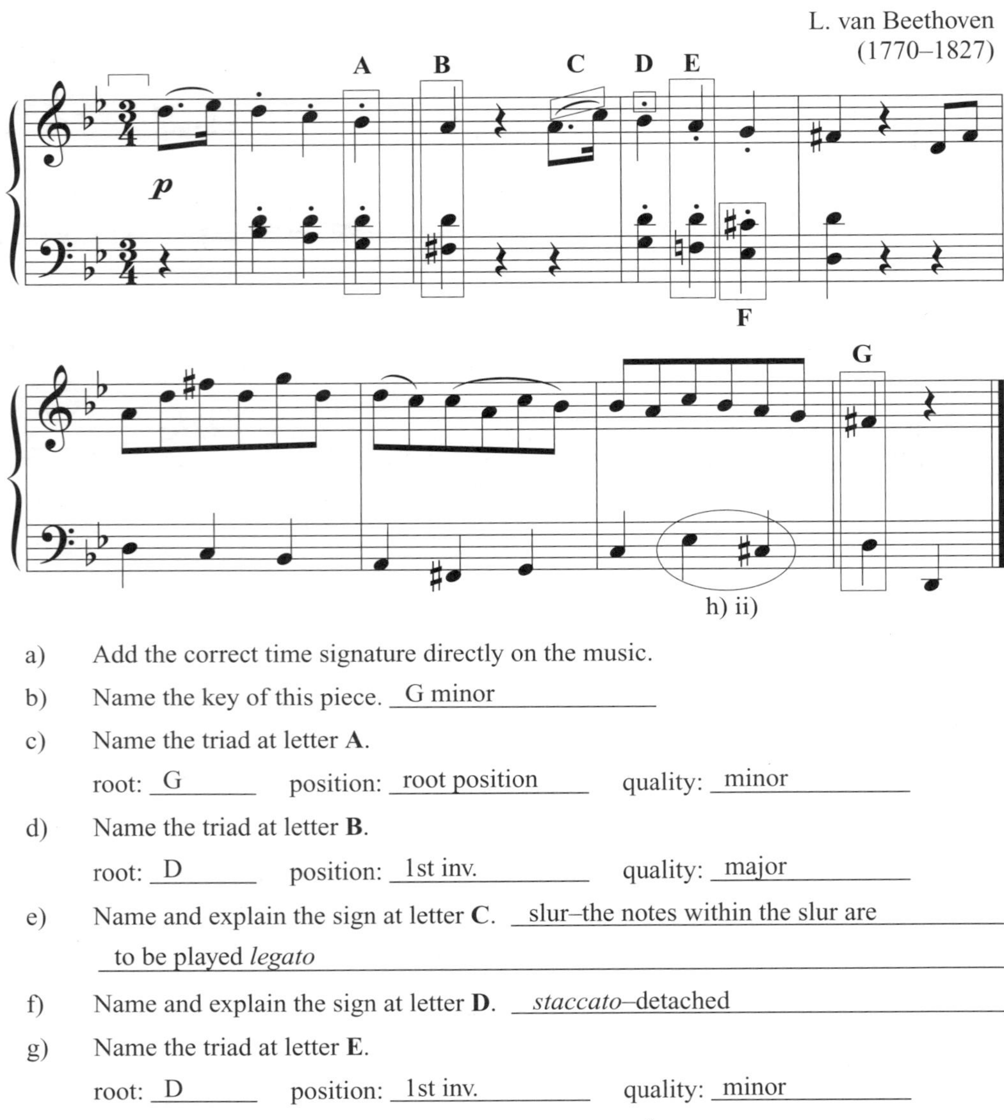

a) Add the correct time signature directly on the music.

b) Name the key of this piece. G minor

c) Name the triad at letter **A**.

root: G position: root position quality: minor

d) Name the triad at letter **B**.

root: D position: 1st inv. quality: major

e) Name and explain the sign at letter **C**. slur–the notes within the slur are to be played *legato*

f) Name and explain the sign at letter **D**. *staccato*–detached

g) Name the triad at letter **E**.

root: D position: 1st inv. quality: minor

h) i) Name the harmonic interval at letter **F**. aug 6

ii) Find and circle the *inversion* of this interval in melodic form.

i) Name the interval at letter **G**. maj 10

5. Analyze the following music excerpt by answering the questions below.

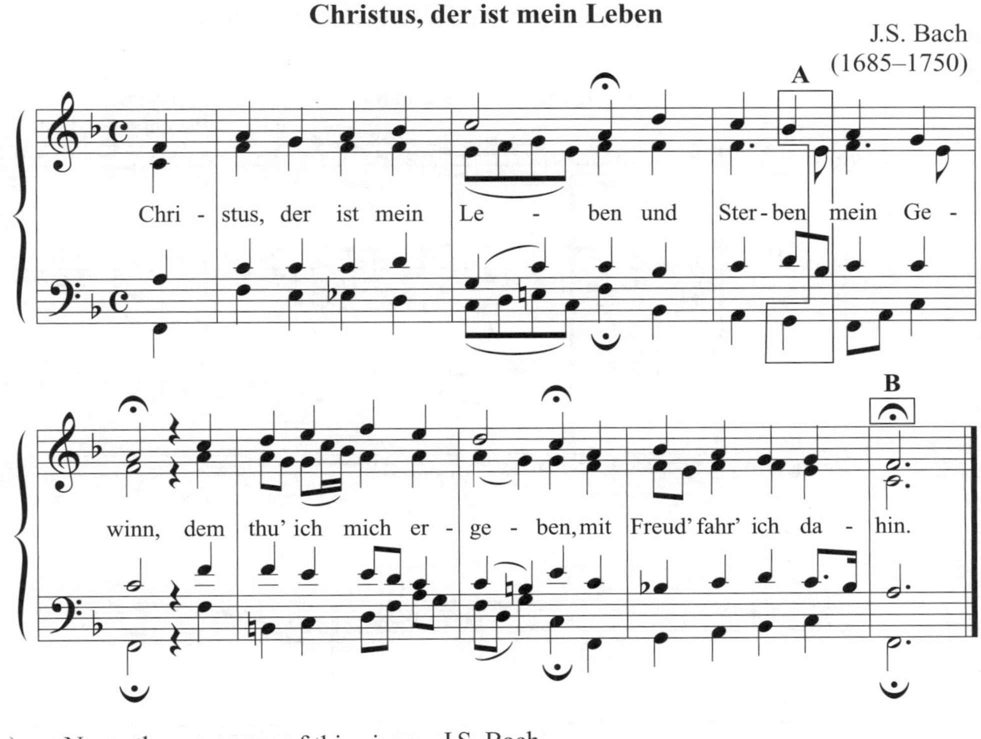

a) Name the composer of this piece. J.S. Bach

b) Name the type of score. short score or condensed score

c) Name the key of this piece. F major

d) On which beat does this piece begin? beat 4

e) For each of the chords in m. 1, name the root, chord type (e.g., triad, 7th chord, etc.), quality, and position.

	root	type	quality	position
beat 1	F	triad	major	root
beat 2	C	triad	major	1st inv.
beat 3	F	7th chord	dom 7th	3rd inv.
beat 4	B♭	triad	major	1st inv.

f) For the chord at letter **A**:

Name the harmonic interval between the soprano and alto parts. dim 5th

Name the harmonic interval between the alto and tenor parts. aug 4

Give the word that describes the size of both of these intervals. tritone

Name the chord (considering all four voices).

root: E type: triad quality: dim position: 1st inv.

g) Name the cadence at the end of this piece. perfect cadence

h) Name the explain the sign at letter **B**.

fermata–a pause–hold the chord longer than its written value

6. Analyze the following music excerpt by answering the questions below.

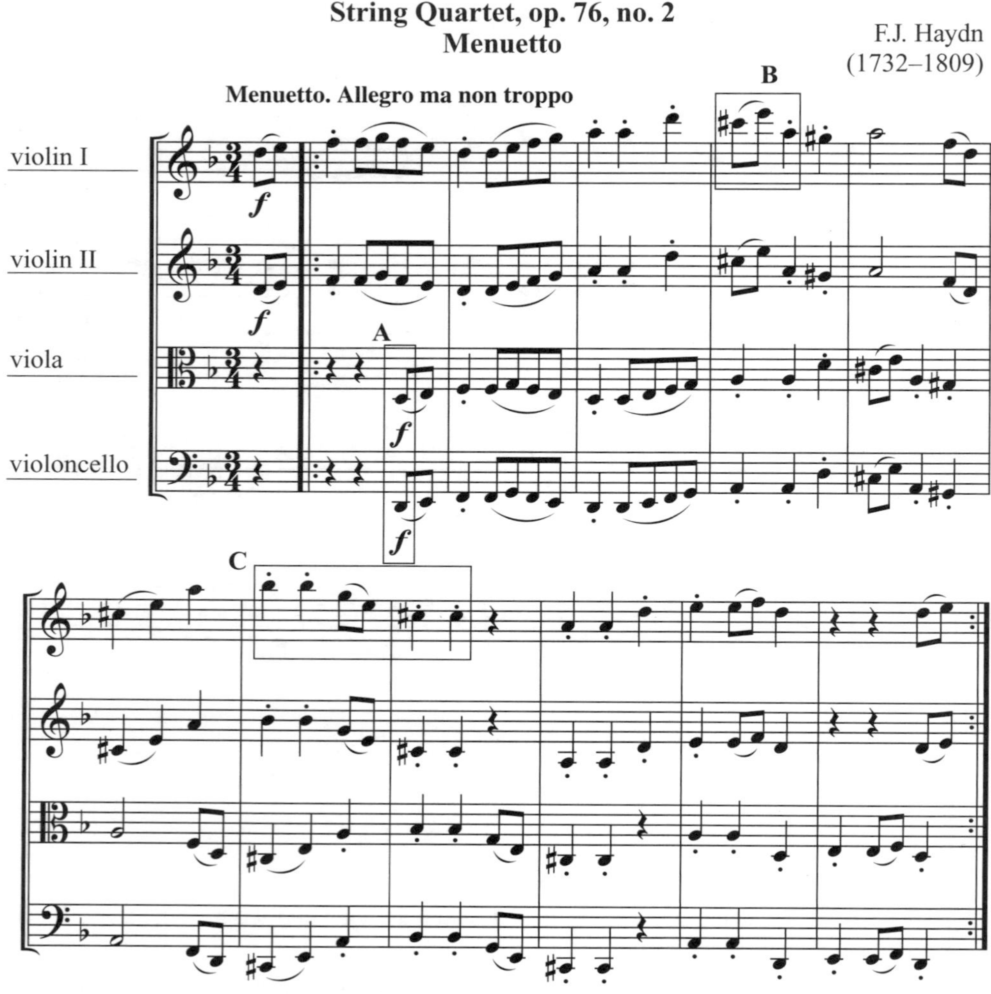

a) Name the composer of this piece. F.J. Haydn

b) Name the type of score. string quartet score

c) On the blank line before each of the four staves at the beginning of the excerpt, write the name of the voice or instrument that performs each part.

d) Name the key of this piece. D minor

e) Give the term that describes the relationship between the two upper parts and the two lower parts in this excerpt. imitation

f) Name the interval at letter **A**. perfect 8

g) For each of the following chords, name the root, chord type (e.g., triad, 7th chord, etc.), and quality.

at **B** root: A type: triad quality: major

at **C** root: C♯ type: 7th chord quality: dim 7

h) Explain the meaning of *Allegro ma non troppo*.

fast, but not too fast (literally–fast, but not too much)

7. Analyze the following piece of music by answering the questions below.

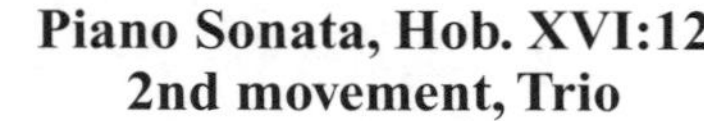

F.J. Haydn
(1732–1809)

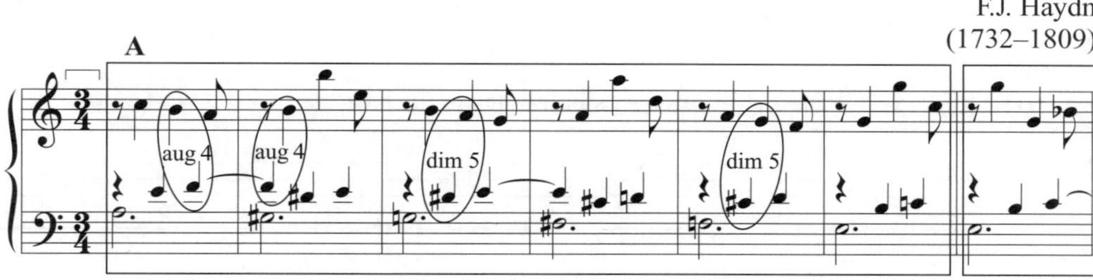

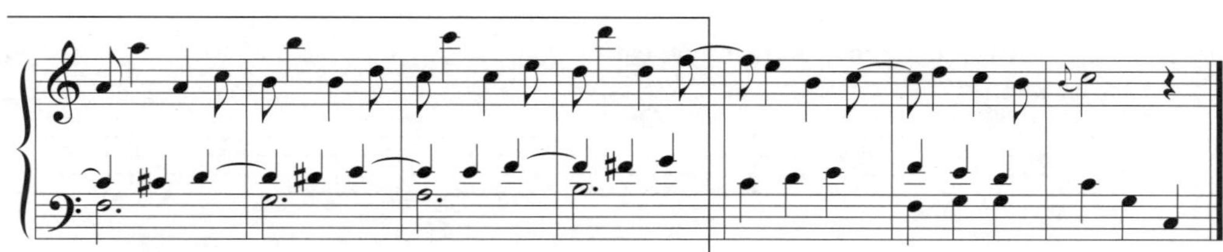

a) Name the composer of this piece. F.J. Haydn

b) Add the correct time signature directly on the music.

c) Name the type of scale in the bass line of the passage at letter **A**. chromatic

d) i) Give the term for the technique used in the passage at letter **A**. sequence

ii) Draw a box around another passage that uses the same technique.

e) Name the key and type of the cadence at the end of the excerpt. (Note that the excerpt does not end in the same key in which it began.)

key: C major cadence: perfect

f) Find and circle three different examples of a harmonic interval of a tritone. Label each of the examples directly on the score with the numeric size and quality of the interval.

CHAPTER 12

TEST PAPERS

Marks **BASIC TEST PAPER** (p. 296)

(10) 1. a) Write the following as half notes in the bass clef.

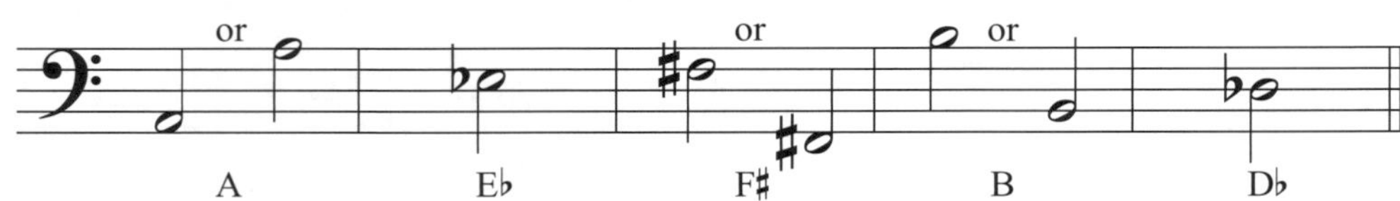

b) Name the following notes.

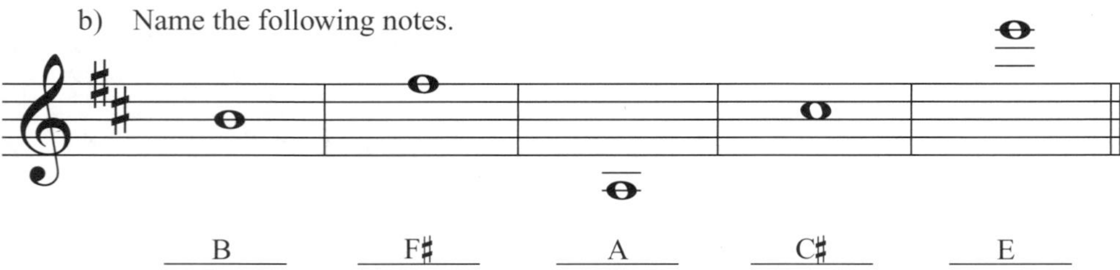

(10) 2. a) Write a whole tone above each of the following notes.

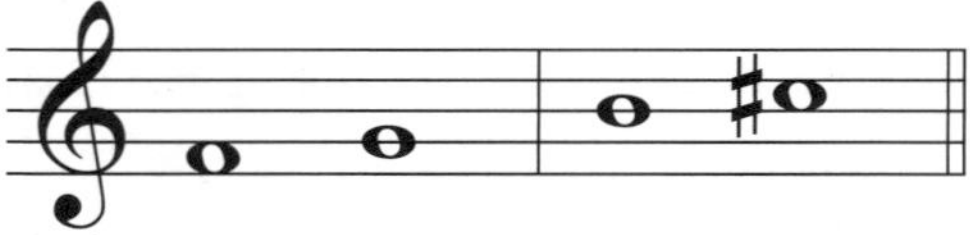

b) Write a chromatic semitone below each of the following notes.

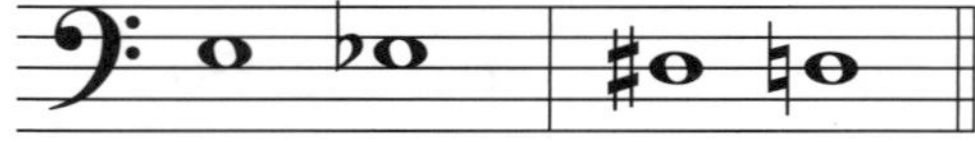

c) Write a note that is enharmonically equivalent to the following note:

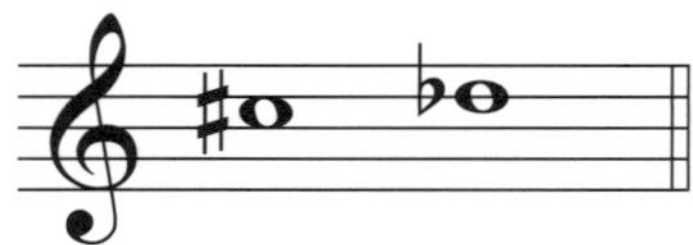

(10) 3. Write the following scales, ascending and descending, using whole notes.

a) E major in the treble clef, using accidentals
b) A♭ major in the bass clef, using a key signature
c) F♯ minor, natural form, in the bass clef, using a key signature
d) G minor, harmonic form, in the bass clef, using accidentals
e) C minor, melodic form, in the treble clef, using a key signature

a)

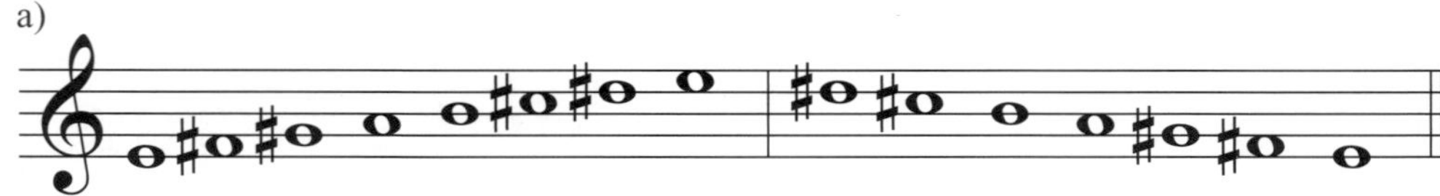

b)

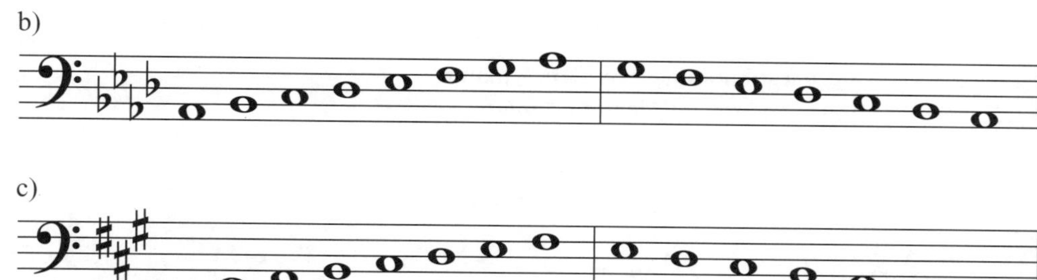

c)

d)

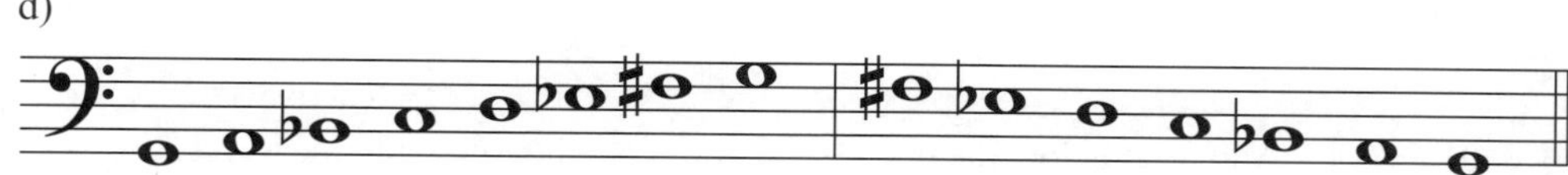

e)

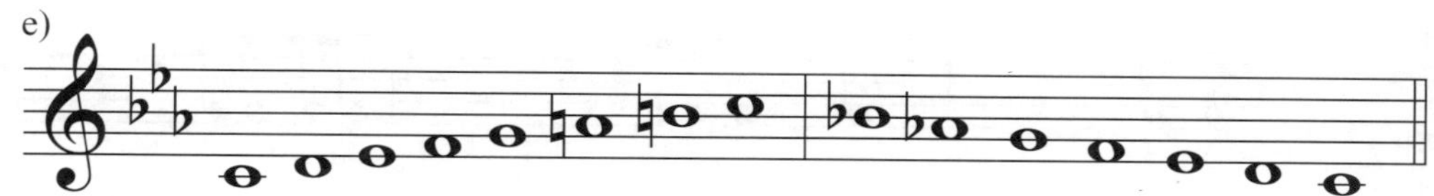

(10) 4. Write the following notes in the bass clef, using accidentals.

a) the tonic of E minor
b) the subdominant of F major
c) the dominant of B minor
d) the tonic of A♭ major
e) the dominant of F♯ minor

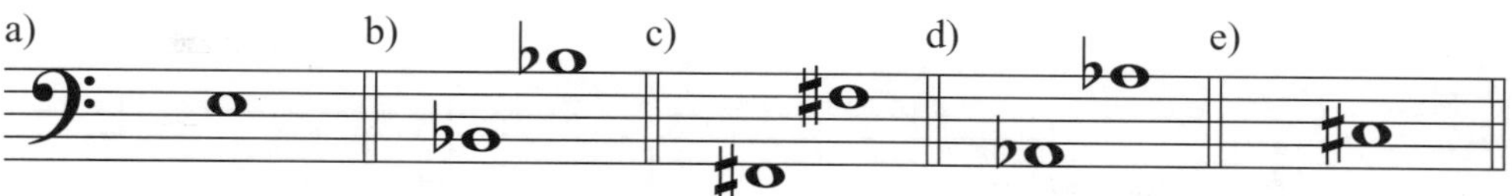

(10) 5. a) Write the following intervals above the given notes.

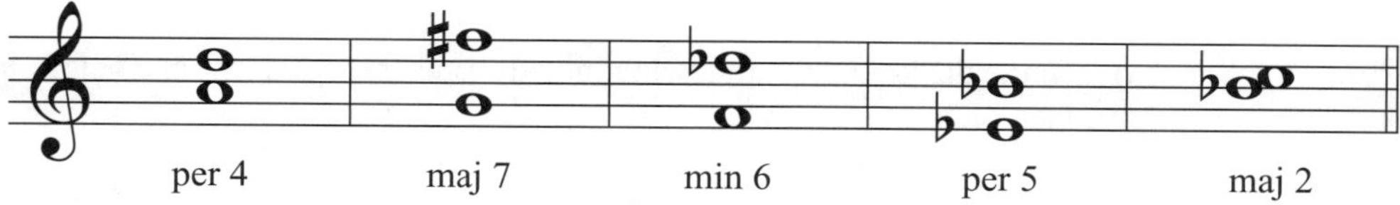

b) Name the following intervals.

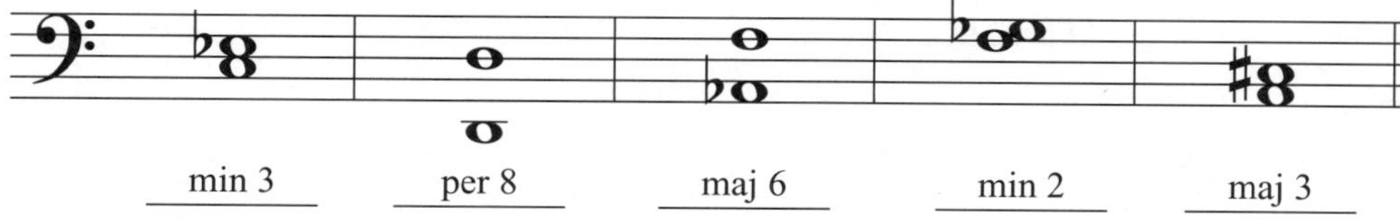

(10) 6. Write the following triads in the treble clef, using key signatures.

a) the subdominant triad of A major
b) the dominant triad of C♯ minor harmonic
c) the tonic triad of B♭ major
d) the dominant triad of E♭ major
e) the subdominant triad of D minor harmonic

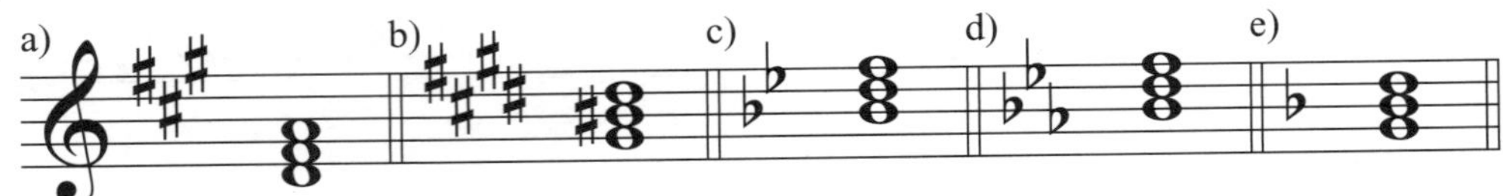

(10) 7. Add rests below the brackets to complete the following measures.

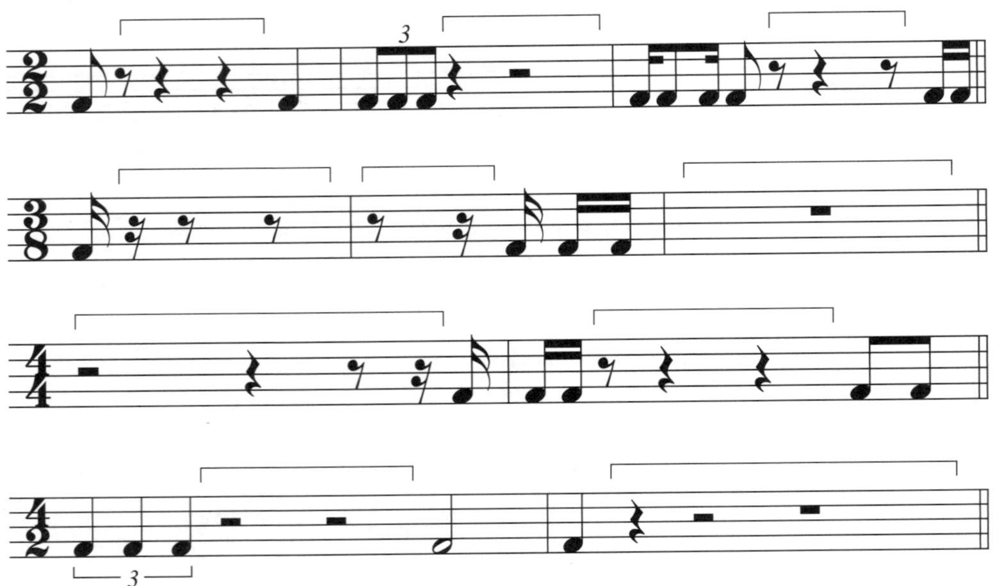

(10) 8. a) Name the key of the following melody. Transpose it down one octave into the bass clef.

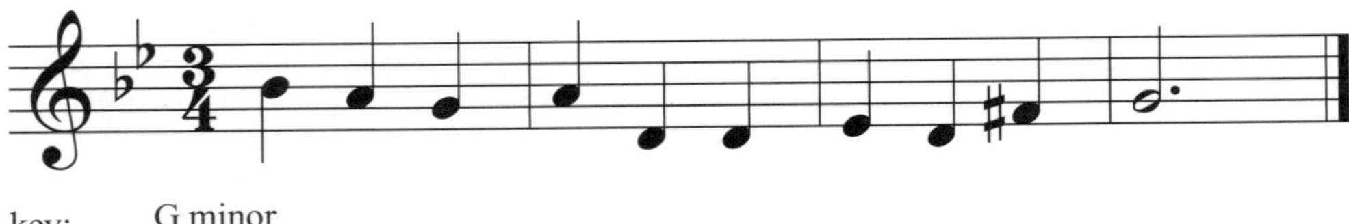

key: G minor

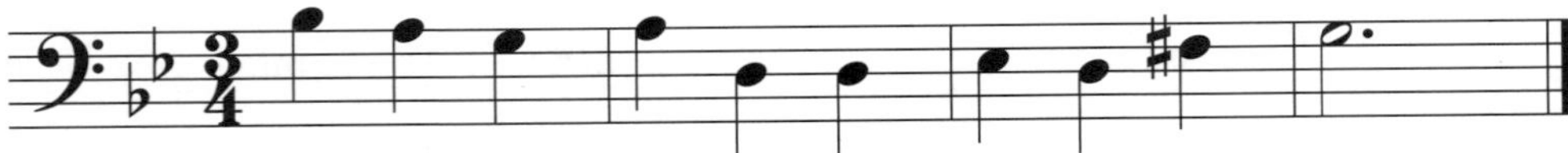

b) Name the key of the following melody. Transpose it up one octave into the treble clef.

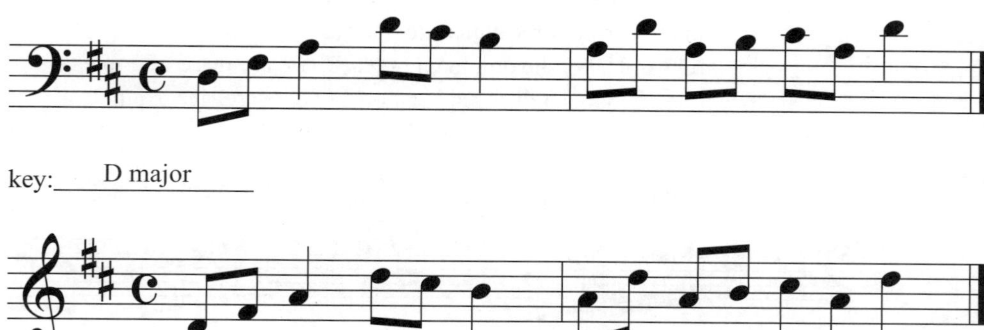

(10) 9. a) Explain the following terms.

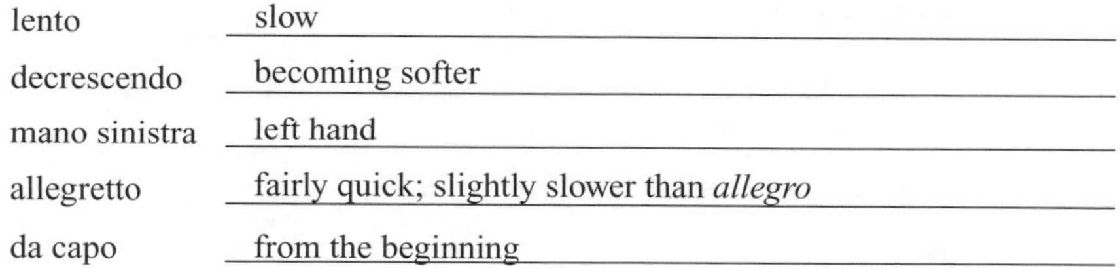

lento — slow

decrescendo — becoming softer

mano sinistra — left hand

allegretto — fairly quick; slightly slower than *allegro*

da capo — from the beginning

b) Draw the following signs on the given notes.

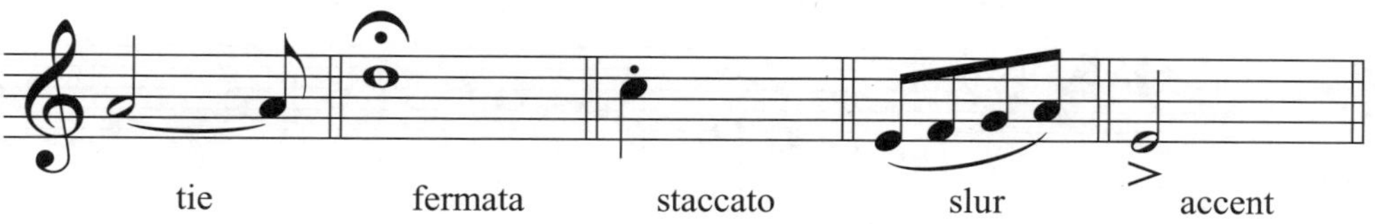

(10) 10. a) Analyze the following melody by answering the questions below.

- Name its key.
- Add the correct time signature.
- Circle and label the subdominant note.
- Circle and label the tonic triad.
- Circle and label the dominant triad.

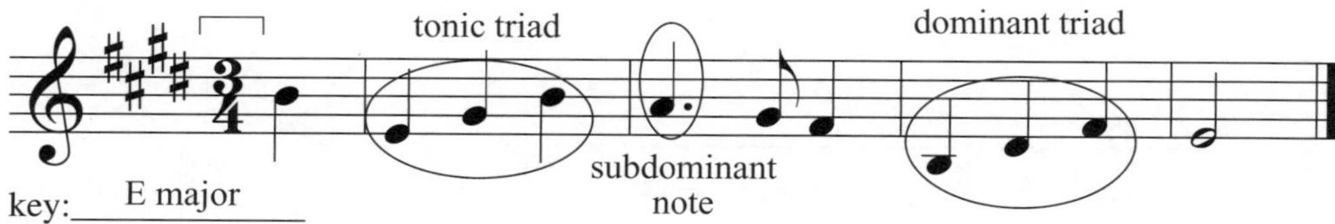

b) Analyze the following melody by answering the questions below.

- Name its key.
- Add the correct time signature.
- Circle and label the dominant note. (There are three examples.)
- Circle and label a diatonic semitone. (There are five examples.)
- Circle and label an interval of a minor 6th.

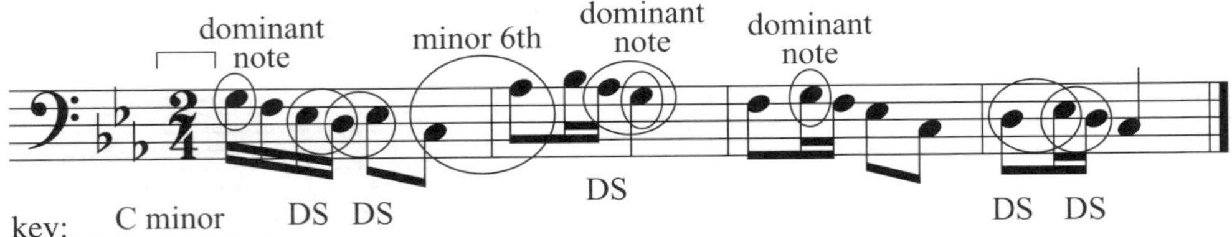

Marks **INTERMEDIATE TEST PAPER** (p. 301)

(10) 1. a) Write the following scales, ascending and descending, using the correct key signature for each. Use whole notes.

C♭ major in the treble clef

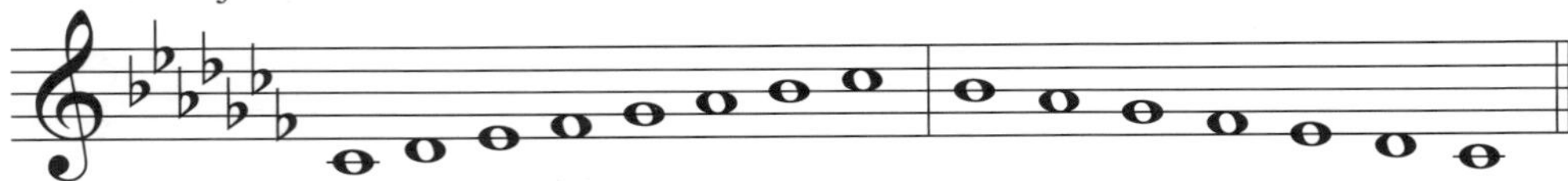

D♯ minor, melodic form, in the bass clef

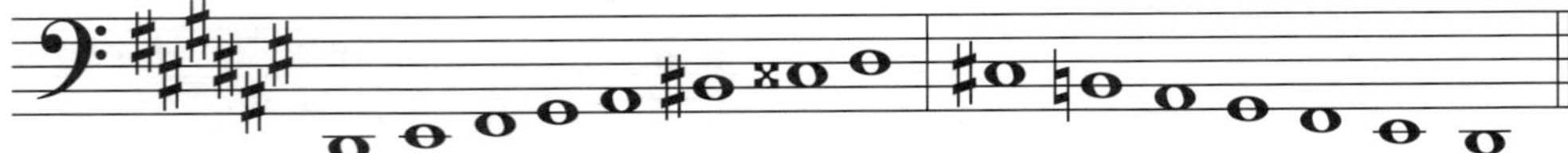

chromatic scale on B♭ in the treble clef

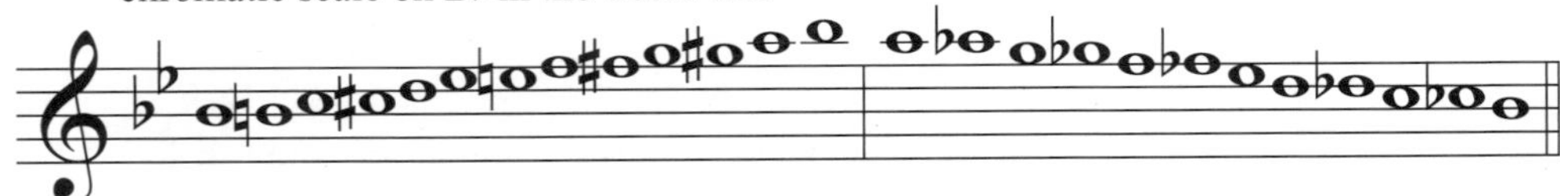

b) Identify the following scale types.

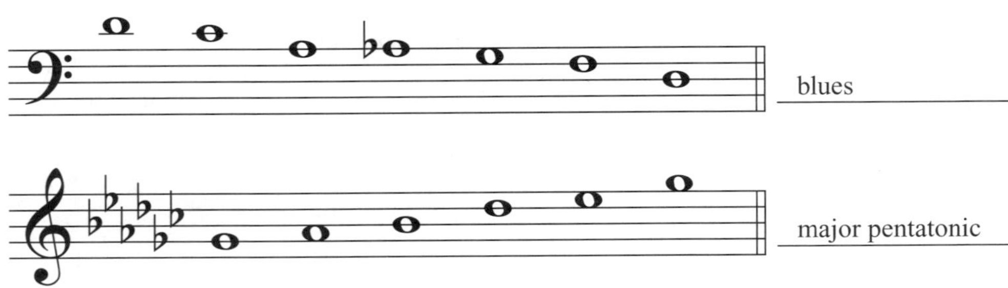

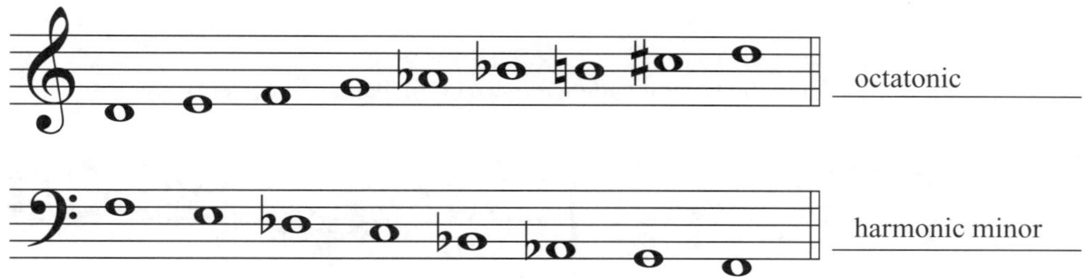

(10) 2. Write the following notes in the bass clef, using accidentals.

a) the supertonic of A♭ major
b) the leading note of G♯ minor harmonic
c) the subdominant of F minor
d) the submediant of B major
e) the mediant of C minor

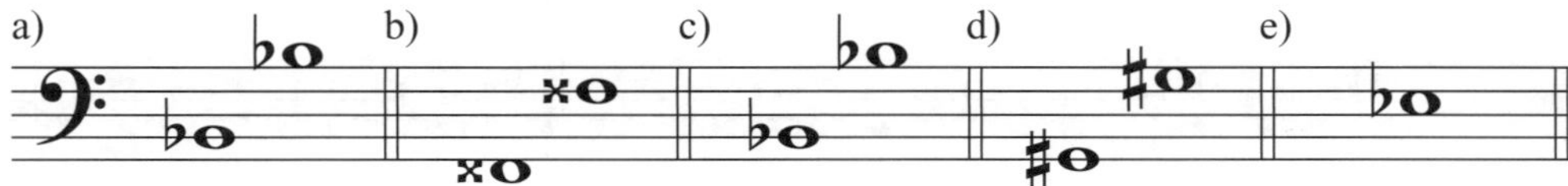

(10) 3. a) Write the following intervals above the given notes.

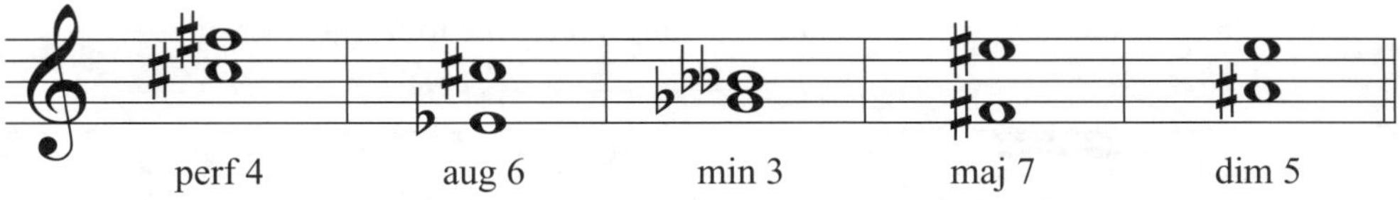

b) Invert the above intervals and name the inversions.

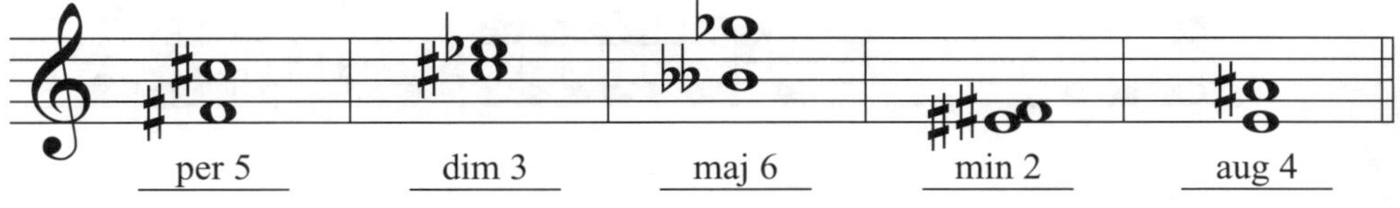

(10) 4. Write the following triads in the treble clef, using key signatures.

a) the supertonic triad of A major in root position
b) the dominant triad of B♭ minor harmonic in first inversion
c) the submediant triad of E♭ major in root position
d) the tonic triad of C♯ minor in second inversion
e) the subdominant triad of G minor harmonic in first inversion

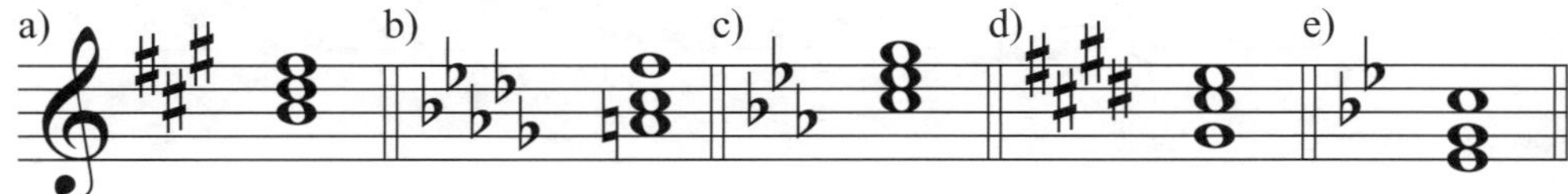

(10) 5. For each of the following:

a) Name the key.
b) Name the type of cadence (perfect, plagal, or imperfect).

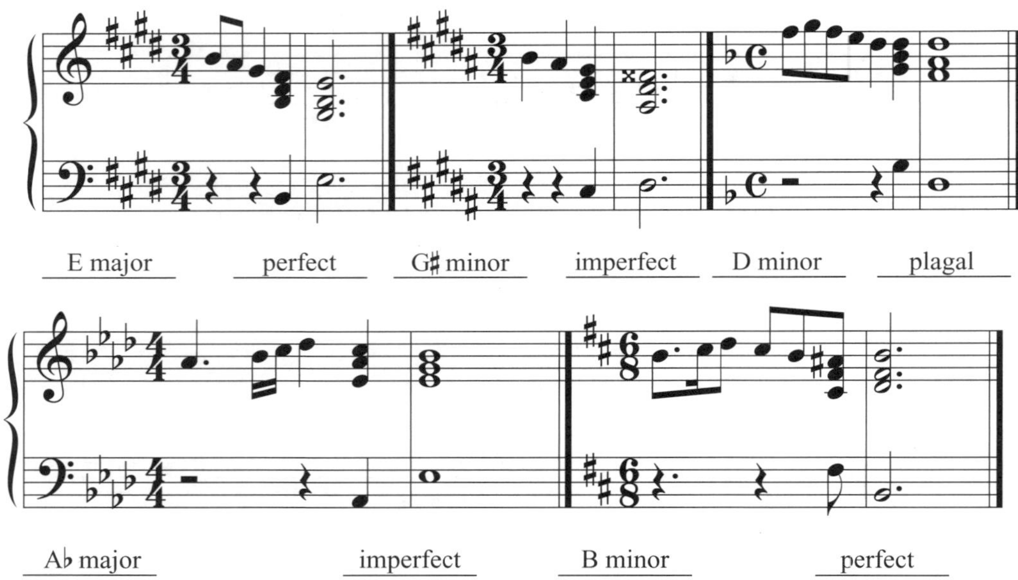

(10) 6. Add rests below the brackets to complete the following measures.

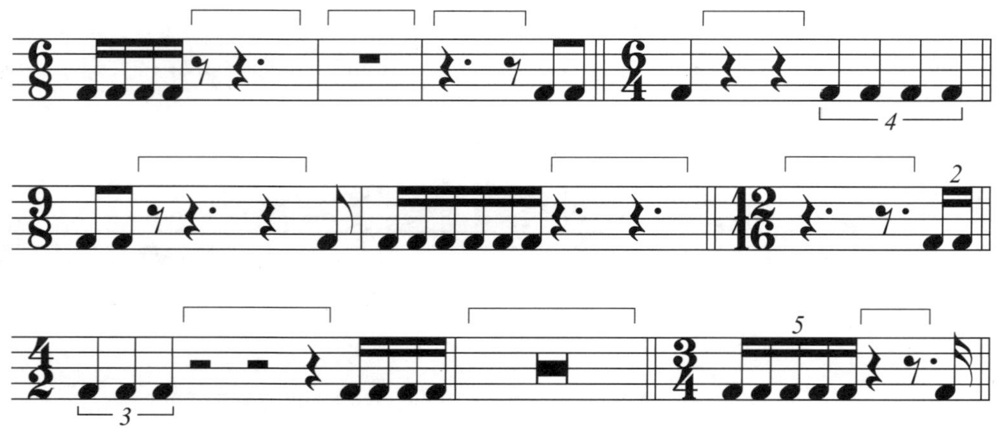

(10) 7. For each of the following melodies, name the key and add the correct time signature.

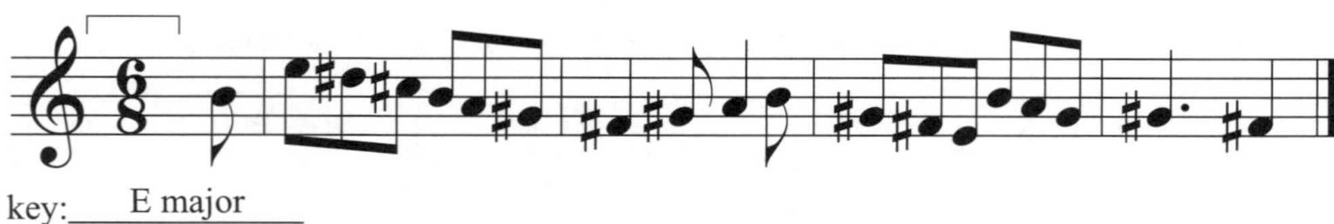

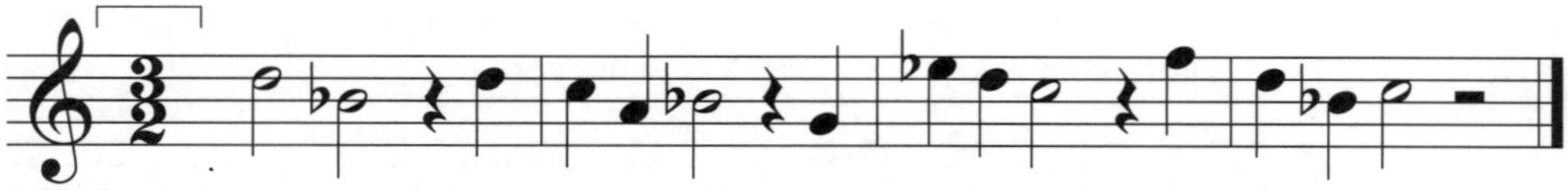

key: B♭ major

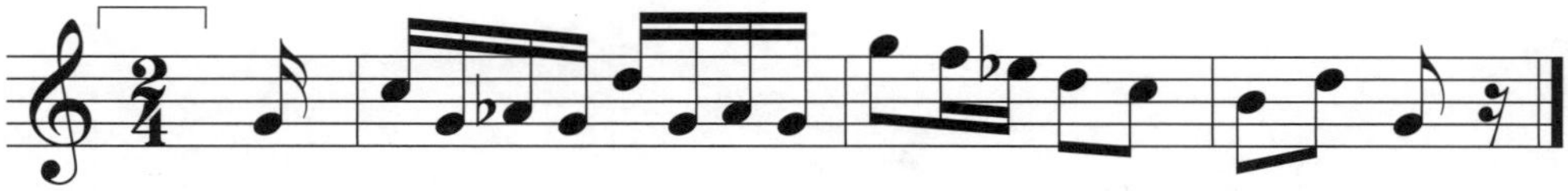

key: C minor

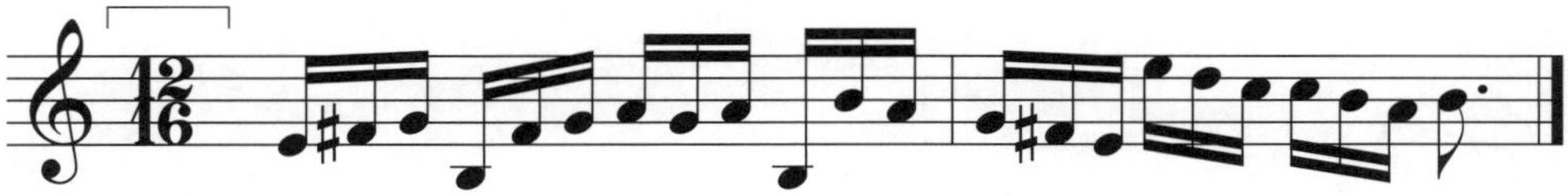

key: E minor

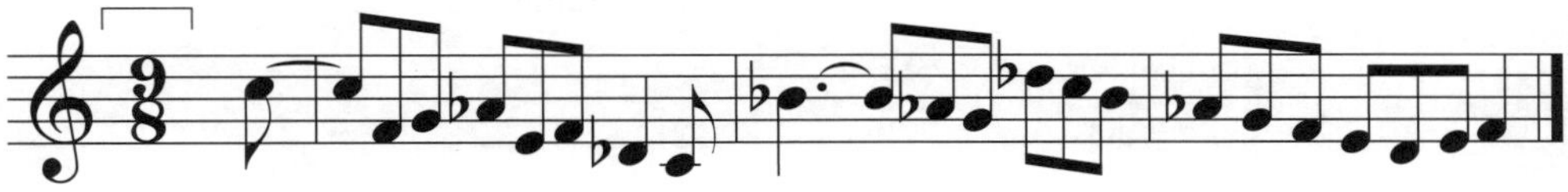

key: F minor

(10) 8. a) Name the key of the following melody. Transpose it up an augmented 4th, using the correct new key signature. Name the new key.

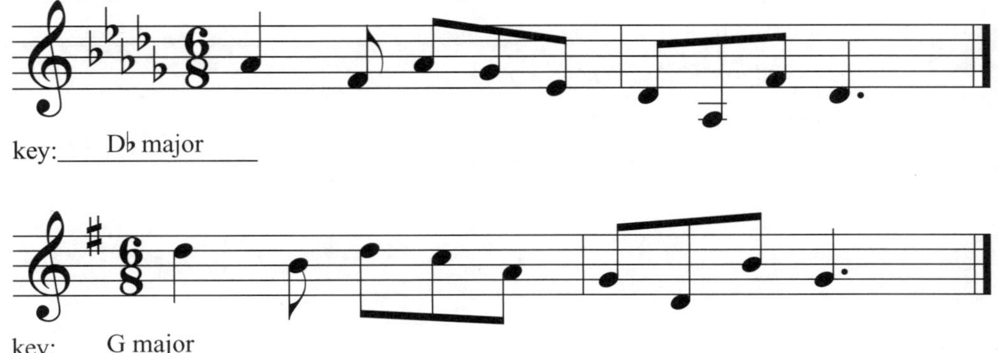

key: D♭ major

key: G major

b) Name the key of the following melody. Transpose it up a minor 3rd, using the correct new key signature. Name the new key.

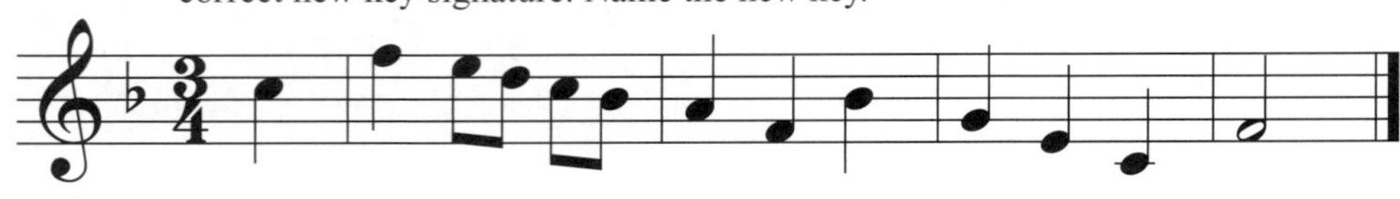

key: F major

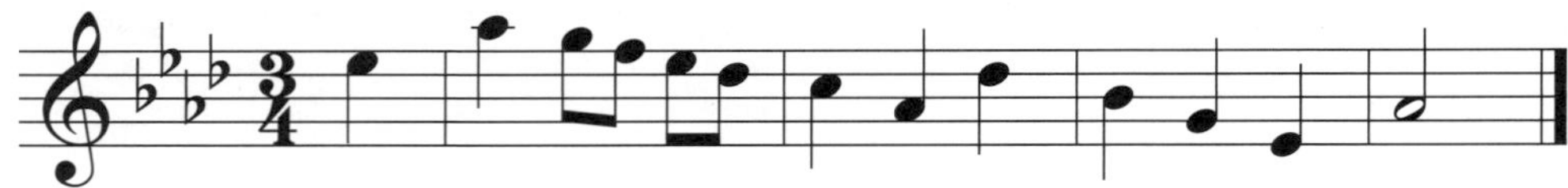

key: A♭ major

(10) 9. a) Explain the following terms.

fortepiano	loud, then immediately soft
vivace	lively, brisk
leggiero	light
grave	extremely slow and solemn
accelerando	becoming quicker

b) Give the Italian word or phrase for each of the following.

but	ma
with	con
little by little	poco a poco
more	più
not too much	non troppo

(10) 10. Analyze the following music excerpt by answering the questions below.

Kinder-Sonate, op. 118a, no. 1
1st movement

R. Schumann
(1810–1856)

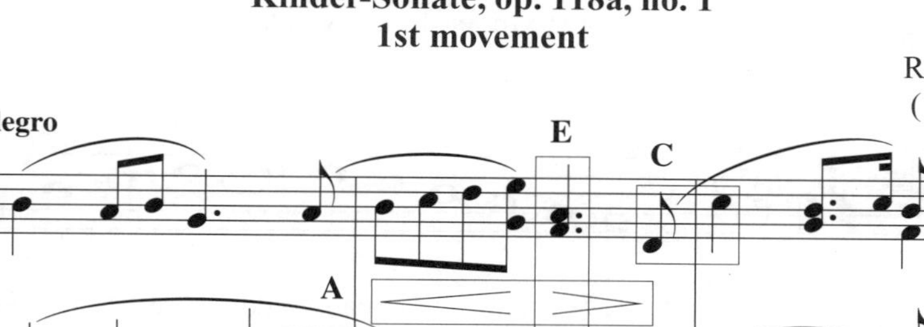

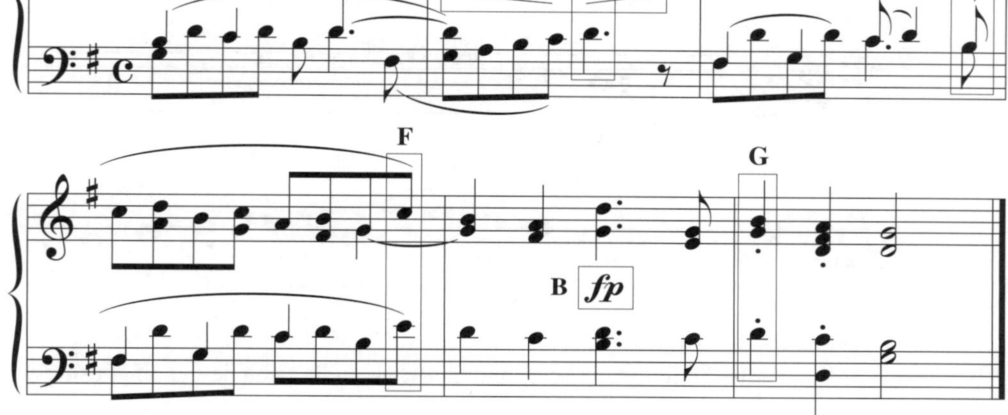

a) Name the composer of this piece. R. Schumann

b) Name the key of this piece. G major

c) How many times is the mediant note played in this piece?

16 times (17 if the unison in measure 3 is counted as 2)

d) Explain the two signs at letter **A**.

crescendo – becoming louder; decrescendo – becoming softer

e) Explain the sign at letter **B**. fortepiano – loud, then suddenly soft

f) Name the interval at letter **C**. min 7

g) Name the interval at letter **D**. min 6

h) Name the triad at letter **E**.

root: D position: root position quality: major

i) Name the triad at letter **F**.

root: C position: 1st inv. quality: major

j) Name the triad at letter **G**.

root: G position: 2nd inv. quality: major

Marks **ADVANCED TEST PAPER** (p. 306)

(10) 1. a) Write the following scales and mode, ascending and descending, using the correct key signature for each. Use whole notes.

C♯ major, from supertonic to supertonic, in the tenor clef

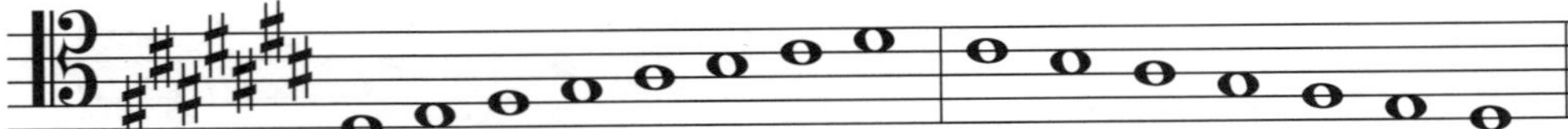

E♭ minor, harmonic form, from dominant to dominant, in the bass clef

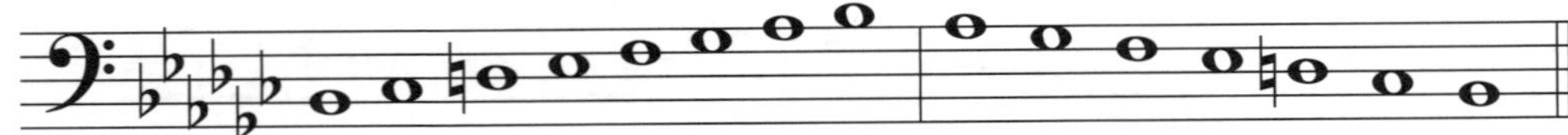

Dorian mode on B♭ in the treble clef

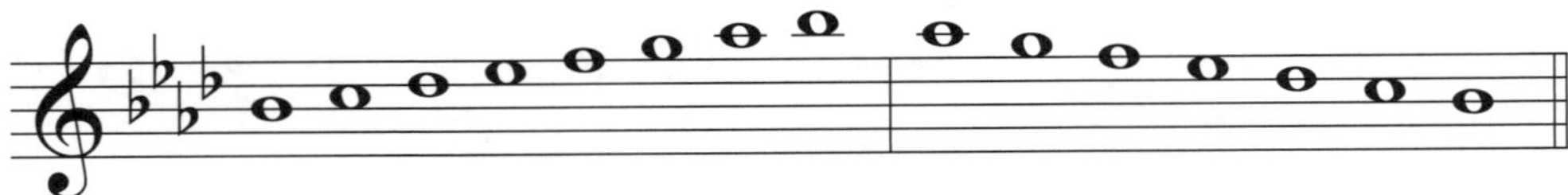

b) Write the following scale and mode, ascending and descending, using accidentals. Use whole notes.

G♯ minor, melodic form, from subdominant to subdominant, in the alto clef

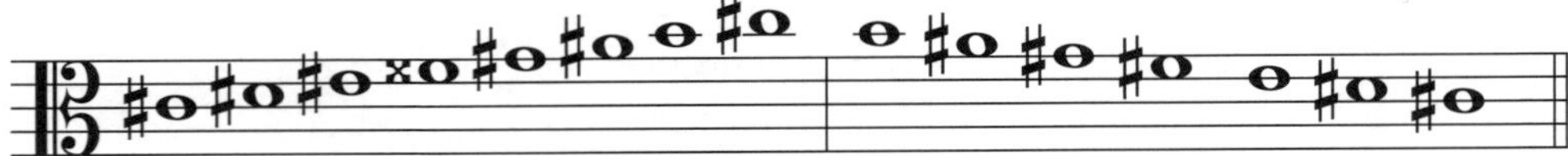

Lydian mode on E in the bass clef

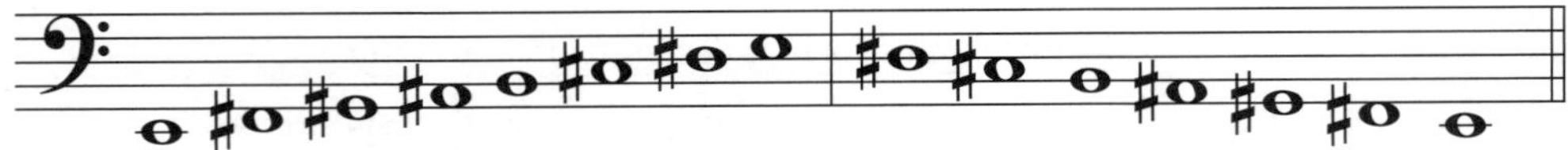

(10) 2. a) Write the following intervals below the given notes.

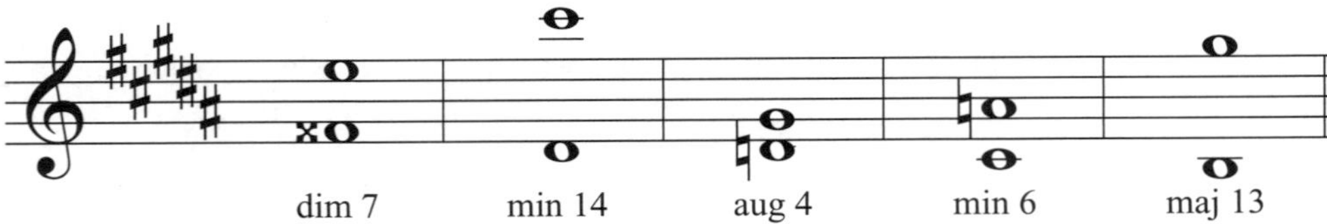

b) Invert the above intervals in the bass clef, and name the inversions.

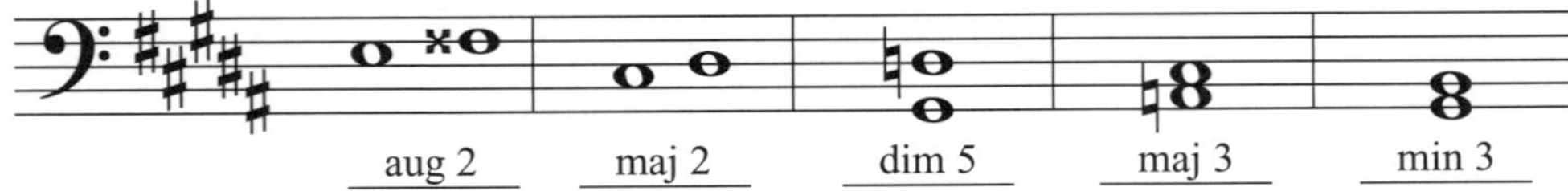

(10) 3. For each of the following triads, name:

a) its root
b) its position
c) its quality

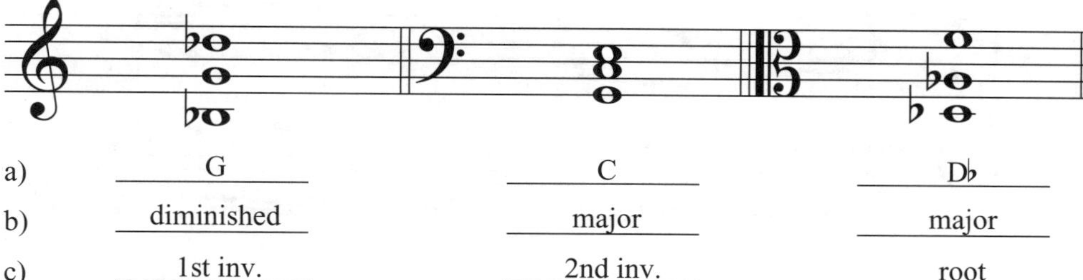

a)	G	C	D♭
b)	diminished	major	major
c)	1st inv.	2nd inv.	root

d) Name the scale that contains all of these triads. F minor, harmonic form

(10) 4. Write the following 7th chords in the bass clef, using key signatures.

a) the dominant 7th of A major in second inversion
b) the dominant 7th of C minor in first inversion
c) the dominant 7th of B major in third inversion
d) the dominant 7th of D♯ minor in root position
e) the diminished 7th of G minor in root position

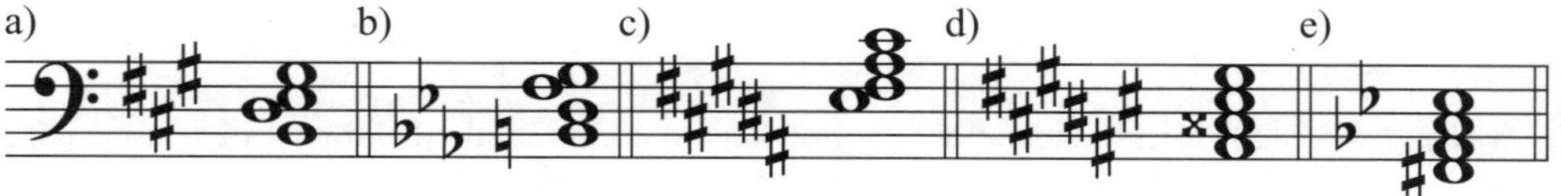

(10) 5. a) For each of the following melodic fragments:

i) Name the key.
ii) Write a cadence at the end of the fragment and name the cadence.
iii) Complete the unused portion of the bass staff with rests.
(Sample answers. Other arrangements are possible.)

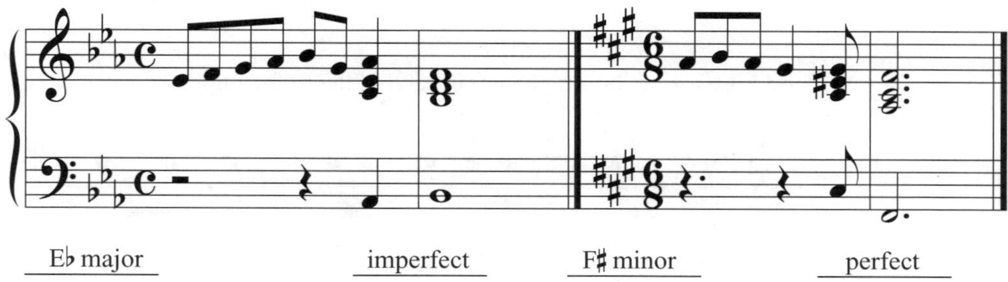

E♭ major — imperfect — F♯ minor — perfect

b) For each of the following excerpts:

i) Name the key.

ii) Name the type of cadence at the end of the excerpt.

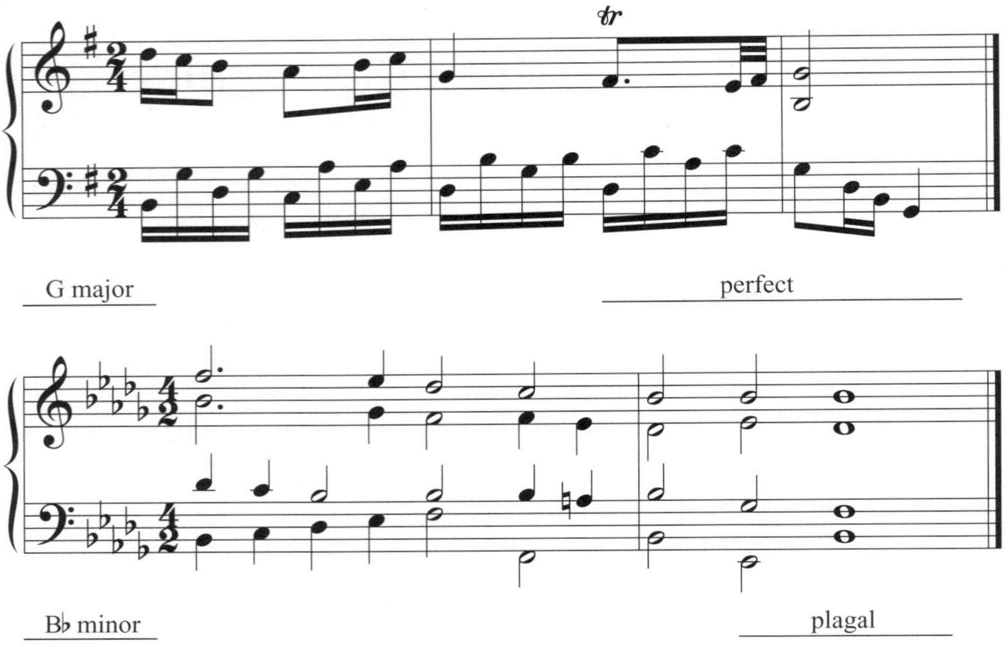

(10) 6. a) Add rests below the brackets to complete the following measures. (Sample answers. Some alternatives are possible.)

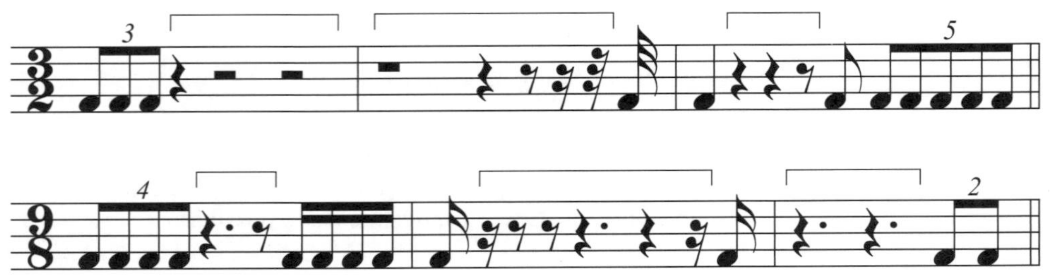

b) Add the correct time signature to each of the following.

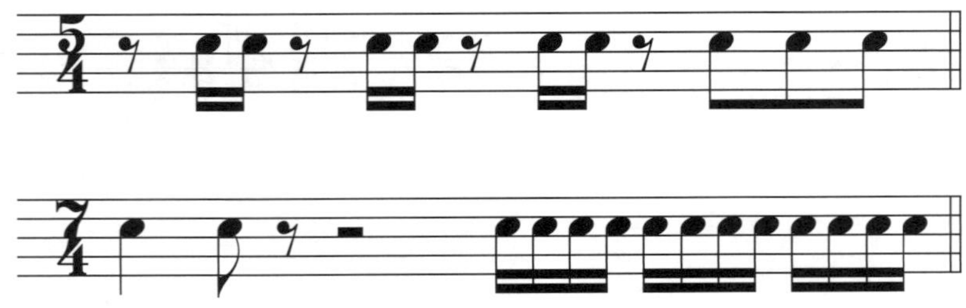

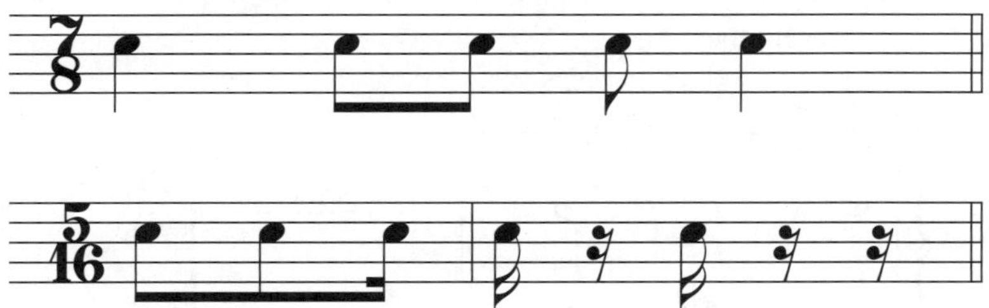

(10) 7. a) Name the key of the following melody. Transpose it up an augmented 6th in the same clef, using the correct new key signature. Name the new key.

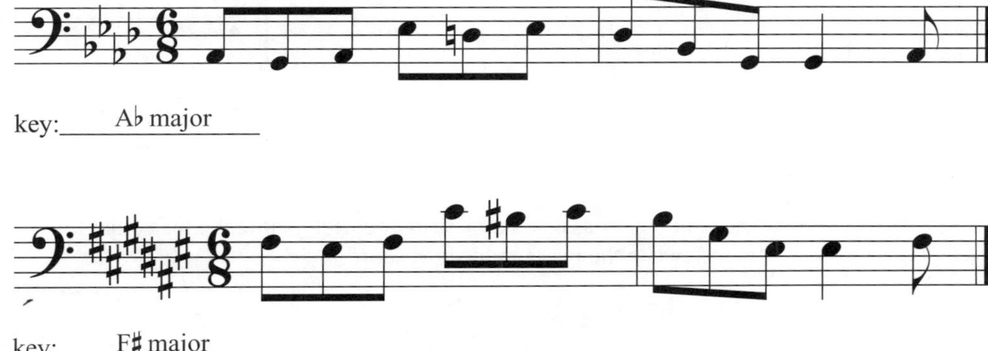

key: A♭ major

key: F♯ major

b) The following melody is written for clarinet in B♭. Name the key in which it is written. Transpose it to concert pitch, using the correct new key signature. Name the new key.

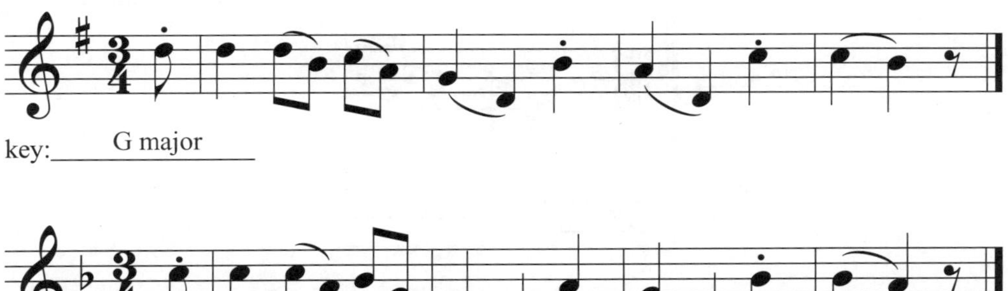

key: G major

key: F major

(10) 8. a) Rewrite the following passage in modern vocal score. Name the voice that sings each line.

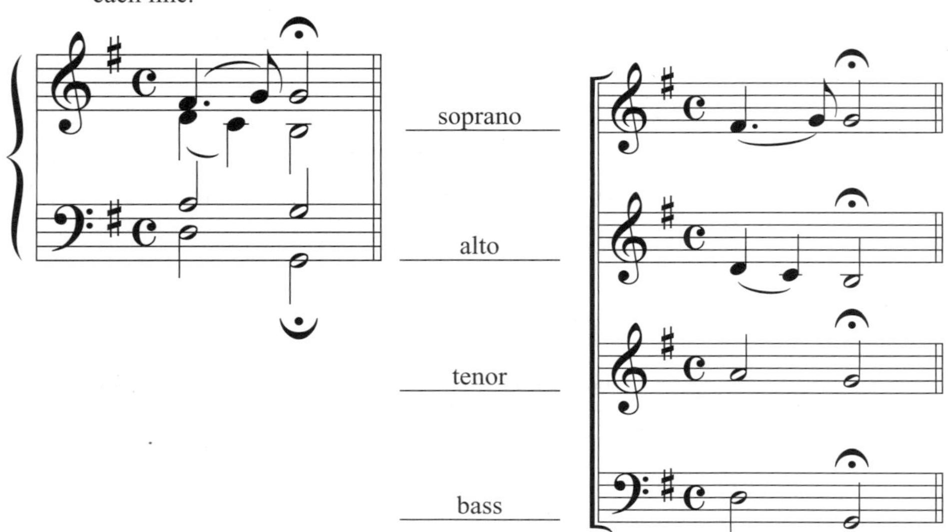

b) The following passage is for string quartet. Name the instrument that plays each line. Rewrite the passage in short score.

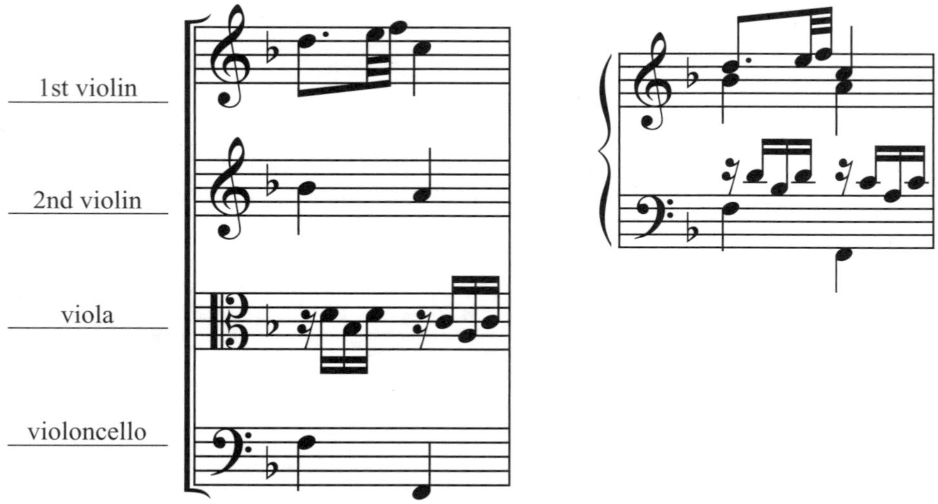

(10) 9. a) Give an Italian term that has the same meaning as each of the following.

léger leggiero

vite allegro

langsam lento

mässig moderato

mit Ausdruck con espressione

b) Define each of the following.

triad	a chord consisting of a root, a third, and a fifth
7th chord	a chord consisting of a root, a third, a fifth, and a seventh
quartal chord	a chord built on a series of 4ths
polychord	a combination of two or more different chords
cluster	a chord consisting of at least three adjacent notes of a scale

(10) 10. Analyze the following music excerpt by answering the questions below.

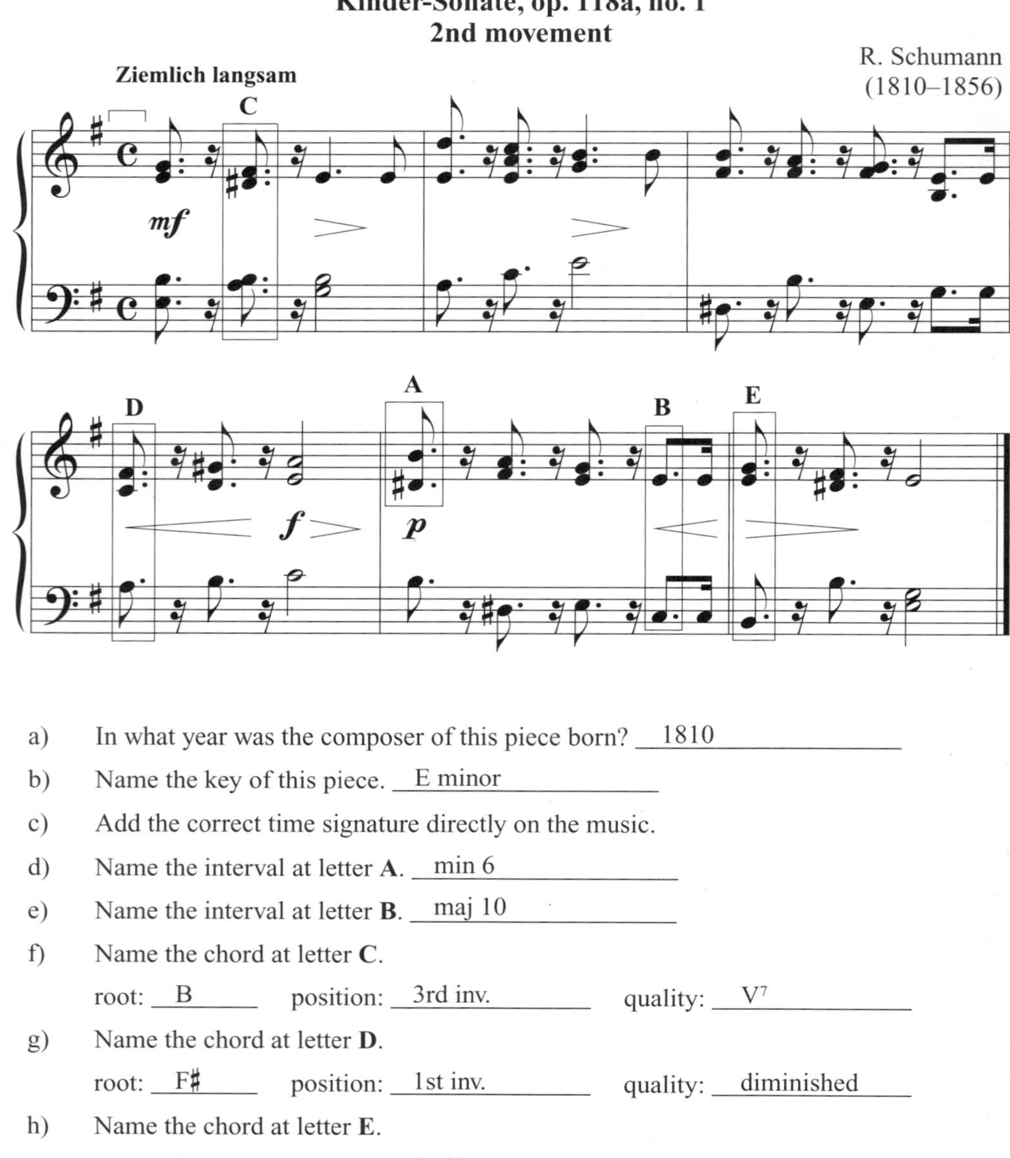

a) In what year was the composer of this piece born? 1810

b) Name the key of this piece. E minor

c) Add the correct time signature directly on the music.

d) Name the interval at letter **A**. min 6

e) Name the interval at letter **B**. maj 10

f) Name the chord at letter **C**.

root: B position: 3rd inv. quality: V^7

g) Name the chord at letter **D**.

root: F♯ position: 1st inv. quality: diminished

h) Name the chord at letter **E**.

root: E position: 2nd inv. quality: minor

i) Name the type of cadence at the end of this excerpt. perfect

j) Explain the meaning of *langsam*. slow